SAVING the
NEIGHBORHOOD

You <u>Can</u> Fight Developers and Win!

WOODBINE HOUSE • 1990

For information regarding bulk sales of this book, please contact:
Woodbine House
5615 Fishers Lane
Rockville, MD 20852
301-468-8800

Copyright © 1990 Adler & Robin Books, Inc.
All rights reserved under International and Pan-American Copyright Conventions. Published in the United States of America by Woodbine House, Inc.

Photo credits: p. 173—Dith Pran/The New York Times; p. 186—Cleveland Park Historical Society; p. 189—Jack Manning/The New York Times; pp. 213, 273—The New York Times; p. 233—Bill Adler, Jr.; p. 238—Terrence McCarthy/The New York Times; p. 306—Penny Davies; p. 313—Hanz Wirz; p. 325—Chester Higgins, Jr./The New York Times; p. 364— Bill Rice; p. 367 —Sharon Farmer

Cover Design and Illustration: Gary A. Mohrmann

Library of Congress Cataloging-in-Publication Data

Robin, Peggy.
 Saving the neighborhood: you can fight developers and win / by Peggy Robin
  p. cm.
 Includes bibliographical refererences.
 ISBN 0-933149-33-6 : $12.95
  1. Community development, Urban—United States—Citizen participation. 2. Real estate development—United States. 3. Neighborhood—United States. 4. Community organization. I. Title.
 HN90.C6R625 1990
 307.1'416'0973—dc20   88-40659
                                                  CIP

Manufactured in the United States of America

This book is printed on acid-free paper.

1 2 3 4 5 6 7 8 9 10

For my mother, who taught me always to stand up for what I believe, even if it means lying down in front of a bulldozer.

Table of Contents

i

Acknowledgements

This book could not have been written without the help of many experts in the field of law, architecture, historic preservation, and politics.

In matters historical I owe a debt of gratitude to Kathleen S. Wood, Professor Richard Longstreth, and Richard Striner. I would also be remiss if I did not thank the staff of the District of Columbia Historic Preservation Division, including Director Steve Raiche, Suzanne Ganschienitz, Nancy Witherell, and David Maloney, for supplying answers to the questions I continually asked.

As regards zoning and the law, I could not have done without the guidance (and prodding to action) of Tersh Boasberg.

Help in understanding the political maze was provided by Washington, District of Columbia Councilmember Jim Nathanson (and his always-helpful office staff) and George Colyer.

For excellent examples of community leadership I freely turned to Joel Odum, Margaret Hare, Charles Warr, and Lisa Koteen—but especially to Phil Mendelson and Patricia Wamsley, whom I met when I knew almost nothing about the slow-growth movement, and who patiently undertook to train me. I should also thank (or blame) Sheldon Holen, the late Tilford Dudley, and the board members of Friends of Tregaron, who first put in my head the idea of volunteering to work against a dense development scheme.

But most of all I am grateful for the encouragement of my husband, Bill Adler, who listened to me talk on for hours about what's wrong with the way development is done today, who sat home when I went off to meetings and marches, who held my hand all through my court appearances after my civil disobedience arrest—and who told me he thought there was a good book in what I was doing.

Introduction

Do our neighborhoods really need saving...from *developers?* If you're like me, then you grew up thinking that developers generally do good things for our neighborhoods. They build us our homes and apartments; they give us more and better places to shop; they put up bright new office buildings that bring more jobs and revenues to our cities and give us modern, convenient places to work; they build new roads to relieve traffic congestion; new schools to educate us; new hospitals to heal us: How could there be anything wrong with any of that?

It's taken some time for most of us to begin to see the truth: There can be too much of a good thing. Another dense subdivision isn't a plus for a neighborhood if it's built over that last bit of meadowland. The jobs and tax revenues provided by the new office building are no consolation to the apartment-dwellers who have just had all their sunlight cut off by their towering neighbor. Even the hospital or the school may not be welcome, if its construction spells the end of a two hundred-year-old oak tree, the dislocation of essential neighborhood stores, or the demolition of a beloved building from another era. It's not that development *per se* is bad, but that a particular development may have bad consequences for a particular neighborhood.

People generally know bad development when they see it—*after* it's built. You don't need any formal training in planning to find it. Just drive around whatever city or suburb you're in and look around. Here's a street so choked with traffic that it takes three light cycles to move one block at rush hour. There's a massive concrete monolith built slam up against someone's little brick house. See those long, depressing blocks of faceless boxes of glass and steel. And think of all those in-town neighborhoods where it's virtually impossible, day or night, to find a place to park.

I think perhaps the best description of bad development came from novelist (and neighborhood activist) Tom Wolfe: "It looks like a Lego set gone amok." After which he added, "It can't go on forever."*

---

* *New York Times,* Jan. 12, 1989, p. B–1.

In more and more neighborhoods, development *isn't* going on unchecked, because the people who have to live with it, like Tom Wolfe, have had enough. They're organizing, pooling their strength, and making their opinions heard. *And they're winning.*

For the past dozen or so years, in all parts of the United States, a clear trend has emerged. Neighbors have been able to unite, to challenge the developers of unwanted, ill-planned projects, and to save their own neighborhoods.

They did it in Denver when new office development was just about to obliterate the oldest section of the city. Residents banded together and fought for a twenty-two-block historic district that gave protected status to the low-scale Victorian buildings still standing in the heart of their neighborhood.

They did it in the former desert towns north of Los Angeles, where it had once seemed suburbanization knew no limits. Citizens of the town of San Gabriel have voted a temporary halt to all new construction. And in nearby Alhambra, Monterey, and Sierra Madre, they've won a moratorium on all new apartment developments.

They did it in Prince Georges County, Maryland, when a developer proposed turning a quiet, semi-rural community into a mini-city on the Potomac. The neighbors joined together with environmentalists and national preservation activists to limit the new construction to just what the fragile shoreline could accommodate.

Who are "they"—these people who have won these victories? Are they, like Tom Wolfe, rich and famous? You might think they'd have to be, to take on the powerful, moneyed development interests. But I haven't found that to be the case. In my ten years of working in the slow-growth movement (and that's what we call it; we dislike the negative-sounding term "anti-development), I've met dozens, maybe even hundreds of successful neighborhood campaigners. They've all been fairly ordinary people, middle-class people with regular jobs. I've met teachers, managers, small-business people, corporate employees, housewives, retired people—some lawyers—but more often, people without professional degrees, people without any background in planning and policy making. They're not normally activists. The fight for their neighborhood is usually their first foray into local politics.

This was the case with Joel Odum, the best, most successful neighborhood-saver I ever met. He had moved to the quiet Tenleytown section of Washington, D.C., from his hometown in Alabama, and he'd just sunk his life's savings into an old house he was intending to fix up as both his living space and art studio (he was a painter, a career-choice that gave him a precarious income in the best of years). He had hardly settled in when he looked out his window one day at the park across the street and saw workmen removing the sign that said, "Welcome to Glover-Archbold Park."

"Whatch-y'all doin'?" asked Joel (whose Deep South accent goes perfectly with his wide-eyed-country-boy looks and style). The crew foreman told Joel that a developer had acquired a segment of the park and it was going to be paved over as a roadway. A large office building, headquarters to a national corporation, would be built along the main avenue, and the new road would serve as its rear access-route for delivery trucks and cars.

Joel was horrified—so horrified that he didn't stop to think about the situation in any detail. He didn't stop to think that he knew nothing about city government, or zoning laws, or leading a crusade. He didn't sit back and reflect that, if he got involved, he'd be going up against one of the biggest corporate powerhouses in America. He just ran to the phone and began calling. He called his neighbors, he called his councilman, he called anyone and everyone he thought could be of help. He called me, because I was known as a neighborhood advocate and was head of a local citizens' organization that had already had some successes in dealing with developers.

In the beginning, I and all the other "experts" Joel consulted were discouraging. The developer was already far along in the building permit process. He had a "vested right" to build both the office complex and the road through the park. Joel was undeterred. He just kept repeating over and over, to anyone, anytime, anywhere he could, that the development would destroy the neighborhood and had to be stopped.

For two years he waged his campaign. He petitioned the administrative agencies, he filed court cases, he generated letter-writing campaigns, and he lobbied politicians. And for most of that time he seemed to be getting nowhere. "Cooler heads" kept telling him to accept reality, make peace with the developer, and cut his losses.

But Joel just kept looking at the ravaged parkland—the bulldozed trees—and shaking his head. When a local reporter asked him, why, after so many defeats, he was still at work trying to keep the park from being paved, he replied "...because it's wrong, it's wrong and it's wrong!"* In the end, he turned out to be right. Because Joel wouldn't give up, the people of the neighborhood (and most importantly, the voters of the city) didn't give up either. The Mayor (after a reelection bid that saw him losing Joel's ward by an 85–to–15 percent margin) decided it was time for a policy change. He directed his planning officials to put pressure on the developer. By denying the developer other favors in other projects, the city was able to force concessions that gave the neighborhood back what it had lost. The developer had to agree to tear up the road he had already built through the park and move it onto his private

---

* *City Paper*, Aug. 21, 1987, p. 14.

property; he further agreed that any new construction in the neighborhood would be only *half the size of the first building*.

This was a victory of unparalleled proportions for the neighborhood—and it was also an important lesson for me. I was just beginning to think of putting my own experiences in dealing with developers into book form, so that residents of other neighborhoods threatened by development could learn from my experience, instead of having to pick it up as they went along—as I did, as Joel Odum did. I was going to put a lot of emphasis on acquiring certain skills: learning the specialized jargon of planners and architects; raising a war-chest; negotiating through a maze of administrative regulations. I will still cover those areas in this book. But I know now they're all secondary to the main ingredient. Commitment.

If you've got the commitment, and your neighbors have it, too, you're more than halfway there. Another quarter of the way comes from good judgment and perseverance. These are things you can't learn from a book, though you may be able to pick up some tips and encouragement by reading about others' success.

Knowing the technical side, having the organizational structure, being able to raise the money, of course will make the struggle much easier. But as Joel has demonstrated, with a lot of determination and some good sense, you can succeed—even if you never saw a zoning map before in your life, even if your neighborhood doesn't have (and has never had) a citizens' association to fight for it, even if you've got very little money and no prospect of raising much more.

Joel won, despite his disadvantages at the outset. With the help of this book, I hope you'll start out a few steps ahead—and do as much good for your neighborhood as he did for his!

Why It's Up to *You* (Government Won't Do It for You)

When faced with unwanted development in the neighborhood, the first, most natural reaction is often a shrug. "I just *live* here. It's not *my* job to deal with planning matters. That's for government planners. That's what we have regulations and administrations *for*."

That was exactly how I felt, about ten years ago, when I first found out that a developer wanted to build two hundred townhouses in the woods across from my house. "He can't *do* that! The city will never let it happen."

But my neighbors were still worried about it, and when they invited me to attend a meeting to discuss the question, I went and listened. What I learned was shocking. The developer had already met with the city's top planning officials. They hadn't said, "No, out of the question!" They hadn't raised a cry about the proposed destruction of so many full-grown trees. They hadn't pointed out that the land was zoned only for about a third the number of houses the developer wanted to put up, nor had they discouraged him from seeking a zoning change of such magnitude. Instead, they had steered him to a special development process. The city had an incentive program meant to ease the way for developers to accomplish certain desirable social ends: to create "affordable housing," to promote architecture of "superior design," and of course, to bring in more jobs and revenues. Though his new townhouses were to cost $300,000 and up, somehow the developer managed to convince the city that his project qualified for consideration under the housing provisions of the program. The planners merely suggested that he ought to meet a few times with the neighbors to find out what they wanted in the way of minor changes to the plan.

Before giving their go-ahead to the application, the city planners never thought to ask us about the *major* change. We didn't want so large a development on our block—period. When we told the planners this, they were not surprised. They seemed to expect neighborhood opposition to development— and to be bored to death with it.

But I was still inexperienced and naive. How could the city planners be so indifferent to the threat that we saw in the development proposal? As public servants, it was their job (so I assumed) to guide the developers into doing what the people wanted. So it was obvious they had either made a glaring error in this case, or else they did not understand their jobs quite as I did.

Unfortunately, the latter turned out to be true. And it's so, I'm afraid, in most American city and county planning departments. Those with authority over land-use (whether city planners, county officials, or elected representatives) generally do *not* see themselves as advocates for the citizens. They see themselves as an impartial body, pulled on the one side by development interests, on the other side by the citizens. They try to maintain "balance" between these two equally competing interests.

When I first heard this explanation, I was incensed—and I still am! Consider what this attitude means to you, the citizen, in practical terms. When a developer comes up with a new plan that will alter your way of life in your neighborhood forever, it's as if you're at the start of a race with him. Your city/ county officials are merely referees. You have the responsibility to do all the preparation for the race, even if you've never trained for an event before. You may have to pay for professional help to get in shape for it; you'll certainly have to take time out of your schedule to devote to the contest. Meanwhile, your opponent, the developer, is only doing the normal day-to-day work of his business in preparing for the contest. He has people on permanent retainer to help him negotiate the hurdles. He's been there so often he knows all the referees by their first names, too (they may even go to work for him when they're finished with their present government service).

Does this strike you as unfair as it strikes me? In the last chapter of this book, after I've already discussed ways to take on a specific development challenge, I'll go into some reforms I think need to be undertaken to change the way the system works, to get public servants to act on behalf of the public at large, and to drop this pose of neutrality.

For now, though, you should act on the assumption that the planning functions of government are not going to work automatically on your behalf. You should be looking to your own neighborhood to come up with the resources (mostly in the form of people, not money or special skills) needed to look out for your own interests.

You may wonder: Doesn't it depend on the administration that's in charge in my particular city or county? Doesn't it matter if the authorities are elected or appointed? Doesn't it help a lot if you know you have people in charge who seem sensitive to citizens' needs? How can you say that citizens have to fight to be heard, when their degree of influence in the process can vary so greatly from jurisdiction to jurisdiction?

Well, I *can't* say absolutely. There is, clearly, a great deal of variation in treatment of citizens and developers, depending on where you are and how they do things in your neck of the woods. In some systems citizen input carries a lot of weight; in others...it will be like butting your head up against a stone wall (or should I say, a concrete high-rise?). Then, too, some kinds of development are easier to take on than others. Luxury vacation condos, to pick an obvious example, will be far more attackable, than, say, a hospital for sick children. There is one thing I can say with certainty in all cases, however: Whether the system works well or badly in your area, you'll still be much, much better off trying to get what you can out of it for your neighborhood than if you just sit back and let the government process work its way through without you.

A (Very) Short History of Planning in America

Before you start looking into how the development process works in your particular part of the country, it's useful to know a little bit about how development has traditionally been handled from the founding of this country onward. Of course, it would take a book in itself to cover this subject in any detail, and I intend for this book to be not a scholarly work, but a hands-on guide. Still, I must touch on a few key historical facts to lay proper background for discussion of several specific development problems in the later chapters.

The first and most obvious fact is that America is a comparatively new country. Our cities are only a few hundred years old (our very oldest, St. Augustine, is coming up on its 425th birthday). So we haven't had long experience of living together in densely populated areas. In Europe, on the other hand, city-dwelling patterns are discernible almost 3000 years ago! In areas of early Roman settlement, archaeologists have discovered evidence of street grids, sewage lines, and uniform foundation construction indicating some level of formal planning in use. Paris, nearly two thousand years old, has had municipal regulations governing the placement and use of buildings since the Middle Ages. (Developers today complain that some of these medieval regulations are still on the books!) A long history of close-quartered living naturally leads to a certain acceptance by residents that rules are necessary to ensure that limited space is used rationally, for the good of all.

But the New World seemed to its settlers to be, above all, a land without limits. The men and women who came were people fleeing their own crowded lands, or seeking refuge from governments that imposed too many rules: on how to worship, how to work, how to live the whole of life. From the very first the new country seemed to promise that here, government would be limited, that "a man's home would be his castle."

But as the cities of the East began filling up with the waves of immigrants in the 19th Century, problems of unplanned growth began to be marked. Factories and sweatshops, built with no regard to health or safety, collapsed or burned, killing all inside. In poor neighborhoods, poor sanitation led to regular summertime epidemics of TB, cholera, diphtheria, and flu, which sometimes spread to the "better" parts of town as well. Construction workers were always at risk of dying on faultily built scaffolding or in insufficiently shored-up excavations.

These conditions led to cries for reform. From the turn of the century onward, cities enacted hundreds of health and safety regulations. Fire prevention, building safety, worker protection, and public sanitation were all codified and minimum standards set forth. Great public works projects were undertaken so that overcrowded cobblestone streets could be replaced by broad, sunny, tree-lined avenues. Bridges, tunnels, trolleys, and subways were planned to allow citizens to reach any part of town with speed, safety, and convenience.

In this same period, another reform—the regulation of the amount of new building that could be put up on a piece of property—was tried for the first time. The idea of **zoning**, as the concept was called, had already been in use in parts of Great Britain, Sweden, and Prussia. New York was the first city to enact a zoning ordinance, in 1916. No longer could developers build to any height they chose, or block off the entrance to someone else's property, or build without windows or out over the public sidewalk. The idea seemed to work, and was soon adopted by most other big cities. By the 1920s and '30s, most of populated America was zoned.

But in each place zoning was tried, court challenges were also tried. Property owners charged zoning was a "taking" of their fundamental rights; it was "communistic" and unconstitutional. The Supreme Court, however, has always found otherwise. Though it has on occasion struck down a particular locality's law as "unfairly restrictive" or "too vague" in its wording, or "inequably applied" in practice, the basic concept of zoning has passed constitutional muster, and is now an unchallengeable tool of city and county governments.

But each state, and quite often, each county or city within a state, is free to adopt zoning codes as stringent or lenient as the lawmakers deem appropriate. Perhaps not surprisingly, in light of our patterns of settlement, our older, more densely populated areas have tended to have the strictest zoning codes; the newer or sparsely populated places have tended toward fewer restrictions. The West generally has been freer for developers than the East, and politically conservative communities are generally less bound by zoning than liberal ones. Southwestern, conservative Houston is a case in point: It's the only major U.S city to have no zoning at all.

While nearly all cities, big and small, have had some form of zoning code for most of this century, the codes have not remained static. Changes in economic conditions lead to revisions, and when the whole country undergoes a major change, zoning in all the individual jurisdictions across America will often follow suit.

This happened at the end of the Second World War. Millions of GI's were returning home, and patterns of living and building were changing rapidly. The young men married in unprecedented numbers and a baby boom soon followed. Thousands of new families were seeking housing, not on the farm and not in the cities as their parents and grandparents had done, but on the outskirts of cities, the suburbs. Zoning was seen as a great helper in bringing about this population shift, and vast tracts of once-placid pastureland were swiftly redesignated to accommodate the sprawling tract-house subdivisions like Levittown and its imitators.

Along with the boom in families and suburban living, came the boom in private car ownership. Zoning codes had to be rewritten to include parking requirements, traffic circulation provisions, and truck delivery unloading points. Widespread car ownership also changed shopping patterns. With the creation of the shopping mall, suburbanites no longer had to drive into the city and find some place to park while they shopped; one single nearby development allowed them to do it all in one place. It also created a whole new zoning category.

But perhaps the most troubling changes came about in the mid-'60s to early '70s. These were the years when the exodus to the suburbs reached its peak, when our cities were torn by riots, when the economy was crippled with "stag-flation," and urban development seemed to be at a standstill. New York, it was well known, was sinking under the weight of its debts, and it looked as if the other big cities would soon follow suit. "The death of the cities" was a common catch phrase of the times.

But zoning seemed to offer, if not a cure, then at least some medicine for the ailment. By raising the limits on development, city governments could make urban development a more attractive proposition, and bring economic vitality back to city streets. From San Francisco to Chicago to New York, and all points in between, a variety of "incentive" programs were tried out. Some included tax abatements for residential development (whether luxury or low-income), some allowed building to greater heights, or greater mass, in exchange for specific public benefits (fixing up a nearby subway station, for example, or building a public sculpture garden).

These programs worked, or the economy as a whole worked—or both worked in conjunction with the other—to turn our cities around. However it happened, by the mid–1980s there was no doubt that most cities were booming—building cranes were everywhere. The trend was clear enough that *Time* magazine could feature on its cover a picture of a beautifully restored city block, under the triumphant heading "BACK TO LIFE."*

But the same development boom that brought back needed housing, created new jobs, and rescued the dwindling tax base also brought problems for citizens. Once construction was going again, the city planning agencies didn't remove the incentive programs that helped to fuel the boom; in the most densely developed downtowns of many of our cities, developers can still take advantage of all kinds of government programs meant to bring economic growth to "neglected" areas. Citizens facing office building after office building going up in the midst of their once-quiet, residential in-town neighborhood may be stunned to find that developers are being steered there by an unrevised 1970s–era city plan.

When a great many people in an area make the same discovery, and face the same development threats, that's when they begin to work for change. And you can see this force growing in all parts of the country where development has been strong. In the same *Time* cover story that cheered the city's

---

* November 23, 1987.

rebirth, there were dozens of mentions of local citizens' groups that had formed to try to protect their neighborhoods from too much new development.

Government rules are nearly always slow to respond to change, and developers are nearly always better equipped to press for what they want than are individual citizens; nevertheless, the citizens' groups have been steadily gaining ground.

However, each group generally works in isolation, and has no way to pass on the knowledge and experience it has gained to slow-growth advocates in other areas. It's my hope to be able to take the experiences of many groups, from all parts of the country, working on all types of development problems, combined with my own ten years of dealing with (and against) dozens of over-scaled development proposals, and shape it all into one all-purpose, easy-to-follow guide for the non-specialist citizen to apply to his or her own neighborhood.

What Is *Zoning?*

Already I've used the word *zoning* sixteen times. If you're getting involved in any kind of anti-development fight for the first time, you'll be hearing this and other planning terms a lot more often, and you'll want a more complete explanation than a dictionary definition can give. Though I'll try to keep this guide as free from specialized jargon as I can, the following vocabulary is essential.

Zoning is the way governments regulate the amount and type of building allowable on a parcel of land. Zoning regulates:

- How tall a building can be
- How big it can be (called **density, bulk, mass,** or **square footage.** Also see **FAR,** below)
- How much of its ground-space it can take up (**percent of lot occupancy**)
- How far it must be set back from the property line, or street, alley, or other public right-of-way or **easement** (building setbacks)

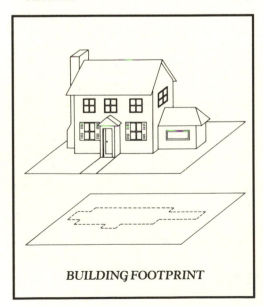

BUILDING FOOTPRINT

The zoning code's restrictions on the percent of lot occupancy and on the maintenance of set-backs work together to establish the maximum building **footprint,** or outline of the built area at the ground level, for a given piece of land. (See sketch on previous page.)

Density is measured in **FAR,** which means **Floor-to-Area Ratio.** This term is used by developers everywhere, and so needs to be learned.

To figure FAR, you total up the square footage of all the floors in the building combined (usually excluding below-ground space) and divide by the square footage (or area) of the lot you're building on. Example: A building has a total floor area of 200,000 square feet (often depicted by⍾). The area of the lot is 50,000 square feet. The FAR for this building will be 200,000:50,000, or 4:1—but will be spoken of as 4.0, or just 4.

FAR works with allowable height and percent of lot occupancy to create a maximum building **envelope.** Developers like to speak of their right to "fill the envelope"—that is, to build to the fullest height and mass permitted under the site's zoning classification. Let's say that a developer has just bought an empty lot measuring 4,800 square feet. The zoning allows 75 percent lot occupancy, an FAR of 3, and a building height of 50 feet (not counting "roof structures," such as ventilating equipment and elevator "pop-ups"). Each story of a building requires about ten feet of height. The developer can "fill his envelope" with a total floor area of 3 x 4,800, or 14,400 square feet. How he gets to this total is up to him: He can build four stories of 3,600 square feet apiece, to a height of 40 feet, or he could build five stories, each of 2,880 square feet, to a height of 50 feet. He is also, of course, allowed to build *less* than the envelope, and so could do four floors of 2,880 square feet each, if he so chose; but he could *not,* for example, do six floors of 2,400 square feet each, even though the FAR still works out to 3—because that would exceed the 50–foot height limit.

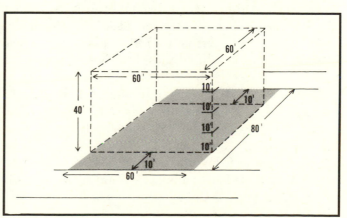

FILLING THE "ENVELOPE"

Four floors of 3600 s.f. each = 14,400 s.f., the maximum building "envelope" for this 4800 s.f. lot when FAR = 3 and lot occupancy = 75%

Zoning regulates more than building size. It also governs **use.** Some areas are zoned for **residential** use only; that means housing, whether detached single-family, attached single-family (rowhouses), multi-family low-rise (duplexes and triplexes), mid-rise (usually garden apartments and buildings up to about ten stories), or high-rise apartment buildings with ten or more floors.

Or an area may be zoned for **commercial** use. That means stores, restaurants, service-establishments, and offices are permitted, and generally, residential building is allowed as well (although it tends to be less remunerative to the developer and for that reason is seldom built in commercial zones, unless done under some sort of government incentive program). Within a commercial zone there may be a distinction made between retail and office use; and within the retail class, subcategories to distinguish establishments that draw customers from the whole city (e.g. a department store, or an automobile dealership) from those that draw just from the immediate neighborhood (a dry cleaners or a shoe-repair shop), and those that fall somewhere in between.

Or an area may be zoned **industrial,** to allow factories, power plants, warehouses, and other large-tract manufacturing uses.

Many zoning codes also allow **mixed-use** districts, that set a fixed ratio of residential to commercial development, for example, or allow commercial uses to be mixed with light industrial. The number of combinations is as large and varied as the number of separate local zoning authorities in America.

Equally varied and numerous are the types of symbols used to designate zoning categories. But there is at least a general pattern observed in most localities. When you see notations beginning with the letter **R** on a zoning map, it usually means residential, **C** means commercial, and **I** means industrial. Numbers following the letters tend to rise as the level of permitted density goes up. So an R–1 zone should be the least dense type of housing (probably detached single family houses on relatively large lots), R–2 could be rowhouses, R–3, garden apartments, and R–4, mid-rise apartment buildings.

Additional numbers or letters add desired refinements. Example: A house in an R–1–A zone will require a 7500–square-foot lot, leaving generous front, side, and back yards, while a house in an R–1–B zone requires only 5000 square feet.

Similarly, in a C–1 zone, only neighborhood-oriented shops like grocery stores and drug stores are allowed, and as the numbers go up, the list of permitted uses expands, up to the highest density category, C–5, the "central business district"—downtown.

The only way to know what symbols are used to describe the zones in your area is to call your local zoning board and ask for a list of the categories and a definition of what goes in each. This will be an easily obtainable public document.

But first you'll have to know what your local zoning authority is called. It may be called the Zoning Commission, or the County Land-Use Board, or it may go by some slightly misleading name like the Regional Parks and Planning Authority. The possibilities are endless, but if you call your local government's general information line and describe the type of board you're looking for, you should be able to get a fast answer.

You may find that zoning is handled by more than one agency. This is the case in my own city of Washington, D.C. The authority that determines what zoning category fits what piece of land is called the **Zoning Commission.** Whenever property owners or neighborhood organizations want to change the zoning category assigned to a piece of land, they apply to the Zoning Commission to have a case heard. This is called a **zoning map change case.** But whenever a property owner wants to do something other than what the zoning allows, *without changing the zoning*, he must go to the **Board of Zoning Adjustment (BZA)**. The adjustment he seeks is called a **variance**, or sometimes, a **special exception**. Development that fits within the zoning "envelope" and thus needs no special review by the zoning authorities is called **matter-of-right (M-O-R)** or **as-of-right (A-O-R)** development.

All of the specific provisions of the zoning code—the FAR limits, the use categories, the way map changes or variances are granted—are spelled out in laws and amendments passed over time by a legislative body—probably in basic form by your state assembly, which then delegates authority to the various local legislators, either county or city councils, to write specific provisions needed to address local conditions and desires.

Certain powers over zoning may also rest with the top administrative official—either the governor of the state, the chairman of the county council, or the mayor—through use of **executive orders**.

Chapter 4 will discuss in some detail how to find out who has zoning authority over your own neighborhood and what role you can play in the process.

How to Use This Book

Novice to Expert

It's my intention that even the least politically involved person—someone who's never contested a parking ticket before—could pick up this book, and by the time he or she is done with it, have a pretty clear idea of what to do when faced with almost any type of development threat. But because I begin with no assumption of reader experience, I've included information that will be too elementary for those who have already worked on, or are now part of the way into a developer-vs.-neighborhood fight (the preceding section on zoning definitions is a good example).

Even so, I hope this guide has some helpful words for the more experienced neighborhood advocate. If you are that person, then I don't recommend reading it in chapter-by-chapter order. If you already understand the regulatory process used in your area, you can certainly skip over Chapter 4. If you already know what development threat is on the horizon, Chapter 1 will be superfluous. Let's say you already know that your developer's proposal looks like this: He plans to tear down a nineteenth century, four-story brick house on your block and replace it with a ten-story office building. You might want to go right to Chapter 10, dealing with historic preservation, or read Chapter 9 on zoning. If, in addition, you will need to have a strong show of community support at your development hearing, you might look over Chapters 5, 6, and 7.

If you're not sure just what elements your development problem will ultimately involve, you may want to read through some of the seemingly "irrelevant" chapters, too—such as Chapter 11 on government development, or Chapter 13 on retaining neighborhood stores. Throughout the book I cite different cases that have been won (or lost) by real neighborhood groups using clever or innovative techniques; though the problem may not be exactly the same, you may be able to learn something from the method. Also, you may not face this particular development threat now, but who knows what the future could bring?

What if your neighborhood doesn't have any particular threat looming right now, and you don't see any in the near future either? I can't imagine where you must live! If you're in a house in the suburbs, an apartment in town, or are a student in a dorm, or a patient in a nursing home, or even if you're homeless on the street, you are affected by what developers build (and what they don't build) near the place you call home. It may be that nothing is going on at the moment—but that's not to say that change isn't on the way. And when development does get going, it often comes more rapidly than you can take in.

I've seen it happen: Suddenly, all in a bunch (the way buffalo move from one grazing area to another) developers "discover" a place. Even if you live in the most remote mountain village, you could wake up one morning and open your newspaper to a real estate ad hyping your hidden wilderness retreat as the next Aspen or Vail. "Coming Soon! A 2000–room luxury ski resort!" Before you have a chance to think twice about the prospect, you find out that the land's already been rezoned and the developer's got his backhoes and bulldozers all set to roll. Then there's little time to sit back, read a book, learn the lingo, and figure out what to do next.

But even in this worst-case scenario there will be things you can do (see Chapter 16). Naturally, however, you will be much better off to be able to anticipate development well before it occurs, and have the time to react thoughtfully, to pick which of the methods, or combinations of methods will work best for you.

Different Cases, Different Places

You will notice I use a lot of examples from the Washington, D.C., area. That's because I've lived in the nation's capital and its suburbs since 1968 and can write with most authority about the system as I've seen it work. But that doesn't mean you can only learn about one system from this book. There are nine different counties, two states, and the District of Columbia in this area, and each has its own special way of handling development cases. One of them will most likely handle cases the way they are handled where you live.

There is also more than one way to try to win any particular case. You can work strictly within the rules of the system, you can try to go around it by a variety of maneuvers, or you can try to change the rules to make the system work for you. This book will cover the broad spectrum of approaches: the administrative, legal, political, financial, moral, and (if absolutely necessary) obstructionist ways to see to it that your neighborhood is not destroyed by overdevelopment.

I've had personal experience, and success, with all of these approaches, including the last-resort tactics of civil disobedience (discussed in Chapter 16). Since 1979, I've organized, fought, negotiated with developers, lobbied for legislation, and testified in the courts about developments of all different shapes and types. It hasn't always been fun (truthfully, sometimes it's been a major pain), but now, a decade after I got started, I haven't a doubt that the effort was worth it. My Washington, D.C., neighborhood of Cleveland Park is now very well protected by city laws and regulations against any further out-of-scale development. The fight is finally over, the citizens have won, and my neighborhood has been saved.

Now what about yours?

PART I

DEVELOPMENT

BASICS

FINDING OUT WHAT'S COMING

The Secrecy of "Public Notice"

You can't fight what you don't know about. So before you even get to step one—making that important first contact with the developer—you have to get beyond step zero: You must know how to find out if there *is* a developer, and if so, who he is,* and what he's up to.

This *sounds* relatively straightforward, right? And it might well turn out to be, if you live in a neighborhood where you're *expecting* development to occur on a particular piece of land. You can monitor that land in the building-permits process and watch closely for the first signs of movement. But if you don't know where or when a part of your neighborhood might be developed, unfortunately, in most places, you're going to find it a tough problem to tackle.

This may come as a bit of a shock to you. You probably have assumed that your local government, like nearly all public bodies today, works under a "sunshine law" requiring that all public business be conducted openly, so that the public can find out what's going on. Any kind of development, no matter how small, will require government approval for construction, even if the project is entirely within the current zoning (that is, no special exceptions, zoning changes, or variances are involved). The reason for this is to ensure that health and safety standards are met, both during the construction and after the building is in operation. So when a developer has a plan to do something in your neighborhood (unless he's a sleazy operator or some kind

---

* Or she. But though I've met a couple of female developers, the overwhelming majority have been male, and for that reason, whenever I use a pronoun for members of the profession, I will always say "he."

of racketeer), you can be sure he will have filed an application with the government for all the necessary permits involved. The fact of that application must somehow be made known to the public. Now comes the problem. Here is the way that this "public notice" will probably be handled in your county or town.

The developer will have to put an advertisement in the newspaper describing what he wants to build and where. You might think this would take up a full or at least a half-page of a newspaper, with pictures of the planned building and a map showing its location. You should be so lucky! The public notice provision will likely be satisfied if the developer takes out a few lines in the "Legal Notices" section of the classifieds. The ad may go something like this:

FILLINTHEBLANK COUNTY, ANYWHERE CITY

Application No. 1234567–89 for Lot 1234, Square 567 (888 9th Street) development in C–3–B zone received on September 11, 1989 from B.D.G. Real Estate Investment Partners. Case file available for inspection at County Hall Buildings, 22 Civic Avenue, 2:30–4:30 pm on Wednesdays. All persons wishing to comment on the application must have their comments in to the Permit Processing Division of the Building and Land Regulation Department by 5:00 pm on Friday, September 29.

Or there's another way "public notice" might be given. This places the announcement in an even more out-of-the-way publication: the state, county, or municipal Register. Like the *Federal Register* but on the local level, this limited-circulation, subscription-only journal carries the daily record of every official act of government, from the text of major pieces of legislation to proposals for a new stop-sign at a particular intersection. Buried somewhere amid pages and pages of notices of building permit applications—for additions, swimming pools, awnings, and other small homeowner projects—could be the permit application for a new building the size of one of the World Trade Center towers!

Even if you were extremely diligent and subscribed to your local government Register, and read it cover to cover as soon as you got it, you could still miss the notice of new development. It may not be listed under the project's street address, or even include that information in the text. It will most likely be listed in order of file number, or by property lot and square number (a number assigned by the Property Tax collection division for their records), or it could be in alphabetical order of the applicants' names, or listed under their corporate address.

And then even if you were able to recognize a listing for a property in your neighborhood, you still would not know very much at all. Under purpose or type of application, the listing could say only: "New construction"—perhaps giving an estimated cost for the new building, perhaps giving only the amount of the filing fee paid.

To make matters still *worse*, by the time the notice is in the register or in the classifieds, the project review period could be nearly completed, or already over. It will be too late in the game for you to get the building plans disapproved or even modified.

Sounds hopeless, doesn't it? Sounds like a developer with reason to be wary of public comment can go a long way toward getting his plan approved before anyone in the neighborhood knows anything about it. That, of course, is just the way most developers like it, and why they don't want to see the system changed—though most neighborhood activists would dearly love to see reform. (The last chapter of this book will deal with ways to approach this problem, as well as other systemic reforms that are needed.)

There's no doubt if you rely on the legal concept of "public notice" to learn of your development, you'll learn too little too late. But "hopeless" is too strong a word for the situation. At least it was for a group of neighbors in Washington, D.C., who found out about a massive new development many weeks after the public notice had appeared in the *District Register*.

The developer already had his permits in hand and had already demolished the old garden-supply shop that had stood on the site, when the neighbors learned that its replacement would be an office building of some 800,000 square feet. The local planning officials told the disgruntled neighbors that there was nothing they could do to stop it: The developer was fully **vested,** meaning that he had established a legal right to proceed. The mayor had the *executive power* to hold up the construction temporarily, but claimed he had no authority to stop the project altogether.

But the neighbors looked at it this way: The law says a developer is **vested** only after he gives public notice of his intention to build a building within the limits of the zoning. We're the public, they reasoned, and no one ever notified us! Therefore, the notice he gave must have been defective—not up to the standards required by the wording of the public notice law. On that basis, they hired a lawyer and sued the city to have the permits revoked.

Over the next eighteen months, the question was debated in the courts, and for much of that time, development was at a standstill. The delay in his construction timetable was costing the developer millions. And though he ultimately did win the argument on the validity of the notice, by the time he won it the point was moot. The expense of the lawsuit had forced him to seek an accommodation with the neighbors, to change the plans for traffic circulation around the building to suit their needs. It wasn't everything they had wanted, but it was still far more than they would have gotten had they simply accepted the government's idea of "public notice."

While it all came out fairly well for that neighborhood, they resolved never again to be caught in the same bind. Now they know it's up to them to be vigilant for any signs that development is coming. They have appointed a **neighborhood monitor,** a volunteer who has learned how to read the permit listings column in the local government register. Once a week she reads through them thoroughly, noting any lots and squares numbered with the code used for the neighborhood, and if there are any applications that seem significant, she calls the building permit processing office and gets more details.

A monitor system can work wonderfully, and if you can set one up for your neighborhood, I recommend it. But you may not be able to find volunteers with the time and patience to keep at it. Still, there are plenty of other ways, unofficial as well as official, for you to get information on what will be happening in your area.

Sources, Official and Unofficial

Private Contacts

Agents. Do you have any friends in the real estate industry? Sales agents have access to vast amounts of useful information through their computerized networks. When large lots change hands for high prices, that's often the first sign of big new construction in the planning. Or when a number of smaller lots on the same block are sold to the same person or company—called **assemblage**—that's another clear signal that development is on the way. If you do have friends who are in a position to learn about these sales, by all means, ask them to keep you posted. There's nothing improper about this. Completed sales are a matter of public record. It's only when deals are being worked out between the parties that the state of the transaction may be guarded as proprietary information.

If you don't have any friends in the real estate business—well, it's always good to expand your social circle, isn't it?

But even without inside friends, the real estate world can yield a wealth of information. Your local newspaper or business journal carries ads for large tracts of commercial and residential lots for sale. When you see a piece of your own neighborhood being touted as a "PRIME OPPORTUNITY FOR COMMERCIAL DEVELOPMENT," or see an ad that goes something like this: "Joint Venture Offering! Will Rezone to Suit Your Development Needs!" or uses any other wording that suggests big buildings and big profits are to be had in your own neighborhood—CLIP THAT AD!

Now, I have to admit, I was never one to pore over the back pages of the ads section, on the off-chance that a piece of land near me might turn up on the market. But I had a friend who always reads the whole paper from cover to cover; he happened to notice that a large parcel of land very close to my house was on the market, and he very thoughtfully pointed it out to me. As soon as I saw the real estate agent's number, I called to express my inter-

est in the property (not, of course, specifying that my interest was that of a nearby neighbor, not of a prospective buyer).

The sales agent asked me, "Are you calling on behalf of a company?"—to which I answered, truthfully, that I was speaking for a group of individuals who were interested in the property's long-term investment potential. (My neighbors and I were certainly as concerned as any buyer would be to learn what kind of profit-potential existed on land in our own backyards!) I don't believe in lying to get information, so I didn't say anything further to the agent to describe myself; I let the agent do the rest of the talking.

He was very helpful. He told me the asking price for the undeveloped acreage ($7 million), told me what it was zoned for, and tossed out some ideas on how the land's restrictive zoning category might be changed. He even gave me some hints as to how I might deal with "that anti-development neighborhood group"!

I thanked him, but told him I considered the property vastly overpriced. So, apparently, have most developers who have taken a look at the property, and it still sits on the market, several years later, with no price reduction and no current offers pending. But so long as it does, we can easily keep track of it, by checking every so often with the agent or in the public land records to see if the situation has changed. And when a new owner/developer comes in, we'll be ready to deal with him—well before he gets any permit applications in the works!

The Developer Himself. You may not have to go to him, or wheedle information out of his agents, to find out what the developer wants to do. More often than you'd think, the first news of a major project in the works comes when the developer himself picks up the phone and calls you.

If the secrecy of the public notice process generally works to the developer's advantage, why should he ever be the one to make the first move? I can think of six possible explanations right off the bat.

1. The developer really thinks he has a terrific project which nobody in his or her right mind is going to oppose, and he wants the neighbors to hear all about the wonderful development he's going to build for them.

2. He knows there's going to be substantial opposition from certain quarters, and he wants to start disarming that opposition now. So he will probably begin by contacting the people within the community he feels are most likely to be receptive to his plan, in the hope that they will start spreading the word on it in the most favorable terms. The opponents will then be put in the position of having to fight against the positive image already formed in the public mind.

3. He's not yet committed to all elements of the plan. If opposition emerges in response to certain aspects, he's still free to alter the plan to eliminate the objectionable elements and so effect an early consensus in the plan's favor. (This is the best motive for a developer, from your point of view, and the easiest sort of person for you to work with.)

4. He needs to know which way the wind is blowing in order to set his strategy properly. If there is early opposition, he can better prepare his counter-arguments; and if the opposition seems too strong, he can abort the project before it costs him too much money.

5. He's got at least one other big project planned for the same neighborhood. He's trying to establish a good working relationship with the neighborhood on *this* project (probably the most palatable of the several he's got on the drawing board) in order to foster a sense in the community that he's a decent, responsive sort of guy, someone you can trust now and in the future. He knows that the second and third projects will undergo much less scrutiny than the first, if he succeeds in securing this good image for himself.

6. There is no ulterior motive. He wants nothing other than to keep the neighbors well-apprised of matters that he understands concern them deeply. He's just an honest, thoughtful, helpful kind of guy. (I haven't met this type of developer yet, but I still want to believe that, along with Tinkerbell and the Tooth Fairy, he really does exist somewhere.)

Leaks. There is a far more common way to hear the first rumblings of development on the way—through the **rumor mill.** If you live in an area where real estate is hot right now, and you keep your ears tuned, you're bound to get some snatches now and then of big projects in the works (maybe even before the developer himself is sure of what he's doing!) Development information, because it necessarily involves so many people, is hard to keep under wraps. Architects and their assistants may be approached about design concepts; people in banking will be asked about financing; consultants in engineering, landscaping, traffic, and a host of other specialties will be contacted and asked for preliminary opinions. If just one of these professionals or clerical employees is unhappy with some aspect of the work, he or she may break the secrecy of the project. (It's happened before on a project my neighborhood opposed, but I'm sworn to protect my source.)

The leaker may live in the neighborhood where the problematic development is to be located, or may have a close friend or relative who does, or be acting on less benign motives, like a desire to get back at his or her boss or client. I know of one case where cut-throat competition was the motive. A sandwich-shop operator gave the neighborhood advance warning that a nationwide fast-food chain was set to develop a building on the block. Frightened of the prospect of more litter, cooking fumes, and cars idling at all hours while customers waited for their take-out orders, the community quickly organized a campaign against the development of the site. The leaker had no interest in any of these issues; his only goal was not to share his location with another, better-known purveyor of hamburgers and fries.

A rumor need not be absolutely verified to be useful to a neighborhood. I saw how this worked in my own neighborhood. I live one block away from a 2000–seat movie theater, and within a two-mile radius there are (I counted) twenty-three other screens. On weekend "date" nights, it's all but impossible for the neighbors to find a place to park their cars within ten blocks of their own homes. We had all heard that a new retail/office complex was planned for a large commercial lot just across the street from the 2000–seat moviehouse. Somehow a rumor got started that this new development was to include a six-screen cinema below-ground. The neighbors couldn't pin the rumor down, but it seemed plausible enough: The site zoning permitted the usage, and a spokesman for the movie-exhibiter's association had been recently quoted as calling the city "under-screened"—that is, able to profitably support a big increase in the number of theaters.

But just the remote *possibility* of getting another six screens—and God-knows-how-many-more cars circling around the neighborhood every night for parking—caused an immediate outcry against the idea. The developer's spokesman was quick and repetitive in his assurances. No, no, there was not, and never had been, a plan to put any movie theaters in the complex.

Maybe that was so and maybe not, but one thing was clear: The fast, heated community reaction to the rumor had caused the developer to make a public promise that there would be no theaters in the complex.

But while a rumor of something bad coming (whether valid or not) can help to rally neighbors against a common threat, hot-headed, half-cocked reactions to rumors can also do some harm. Residents of the neighborhood just to the south of mine hurt their own credibility this way. They'd heard that a commercial landlord had a plan to redevelop his storefront property, which had been left vacant when the former leaseholder, a small deli-gourmet shop, had suddenly moved out. The talk on the street was that the landlord had forced the turnover because he wanted to get a higher-rent user in the space—possibly something like a nightclub, disco, or bar (whose patrons would have come from either of the two huge hotels that were in the neighborhood). But nobody apparently, thought to call the landlord and ask him what was coming. Instead some neighbors called up their city councilwoman complaining bitterly that greedy landlords were yet again driving away small, neighborhood-serving businesses for their own profits. When the councilwoman called the landlord to discuss the problem, he was baffled and upset. The former tenant shopkeeper had moved of his own will; a long-term lease with a new, nicer, cleaner deli-gourmet store had already been signed. The new place would be opening in a few weeks' time.

The councilwoman was left to apologize—and doubtless to wonder if she should in future be so quick to come to the aid of her anxiety-prone constituents.

In this case, it would have been quite a simple thing for the neighbors to have asked the landlord directly what his plans were as soon as the empty storefront appeared.

Still, there will be times when you can't find any way to track a rumor down. In those instances, you'll have to judge for yourself whether it's best to ignore the rumor or repeat it, and see what response it gets. There are three factors to weigh in the use of rumor:

1. Consider the source. Is the person telling you the rumor likely to be in a position to know something true? Or is he or she just passing along something picked up from someone else, who's in no better position to know?

2. Consider the substance. Let's say you hear that a developer has a plan to build a twenty-story hotel next door to your house. But you know that the zoning for the site allows only three stories. Don't even think twice about the rumor. The disparity between what's rumored and what's allowed is so great, it would be highly improbable, if not impossible, for any developer to get permission for such a structure. On the other hand, if the zoning allows sixteen stories already, an application for a four-story variance does not sound so far-fetched—and you had better start checking into it!

3. Consider the harm that could be done if you act on the rumor and it turns out that you're wrong. If people are likely to get emotional and start shouting out accusations that may well be unwarranted, you had better keep quiet. If you have confidence that your neighbors will act responsibly, then you can offer up the rumor, with appropriate caution, as a possibility, (perhaps one of many) and start formulating a prudent response, which you will then have ready should the rumor prove true.

Government Contacts

Elected Officials. The people who represent you at the local level—your city or county councilmember or state legislator—often hear of pending development in their electoral districts long before their constituents do. This is especially true if the project will entail public costs (the construction of new roads, sewer hook-ups, more classroom space for children of new residents, and so forth). If your elected officials are doing their jobs, they'll waste no time in informing and consulting with the most affected neighbors. Even the most pro-development politicians by reputation (if they have any political savvy at all) know it's bad to be caught off guard by negative constituent reaction. So they set up meetings, invite the residents in to hear the developer talk about his plans, and in some cases, act as go-betweens to iron out differences between the developer and the community.

When the politician is well-versed in land-planning and well-attuned to the needs of the people he or she represents, the politician is quite likely to make an excellent first contact for development information. But I can think of three circumstances in which it would *not* be desirable for a neighborhood to rely on the politician to fulfill this function:

1. —when the politician and the developer are known to have a close relationship (evidenced by the fact that the politician has received substantial campaign contributions from the developer, or has supported the developer's work in the past). Chief danger: The politician may give the neighbors the impression that the plans are moving on the preferred track through the government permit process, leaving them hesitant to make the effort to organize and object.

2. —when the politician has limited ties to that part of his constituency affected by the project. He or she may not get the information through to the people who can act on it, or he or she could simply sit on the information and do nothing with it. Meanwhile, the developer thinks,

because the politician is not reporting any objections, that the plans must have been well-received in the community.

3. —when the politician has the right intentions and promptly does inform the most prominent members of the community, but those community leaders happen not to be well-attuned to development sentiment in their own neighborhood, or simply have no idea what to do with the information.

Chapter 6 will address some of the steps you can take if either your recognized community leaders or your elected officials are unresponsive or ineffective in their handling of development problems in your neighborhood.

Your politicians will be far more likely to come to you quickly to let you know what they've heard about development if you've let them know in advance that you'd appreciate it. The same is true for the heads of any citizens' associations or other recognized community figures. Then, when they do get that first nibble of information, they'll be on notice that you expect to hear from them soon, and be brought into the process long before any bricks are laid or concrete is poured.

When you go to "touch base" with your elected representative, let him or her know at the start what type of development would cause you the most concern (office construction encroaching on a residential area? another shopping mall? loss of remaining open space?) This helps the politician understand what you want him or her to do. Extra suggestion: Be quick and to the point with the politician, but spend the longer part of your visit briefing the staff people. When something new comes into the office, it's usually the staff who see it first; how the boss hears of it, how he or she approaches the issue, typically will have more to do with the way the staff presented it than with the politician's own ideas.

Administrators, Regulators, and Planners. If your elected officials don't get the word first, it's probably because the system in your area doesn't work that way. Some time ago, someone decided that development should not be allowed to become a "political football," that the issue needed to be dealt with rationally, scientifically, without prejudice or favoritism—as only professional planners and trained public policy experts could do. So a department is set up within the government bureaucracy and all development applications are routed to it first. This department could be called the County or City Planning Office, the Land Use and Development Department, the Office on Economic Growth—every government invents its own term for this agency. In low-budget systems, there may not be an entire department, but the mayor or county executive will simply have an assistant on staff who functions as the reviewer of new plans.

The fastest way to find out if there is such an agency and what name it goes by, is to call up your mayor or county supervisor's office and ask. (The planning office will normally be found within the executive branch of the government.)

Once you've established that your jurisdiction does have a special planning department, you should quickly seek out the staff member assigned to handle your neighborhood. In all likelihood, if there is a developer interested in doing something near you, he will have already started exploring the matter with the planning staff. Government planners could well have begun to study how *they* think the project will affect you and your neighbors, without consulting you. If you want to get "into the loop" (the circuit of consultations) as soon as a development is under consideration, you'll need to let the planning office know you're there. You will probably have to be part of a recognized neighborhood organization to receive this courtesy. It's too much to expect that officials will call every interested resident, every time a new development is under discussion. But an organization is a different matter.

Physical Signs

Suppose you miss the public notice in the paper. Your elected representatives haven't heard a thing, and your local planning officials never thought to get in touch with you. The very first clue you may get of the new development will probably come from your own eyes and ears. You will see physical evidence that development is on the way.

To catch it in the early stages, you will need to be alert. Keep a regular watch on any vacant lots or empty storefronts in your neighborhood. Have you ever seen people looking over the property, or walking around with clipboards, or using surveying equipment or other accouterments of the site-planning and engineering trades? Be nosy! Ask them what they're up to. The worst they can do is refuse to answer. They may well be willing to tell you exactly what the future holds for the site, or at least refer you to a boss or landlord who can tell you.

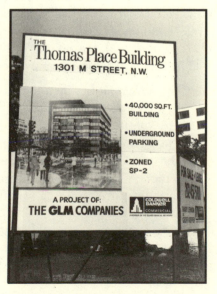

If you don't see the development people at work yourself, you could still find the physical signs that they've been there. Keep an eye out for stakes in the ground, paint markings on the sidewalk (identifying where utility lines come in from the street), and cuts in the asphalt or borings in the earth (to test the soundness of the foundation or the condition of the soil).

The most unmistakable signs you already know: construction fences, construction trailers, backhoes, and bulldozers. Quite often the fence has a giant poster on it with a full color illustration of what the project will look like when finished—usually complete with mature trees drawn in and happy pedestrians strolling down the sidewalks. By the time you see these signs, the permits will all have been granted and the development will be well underway. Though it's pretty late for you to hope to have much impact on the plans, you can at least ask to see the permits.

They should be available for you to check on site. The typed-up permit will list the name and address of the issuing agency of government, and the file number, so you will be able to visit the office and take a look at the actual plan in the file (as opposed to what's on the glossy poster), which will tell you all the specifications of height, density, traffic circulation, and so forth.

What if you don't see any permits displayed anywhere (you checked first on the window of the construction trailer, the most likely spot) and then you asked the foreman or site manager and they couldn't (or wouldn't) answer your questions?

First, you should know the law about public access to permits in your area. In a few places there is no requirement to post or make permits accessible to the public. You'll have to go to the government hall to see whether or not approval for construction has been granted.

But if you know there is a law requiring permit display (and that's *very* likely to be the case), but no one will let you take a look at the permits, you should be concerned, for one of two reasons:

1. The developer has instructed his employees to disregard the law and treat the public like intruders. This signals a basic insensitivity to the rights of the community. You will undoubtedly have a very hard time trying to work with this developer.

2. The developer is proceeding entirely without a permit, or doing some extra construction not authorized by the permits, or doing the permitted construction in a way that doesn't meet the building code. If you have reason to think any of these illegal acts could be going on, don't hesitate: Call the police at once! They will put a **stop-work order** on the building. Un-permitted construction is a serious offense. To give an idea of how serious, consider how New York City handled one

violator. In 1985 a developer, overnight and in secret, tore down an old, crumbling welfare hotel; for his failure to obtain a proper demolition permit he was fined *two million dollars* and barred from any further work on the site for a period of *four years*.

Now let's assume you are given no trouble about your request to see the permits. The site manager or foreman is willing to talk to you and lead you over to the corner window of the construction trailer where the government approvals have been put up with scotch tape. Unless you have training in the construction business, you probably won't be able to tell very much from seeing these slips of paper. But if they're willing to help you this far, it's a good bet they're willing to answer a few other questions as well. Ask the man in charge to describe the project to you as fully as he can. You may be told, "It's company policy not to talk to unauthorized persons." But they should still be willing to give you the name and phone number of someone in the developer's office who will be willing to answer your questions.

Once you've got the name of someone to contact, make that call without delay. It's a universal principle: The earlier you catch the development, the more impact you can have on its final form. So even if the people on site say something that sounds reassuring ("No, there's no construction plan yet. We're just surveying the site to get an idea of the lay of the land" or "We haven't applied for any permits yet. We'll be sure to call you before we do")—don't sit back and wait for development to start. The time before applications are filed is far and away the most valuable time for neighbors to meet with and try to influence a developer. Don't let it go to waste!

Special Notice for Special Projects

In all the situations discussed so far, where clear warning is lacking and signs of development need to be ferreted out, it's because no special exceptions or changes in the zoning are necessary (that is, the construction falls within the developer's **matter-of-right**).

Public notice is generally not a problem when a developer seeks to build *more* than the current zoning permits. Variances and "bonus" allowances must be granted by a quasi-judicial agency of the government, after a full public hearing on the merits, in which all affected persons will have the right to participate. The public hearing can only be scheduled if all those affected are duly notified according to procedures set down by law.

This notice most often comes in the form of large signs tacked up on fences or utility poles on or around the potential building site, starting a fixed number of days in advance of the public hearing date. (It might be 30, 45, or perhaps

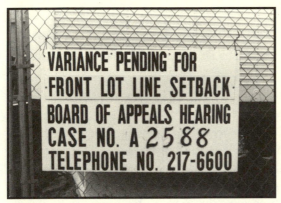

VARIANCE PENDING FOR FRONT LOT LINE SETBACK BOARD OF APPEALS HEARING CASE NO. A 2588 TELEPHONE NO. 217-6600

60 days beforehand.) The sign will look something like this. However, the exact wording will vary greatly from town to town.

Requirements for posting also vary. Some rule books call for just one sign posted on-site; others mandate signs to be placed one on every block up to 200, 300, 500 feet, or even further from the property. Generally, it's up to the applicant to do the posting and to certify by affidavit that the sign stayed up through all of the pre-hearing notice period. (The legitimacy of the hearing is subject to attack by development opponents if they can show the applicant did not meet the hearing notice requirements.)

While big signs with big, black lettering are hard to miss, some localities make development notice even more certain by requiring a mailing to go out to all property owners within so many hundred feet of the site. This method may fail to get the word out to renters, however.

Whether by sign-posting, by mailing, or by both methods combined, notice of a scheduled public hearing will contain several pieces of crucial information. It will of course give the date, time, and place of the public hearing. It will identify the location of the property to be developed (maybe in terms of lot and square number, rather than street address) and tell the name and address of the applicant (not necessarily the same company or persons as the developer), and describe, more or less, what the hearing will be about—though it probably will do so exclusively in technical zoning language (e.g., "Request for 27 percent variance from lot occupancy requirements in a C–1 zone," or "Special Exception to allow a mixed-use development, C/R–3, in an R–2–B zone").

You may feel you need to be a zoning lawyer to decipher the code of the public notice. Don't worry. The notice will carry a telephone number to call for more information. Anything in the notice that isn't crystal clear, you should ask the staff person who answers the phone to explain to you. Don't hang up until you're sure you understand everything the notice tells you, because you will be held responsible for your ignorance if you misstate any of the facts about the case at the public hearing. Above all, you should find out what you need to do to be recognized as an "affected person" and allowed to participate, either as an individual or as a member of a recognized community organization, at the upcoming hearing.

You may need to put your request to participate in writing so many working days before the hearing is held. Whether or not you're sure you intend to get involved in the case, go ahead and send in the letter. You can always cancel later, but it will be hard to be allowed in after the deadline has passed.

When you first see a notice of a public hearing on development, you may feel the 30, 45, or even 60–day period gives you sufficient time to act. You'll think you have time to find out what the proposal is for, and study how it will affect your neighborhood, and prepare a measured response. But be warned: large-scale projects often pose a multiplicity of problems that need to be analyzed with some thoroughness. The developer has probably had his plans in the works for many months, if not years. You're only being given a few short weeks to decide how you will deal with something that will affect living conditions in your neighborhood for decades to come, and maybe for the rest of your life.

Seen in this light, the 40– or 60–day lead-time will seem inadequate. So even in cases where mailings are done and signs are well-placed and in large, legible type, you are still going to be much better off if you can find out about the pending special project well in advance of the formal filing. So keep your eyes and ears open, read the ads, pay attention to whatever real estate talk you hear...and good luck!

Two

TELLING THE PEOPLE WHO NEED TO KNOW

You have learned (through any of the methods discussed in Chapter 1) that a big change is coming to your neighborhood. You're not sure whether it's a good change or a bad change, but whatever it is, you want to have something to say about it. You're ready to start making contacts, and you can begin by moving in any of three directions:

1. Get together with the people in your neighborhood you feel are most likely to share your interest in the development proposal, and who will be willing to help you do something about it;

2. Contact an existing organization that has in the past dealt with development problems of this type, or which might be willing to tackle this one;

3. Contact the developer yourself, find out all you can about the proposal, and based on what you learn, decide on your own whether the proposal should be opposed, and if so, what individuals or groups should be asked to work on the issue.

All three courses of action have their merits. If you're the aggressive type and have the persistence to keep trying to get through to the person in charge, and you don't mind being as nosy as it takes to get your answers, then by all means, follow the third course. You just might find that the project is exactly the sort of thing your neighborhood wants and needs, and in that case, quit right there and relax. But consider: If you don't know enough about planning to know how to interpret what the developer tells you...(if, say, he's describing a building with an FAR of 7 and an 80 percent lot occupancy and a footprint of 59,000 square feet, and you're not sure what that means) for God's sake, *don't* relax! Take down what you've learned and discuss it with people who have some experience in dealing with development terms before you agree to anything. Keep in mind that all developers, even the most responsible of the breed, will use the blandest, most soothing, least alarming terms to describe their projects. "Public benefits"... "compatibility with neighborhood character"..."extensive landscaping"..."sensitive design"... "job training for unemployed youth" and other high-sounding phrases can (and will) be used in connection with any development, even if it's for another Alcatraz! So question all aspects intensively, and don't accept vague assurances. There can be no substitute for the numerical data.

Let's assume you don't have the time or expertise needed to go over the proposal on your own, or you don't want to take on the responsibility yourself of judging whether a plan is good or bad for your neighborhood. Then you'll want to get in touch with others who will share the burden with you, and as soon as you can. But how can you know who these people are? That will depend in large part on what kind of neighborhood you're in and what kind of development problem you're facing.

Who to Call First: Three Problems

Problem 1. Too Few Neighbors. Ellen S. lives near a twenty-five-acre tract of woodland. She's found out it's been sold to a developer with a contract to build a hospital. Her neighborhood is semi-rural, and there are only a handful of homeowners nearby who are likely to be as upset as she is. In her tranquil corner of the county, there isn't a homeowners' or community association to deal with these types of problems, because they've never had them before. The closest local citizens' group, representing a dense, suburban subdivision a few miles away, has already held a reception to welcome the planners and administrators of the hospital, which they consider to be far more beneficial to the public than the forest that's there now.

Ellen is worried that the lack of nearby allies to take up the cause will mean defeat before she's even begun. But then she starts to think of others who might share her feelings about the land. She remembers that there are hiking trails through the forest, and that the local branch of the Audubon Society has been leading bird-walks there on a regular basis. She recalls having heard the bird-walk coordinator speak of her doctoral work on a particular species of bird that nests there, but nowhere else in the region.

So Ellen goes right to the phone and calls the bird-person, who immediately offers the help of her fellow members in responding to the development plan. She also gives Ellen the names of some people at the Sierra Club and the Nature Conservancy she thinks will want to be active on the development question.

Meanwhile, Ellen's closest neighbor, Tom D., has had an idea. He's been walking through the woods every morning and talking to everyone he meets. He's discovered that people from all over the county use the woodland—many more than he'd imagined. He's met joggers, dog-walkers, picnickers, plant biologists from the state university, and a scout troop and their scoutmaster doing trail maintenance. Each of these, when told the trees would be coming down, has expressed some desire to help save them, and a few of them have some special skills in land-use planning, politics, or community organization to contribute to the effort. One of the joggers he talked to was a lawyer. So, despite the sparse population of the area, Ellen actually had little trouble getting enough people together to form a working group to start dealing with the development plan.

Problem 2. Too Many Neighbors, Too Little Known about Them. Sam F. lives in an apartment building in an already densely populated urban neighborhood. He figures most people won't mind that another tall apartment tower will be built; if they're like him, they moved there because they prefer the lively, bustling quality of this part of town. But the new apartment building will be sited so that it will throw a long shadow every afternoon over the only baseball-sandlot in the neighborhood. *And* they'll be building it on land that the school system has leased for the past fifteen years to be the recess grounds for the elementary school next door.

But Sam doesn't know any of the other people in his building very well. Nor is there an active neighborhood association around to deal with the matter. But there *are* two obvious pre-existing organizations that will rally around the cause: the weekend baseball players' leagues, and the parents of the schoolchildren who will be losing their only playground. Sam has only to drop by the sandlot on Saturday morning and tell the team captains what's going on, and then contact the head of the PTA and tell her what the plan will do to the school kids, to be sure that the issue will not be neglected.

Problem 3. Some Neighbors Are Timid. Bill J.'s in a fairly common situation. He's lived in his neighborhood for years and he knows most of the people. He's heard a developer has plans to put up an office building on the major avenue nearby—but the loading docks and the driveway to the parking garage will be located on the alley that feeds into his all-residential side street. Seven hundred extra cars a day will be entering and exiting the alley past his house.

He's contacted his local citizens' association, but he's found its small membership to be nervous about getting involved in anything controversial—besides which, they have no practical experience in dealing with development. Bill soon discovers that their hesitance is less of a problem than he'd thought. The minute *most* of his neighbors find out about the projected increase in traffic, they are up in arms over the development. By the time Bill's finished explaining where the trucks will be parked to unload, he can tell that he's talking to people willing to help him do something about it. A new ad hoc citizens' group comes into being that will take a stand where the existing one would not.

Of course, Bill did find one or two of the homeowners on his block who were hesitant to join in. But he expected this and didn't push them, thinking it was better not to antagonize anyone. Some people believe so strongly in private development rights that they're against any attempt by neighbors to have influence over nearby growth. Others simply don't have the time or the inclination to focus on a neighborhood issue. Still others will find the proposal—however frightening it may seem to *you*—nothing to get worked up about.

It's far too early in the process to be worried about a few refusals to your invitation to get involved. As long as you are able to find at least five or six others who feel more or less as you do about the neighborhood, you will be able to get started on dealing with the developer's plans. Chapter 5 will go into ways to attract others to the group and turn it into an effective defender of your neighborhood's interests. Chapter 7 will deal with building and keeping consensus within the group.

Your First Meeting

Now you've figured out who besides yourself is interested in the problem; you've perhaps even talked to the developer or to city officials to find out how fast the plans are moving and how much time you have to react. Whether the development is going fast or slow, you should take the same next step: You must call a meeting.

It will—unfortunately—be the first of many meetings you can expect to attend if you're going to be a player in this field. But with a little forethought and a few easily learned management tips, you will be able to hold the length and the number of your meetings to a bare minimum. Some groups exhaust themselves meeting endlessly and pointlessly into the night, and that's a fate you'll want to work hard to avoid!

Each meeting should have a stated purpose, a written but *brief* agenda, a designated person to run it (not necessarily given the formal title of "chairman" but at least understood to be in charge of the flow of discussion), a set time limit (say, two hours) and, by the end of the meeting, a common understanding of what each participant is supposed to do next.

If you start out your first meeting under these terms, you'll find all subsequent meetings that much easier to handle. But start off with sloppy meeting procedures—no person in charge, everybody talking at once, no agenda, no time limit—and you'll waste hours, days, weeks of your life re-explaining things, arguing, trying to figure out who was supposed to do what—and generally going in circles. Good people will get frustrated and drop out, or worse, be recruited over to the developer's better-run, seemingly-more-sensible side. So be warned now!

A Practical Starting Point. The person with the most spacious house or apartment hosts the first meeting. Alternate plan (for a larger first meeting): The person who knows how to get permission to use the church basement or the school auditorium will make the arrangements for time and place. Whoever called for the first meeting to take place will act as its (temporary) chair. That person will also type and photocopy a simple agenda.

Method of Announcement. If the number you're starting out with is small enough (under twenty), don't bother with written announcements. Call the people you think most likely to want to get involved and ask them to attend. (If you don't know them all personally, either ask someone who does to extend the invitation, or go right ahead and introduce yourself. Most people are only too happy to get to know their neighbors.)

Calling Out the Whole Neighborhood. In some cases the harm of the proposed development will be so clear-cut, and the time-frame for neighborhood reaction so short, you won't have the luxury of inviting a small circle of neighbors in to mull the problem over. You'll want to cut the preliminaries and get the whole neighborhood out to deal with the crisis.

In the fall of 1987 my neighborhood was faced with just such a situation. Our only grocery store was on the verge of closing and it seemed certain that the site would be redeveloped as a mid-rise office building. No zoning change was required. Neither I nor any of the other regular community activists knew what we could do to prevent this from happening. But we did know how to put an emergency meeting together. Here's what we did.

The minute I had confirmation from the Safeway manager that the grocery chain was definitely pulling out, I called a few people who I knew would be upset by the news. One was the president of his apartment complex's large tenants' association. Another was simply a neighbor who was willing to call around to find a large auditorium to hold our town meeting in. A third owned a personal computer and some simple graphics software, and was able to put together an eye-catching flyer on short notice, to let the neighbors know that there would be a meeting on the matter, and when and where it would be.

A fourth was active in senior citizens' issues, and would be a moving public speaker about the hardships facing the neighborhood's elderly (few of whom had cars), should the area's only grocery store in walking distance shut its doors just before Thanksgiving (as Safeway was set to do).

SAVE OUR SUPERMARKET

SAFEWAY has announced a closing date of Oct. 17 -- not much time to press for Safeway's retention or work for its replacement with another grocery store. So we need everyone's help!

IF YOU CAN, PLEASE ATTEND

● AN EMERGENCY MEETING ●
== ========= =======

Saturday, Sept. 12
10 a.m.
Cleveland Park Library Aud.

If you can't attend, you can still write letters of protest to:

Peter A. Magowan
Chairman of the Board
Safeway Stores
4th and Jackson St.
Oakland, CA 94660

sponsored by the SOS Committee, an ad hoc citizens' group. Margaret Hare, Chairperson. Call   for more information.

Within a few days of that first round of phone calls, a meeting date just a week away was set, the library auditorium reserved, and the flyers were out to spread the word. We five volunteers posted them on phone poles and in the store windows of helpful shopkeepers, on bus shelters and on community bulletin boards, and we left them in the common areas of the large apartment buildings (there was no time to do a door-to-door distribution).

We had our three speakers lined up: the Tenants' Association President, serving as temporary chairman; the elder spokesman of the neighborhood; and our ward representative on the city council to talk about what, if any, help the political system could give.

Safeway officials were *not* invited. Why not? We considered the question carefully. The main reason to invite them would be to give them a chance to explain what they were doing. But they had a store that was open to the public fourteen hours a day, seven days a week, and could have used it any time to post a letter or flyer giving their point of view. We figured this meeting was *our* forum. Also, we intended to use the large meeting to solicit volunteers, get some ideas for how to proceed, raise some money, and begin to strategize. One doesn't ordinarily invite the other side to one's internal policy-setting sessions. Then, too, we considered how Safeway would likely use any time given them. They'd send a vice-president in charge of public relations to go on at length about Safeway's years of service to the community, and all the charitable endeavors they supported. We didn't want the meeting to be sidetracked onto the question of Safeway's corporate record; whether they'd been generous or stingy had no bearing on how we all would cope with their closing of that store.

So we focused our agenda on that question. Here's how it went:

SAFEWAY CRISIS EMERGENCY TOWN MEETING
SEPT. 12, 1987, CLEVELAND PARK LIBRARY AUDITORIUM

Agenda

I. First speaker, Tenant Assoc. Pres. 10 minutes.
1. Introduces self and others who called the meeting as members of the Save Our Supermarket (SOS) Committee.
2. Reports what's known so far about the Safeway closing.
3. States the purpose of the meeting (intended to get the whole community working together on solutions).

II. Second speaker, Ward Councilman. 10 minutes. Discusses role of city government and legislative help possible under the circumstances.

III. Third speaker, advocate for the elderly in the neighborhood. 5 minutes. Discusses the special problems the store's closing poses for the elderly, handicapped, and those without cars.

IV. Questions and Answers. 15 minutes. Gives everyone the opportunity to ask about issues not covered by the speakers and to offer up his or her own ideas.

V. Call for Action. 30 minutes. Members of the audience who wish to volunteer are asked to sign up for subcommittees that will take on various tasks (publicity, fund-raising, petition-drive, letter-writing campaign, replacement store search, and several others).

VI. Adjourn. Approximately an hour and a half after starting.

The flyers worked to get over 200 people to turn up on a nice Saturday afternoon and overfill the 100–seat meeting room. The agenda worked to keep them all focused on the facts as known, the need for action, and the practicality of the various ideas for action that were offered up. By the end of the meeting the newly formed SOS Committee had some forty volunteers, many of whom had special skills in communications, legislative work, and management, who were willing to serve as heads or members of the subcommittees. A schedule of meetings and a network of phone consultations were devised so that the different groups of volunteers could keep up with what the others were doing.

From this beginning—a meeting called on just one week's notice—a campaign that ultimately counted *seven thousand* supporters got moving.

Legislation to give property-tax relief to the operators of grocery stores in "under-served" urban areas was pushed in the city council; the process initiated to change the zoning from the mid-rise office classification to neighborhood-oriented-shopping; and of most immediate help, a new grocery store operator was found who was willing to purchase the site at the landowner's asking price.

I wish I could promise that any neighborhood group calling people out in response to a development crisis can get them working together with equal success if it will just run its meetings the same way. More likely than not, when virtual strangers decide to work together for the first time, there will be some rough spots that will need smoothing out. People have different working styles, they rub each other the wrong way, they have different internal timetables, and many other individual personality quirks—all of which help to make it a rare thing for a group to have smooth, efficient meetings from the start.

But if you will just anticipate a certain roughness at the beginning and allow everyone a little time to get used to each other's style, you'll be better able to work out the best meeting patterns for you and these other people, who are going to be seeing so much of each other in the weeks to come.

Pick a Name—Carefully!

You have the people, ready and willing to work (you hope they're good!)—now you need something to call yourselves. The name you pick will shape the way your fellow citizens and political leaders view you from the time they first hear of your efforts ever after. So please take the time to think this step out fully. A few considerations and suggestions follow.

Positive associations are better than negative ones. If, for example, it's your goal to prevent a new highway from slicing through the middle of your residential area, don't call yourself "Citizens Against the Northeast Freeway." Better something like this: "One Neighborhood Indivisible." It has something of a patriotic ring to it, doesn't it? And it implicitly puts the highway's advocates on the defensive, suggesting they're for divisiveness and discord.

If the fate of a piece of land or a particular building is at issue, you might consider identifying yourselves as the "Friends of ..." that property. Without saying one word to attack the developer, you've just conveyed the idea that he must be the "Enemy of ..." the same site.

You also want your name to be *easy to remember*. Imperatives tend to be good for that purpose. Washington, D.C.'s, best-known, most effective preservation group went by the commanding title "Don't Tear It Down." And many think when they changed their name to the blander, more forgettable "D.C. Preservation League," they immediately lost a lot of their oomph.

Acronyms and abbreviations are a common way groups seek to telegraph their purposes to the public. "Save Our Supermarket" abbreviated to the distress call SOS. A coalition of golfers and neighbors fighting the conversion of a public golf-course into a football stadium chose the apt initials GRASS: "Golfers and Residents Against the Stadium Site."

Even though positives are generally better than negatives, if use of the word "against" or "opposed" spells something clear and memorable, by all means use it! The residents of Paramus, New Jersey, did this when they wanted to call particular attention to the name of the big developer they were fighting: Donald Trump. The head of the multi-billion dollar company is trying to win approval for a gargantuan shopping mall in the town. STOP (for "Stop Trump's Overdevelopment of Paramus") leaves no doubt as to how the unhappy citizens feel about his company's plan.

You wouldn't doubt the long-term staying power of the group that's called CONTINUE, would you? They're the Committee Of Neighbors To Insure a Normal Urban Environment—and in their little section of Manhattan, that's definitely a long-term project.

On the other hand, it's best to avoid an acronym that seems *too* labored or one that spells something unsuitable. The residents of Lower Ealing, for instance, should not fight off unwanted suburban development as "Homeowners Allied to Stop Subdivision of Lower Ealing." A HASSLE is something caused by a troublemaker, not a responsible group of citizens who care about their neighborhood.

In any case, you'll want to avoid terms like "homeowners" or "property-owners"; they're too exclusive-sounding to do you good. "Residents," "citizens," "neighbors," or just plain "people" will make clear that you welcome support from the whole community—renters, shopkeepers, students, and visitors included.

Once you've picked the name that suits you, it's very difficult to change it, so try out the sound and feel of the name among your neighbors for a few days before you commit yourselves. Be creative, and then after that, be reflective about the choice. You may be living with it for a long time to come.

About Existing Groups

Want to avoid the trouble of forming a whole new group? You can if you're fortunate enough to live in a community that already has an effective organization to press for its goals. But what if you've never heard any mention of any local **citizens' association?** (It may also be known as a civic federation, neighborhood committee, or any similar sounding name.) Then you probably don't have one in your area, or else the one you have hasn't been very active on issues that matter. *Better to start up a new group than to rely on an existing organization that's never accomplished anything significant, or worse, is regarded by government officials as incompetent, fuzzy-minded, or off-the-wall.*

How can you tell whether an existing group is effective or useless for your purposes? It's a matter calling on your powers of judgment, your ability to size people up quickly and accurately. When you talk to the officers of the association about your development problem, listen closely to their responses. Do they sound knowledgeable about this type of situation? Can they cite other cases that seem similar? Are they interested in being helpful? Or do they sound nervous, hesitant to get involved in something so "complex" or "controversial"?

I've met a few leaders of citizens' groups who are terrific organizers and fighters for causes; I've met quite a few more who couldn't handle any organizing effort larger than a bake-sale. The latter type see their organization as a nice place for neighbors to get together and have tea and maybe exchange a few gardening hints, or show slides of their members' trips abroad, or pass resolutions naming the Mother of the Year (I've seen it all). This may be fine when there are no bulldozers on the way, but it counts for nothing when there are.

A good way to get a quick sense of the existing association's interests and abilities is to attend one of its regular meetings. Ask to have a few minutes on the agenda to explain your development problem, and see how the members react. In some cases, even though the leadership is not exactly gung-ho, the audience's sympathy and desire to help is enough to prod the organization into action. It may set up a subcommittee to deal with the issue, and let you work on the cause under its aegis, with access to its letterhead, membership lists, and other resources. This will save you both time and money.

But if you conclude that you are better off starting afresh with your own people and your own new organization, you should still take care to keep good relations with any existing citizens' associations. Or at least don't offend them. The very worst thing that can happen is for the developer to court them, and to sway them over to his side. This is the "Divide and Conquer Ploy" described further in Chapter 8, and it works! So pay attention now to what sort of ties you'll have with whatever citizens' association you may find.

Forming Affiliations

There is a middle ground between setting up your own independent group and handing the problem over to an existing one: You can form a new group but attach it, legally and financially speaking, to an existing, respected, larger organization. This will give you the independence you desire—the ability to pick leaders from among your own neighbors and make decisions you know are right for you—but still allow you to benefit from the name, size, strength, and maybe even fund-raising abilities of the nationally or regionally prominent organization.

You need to make yourself aware of which of the established organizations in your area (or local branches of national organizations) are willing to enter into partnerships or affiliations with groups such as yours on problems of mutual interest. In my own part of the country there is one of the oldest citizens' planning associations, the Committee of 100 on the Federal City, which concerns itself with any development touching on the aesthetic qualities of the nation's capital; it has taken on as its special projects the efforts of a dozen or more neighborhood groups fighting off ungainly projects, both public and private. When a neighborhood forms a new group, for example, to oppose a project that will be a visual intrusion on the Capitol dome, the Committee of 100 lends its highly reputable name to the effort. So when the neighbors sit down to talk to the developers and to city officials, it's clear they are not just some group of obstructionists, but reasonable people who have already won over the support of a well-known and influential body. The Committee of 100 also sets up a bank account so that money to be used by the development opponents can be funneled through a recognized non-profit organization, and be tax-deductible to the giver.

However, the Committee does not assume any control over the day-to-day handling of the case. It is still up to the neighborhood opponents to attract and keep new members, to decide how they will prepare for the public hearing and who would say what, and to come up with most of the money to pay for the effort. The relationship lasts until a satisfactory (or at least final) conclusion of the case, after which the smaller, cause-driven group dissolves.

A similar relationship is possible between the Sierra Club and a neighborhood group, provided the environmental implications of the development at issue are severe enough. One of the organizations I helped to found, TACPEC (the Tenley and Cleveland Park Emergency Committee) was protesting the development of an office building with an access road that cut through a federal park. As soon as the board of the local branch of the Sierra Club heard of it, they voted their support and allowed the affiliation to take place. This meant a great deal more than the tax-deductibility of donations. We were able to publicize our events regularly through the Club's attractive newsletter; Club sponsorship of our "camp-in" overnight-protest on park grounds helped to draw all the local TV stations to cover the issue; and branch-to-branch networking within the organization helped to turn our small local case into an issue of national interest, worthy of the remedy of federal legislation.

And so with that experience, I highly recommend affiliation for any new group (if you can get it). But don't be discouraged if no one will take you on at the start. Old, reputable organizations are right to be worried about who you are and what you might do in their name. So allow sufficient time to show that your group isn't up to anything underhanded, wasteful, or foolish. In the meantime, while you're establishing your trustworthiness, accept any lesser degree of support that might be proffered (such as access to relevant files, maps, or books; advice on legal or technical matters; supporting testimony or letters to be entered into the record at your public hearing; contacts with government officials on your behalf; or contributions of any size).

Consider, too, that affiliation may be prohibited by the charter of the well-known large organization you approach. So accept any turn-downs you may get with good grace, but keep looking for others that might work out.

Incorporation

This is important: If you are forming a new organization that is not under the umbrella of an existing organization—unless you expect it to be dissolved after only a few months—*incorporate as a non-profit organization.* If you don't have a lawyer in your group to volunteer to handle the relatively simple paperwork for you, you must raise the money and pay to have it done. *If you take only one piece of advice from this whole book, this should be it.*

Why? Without a corporate structure to protect you, the individual leaders of your group could be held personally liable by the developer in a lawsuit. You could be risking your house and your whole life's savings, when a few hours' legal work could afford you full protection.

Just imagine your group has filed for an injunction against a developer, claiming that he cannot build because he obtained his permits by illegal means. Then suppose the developer is able to poke holes in the evidence you've brought, which you believed to be solid. Just think of the damages he can show: Your injunction has cost him hundreds of thousands of dollars in carrying charges, wages, and fees. If he loses his financing because of the delay, he could sue you for the *millions* that the lender was supposed to have given him. So find a volunteer to draw up the papers, or raise a couple of hundred bucks—but don't neglect this essential step.

You should become a 501(c)(3) non-profit organization. This means you cannot be a partisan political organization. You must write a charter or a set of by-laws that sets forth a legitimate public purpose for your existence. This can be quite vague: a dedication to the promulgation of sound land-use planning principles, for example; education of the community about its built environment and/or natural resources; historic preservation; and so forth—though the immediate application of these lofty ideals may be on one specific plot of ground on your block. Your group can still lay legitimate claim to a broader public service, because the case will doubtless have precedential impact on development in the rest of the state, or the area to be preserved from excessive development could be of value to the citizenry at large, not just its immediate neighbors. Your lawyer will explain to you in more detail how your organizational goals need to be framed in order to qualify for recognition as a non-profit organization under the 501(c)(3) regulations.

Your incorporation will call for a formal structure: a Board of Directors, a President or Chairperson, a Vice-chair, a Treasurer, and a Secretary, and election procedures for each. You may not want to use these exact titles, and there will be some leeway for you to call those in charge by whatever terms you find most fitting—just as long as you've made clear who assumes responsibility for calling meetings, running them, keeping records, and accounting for the money. If you know of any non-profit organizations of similar purposes in nearby neighborhoods, call and ask the chairperson if you can use their by-laws (adapted, as necessary) as a model for your own.

When you write your by-laws, pay attention to the method of removal of officers/directors and the selection of their replacements. This could save you some trouble later on, if it should turn out that one or two individuals on your board are incapable of going along with the consensus. Then you'll be glad you have some formal method for their removal. It can be terribly sticky business to try to add such procedures by amendment, once the difficulty with a member has already begun.

Consider, too, how a developer might be able to bend your rules for his purposes. Will he be able to acquire memberships for people on his side and, with just a small block of votes, get someone elected to your board? You need to write rules with the prevention of this remote (but catastrophic!) possibility in mind.

What constitutes a quorum is another matter for serious thought. You will not want it to be so large that you will have difficulty assembling that number often enough to make decisions. On the other hand, you don't want the number so small that just a handful of individuals can get together and vote policy changes on the organization's behalf. The problem is magnified if your neighborhood contains more than the usual share of **flakes, oddballs, and eccentrics** (I use the abbreviation F.O.E. to describe these types, collectively). Unless your quorum and election rules are written with their number in mind (assuming you have more than one or two of them), they can take over your organization and discredit your community's whole effort! (This problem, and ways to prevent it, is discussed in a separate section of Chapter 5.)

Incorporating, writing a charter, affiliating with other groups...it all sounds a bit daunting, doesn't it? It isn't really. I'm neither an M.B.A. nor a lawyer (just a B.A. in Chinese history, of all things), but I've now helped to found five distinct neighborhood organizations. One, the Cleveland Park Historical Society, is an independent non-profit organization formed to promote historic preservation in the neighborhood, funded by tax-deductible contributions. Three others (the Friends of Tregaron, the Tenley and Cleveland Park Emergency Committee, and the Wisconsin Avenue Task Force) were begun in affiliation with wider, national or regional organizations, but focused on a specific local development problem. The last, the Save Our Supermarket Committee, was an *ad hoc* group which dissolved within a few months, as soon as its goal was met and a new grocery store was in business on the block.

In no case was it hard to get these groups going. Once people understand that over-scaled or problematic development is on the way, they get moving. They turn out for meetings, they cough up the initial $10 or $20 apiece needed to order letterhead and stamps, they use their home computers to set up mailing lists, they hand-deliver photocopied notices door to door, they study up on the zoning laws and regulations they need to know for the case, and they learn all the other arcane skills they need in order to meet the challenge to their homes. It's thrilling to see how quickly a previously sleepy little community, when roused, can turn itself into a well-oiled machine. I've seen it happen again and again. And I know that no charismatic leader-figure is required; no wealth, no brilliance, no experienced activists need be involved.

Of course, if you've got them, they help! But not nearly as much as it helps to have good, plain sensible people who care deeply about the place they call home. When you've got that, you can acquire the rest of what you'll need from many sources, including books like this one (many of the others I've found helpful are recommended in the Select Bibliography at the back). Without neighborhood commitment, you might as well quit now and save your breath.

THE DEVELOPMENT PROPOSAL—A FIRST LOOK

Seeing the Plan: When, Where, and How

By now you presumably know the general nature of the development proposal, and you're in touch with others who are willing to work with you to delve more deeply into the matter.

Your next step: Sit down with the developer and learn firsthand what he wants to do.

By this time, you or one of your neighbors will have had some telephone contact with the developer, his attorneys, or his public relations people—most likely when you were trying to confirm those first rumors of pending development on the site. Whoever has already made the initial contact (assuming that conversation did not end on a hostile note) should be the one to call back and set up the meeting. Continuity of relations counts for something at this stage.

Two exceptions:

1. There is someone in your group of interested citizens who has some previous connection to the developer; someone, who, for example, is friends with his wife through their volunteer work at the same animal shelter, or who knows him through activities of the alumni association of the school they both attended. If so, ask that person to handle the meeting set-up. A familiar name and a shared interest will help to get things started in an atmosphere of cordiality, which is often conducive to fair dealing and candidness later on.

2. There is someone in your group who is a widely known and respected figure in the city or in a particular field. That person would also be a good one to invite the developer to a meeting; it would instantly establish that your group is no bunch of hysterical crazies but is composed of serious, intelligent people whom he cannot afford to ignore. You may in fact have total blockage of his plans in mind, but you'll seem to him more moderate and reasonable if his first association with your group is through someone whose name he knows and respects.

How you handle your first contact with the developer affects more than his impression of you; it also has bearing on how the public at large begins to perceive your cause. If you make no effort to get in touch with the developer, or if you wait too long to meet him, or if your first approach to him is hostile and suspicious, you'll have trouble with your public image right away. The developer will be able to tell people, quite accurately, that you never gave him a fair chance to win you over. This will hurt you, even if the sort of development plan is so awful, so outrageously over-scaled for your neighborhood, that you just can't imagine what a meeting can hope to achieve. All the same, *you must show a willingness at least to hear him out, and give him a chance to hear your ideas about development and act on them.*

There may be those cautioning you: Meet with the developer, but do so only after your side has had time to prepare fully. Wait until you've formed an official position on the development plan, or until you've got answers to any technical or legal problems the development plan poses. Wait until you've had a chance to meet with government officials and learn their attitude toward the proposal. You may also hear: Meet only on your own turf—never in his office, where he will be surrounded by, protected by, a whole back-up team of lawyers, architects, engineers, and other degree-laden professionals.

But I disagree with these prescriptions. I say, the sooner you have any sort of face-to-face contact with the developer, the sooner you can establish your presence as a force to be reckoned with and be counted as a major player in the game. If you wait until you're sure what position you'll take, what legal theories you'll rest on, you may well be working out your internal policy questions while the building is going up! So my rule is: There's no such thing as Too Soon to Meet. Even if it's only yourself, your next door neighbor, your children, and your pets at the start, go ahead, ask the developer to come and to bring along his blueprints. This will, if nothing else, leave you with a sense of who and what you'll be dealing with. You'll be able to ask direct questions and take notes on the answers (or non-answers, if he's evasive). Armed with this information, you will then find it much easier to make clear to others what's going on and to ask for their support.

What if the developer agrees to meet only in his office, on his terms? Experts tell us there is a decided psychological advantage to the side which names the place and time when adversaries get together. You can see how this can be so when you first arrive at the development company's headquarters, and find yourself led up to a richly paneled conference room, with the trappings of power all around you. The receptionist serves you coffee in china cups while you wait for the busy executive to appear. On the walls hang pictures of the many successful multi-million dollar projects the developer has already completed. You also note the number of engraved plaques and awards for his philanthropy and civic good works. In a plexiglass case on the sideboard at the end of the room there is a wonderfully detailed scale model of the project he's planned for your neighborhood, complete with pretty sponge-tipped sticks for trees and cotton-wads of shrubbery, and Matchbox cars on the streets. The vision appears fully realized even before you've had a chance to say one word about it. Everything together conspires to give you the impression that he's a savvy, experienced mover-and-shaker in this world, a proven winner...and you're out of your depth.

Should you meet with the developer under those circumstances? I still say yes. Go, and when you're there, keep telling yourself you know what he's up to, because you've heard it from someone who's been there—me. Many times have I sat in plush offices and been told, this project is going to go forward exactly as planned, just as it appears in the model, and (despite the intimidation I may have felt at first), have determined to do what I could to see that it didn't—and won.

But of course, if you *can* persuade the developer to come to a meeting in your neighborhood, on your terms, so much the better for you. And in most cases, you will find him willing, because the developer, just like you, has to be thinking about his public image. It doesn't sound good if you can say that you've been denied so simple a request as a meeting. In general, the more successful and reputable the developer, the more agreeable he will be to come out and talk to concerned citizens without preconditions. Especially if the invitation (as already suggested) comes from someone he knows or has heard of in a good context.

What if the contact between you and him has already gotten off on a sour note? This can happen all too easily. Say the newspaper has done a story on the planned building, and someone from your neighborhood has been quoted calling the developer "a greedy pig." Then you should consider an approach that can't be construed as an invitation to take more abuse. You could look for a neutral setting for the meeting, and you might want to have a third party present who's used to working with people of opposing views. City Hall might be the place, in that case, and officials of the planning agency could serve as the hosts. Your local elected representative is another likely choice to set up the meeting.

But there are three pitfalls to this approach:

1. It signals your public officials at the outset that you've failed to establish a civil dialog with the developer. Unfair as it may seem, the blame for the poor atmosphere will fall on the neighborhood, since it's most often assumed that the citizens react too emotionally in these situations, while developers maintain a businesslike cool.

2. Casting your public officials in a seemingly "neutral" role of meeting-sponsor may work against you later on, when you want them to function as advocates for your neighborhood's interests. If the outcome will depend heavily on strong, reliable support from your government officials, perhaps it's best to begin as you hope to continue, and approach them only when you want them to take a stand, not serve as a referee.

3. Problems that you may have wanted to discuss only in private with the developer will be brought out in front of your "neutral" official sponsors. What they hear from you at this early stage may prejudice the way they feel about your side's position as the case progresses. Additionally, in many jurisdictions, where elected officials double as zoning case hearing examiners, your representatives will not be permitted to play any part in these private talks. To do so would be considered **ex parte communication** (see Glossary for definition), from which they are barred by law.

If, however, your government representatives are allowed to act as go-betweens, and you have confidence that they will do so fairly and competently, and keeping your legitimate constituent interests in mind—then by all means, ask them to do so. But to make this determination, you will, of course, need to know your local officials *very well*. I can think of a few terrible instances in which the citizens' group allowed their elected representative to negotiate a difficult point with a developer on their behalf, and found, to their dismay, that their councilman had struck a deal they never approved. He'd sold them down the river! (The problem of unreliable or back-stabbing politicians is discussed at more length in Chapter 6.)

Who Says What. Though I urge every group to have at least one face-to-face session with the developer (even if it seems to you there is little common ground for discussion), it's very important from the start onwards that you have some control over what your side lets out. Though the meeting may be hastily put together, or informal in tone, or as casual in setting as a stroll through the development site—don't be surprised if the comments your people have made off-the-cuff are quoted back at you word for word in the record of the public hearing (where courtroom rules excluding hearsay will not necessarily be observed). So keep in mind what they say on all the cop shows: *Anything you say can and will be used against you!* And make sure everyone on your side knows it, and is well briefed beforehand on any aspects of the case for which discretion is in order.

To reduce the chance that imprudent comments may be made, it would help if you could arrange to have present only those neighbors of the initial group who you know to be responsible, closed-mouthed types. But you probably won't know the people who have come together over the development issue all that well, or you won't have the authority to invite whomever you'd like to the first meeting. But if you *do* get to pick and choose, here are some criteria:

Number. Find out first how many people will be there from the developer's side. Let's say he wants to have a business partner present, his lawyer, his architect, and his landscape planner—five people. Your side ideally should have six. A larger number will make it look as if you're trying to pack the room. A smaller number, and he will have the slight psychological advantage of being in the majority. If you don't know how many he's bringing, you still might want to bring six; it's a large enough number to let him know that you had no trouble rounding up people who want to get involved. If any fewer come, he may think that you just couldn't get any more to show up.

Variety. Assuming you've been in touch with at least ten or fifteen people who want to work on the problem, you'll want to bring to the meeting the ones you think will contribute the most to your understanding of the case. As said above, you will want to exclude if possible any you think will be unpredictable, rude, or intemperate in their reactions, but seek out those you believe to be level-headed and sensible. Whatever their personalities are like, you should certainly include the neighbors who would be most directly affected by the development if built as planned. And if the project has stirred up interest from any established groups (environmental, historic preservation, traffic watchdog, whatever) you should invite a representative from that group to participate.

It's always a good idea to make use of whatever talents or professional qualification you can find among those who have expressed an early interest. Are there any lawyers in the group? Even if they've never dealt with land-use matters before, lawyers, by their training, will still have an edge at these sessions, being familiar with the situation of sitting across a table from an adversary and talking about matters where there are big dollar amounts at stake. Of even more immediate utility will be any architects, engineers, designers, or others with the training in spatial relations crucial to the understanding of site plans and schematics. An economist, accountant, or budget analyst can similarly help to make sense of whatever figures the developer throws your way.

Whoever the people are that will be in attendance, whatever their level of experience or skill, make sure they all understand beforehand what the basic parameters of the meeting are. If it's just to find out about the plan, then agree that everyone will just ask questions, and not make any speeches. But if you decide to deliver to the developer some kind of statement of position or guiding principle of your group, make sure you know who's going to do the talking and just how far the statement will go. From my own experience, I generally counsel that the less your side says at that first meeting, the better. The developer's the one who wants to do the changing, so it should be up to him to do the explaining.

Meeting Mr. Bilderbig (A Story)

It's 7:30 p.m., and Linda and Len Cottager are getting the living room of their little bungalow ready for all the neighbors they have invited over to meet with the developer, John Bilderbig and his staff. Only five days ago the Cottagers saw the placard posted on the wooded tract next door to their house announcing that the Bilderbig Development Corporation had applied for a change in zoning to allow the construction of a 600–unit apartment building on land that now permits only single-family detached houses. Linda immediately called Mr. Bilderbig (whose office number was given to her when she called the information-line listed at the bottom of the posted notice) and asked him to come and talk about his plans.

She also called several neighbors and interested others, who are arriving one by one. Linda's next-door neighbor, Sandra Cape-Cod, a patent attorney by profession, is the first, closely followed by Bob Feltip, who lives on the street just on the other side of the proposed building, and works out of his house as a freelance graphic artist (he's particularly alarmed at the prospect of having his natural sunlight cut off by the long shadow of the new building). Linda has also invited Jane Matronly, who is the chairperson of the neighborhood civic association, and Roger Thistlewood, the president of the local chapter of the Audubon Society. (Linda knew he'd want to be involved because the Audubon Society had for years had an informal understanding with the previous property owner that the creek bed that runs across the land would remain undisturbed, as an unofficial bird sanctuary.)

Soon after all of Linda's people arrive, the developer and his "team" show up as a group. In addition to Mr. Bilderbig, there is Arthur Yakalot, Senior Vice-President—essentially the top P.R. person at the company—followed by

Yvonne Artsy, a young architect with Hotstuff, Flashy & Glitzy (or HFG Associates), an internationally known firm associated with the neo-post-retro-constructionist school of design); Tom Yew, an arborist and partner in Broad-leaf & Yew, landscape consultants; and Miles Hourglass, a zoning attorney with the firm of Dunning, Billing, Padding and Hourglass.

Linda, as organizer of this get-together, assumes the role of chairperson as well as hostess for the evening. She begins by offering everyone coffee or tea while allowing each to do his or her own introductions. Then she welcomes the developer and his people to the neighborhood and thanks them warmly for agreeing to come out and talk about their plans on such short notice.

John Bilderbig thanks her for the invitation and says he's always happy to get to know the neighbors of the projects he builds. His company has completed many other buildings of quality in similar neighborhoods to this (he names two) and he was pleased to be able to gain neighborhood cooperation for each one. He hopes those present will be as pleased in the end by the new and striking addition to their neighborhood as he will be himself.

He then launches into a long speech on the history of his company, its sterling reputation for sensitivity and civic responsibility, and that of the architects and all the other consultants he works with.

He next moves on to the site itself and the design considerations taken into account in creating the plan he has yet to present. He stresses his belief that the site is a "special" one, requiring extra care and respect from its developer. So before he even made a purchase offer on it, he had a study commissioned by top environmentalists and land experts to guide him toward the best approach to building there. He also learned from the past mistakes of others; he knew that in the mid '70s there had been a plan for a 100–single-family-house subdivision, but the development company had been caught up in the spiral of interest rates at the time and in the end couldn't afford to build them. Not long afterwards, another developer came up with a plan to do a shopping mall (some of those present remember it well), but initial reaction, both from the planning authorities and from various citizens' groups, was so negative that the developer eventually withdrew his application. Of that plan Bilderbig says, "Of course you were right to fight that one off. Your roads around here just aren't built to take all those thousands of cars coming in and out, and you couldn't stand for them to destroy all the trees and just cover the land with asphalt. If I'd lived here, I'd have been right there fighting it with you!"

With that nod to the neighborhood's wisdom, he leads smoothly into how different *his* development will be from those horror-stories of the past. "This will be a hundred percent residential—fine homes for people just like yourselves. People from all over who have discovered what a beautiful place this neighborhood is. They want to live here, but they're single or they're couples without kids, they're retired people—people who don't need a big house and a yard. They're looking for all the benefits of fresh air, trees, and all the other things you have out here, but without the hassle and expense of upkeep. That's what the market studies tell us, at least. So we planned an apartment building, designed it to suit this parcel perfectly. It'll be set back so far from the roadway you won't even know it's there. The way we'll build it, set into the slope that comes down to the creek bed, we'll be leaving that whole grove of trees between you and the building just as it stands now. The people in these apartments will have great views, but you won't be losing any of your own views ..."

At this point Linda, realizing it's getting late, and they still haven't seen the plans, interrupts, saying, "Maybe it would be a little easier for us to visualize what you're saying if you could point to the drawings on paper and we could follow along while you talk."

Yvonne Artsy unrolls the eleven-sheet set of blueprints from their container and spreads them out on the coffee table. She starts with the top sheet and begins describing, layer by layer, what the plans show. First is the "topo"—the topographical map showing the site marked out with lines to indicate the degree of slopes at given points on the site, and dots of varying thickness to indicate the size of all existing trees over ten inches in caliper (diameter). The developer remarks that 80 percent of all the trees shown will be retained. Bob Feltip, who has quietly been taking minutes for the group, duly records this promise in his notes.

The second sheet shows the lowest floor of the building, called the "third sub-basement" on the plan. It's actually the lower of two levels of the underground parking garage. It takes a few seconds for Linda and the others to catch on to the fact that they're being shown the floor plans of the building in order, from bottom to top, and that they'll have to wait to the end to see an actual drawing showing the building as it's seen from the front, the sides, and the back (called the **building elevations**).

Then Linda interrupts again and says, "Maybe instead of going through the blueprints floor by floor, it would help us to understand the whole thing better if we first took a look at the north elevation, the side that faces the road. And also, if you have a **perspective drawing,** showing two sides of the building from an angle, in relation to the street, that would help us to see how the building fits into the site. That way it will be easier for us to understand what all these floor plans add up to."

Fortunately, the architect has prepared a perspective drawing and the developer is prepared to present it. The picture is done as if it's springtime, with all the ornamental trees and shrubs proposed in the landscape plan fully matured and in bloom. The view from the street shows one car stopped at a traffic light while pedestrians stroll casually across the crosswalk-marked pavement.

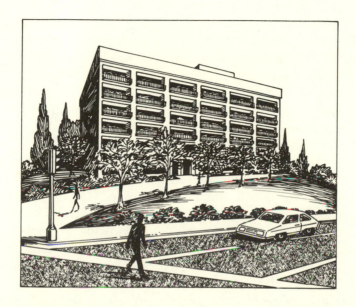

While Linda, Sandra, and Bob are thinking, "Actually, that looks rather nice," Len Cottager suddenly notices something odd about the picture: "We don't have a traffic light on Creek Road now. Do you mean to have the city install one?"

Mr. Bilderbig: "No, no, we don't have any definite plan for that. If you all don't want it, we definitely won't ask for it. We just thought, since the driveway to the garage comes out right there, it might be a good way to keep the traffic flowing smoothly in and out. But we're open to any other traffic management measures you want us to study."

Len: "There's very little traffic on that road right now. How many cars per hour will be added?" Len is very tempted to get started on his objections to any additional traffic volume, and warn the developer that the neighborhood will never stand by while their country lane gets turned into a commuter highway—but then he remembers what he agreed about keeping first impressions to oneself and not revealing anything about possible grounds on which the project might be opposed, and so he says nothing further while the developer replies:

"We've just hired a traffic consultant who'll be working up some data. We'll get that to you as soon as we have it." Bilderbig was aware before he came that traffic was going to be a major sticking point in his application, so he's trying to look as cooperative as possible to deflect the neighbors' concern. But in fact he already knows what his traffic consultant's report will conclude: "This development will have no adverse impact on neighborhood streets." He knows that, because that is how *all* developer's traffic consultants' reports conclude, from the time the first such study was commissioned, and ever onward.

Linda sees the potential to get bogged down over traffic before the group has seen the rest of the plans, so she abruptly changes the subject by asking to see the building facades.

The blueprints give some information about the overall design, but certain details are lacking. What color will the brick be—dark red? Beige? What about the balconies, are they faced in poured concrete, or is that a stucco finish? What's the glass going to be like? Tinted black? Mirrored? What's this box-like thing shown on the roof, and how tall will it be?

Bob Feltip takes careful note of all the answers. The brick will be a standard red, about the color of the school building down the road. The balconies will be faced with a synthetic compound that is virtually indistinguishable from the stucco found so often on neighborhood houses. "We wanted to have the building pick up some of the historical detail of the neighborhood," notes the architect, "and so relate it visually to its surroundings." The windows will be slightly tinted but they won't appear dark from the outside. The "roof structure" houses the "elevator pop-up" and the heating and cooling equipment. The building code allows for it to be eighteen feet tall, but this one is only going to require sixteen feet.

The architect and the developer are both speaking as if what they're proposing is exactly what's going to go up, without modification or reduction of any kind. The neighbors, at least initially, are careful to frame their questions like this: "*If* you get permission to build this…" but after a few minutes this gets cumbersome and they simply talk as if what they're shown will be what they'll get. They may already feel determined not to let one single brick of that building be laid, but they are wise to keep the thought private at this stage. Any hint to the developer that he's with people who are out to block his plan entirely, and in all likelihood, he'll stop being so open, stop giving out information so freely, and dig in his heels and prepare to fight.

Until the breach becomes open and un-ignorable, both sides will continue to act as though a compromise is the goal, and that a building fairly close to what's drawn on the plan will result. The neighbors know they can't even decide how much or how little of it they feel they can live with, until they've got all the technical information about it, analyzed its practical impact on their lives, and figured out how the zoning process allows them to present their views.

So they concentrate now on getting the numbers right. They take down the total square footage of all floors combined (the gross square footage) including underground space, which they learn for the first time, is not counted by the county in the calculation of FAR (that's based on the net square footage only). They note the square footage of the average unit, the square footage of the building footprint, and the total square footage of the lot it occupies. They ask the number of parking spaces and the method of allocation (residents can rent one space per unit, at a not-yet-determined price).

They learn how many of the 600 units will be one-bedrooms, how many efficiencies, how many one-plus-den, and how many two-bedrooms are planned. They try to get as much information as they can about the type of residents the building will attract. Will any be subsidized by state or federal housing programs? How many children are likely to be added to the school rolls? How many will be senior citizens? What about residents' attendants, domestics, or other employees? Where will they park? What about guests?

They look at what the developer calls the "amenities"—the lounge in the basement where the residents can hold large parties; the fountain in the middle of the semi-circular driveway; and the brick-paved "promenade" that will follow the creek's path.

They are equally concerned with uses. They soon discover that in this "100 percent residential" complex, there are to be several commercial establishments—a small convenience store, a dry cleaners, and a beauty salon—but that these are considered "accessory uses" under the county's code and so allowed in a residential zone. In addition, they learn that the ten units on the ground floor toward the rear of the building are to be leased as doctors' and dentists' offices—and these don't actually count as commercial space either.

Next they go into landscaping and maintenance of the grounds. From what's drawn on the site plan map it looks as if the flow of the creek is to be shifted a few feet over to the west. Have they consulted with the Army Corps of Engineers about the feasibility of doing this? What about the brick wall shown along the promenade? Will the neighbors no longer have any access to the creek? Will there be an Environmental Impact Statement (usually referred to by its abbreviation, EIS)? How soon will it be available?

They also want to know how far along the developer is in the process. Has he had any feedback from the county planning agency? Is a particular official assigned to review the project and make a recommendation to the Zoning Board? Has the developer's private traffic consultant met with the County Transportation Authority? Will that agency be issuing a report, and when?

With that they're back to the issue of traffic patterns. How wide is the driveway where it meets the road? Where will cars wait when coming to pick up residents? Isn't that area part of the fire lane, to be kept clear at all times?

How many residents are expected to own one car? Two cars? Where will they park if they decide not to rent an indoor space?

During all the give-and-take, the neighbors aren't the only ones taking in data. The developer, too, is finding out some facts of interest. He learns that the neighbors haven't yet had any contacts with the county planning office themselves. He can see that the "synthetic stucco" on the balconies didn't go over all that well, and he'll direct the architect to substitute a glass facing instead. It's also apparent that the worst protests about traffic are going to come from the residents along Creek Road to the front, and not so much from the people on the intersecting side-street. This will all help him to better prepare his application for the opposition he's now sure he'll be encountering at the public hearing.

When all the questions that the neighbors can think up are finally asked, from the sub-basement to the roof, and the developer has given as many answers as he seems willing to give at one sitting, Linda decides the time has come to start wrapping things up. She thanks the developer and his team for being so forthcoming.

Mr. Bilderbig thanks her for her hospitality and promises to get back to her soon with some of the additional technical data she and the group have requested. It was a great idea, he adds, to check with the Army Corps of Engineers before trying to move the creek over, and he'll get on that right away. And of course, he'll send over the EIS report and the traffic study as soon as they're both ready. But he's neglected to mention a few of the other requests that were made. He hasn't said anything about supplying some of the costs and projected rents he was asked about. The neighbors aren't too bothered that he won't tell them what price he paid for the land, because they know that they can find out that information from the recorder of deeds in the municipal building. But they would like to have some kind of guess-timate on his projected return on his capital. This would help them to gauge just how much "give," or room for negotiation, there really is in the project.

But the developer's staunchly taking the attitude that to let anything about that out would simply "give too much away to the competition." He adds, a bit too coyly for some, "Let's just say I'm not in this thing to lose money. I expect to make a comfortable profit. And it wouldn't be good for any of us if I built a building that cost too much per unit for me to rent out to anyone. It would just sit there empty, and we'd all be in big trouble."

None of the neighbors will dispute that point, though none of them thinks that's sufficient reason to allow the developer to build to whatever size he needs to make the investment pay off. Linda simply says blandly, "We all want to do what we think is right for the neighborhood," and she adds that it may take a little time for the neighbors to consider what they've heard tonight and get back to him with their reaction. She asked if they could perhaps keep the set of blueprints to study, and is pleased to be told "They're yours."

After a final round of pleasantries and goodbyes, the developer and his "team" finally leave, and Linda and her neighbors can begin the harder business of doing an intelligent critique of what they've seen.

Linda first goes around the room and asks for a quick impression from everyone.

Len: "That building's gonna stick out like a water tower over a turnpike. There's no way it will be "screened" as he said by those little dogwoods on the north."

Sandra: "I can't imagine who they expect will live in a high-rise so far from downtown, and not on a major transit line. I wonder if they haven't seriously misjudged their market."

Jane: "I don't know...Many of our older residents, after their children are grown, might welcome a way to remain in the neighborhood without the expense or work of maintaining a large house. I think the idea is attractive myself. It's just that this building is so big! Maybe if they made it a few stories shorter, it would be all right...."

Bob: "Even so, the traffic will be a nightmare. It can't all go down Creek Road. It's bound to spill over onto the side streets, to avoid the back-up at the intersection of Creek and Grove. If the thing gets approved, I'm sure we'll need a "No Left Turn" from the development driveway onto Creek."

Roger: "I don't care where the traffic goes, or if the building is made smaller or narrower or whatever. I don't want it there, period. That land is practically the only open space left in this county. It's been a bird-sanctuary for years, in fact, if not by law, and if we don't work to keep it so, you'll hardly be able to find a songbird for miles around here anymore. There's no use in trying to compromise about size or roads, since none of that matters to the birds one bit!"

Though it may seem that everyone has expressed a different reaction, there is actually a fair amount of consensus going on here. No one can stomach the plan just the way it is. It's not necessary to work out now whether the plan is to be opposed in its entirety or just in part. The group still doesn't know what sort of testimony or evidence the zoning hearing process will admit, and of that admitted, which type works best with the particular zoning commissioners who'll hear it. All they need to be able to agree on at this point is that they will keep proceeding along the lines already laid out. They will:

- wait for the developer to provide the additional information he promised, and see to it that it is reviewed by those with the technical expertise to interpret the data and its method of collection;

- report on what they've learned so far to the particular interest groups each represents. Jane Matronly will brief her civic association; Roger will keep the Audubon Society chapter informed; and Linda, Sandra, and Bob will spread the word to all the residents of their blocks of the neighborhood;

- educate themselves thoroughly as to how their local zoning board will proceed with the developer's application. How many hoops must the developer jump through before he has his permits? The number and the criteria for approval at each stage will shape to a large extent the course that the group takes in their opposition to the plan. (How to find this out and how such cases are typically handled will be the subject of the Chapter 4.)

Things to Watch Out For

Though the Bilderbig story covers a great many of the questions you'll want to ask when you first see the developer's plans, it necessarily leaves out a few. No single example can show you everything to look out for about every type of development. So here are a few extra tips you may want to keep in mind when you see whatever plans may be in store for your neighborhood.

Visualizing Size

Unless you're an architect or designer, you probably have no idea what size a building is in real life, just from hearing its square footage. But unless you've got some real physical sense of the amount of space it will occupy, you won't be able to gauge what it will feel like to have it in your neighborhood. You need a visual yardstick against which you can judge the plans. One way you might get this is to find an existing building of similar square footage, height, and footprint. You might even ask the developer to point one out to you. When you've found an approximate equal, go and visit it; walk around the site; view it up close and from a distance. Only then can you begin to imagine what it will be like to have something like it in your neighborhood.

Finding a comparable building can also be a big help when it comes time for you to communicate what you've learned of the development plan to your neighbors. I found this so when a developer first told me of a plan to build an office complex of 200,000 square feet on an acre lot up the street from my house.

Just a few blocks away from the proposed development site was a recently completed office building of some 50,000 square feet in all. So when I went to a community meeting and reported on the plan, I put it this way: "This office building will be the size of *four* of that new building that's on the corner of Van Ness Street." No one had any difficulty imagining four of the new buildings stacked up together on the site. There was no question in anyone's mind that the project would be enormously over-scaled. It didn't hurt, either, that the building I picked for comparison's sake was almost universally regarded as a wretched eyesore!

What Goes on Top?

When you're not used to looking at plans, you tend to focus on what's immediately apparent—the exterior facades, the height, the lot coverage—and assume that other elements, like what's on the roof, won't be seen. This happened in one case I know of: The neighbors saw plans and after some dickering over the front facade, agreed to support the developer's design. After the building was completed, it didn't look quite as the neighbors expected. On top of the building, there appeared to be a thick sort of crate, a full story high. As one of the neighbors described it, "...like a giant hat someone had stuck up there." When they asked the developer what it was, he told them it was just the 'mechanical roof'—it was shown on the plan they had approved. But had they imagined that the housing for the heating and cooling equipment was not going to fit under the roof, but sit up on top of it in a big, ugly, blank-walled box, they certainly would have objected.

Roof struc-
tures, or
"What's that
funny 'hat' on
top of the
building?"

The "mechanical roof" may also be referred to as the "penthouse," which can easily lead you to believe there will be another apartment unit on the roof, not a covering for that noisy, smoke-spewing system they're hoping you won't notice.

In addition to ventilating equipment, you should also pay attention to other "roof structures" that may be visible when the building is done. Satellite dishes are almost obligatory these days, and with a little care, can be sited and screened so that they're not a visual intrusion. Other potential problem-causers include radio towers, TV antennas, weather balloons, and helipads.

Private vs. Public Space

Unless a plan shows a clear demarcation between the developer's private land and the public space (or you've seen the *plat*, the official map showing where the private boundary lines start and end) you may not be able to tell if all of the construction is to stay within its own lot. It's getting more and more common for developers to build out into the public space (into the sidewalk, onto the street, or over it). In Washington, D.C., we've found that the public-space permit process is closed, without notice to affected parties, and without providing a way for citizens to comment. So "sidewalk cafes" suddenly appear that are in reality extensions of enclosed restaurant space built with permanent walls out into the sidewalk. "Skyways"—exterior office corridors—are built to connect one big office building to another; and walls, fences, courtyards, pillars, and awnings are put up to give the impression that an area at ground level, once accessible to pedestrians or cars, now belongs to the owner of the building adjacent. It's essential to catch these intrusions early in the planning stage, when the zoning authorities still have the matter under consideration, because if your city is like mine, you won't get a chance to have any kind of input in the subsequent public-space approval process.

Details, Details

There are a mass of other seemingly minor things to watch out for; some of these can suddenly loom rather large when you discover them after the building's in operation. Truck delivery hours, for example. When those monster eighteen-wheelers come rolling down your street at 5 a.m. to unload the day's supplies for the building, you'll be cursing yourself for not having paid attention to that detail. Here's a partial list of these things to worry about:

Trash Operations. Location of dumpster, time and days of pick-up, route used to get to and leave site for pick-up.

Lighting. Exterior: brightness and direction (out toward residential streets or alleys, or in toward the new building only?); interior: Will late working hours of some employees cause the building to be lit up on many nights?

Window Treatments. Extensive use of mirrored or black glass has been found to contribute to higher urban temperatures in summer. Use of Venetian blinds and shades: Some building managements will mandate that blinds and shades be kept at a uniform level, to prevent the building's rows of glass from appearing too hodge-podge from the street.

Grounds. Will landscaping be sufficiently maintained, dead trees replaced, litter picked up, etc.? Are there any guarantees that the trees and shrubs planted will be the same varieties shown in the landscape plan? (Cheaper substitution is a common way for developers to cut corners.)

Fire Prevention and Public Safety. Where are the standpipes or fire hydrants? Will the fire lane be kept clear of parked cars? Is there a sprinkler system? What's the building security going to be like? Private guards? A check-in desk?

Interference. Will the building be used for any activity or allow any equipment that will interfere with normal TV and radio reception of nearby residents? Building intercom or walkie-talkie systems, microwave-producing devices, and many different types of machines for data transmission have been known to produce this effect, and neighbors are left without aid in their search for ways to bring back their formerly good reception. You don't know just how upsetting this problem can be until it happens to you!

Signage. This is planners' jargon for the plastic, neon, or carved lettering that proliferates on our commercial buildings these days. Ugly, badly placed, confusing, overlit, or too-obtrusive signage should not be ignored in the planning stage—though it's usually one of the easier problems to correct once the building is complete. You can just take it down and redesign it.

Noises and Odors. Restaurants and fast-food places in particular should be scrutinized for these problems. Frying fat produces a strong smell which can permeate a neighborhood, and only an expensive state-of-the-art ventilation system can contain it. Noise control measures can also be added to new buildings under construction for the price of extra wall thickness and insulation; the planting of certain varieties of dense, sound-absorbing trees or installation of a fence of an absorptive material can also significantly diminish noise transference.

Most of these problems are discussed in more detail under those chapters dealing with specific types of developments and how they can be approached (the chapters on big institutions, on small businesses, on suburban development, and others).

It may seem that there are just too many little parts of any plan for one person to keep track of. That's why you'll be glad to have a large number of neighbors going over it with you. Odds are, what you let slip by you, someone else will catch.

You can also benefit from the experience of others who have gone before you. If the plans are for an ice-skating rink and concession stand, for example, get the names of the neighbors who already have one in operation near their homes. Ask them the sort of questions the developer can't (or won't) answer. What's it like on a busy Saturday night? Over the Christmas holidays? Is noise a problem? Do they wish there were more parking spaces? Do rowdy patrons ever get into fights or drive recklessly on neighborhood streets? Could security be improved? When you raise these questions with the developer, you show you're not being overanxious and paranoid; you really know what you're talking about. When you demonstrate at the public hearing or in meetings with public officials that you've investigated the proposals with such thoroughness and considered the real impact of every detail, they are bound to pay close attention to your assessment of its merits.

UNDERSTANDING THE PROCESS

The Public Side

This *ought* to be a straightforward chapter. This should be the part where I outline, step by step, the sequence of events that a development application will go through from the moment of filing to the ultimate granting or denial of the permits to construct a building. Would that it were so simple! In the first place, the process will be very different in one state than it is in another, and it may even be different from county to county within the same state. And second, in all states and counties, there's a whole lot more involved in getting a major development project approved than what's laid out in the regulations and is there for the public to see. A savvy developer will be at least as good a player behind the scenes—making contacts with the right people, building up helpful relationships, creating a good "climate" for approval of his plans—as he appears to be in the public hearing room. If you hope to beat him, or at least hold your own on the stage, you will need to be, too.

But first you have to be up on the visible, public side of the process—or processes. Your local government will have at least two different ways to handle development applications, and it may even have three or four. Development within the zoning "envelope" (within the **matter-of-right**) will be handled according to one set of procedures; development applications for **variances** will be treated in quite a different way; those involving changes to the **zoning map** might be heard according to yet another set of rules; and those seeking to be granted density **"bonuses"** or be considered under special development **incentive programs** could be considered in a separate forum altogether. (All of these terms describing types of development applications are defined in the Introduction, and again in the Glossary at the back of the book.)

Presumably you have learned from your previous talk with the developer or your public officials which of these types is being planned for your neighborhood. Now you need to find someone who is knowledgeable about the workings of the process crafted to deal with that method of development in your area. An obvious place to start looking for a person to answer your questions is at your local government offices.

You may be so new at this that you don't yet know the name of the agency that handles planning and land-use questions in your area. Start by calling the general information line of your local government, describe what you're looking for, and get the name, title, and phone number of someone with responsibility in that field. We all know it's sometimes difficult to get hold of the right official to answer your questions, but be persistent. If the clerk who first picks up the phone seems unwilling or unable to help you, ask to speak to someone who can help, or to the boss. And don't be apologetic if your questions take up a lot of time. The system is there for you, the citizen, but you can't use it unless the people who are keeping it running will help you to understand it. That's what they're there for, and they're paid for doing it with your hard-earned tax dollars.

Even if your city's planning/zoning employees are patient and willing to explain the system, however, you may want to seek information first from the office of your local *elected* official. If development has ever been an issue before in your district, you will undoubtedly find your representative and/or the staff people well-versed about the system's rules and procedures. As you are a constituent and a voter, you should find your questions more courteously received and more speedily answered than if you brought them directly to the civil servants of the agency involved. You might also find it a plus to have this additional contact with the staff or the politician who serves your electoral district. Later, when you come back seeking support for your neighborhood's position, you'll be a familiar name, and your concern about the development will have been noted early on.

Yet another source of information—and in my opinion the best—is from other citizens in your area who have dealt with the process before. I get calls of this sort from time to time, either from people who have been given my name by a friend or acquaintance, or on a few occasions, from someone who's seen my name in a newspaper article about a neighborhood development problem. However they get to me, I always take the time needed to brief them fully on how development applications are handled here in Washington, D.C., and just what role the citizens are allowed to play in the process. And I think

I'm no exception; most veterans of development wars I'm sure would be glad to do the same.

Once you've got a reliable source of information to talk to, you need to know what to ask. Assuming your case will involve a public hearing, here are some (by no means all) of the things you will want to find out:

Who holds the hearing? You need the exact, capitalized name of the body, not some generalized term—e.g., not "the Zoning Board" but "The Anywhere County Board of Zoning and Land-Use Regulation."

Who are the hearing judges? How many are there? Are they elected? Appointed, and if so, by whom? What are their qualifications/backgrounds/special areas of interest?

What's the date, time, and place of the hearing? What are the deadlines for submission of letters, petitions, or requests to be given the opportunity to speak?

Is it possible for a neighbor, interested citizen, or organization to be accorded **party status** (that is, allowed to put on a presentation with witnesses's testimony and other forms of evidence, and cross examine the developer's witnesses)? If so, must one first show **standing** (a legitimate stake in the outcome of the case)? What does a person or organization have to do to establish intention to participate?

What kinds of supporting evidence may be introduced? Traffic reports? Soil surveys? Photographs, slides, or videos? Are there any special format requirements (such as, all written reports must be on legal-sized paper; all submissions must be stamped with the case-file number in order to be admitted into the record)? How many copies are required? What are the deadlines for submission?

What other government agencies usually participate in public hearings? Does the city/county planning office enter a recommendation in every case? Does the Department of Transportation file a traffic report or testify as to road conditions? Is an Environmental Impact Statement required (and if not, can it be requested, and by whom)? Do other agencies participate when their special areas of expertise are needed (e.g., the State Office for Historic Preservation; the Parks Department; the Business and Economic Development Agency)? Are these government agency opinions merely advisory, or can they dictate the outcome of a case?

Is there a role for other levels of government in the hearing process or later on in the case? Does the state legislature or governor review land-use decisions? Does some multi-state or regional authority have a role? Is there any federal interest (because the case involves an interstate highway, or other federal facilities or lands, or raises issues covered in federal legislation)?

How long does one have to testify/present evidence? Do the parties get equal time limits? What happens if they go over? Is there a fixed limit on the whole hearing? What if the time is up but there are still people waiting to speak? Will other hearing dates be set?

When does the record close? Do parties get a chance to submit additional information that may have come in after the hearing is over? Is there opportunity to rebut the other side's points?

What about the decision? Is it ever made on the spot ("from the bench," as it's known)? Or is a date set for another hearing with the vote to be taken in public? Or is a written order and decision simply issued whenever it's ready? If a public decision-date isn't set, how does one find out when the decision has been made? Are parties automatically notified?

If you're very lucky, you live in a jurisdiction where you won't need to track down someone who can brief you about all this. The planners, rather than have to give out the same information to new groups and individuals in case after case, will have put together a booklet or brochure outlining the way the system works and will make it available to all citizens on request. If there is such a guide to the process in your area, you've just been saved a great deal of time and trouble. If there isn't one, and you're going to be spending a lot of time on the phone with the planning office anyway...why not suggest that they put such a guide together?

Case File No. 1234567–89 (A Story)

Linda Cottager (the homeowner from the story that began in the previous chapter) is still worried about the Bilderbig proposal to put a 600–unit apartment high-rise on the wooded lot next door to her house, now zoned single-family residential. She knows that a hearing will be coming up in just six weeks, but she has never been involved in a case like this before, and has no idea what the hearing will be like, or how she and her neighbors should prepare. But she's called her county councilman's office, and his assistant has given her some good information and advice.

He suggested that Linda might benefit from going to the County Zoning Commission's next public hearing, so she can sit through a real case and see how it goes. There will be no problem getting in: All hearings are open to the public. They're held during evening hours, too, so Linda won't even have to miss work.

The case Linda's going to hear is known by its case file number, 1234567–89. It's an application by the Cranefield REIT ("Real Estate Investment Trust") to develop an office/retail/ light-manufacturing complex in a mixed-use zone (mid-rise office, retail, and residential are permitted as-of-right). The proposal is for four connected buildings on a seven-acre site, all for the use of the OSRAD Corporation (the initials stand for "Outer Space Research and Development"). The first building will be the six-story headquarters of the corporation; the second will be a three-story building devoted to laboratory space and sterile testing rooms, where new products can be tried out; the third will be a two-story manufacturing plant/storage facility, where the several products the company now makes and sells can be assembled and prepared for shipping; the fourth will be a parking structure, containing four enclosed levels of spaces for cars. In the basement of the office building will be an employee cafeteria, a newsstand, and a small convenience store. There will be about 2500 employees and 1800 parking spaces.

The Commission that will hear the case has six members, all appointed by the County Supervisor and confirmed by the County Council. They serve part-time, meeting just once a month, and receive no salary but a stipend of $100 per meeting. They are by profession: a realtor, an architect, a retired civil servant, a lawyer in private practice, an economist with a think-tank, and a small businessman. At first glance they seem a diverse bunch, but a little digging into their backgrounds will reveal one thing they all have in common: They all worked for or contributed generously to the County Supervisor's last re-election campaign.

The Chairman of the Commission is the lawyer, Anthony DeTale, who's known to run his hearings with an iron gavel, holding the parties to the strict time limits he sets for them. The hearing format is called **quasi-judicial,** meaning that it's conducted very much like an adversarial courtroom case; however, the person in charge is not a judge, and the representatives of the parties do not have to be lawyers (though they very frequently are). The applicant (the developer) has the **burden of proof,** meaning he must show, by a preponderance of the evidence, that the zoning change he is seeking is in the public interest. He gets to put on his whole case first. Counsel for any parties in opposition may **cross-examine** his witnesses after they're done with their direct testimony; but the questioning must stick to subjects raised by the witnesses' own testimony. Cross examination cannot be used to introduce new facts or make arguments on the opponents' behalf.

After the applicant is finished with his witnesses, and all the questioning is concluded, the next order of business is to hear from any organizations or persons who support the application, but are not part of the developer's "team." Cross-examination of these witnesses (assuming any have signed up) may be by both parties, as well as by Commission members.

After the pro-applicant side is finished, the representatives of the various reviewing agencies of the county government may be heard. The county planning office will take up the largest amount of time, and its recommendation is to be accorded what the statute book calls "great weight" by the Commissioners. Other public agencies (Transportation, Fire Department, Police Department, etc.) testify only in cases that the head of the relevant agency sees as problematic. Government witnesses may be cross-examined by both sides just as if they were witnesses for one of the parties.

When all of the supporting players and all of the "neutral" government players have spoken and been questioned, the recognized party (or parties) of opposition are allowed to begin putting on their witnesses, who, of course, can be cross-examined by the developer's attorneys, as well as by the Commission members. Following the opposing party's presentation will be presentations by any other organizations and individuals who have asked to be recognized to speak in opposition, but have not filed for party status. They may be cross-examined by both sides.

At the very end, counsel for both the applicant and the opposition are given a short time to rebut some of the other's points, and to make a concluding statement if they wish.

The Chairman may then close the record (i.e., nothing further will be considered by the Commission when making its decision) or he may leave it open for the receipt of some additional information specifically requested by his colleagues. At the next month's regularly scheduled Commission Meeting, held in the same room, the Commissioners (having been careful *not* to consult privately with one another on their views of the case), may discuss the matter in public for a short time, after which they will consider a motion to approve (possibly with specific modifications) or to disapprove the application.

That action is final and binding (in this state the law provides no executive review or legislative veto)—though if the zoning order is later found to be legally flawed, it could be overturned by a court on appeal. But such reversals are infrequent.

Linda Cottager has learned all these facts about the hearing process just by arriving early and asking the hearing transcriber, who is not too busy setting up the tape recording equipment to tell her what will happen in what order.

Now all the Commission members are present, the parties and individuals have packed the stuffy little hearing room to capacity, and the Chairman has gaveled the hearing to order. Fortunately for Linda, there are no legally obscure "preliminary motions" to delay the real action of the case. The lawyer for the developer, John Loquashus goes immediately into his opening statement. It's only five minutes long (the applicant needs to fit his entire presentation into three hours)—but it's almost lyrical in its description of the OSRAD plan: it will be an ideal workplace, a model of American enterprise, and an architectural statement of man's thirst for knowledge, arranged in harmony with the natural beauty of the landscape. Linda, who had come into this hearing automatically disposed to the opposing neighbors' point of view, finds herself somewhat moved, and she can't help but wonder if the neighbors ever gave the plan a fair chance.

The subsequent parade of highly articulate, well-credentialed witnesses on the developer's side increases her doubts. They are:

The **architect,** who presents a spectacularly detailed scale model of the site, complete with movable garage doors and rolling cars. He also has an impressive array of slides and display boards, to show that development according to the site's current zoning would actually be devastating to the land, while his plan preserves its grades and vistas. (20 minutes)

Three members of the **engineering design firm** discuss how the plan more than meets county development standards, is energy-efficient and non-polluting, and addresses all the needs of the OSRAD Corporation. (10 minutes)

A **transportation consultant** presents his traffic and parking study done under the developer's auspices. Conclusion: "No adverse impact on the road-net of the surrounding community. No net change in on-street parking patterns." (10 minutes)

Because the plan involves the demolition of the two old structures existing on the site, a hired expert on **historic preservation** is called to testify. She finds that the 1880s–era general store is indeed worthy of landmark status and preservation, and explains that the developer has made a commitment to have it picked up and moved to another site, after which he will file a landmark application for it, all at his own expense. The other building, a simple wooden barn of unknown vintage, is an unremarkable structure and can be demolished at no loss to the state's architectural heritage. (15 minutes)

The **demographics expert** is up next. He explains why the OSRAD Corporation picked this county for its site as the most attractive living and working environment for its executives and workers. He discusses the advantages to the county in having a corporation of OSRAD's high quality within its boundaries, and explains that the site was picked after an exhaustive nationwide search for a headquarters, in which many other states and communities were vying to be the chosen location. (5 minutes)

The **economist** further elaborates on this theme, presenting figures on property taxes to flow to the county coffers, sales taxes to be generated by employees' consumer spending in the county, the new jobs and the subsequent income taxes that will result, and other financial advantages to the plan. (5 minutes)

A **university professor** indicates the support of the academic community for the presence of this "important research facility" in the state. (5 minutes)

An **expert in disposal of toxic waste** assures the Commission that the laboratory and manufacturing plant are "absolutely 100 percent safe" and will operate with standards far superior to that required by federal and state law. (10 minutes)

A well-known **"futurist"** expounds on the need for the U.S. to remain competitive in the sort of chemical and biological research and development that OSRAD carries out. He presents a portrait of the world in years to come, that, through the work of the corporation, will be free of many of our most deadly diseases, support farm-harvests double and triple what they are now, and yield its secrets of weather patterns, earthquake frequency, and volcanic eruption to the understanding of science. (20 minutes)

A retired one-star general who serves as a consultant to OSRAD explains its **military** value to the U.S. government as a holder of several essential, top-secret defense contracts. He cannot, of course, divulge their nature, but he does state with certainty that there is no possible hazard to the public involved. (10 minutes)

A former FBI officer, now in the **private security** business tells of the measures to be undertaken to restrict access to the site and protect the classified documents within. The architect has already described the wrought-iron fence around the perimeter as having been given an aesthetically pleasing design. It's now revealed that there will be an inner ring of fencing as well, this one made of chain-link, topped with barbed-wire, and "mildly" electrified after hours. (10 minutes)

The final witness is the President of the OSRAD Corporation. After speaking glowingly of his company's record for achievement and safety since its founding some six years earlier, he provides a summary of the case and handles the concluding remarks, which are often left to the lead attorney in zoning cases. (15 minutes)

The applicant having completed his case, the Chair makes an obligatory call for any organizations or persons in support to come forward—though no one has formally filed a request to testify in this role. The local Chamber of Commerce has sent a letter of support, which is in the case file.

Rather than go on to the witnesses for the government reviewing agencies, the Chair now points out that the hour is late. It's nearly 11 p.m.; some four hours have passed since the hearing began. Though the applicant only used up two and a half of those hours on direct testimony, the cross-examination and the detailed questioning by Commissioners of each of the thirteen witnesses has stretched the time spent on the applicant's side to just over four hours. The Commission members look tired and are ready for adjournment. So the Chairman sets a continuation date exactly one week later, for the same place and time.

At home that night Linda tells Len that, while it was useful to see how the proceedings unfolded, she didn't find the substance at all comparable to the Bilderbig case. The OSRAD plan seemed much more suited to its site. The nearest homes were a quarter of a mile away. She was impressed by the thoroughness and care that OSRAD had given to their architecture, landscaping, and other details. They seemed to have anticipated every reasonable concern the surrounding community might have, and to have ready sensible answers in language that any layman could understand. She was particularly impressed by the clear but scholarly reasoning of the university professor who testified in support.

In contrast, it seemed to her that the opposing counsel wasn't doing too well for his side. She couldn't figure out the point of many of his questions, and he seemed to be trying to pick apart some of the testimony on what she thought were trivial matters. She found herself being put off by his aggressiveness and wondered if the Commissioner-members weren't thinking the same thing. The developer's witnesses answered all questions bluntly and forthrightly. It was hard for her to imagine how the good impression they were making could be seriously undermined by the opposition. But she did want to go back and see how they would try.

One week later, Linda's back in the hearing room. She is expecting that the first witness to be heard will be the chief of the county planning office. Instead, to her surprise, the Chairman welcomes the U.S. Congressman from the district to be the first to speak.

Congressman Tom Handschake begins by noting that he very seldom comments in local land-use decisions. These are matters for county planners and citizens to decide, and he respects their good judgment and hard work. But this case is so important to his constituents, and indeed, because of its national security and public safety implications, to the country as a whole, that he's decided to make an exception and offer his opinion. He is against the project. He's studied it in some detail, and has concluded, with regret, that the dangers outweigh the benefits to his district. He knows that the neighborhood groups, organized as the Coalition of Neighborhoods United to Conserve Our Safety and Tranquility (known by its acronym, CONUCOST), will be putting on a full presentation of expert analysis to back up that conclusion, and he "doesn't want to steal their thunder." But he does want to note for the record that he has found the evidence they brought to him clear and impressive, and he congratulates them on their efforts and wishes them success.

After that speech, the packed room erupts in applause from the neighbors, who are immediately cautioned by the Chairman to restrain themselves from any subsequent displays.

Then the Planning Office goes on. The head of the agency reads in a monotone the report written by members of his staff. Looking at the county's stated goal of attracting new business and encouraging economic growth on appropriate tracts of unused land, the Planning Office finds the proposal consistent with public policy. It will cause no significant strain on the infrastructure. There are, however, certain scientific and public security issues raised by the opponents of the application, which the planners do not feel within their scope of expertise to address.

The only other government agency scheduled to participate is the Department of Transportation. The official spokesman notes tersely that the code regulations governing the ratio of parking spaces to volume of interior floor space have been exactly met. A study of the applicant's traffic circulation plan has concluded that "the ingress and egress to public streets" is "adequate."

No request to testify has been filed by the State Officer for Historic Preservation, the Fire Department, the Police Department, or the State Environmental Protection Department—though each would have gladly been accorded time in the hearing process to enter any remarks or recommendations. But Linda guesses that none of the bureaucrats wants to touch a case that she can see has become something of a political hot-potato.

The Chair proceeds to call on the one recognized party of opposition, CONUCOST, to begin its allotted two hours for presentation. (Another hour has been allotted to the numerous other groups and individuals who have signed up to speak in opposition, though they are not part of the CONUCOST group, and have not been accorded party status. The total time allotted to opponents is three hours, the same as for the developer.)

CONUCOST is represented by an attorney, Richard Causewitz, who has agreed, as he often does in public-interest cases, to handle the matter at a much-reduced fee. In a brief opening statement, he describes who CONUCOST is, how wide the geographic area it represents, and what it stands for. He emphasizes that it's strictly a volunteer citizens' group, and that none of its witnesses (in pointed contrast to the developer's obviously well-paid experts) is receiving compensation for the testimony he or she will give.

His witness line-up is as follows:

The president of CONUCOST, who covers the five basic reasons for opposition that motivated the residents of a diverse collection of neighborhoods in the area to coalesce into one organization. He explains that subsequent witnesses will provide evidence for each of the reasons. (5 minutes)

The most important of the expert witnesses is put on next, to address the unifying issue of **safety**. He is one of the most prestigious scientists in the country doing research in the same field as the OSRAD scientists. (Though he agreed to testify for no pay, he did have his airfare from Cambridge provided by the group.) Having been the first to work with some of the materials that OSRAD will be using in its manufacturing process, he can explain with unquestioned authority that there are not yet any safety standards sufficient to guard workers from the still largely unknown hazards. The manufacturing side of the company's plan, at least, should not be permitted. (30 minutes)

The scientist's argument needs to be framed in land-use terms that relate to the county's **zoning** code—which is what the next witness covers. He has no special zoning expertise but is simply a neighbor with an academic background in public policy issues and the willingness to research the question as his contribution to his neighborhood's case. He has analyzed what would happen if the parcel were to be developed as its current zoning allows—as housing, with some retail and limited office space—and his data on taxes and jobs generated shows a greater return to the county than under the OSRAD plan. (15 minutes)

A CPA who serves on the CONUCOST board continues this line of testimony with a critique of the developer's projected tax benefits. He finds that the OSRAD budget analysis has failed to consider the **costs** to the public incurred through increased use of the county's roads, its landfill, sewer, and other services. Despite the presence of fences and private guards, the high-security nature of the work must be expected to take up a disproportionate amount of police time to investigate possible security breaches. (10 minutes)

Traffic is the next issue. Again, no expensive consultant has been hired, but a committee of neighbors, standing with digital counters at the major intersections each morning, has compiled their own data, which the committee chair reports. The neighborhood count shows traffic volume 50 percent greater than the Department of Transportation study had shown, and when using these figures as the base for projection, the resulting volume when the new traffic is added in will put the road system "over capacity." The parking garage capacity is also found lacking, based on the actual percentage of drivers who arrive in no-passenger cars at a comparable workplace in the county. (15 minutes)

The **historic preservation** problem of the general store and the old barn is addressed by a retired history professor who lives in the neighborhood and who has become something of an expert in local lore. She effectively counters the developer's argument that the barn is unworthy of preservation, pointing out that it is the single extant building from a much larger complex of buildings, the old Chaney Farm, which dates back to the Civil War. The general store, as the developer has already conceded, is a little time capsule in itself—but it will immediately lose a large part of its historical value if it's physically removed from its site, from the view of the people who have grown up with it all their lives. (20 minutes)

The **wrap-up** of all these remarks on specific issues is provided by an average county resident, a mother who stays at home with her two small children. She describes what it will be like to live on a day-to-day basis so close to a high-security office complex and factory. When she and her husband bought their house only a few years earlier, they'd been aware of the zoning, and had taken the mixed residential/commercial classification to be an assurance that they would have mostly other homeowners as their neighbors when the land got developed, and maybe a few useful stores and businesses. They never dreamed that such an incongruous and frightening prospect as a closed, fenced-off, high-tech lab would be considered. Her testimony concludes with an emotional plea for denial of all the permits, an outcome that's clearly in line with the views of the vast majority of her neighbors. (15 minutes)

The testimony of all seven of the CONUCOST witnesses takes a little under two hours, but with the often-lengthy exchanges between the witnesses and the counsel for the developer, the hearing is now three hours in progress. There are numerous groups and individual neighbors still waiting to testify as opponents of the plan. To speed matters along, the impatient Commission Chairman asks if all who have come to express opposition would simply stand, identify themselves and the organization represented, and endorse the position of the CONUCOST group. Those who have prepared written statements are invited to file them for the record.

Not wishing to antagonize the Chair, the fourteen would-be witnesses agree. Five are delegates from other civic action and community associations, and three are from national cause organizations—one formed around the issue of scientific responsibility, a second that promotes the preservation of barns and rural structures, a third that opposes the use of live animals in research— and there are six other individuals who have listed no affiliation.

That concludes the opposition's case, announces the Chair. Counsel for the parties each has ten minutes for rebuttal. After that the Chair is ready to adjourn the hearing. He does not set a date when the vote on the decision can be expected. Because the case has been so long and touched on so many complicated issues, he remarks with a nod to his colleagues, the Commission will probably want to take more than the usual month to be ready to cast its votes. He adds, "When we've scheduled this item on our agenda, the parties will be notified that it's coming up, at least one week prior to the public meeting. That concludes this hearing. Thank you all for coming."

Linda wonders if she'll ever hear the outcome of the case. She's not one of the parties and doesn't live anywhere near the project, so she can't expect anyone will inform her. Still, she's in a state of suspense. After nearly eight hours of hearings, she now has no idea who will win. Yes, the Congressman's presence seemed like a great coup for the opposition—but what real weight does he carry with the zoning commission? The county planning office seemed less than enthusiastic in their support for the development—but they were supposed to receive "great weight." And what to make of the diametrically opposite conclusions of the "experts" on traffic, historic worth, and safety in the manufacturing process?

After a few weeks, as she's getting more wrapped up in the details of her own zoning case, Linda forgets about the OSRAD hearings. Then one day she picks up the local business section of her newspaper and notes a headline of interest:

"OSRAD OUT IN REZONING BID; SAFETY, TRAFFIC CITED AS REASONS." The vote had been 3-3, but a majority of "aye" votes was needed for an application of this nature to go forward. The architect, the realtor, and the businessman on the panel had all voted for; the other three, including the Chairman (who had seemed so impatient with the opposition, in Linda's view) had cast the "nays."

With the Bilderbig case now just two days away from being considered by the same panelists, Linda understands how much of an advantage it is to have been able to watch them reacting to neighbors' testimony and to see how those reactions have translated into votes. She'll now have some useful tips to pass on to her coworkers on the case, and some added confidence on how her neighborhood's points will be received.

Will your case be handled the same way as in the OSRAD story? It may well be. But your zoning authorities could use another model for taking testimony—not an adversarial, quasi-judicial process, but a **legislative** process. In this set-up, there are no parties, and no cross-examination. Witnesses present testimony to the deciding panel, who may question them, but no one else has the right to do so. There is usually no right to rebuttal time to respond to another witness's assertions (though in some instances, it could be granted).

Another widespread method of dealing with land-use cases is through use of the **political** system. Instead of making his case before an independent, non-partisan agency, the applicant offers his land-use plan directly to the city or county council for its consideration and judgment. The members may conduct the hearing according to their usual rules and procedures, or follow a format especially designed for land-use matters.

The kinds of evidence you marshal and arguments you make (or the emphasis you place on certain elements of your case) will vary depending on which of the processes is in use in your jurisdiction. But it's up to you to find out what works best where you live.

The Not-for-Public-Consumption Side

What you see at the public hearing is just a portion of what's involved in the decision-making process of a land-use case. It's the old iceberg problem: You know that 90 percent of the matter is under the surface, and you need to find some way to see it, and shape your activities accordingly. But you really need to have certain skills and equipment for this. The developer of course has them, and this is where he usually gets his big edge. Here, too, is where the system most needs reforming.

Developers have the skills and equipment because they could not stay in business otherwise. They spend eight or more hours a day, five, six, or seven days a week at what they do, so it's no wonder they know how to handle the problems they encounter. And if they don't know, they can hire the best people to help them.

But that doesn't mean they're always bound to win. As we've seen (and it's happening more and more often of late), the community can learn how to use the process, too, and if the facts (and a few of the breaks) are with them, they will beat the developer at his own game. They have one crucial advantage the developer lacks: a driving spirit. They know if they lose, life in the neighborhood will never be the same again. It's their *homes* on the line. For the developer, it's usually all just a matter of money. "You win some, you lose some," most businessmen in the more speculative fields are able to tell themselves, consolingly. They go on to the next project, having learned from their mistakes.

One thing developers all know is that they've got to lay the groundwork for acceptance, long before they're ready to file the application. They have their market analysts go over the idea for the plan; they study the neighborhood and figure out what the most likely objections might be; and their lawyers are always at their elbow telling them just how much the zoning code will allow (or can be stretched to cover). And because the developer can file the plans whenever *he's* ready, he's always got the first move in the game. He's got the element of surprise—which any battle tactician can tell you is a considerable advantage. So you're always in the position of having to react to what's happened, and you can all too easily end up on a perpetual defensive, looking like you're always opposed to things, never wanting any change to occur. (Of course, no developer ever asks you what you'd like *before* he draws up plans.)

A plan could be anywhere from several months to several years in the preparation stages before you and your neighbors have any inkling it's coming; but if the developer's done his homework, by the time you sit down to meet with him, he could actually have a pretty good idea of what you all are going to say.

What's more, he's already been to see the planning officials downtown, and he's told them not only what he's planning, but why a handful of overanxious neighbors may object to it, and why they're wrong. These city or county employees know the developer's track record pretty well. They've worked with him before on other projects he's successfully completed; they may even be on a first-name basis with each other. He's been to their offices and taken them out to lunch. He may have even contributed to a jointly funded government/private study on some special problem that allowed the office to hire more people or get better office machines.

It's also possible (very likely, in some areas) that the developer is operating a **revolving door** for the government employees who look favorably on his work. This means that there are much higher-salaried jobs waiting for these officials at the developer's firm (or in his consultants or lawyers' offices) when they're ready to leave public service. Nothing is ever so openly stated, of course; it's just something that happens. When the new employees of the development company go before their former colleagues on the Zoning Board or at the planning office in support of a development proposal, you shouldn't be surprised if their advocacy is received in a more cordial manner than the advocacy of strangers.

Is this a form of corruption? *You betcha!* But it's a subtle enough variety to pass legal muster in many localities. The law will most likely bar an ex-government employee only from appearing on behalf of an application that he or she had any dealings with while still in public life. New proposals are a different story.

A far less subtle sort of influence can be gained—again, with complete legality in many areas—over elected officials who have a role to play in the approval process. The developer has only to contribute the maximum allowable amount to the re-election campaigns of those politicians with any say in the outcome. If the giving limit is low for each individual, it's not a problem to get each of his partners, secretaries, janitors, and their spouses and children to contribute the maximum amount.

It doesn't stop there, either. In non-election years, there will be countless functions—banquets, parties, galas, performances, and competitions—underwritten in part or in full by private corporations. Unless your developer's very stupid or new at this, you can bet his name will pop up under the "Patron" or "Sponsor" category of donor, every time. None of these gifts ever entail any definite *quid pro quo* ("That would be wrong!" as former President Nixon used to put it), but you should not imagine that he's being so generous for the hell of it.

The Specter of Corruption

What if you suspect real corruption—out-and-out bribery, influence-peddling, or kickbacks? There are, sadly, many critics and towns where the development process is a crooked game. Nobody gets any permits without paying off the right people—it's something that "everybody knows"—and there may even be set "fees" expected as bribes.

If things are so out of hand in your area, it could be very difficult—and possibly dangerous—for your group to try to do anything about it. Move cautiously, by all means! First consider what evidence you have. Is it just vague rumors—without dates, times, places, or names? Or have you specific but secondhand knowledge (hearsay) of a bribe being paid? Or did you actually see, hear, or read proof that something underhanded is going on? If the latter, get some *good legal advice*. If the lawyer tells you you've got real evidence, then you can think about taking the next step

Now consider who is the most trustworthy person to turn to. Is there one official, elected or appointed, known to you to be of indisputable integrity? If not, you may look to the federal government to start an investigation of the case. The FBI or the U.S. attorney's office for your region should be called in.

What if you're afraid to get involved in a criminal investigation? You may be able to avoid it, if there is a strong newspaper or television station in your area that practices investigative journalism. In many states there are "shield laws" permitting reporters to protect the anonymity of their sources. Even in states lacking such laws, a reporter may be willing to pledge to protect your identity at all costs, when you pass along the proof that there's something scandalous going on in a zoning case. Busting a local graft ring can be a story of Pulitzer-prize-winning proportions, so if there's anything at all to what you've got, the newspaper or TV station could be the quickest, most determined force to find it. And if they do, your little "local" problem could suddenly be the subject of national attention.

What if you're not sure whether corruption's an issue or not? Well, under our system, you are going to have to proceed as if everyone is clean until proven otherwise—no matter how strong your suspicions are. Even in towns where corruption is assumed to be rampant—there are some types of cases you can worry less about than others. Surprisingly, it's the really hot, controversial ones where corruption is the *least* likely to occur. Why? Because the high degree of media attention and public interest in the outcome accentuate the risks for the crooks. It's naturally a lot harder to pay for favors when everyone's watching to see what favors are granted and who's doing the granting. Rather, it's in the lower-level aspects of development (the fifty or a hundred bucks slipped into the building inspector's pocket to ignore a minor code violation while a building's going up, or the "grease" applied to the system to get an already-approved but stalled building permit issued faster so that construction can start on time) where corruption most typically enters in.

Still, whatever the level of case you're working on, whatever the reputation of your town, keep your eyes and ears open. If, say, the chairman of your local zoning board changes his mind on an important vote just as his wife has received the anonymous gift of a full-length mink...perhaps you should start making some quiet inquiries. What you find out could not only work toward saving your neighborhood from a crooked developer—you could just be cleaning up the whole town!

Strategies to Try; Pitfalls to Avoid

So what's a poor community to do? With all these unofficial developer-government relationships going on before and during the public hearing process, do you, the citizens, still stand a chance? Yes, of course, or I wouldn't be telling you even to start! But you do have certain obstacles to overcome, and you just need to recognize that they're there—though they may seem a bit hidden, or below the surface.

Once you're aware that they're out there, you can do some things to minimize their impact, if not remove them altogether. (A complete leveling of the playing field can only be accomplished by a full-time effort at systemic reform, and you are probably too caught up in the particular development fight at hand to get into that subject now. Chapter 17, however, examines some legislative and regulatory changes that are needed to put citizens and developers on an equal footing in the development process in most jurisdictions.)

Here are some ideas to try, plus a few pitfalls to avoid.

Playing the Underdog

First and foremost, you have to make use of your status as the little guy. You have to remind everyone, every chance you get, that you *don't* have the money, the influence, the army of consultants and lawyers to guide your moves. Without all this, things are stacked against you, and so allowances need to be made. So you *won't* have the polished speeches and professionally designed graphics in your presentation; so your traffic study was done, not by a Ph.D in transportation management, but by neighbors standing out on the street corners at 8 a.m., digital counters in hand to note the number of cars passing by; so you *did* miss one filing deadline, and didn't have the right number of copies, marked with the case-number in the right-hand corner only, as the rules require. So your group *does* appear a bit disorganized and stuck on irrelevant points at times. Turn all these little weaknesses into your strength! Use them to show how the developer, by contrast, is slick and manipulative with the facts. The natural sympathy goes to the underdog, and you'll want to get every bit of it you can!

The corollary to this advice is that you must not do anything that makes you seem too powerful, professional, or experienced at getting your way. Do so, and you leave yourself open to any of three negative syndromes.

The Rich Neighborhood Syndrome. A neighborhood will be particularly vulnerable to this problem if its residents are generally in the upper- or upper-middle-income brackets, or if it has a few individuals or families who are *very* rich. The developer then attempts to paint his company as a collection of hard-working, solidly middle-class businesspeople—decent people just out to earn an honest day's dollar—who are being unfairly attacked by an "effete corps of impudent snobs." If the neighbors are objecting to an overly dense residential development, he will say they are just trying to preserve their closed-off and privileged enclave. If they're fighting an ugly design, he accuses them of being pompous dictators of taste, caring for "mere aesthetics" rather than the hard costs and real human benefits of growth. This argument poses a particular danger in cases involving historic preservation, where the developer may be able to make it seem as if there's basically this choice: preserve (at great expense) an old building that's of little use to the modern world, or tear it down and build something larger, less costly per square foot, but more suited to the way people live and work today. It's easy, in that case, for the well-heeled advocates of the costlier solution to be perceived as out-of-touch with the needs of working America.

A rich neighborhood is also at a special disadvantage when the developer is proposing to construct a building whose purpose is to serve the needs of the middle or lower class. This could be a school, a hospital, or a low-to-moderate income apartment project. The developer seldom has any trouble keeping the focus on the wealth of the neighborhood comparative to the relative poverty of the residents/students/patients of whatever he is building, and so can appear to be a champion of the underdog himself.

What the neighborhood often neglects to point out is that the greatest wealth by far belongs to the development corporation, the ultimate recipient of the construction project's benefits (its profits). This holds true even in some of the highest-income counties in the country, at least as far as my research has shown. No community organization I've investigated has been able to muster the kind of financial backing and professional talent that would put it in the same league as even a relatively small and weak development company. If you could just get the developer to disclose what he's spending on his quest to get permits, as opposed to what your own organization is spending to block them, you'd see the tenfold or more difference that bears this out. It doesn't matter, in any case, what the total combined wealth of your neighbors may be, since your anti-development organization (even if it's headed by a fund-raising genius) will only be able to tap a very small fraction of the money. It's up to you to keep the real balance sheet a factor in the public mind, or your "underdog" advantage could be usurped.

One thing I've noticed that should work in your favor: In most high-income neighborhoods, the spokespersons and real activists in the anti-development fight tend to be of middle or lower income. Perhaps it's because the people with the fewest options (who can't afford to move if the neighborhood's quality of life declines) are the ones with the greatest incentive to see the case won. Or perhaps it's that activists so often are the retired, the part-timers, or the self-employed (and sometimes *un*employed), who are able to devote more attention to the development problem.

If that's the case in your rich neighborhood, don't let the fact go unremarked. An example: You pick up your morning paper and read a news-story on your case that begins: "In the affluent community of Bucksville, owners of million-dollar houses are protesting the construction of an apartment complex ..." The least moneyed, but most active person in your group should waste no time writing a letter to the editor in response. It should be personal and somewhat ironic (not angry) in tone. Like this: "I see by your article [cite date and headline] that I am one of those Bucksville millionaires protesting overdevelopment. This would be pleasant news if true, but I'm afraid it's not the case. I am a retired postal employee who bought my house in 1956, for $15,000. Like many of my neighbors, I love the place I live, but find it a struggle to keep up with maintenance costs of the house and the ever-rising assessments. Now I have to worry about living under the long afternoon shadow of a thirty-story high-rise ...."

The "Celebrities-Always-Get-Their-Way" Syndrome. What too many rich people can do to your underdog status, just one famous person, if quoted to your disadvantage, can accomplish in a day. Does that mean if Jackie Onassis offers to testify in your neighborhood's cause, or Tom Wolfe is available to meet with the developer, you should say, "Thanks, but we don't need any more help"? Don't be silly! But you do have to be careful to use your celebrity neighbors' time judiciously, or you could be doing your own side some damage. How? The press will swarm around the celebrity and ignore the reason he or she is there. And the developer will say, "Just because she's a famous actress, she thinks the city should preserve her private view...But I'm trying to build housing for the rest of the people of L.A. (or New York, or wherever it may be)."

The way to avoid the problem is not to showcase the celebrity unnecessarily. Allow him or her to participate exactly as would any other neighbor with a similar degree of expertise. So if your actress-neighbor is a good public speaker, she should read the statements on behalf of the group. If the best-selling author who lives in your building has had articles appear in respected architecture magazines, he could certainly draft and present testimony on the design of the development you're fighting. Of course his or her mere presence is going to attract more press to your group's efforts...and that's good—and it will *stay* good if you can show that the celebrity is there to contribute something, not just there as an attention-getting gimmick.

I think Joan Mondale is the perfect model of how a celebrity neighbor should behave. The former "Second Lady," who lives three blocks away from me, was very active in her neighborhood's campaign against an excessively large office/retail complex that was going up on the nearest major cross-street. She faithfully attended all our meetings, which helped to bring out the press. Though she was very quotable, she never hogged the spotlight or made reference to her husband's political career. She spoke just as any other concerned neighbor and citizen would have done. When reporters asked her about technical or legal matters in the case, she referred them to the less-famous leaders of the organization for answers. During the hearing on the case, she sat quietly in the audience, nodding thoughtfully, while the Zoning Board members (who all just happened to be Democratic appointees) heard others arguing the points. The developer thus could not claim she was exercising any extraordinary political influence on the case. She was, after all, "just a neighbor"—but a very helpful sort to have!

The "Too-Smart-for-Your-Own-Good" Syndrome. It's not a good idea to appear to be more experienced at fighting development than you really are. This syndrome befalls, not the group just forming, but the one that's been around for a while and may have fought off a few unwanted construction projects in the past. The developer can easily turn this to his public advantage. "They're at it again!" he says. "These people don't want anything!" Residents of nearby neighborhoods similarly beset by overdevelopment, hearing that you're fighting again, may switch from cheering you on to wondering resentfully, "Why should *we* get stuck with all the big new buildings and the traffic? Why don't *they* take their fair share of the burden?" When you go out seeking other organizations' letters of support, you may find yourself short of allies, or worse, find the developer is picking up some he never should have won.

A related problem is appearing to have greater technical expertise than you do. Your traffic committee has put together such a competent-sounding and professionally packaged report that the zoning panel now wants to judge the work according to the standards of the field. But the co-authors of the study are still just neighbors and volunteers. They don't have the time, equipment, or background to assemble the size of data-base called for, or to perform the number of comparison-counts required, according to the textbooks on the subject. You don't want to fall into this trap. If your witnesses are not certified experts, they should not use the jargon of those who are, but should stick to layman's terms to describe the conditions that they, as ordinary, observant neighbors, have studied.

What to Do? The underdog status will be more securely yours if you take a few simple precautions.

- Don't spend too much money on presentation and hype. Keep your literature simple and informative; it can be eye-catching and pleasing to look at, but not obviously expensively designed.
- Don't raise money in ostentatious or high-profile ways (no balls, galas, or big-name art auctions). Approach the potentially big donors privately, and see if they don't mind receiving relatively little (or no) public credit.
- If it's known that you've amassed a big "war-chest," announce that any money left over after the case is won will be donated to an appropriate charity, or earmarked to help solve some other neighborhood problem.
- Let a variety of people speak for the group, as called for in each situation. The celebrity should be encouraged to speak when he or she has something special to say, just as your poorer, more obscure, neighbors should do, as it suits the circumstances.
- Bring in fresh faces, new workers, to spread the fact-finding and presentation tasks around. The older, more experienced neighbors will still be available to guide the newcomers along, but they'll be less susceptible to "burn-out"; meanwhile, the new people making the neighborhood's case at the public hearing will not have to worry about being tagged as "experts" when they're just diligent volunteers.

Playing All the Bases

You've taken some steps to preserve your underdog standing, but that doesn't mean you'll want to look like a bush-league player. You also need to put forth the best possible effort that you can muster, and you *need to be seen doing it*. And for that, you'll need to get around. You're aware by now that the developer's already got a head start on you at this. He's out there working his regular connections: with the people in the planning office, with the politicians, on the social circuit, and through the various boards and foundations and business associations he serves on.

You might feel like you could use a full-time social secretary for the next few months, but start making appointments, and working the same circuits. Go where the developer goes, and cultivate the same friendships. You'll really be missing out if you let him be the only recognized player in the game. And it's really not hard to start making some impressions. First, call the head of your local planning office and suggest, not a formal meeting, but just some time to talk informally about a variety of planning issues...perhaps over lunch? (You pay.)

Explore with other members of your group what other relationships you might want to build up. Someone in your neighborhood group may already have some good contacts who are important in the development process. Or you may learn of someone outside your group who knows people, someone who has not yet been approached to become a member of your organization. Some people may be worried that they're being asked to exploit their friends or connections in the neighborhood's interest. So you must make clear that you don't want anyone to lobby on any issue in a social setting. That would be counter-productive, and in many cases, illegal. (See the Glossary for a definition of *ex parte communication.*) You really want to do nothing more than establish a friendly connection with some of the people in public life, so that when they encounter you again in an official capacity, they'll already know who you are, where you're from, and what sort of issues concern you. And there's nothing at all wrong with that. (You may also be doing some regular lobbying, openly trying to sway officials to see things your way, which you will do during ordinary working hours in the officials' offices. More on this subject in Chapter 5.)

What if you don't have time to do all this *schmoozing?* You've got a full-time job of your own to attend to, and the case is coming up so rapidly, you can't spare any time just to get acquainted with people. Then let the city planning officials know it. When you meet one of them for the first time, say, "I'm really sorry we didn't get a chance to get together sooner. But we've just had our hands full answering all these misstatements in the developer's application...I'm sure you know how difficult it can be when you've got a crucial hearing date coming up...."

With elected officials you may not have to worry as much about keeping in their good graces. *They* are the ones to do the worrying about keeping their names and faces known and respected. You put them in office, after all. And you can take them out again. And don't think this fact is ever far from their minds. You'll never have to remind them openly (to do so would be somewhat insulting), but they know, if your group is large enough, and committed enough, they had better not offend you if they can possibly avoid it. So while they may disagree with what you're working for, they will at least listen to you with courtesy and attention. You'll find this true, even of politicians who number developers among their biggest contributors. They know, when it comes close to election time, no amount of money, no pull-out-all-the-stops ad campaign, can win back angry voters who feel they've been neglected or betrayed by someone they once supported.

Think this is too romantic a view of our democracy today? Think a more cynical view is in order? Just look around at what's happening at the polls these days. Here's a typical example, from Fairfax County, Virginia. County Executive Jack Herrity presided over the local government for twelve years of the greatest building boom in the county's history. He backed all major construction projects, even though road capacity and social services were hardly able to keep pace. Little-known challenger Audrey Moore took him on over the issue, and though he far surpassed her in fundraising and important connections, she still beat him by a decisive majority. Now the county's on a "slow-growth" track.

A politician doesn't have to lose an election to absorb this lesson. Senator John Warner is a case in point. He was not only a supporter of more commercial expansion, but a close friend of one of Virginia's biggest developers, John T. ("Til") Hazel. When Hazel's company put forward a plan to build a shopping mall next door to the Manassas National Battlefield, in the beginning Warner was all for it. On August 8, 1988 the *Washington Post* reported that 65 percent of all Northern Virginians agreed that the site of the proposed mall should be acquired by the government and so preserved as part of the Battlefield.* Not long thereafter, Senator Warner reported a change of mind. He was now for legislation to accomplish that goal. The people had spoken. With his help, the bill passed and was signed by the President, and the shopping mall was "history."

You may not feel that the "slow-growth" movement in your area is yet able to command this level of attention. When you are meeting politicians for the first time, you won't easily be able to tell how well they're receiving your message. It helps to know how many others like you are coming in to talk about similar problems. How strong are the ties the politician has to the development industry? How entrenched an incumbent is he? (Are challenges a relatively rare thing in your area?) These are not questions to ask the politician directly, but they're things to find out discreetly as you start to move in local political circles. Knowing the answers will enable you to accord each elected official,

---

* "Public Bucks Officials on Proposed Mall," *The Washington Post*, p. 1.

and each potential challenger, the degree of friendliness and seriousness he or she deserves.

Putting the Public and Private Sides of the Process Together

Now to get back to that old iceberg cliche I dished out at the beginning of this section. You see now that the public hearing is just the tip of the iceberg, and that by far the greater part is out of view, in sometimes perilously murky depths. But you're going to have to learn how to navigate in these waters if you want to get anywhere.

Still sticking to the polar reaches, let me now switch metaphors on you and compare the work you'll be doing to building an igloo. First, you'll have to cut the pieces as time and custom require (i.e., follow the rules of procedure set down in your jurisdiction). You'll need to lay your foundation blocks with care, and then build up gradually and smoothly toward the final form (rest your case on sound understanding of the process and bring in pieces of evidence that support your conclusion). You must take care not to leave large gaps anywhere (by neglecting to get to know anyone who has an important role in the process); and you must build with the right kind of snow (you don't want to use expensively imported and packaged materials when the local stuff serves your needs much better); and you'll need good teamwork to put it all together. But when you're all done, you've got the protection you want to see you through the worst part of the storm.

So on to the next building block!

PART II

THE NUTS AND BOLTS OF COMMUNITY ORGANIZING

Introductory Note to Chapters 5–8

You should now know:

- who your developer is
- what he plans to build
- what major problems the plan poses for your neighborhood
- what government process the case will go through before any permits can be issued
- how to approach people, in and out of the government, who will have an impact on your case.

You may also know:

- that there will be a public hearing at which you will need to put on a credible presentation *or* (because there is no public hearing involved in the type of process called for by the plans, or because the development problem seems amenable to a negotiated solution)
- that you will need to put together a credible representative group to speak for the neighborhood at negotiating sessions and other meetings.

In either case, you and your neighbors must know how to organize yourselves effectively. A strong organization rests on the soundness of its three basic components, which are:

1. Its people (its leaders, its general membership, and the special help provided by experts).
2. Its set-up (how tasks are delegated and decisions are made, how different parts of the organization communicate with each other and with the general public, how money is raised and records are kept, etc.).
3. Its purposes (whether goals are set that are reasonably attainable and how the members set strategy to achieve those goals).

These three components may be summarized simply as the **Who**, the **How**, and the **What For** of the organization. Chapter 5 will address the first, Chapter 6 the second, and, once you've got a working group of people and have a structure for their activities, Chapter 7 will tackle the somewhat messier question of just what it is you hope (and can expect) to achieve with the people and the set-up you've got.

After you've got these matters settled for your own organization, you'll want to give some thought to how the developer's company works and what options he may be exploring. This is the subject of Chapter 8.

The Organizational Who

General Membership

Rules for Members

You will want to make your organization easy to join, with as few rules as possible, so that you can attract a large and varied membership and gain strength through numbers. Accordingly, I suggest conferring membership upon anyone who is in basic agreement with the purposes of the organization as stated in your by-laws. Members might check off a box with a statement to this effect when they submit their names and addresses on a form.

Yes, I support the work of the Save the Neighborhood Coalition, Inc. Here's my tax-deductible contribution of:

$100 _____ $50 _____ $25 _____ $10 _____ other _____

Name _____

Address _____

Phone (H) _____ (W) _____

I'm interested in helping out on [sample committees]

flyer distribution _____ fundraising & activities _____

research _____ legal _____ media contacts _____

If receipt of dues is to be made a pre-condition of membership, the amount to join should be very low, so that membership remains within reach of even the poorest segment of the community. (Members who can afford to pay more can always be asked by the fundraisers to do so, and can be offered a different, perhaps more distinguished-sounding category of membership—sponsor, patron, life-member, etc.—for the higher donation.)

What about restricting membership on a geographic basis? Is it a good idea to ensure that all members live within a certain distance of the development site? I think not. It's an advantage to you to be able to show that your case has attracted supporters from all over the area, not just the few blocks directly under the development's shadow.

But what if the developer, who lives in another neighborhood, tries to join? What if he gets all his employees and consultants to become members, too, and pack your meetings? One exclusion you should write into your rules is on memberships by persons who have any financial ties to the developers, owners, or lessees of the development site. That avoids that problem.

What if the developer is able to find someone who isn't an employee, who will join your organization and serve as a **mole**, to keep him informed of your activities? In that case you'll be glad you have as your one requirement for membership an agreement with the basic purposes of the organization. You'll also be glad you have some kind of removal clause (discussed under "Incorporation" in Chapter 2), so that your Board can terminate the membership of anyone found to be working against your stated goals.

The hard part will be not in deciding how to deal with the mole, but in finding out if you have one. You probably won't have any sure way to discover this—but don't worry too much about it. It's a very rare occurrence. The risk to the developer who's caught trying to spy on his opposition is quite high. If exposed for using such KGB-like tactics, he'd surely lose all hope of public sympathy, and official approval along the way. But despite the small likelihood of spying, it doesn't hurt to be a little cautious when dealing with volunteers who are strangers to you. Get to know the volunteers who sign up as well as you can. Be inquisitive about their backgrounds and interests. Where do they work? How and where did they hear about the organization? Don't go overboard with the questioning or get paranoid, but just ask the normal sorts of things you'd ask anyone you'll be working with closely over a period of time. If it should just happen to come up that one of your members is the wife of the developer's nephew...you just might want to steer that person away from any sensitive strategy-making or priority-setting sessions.

Avoiding the F.O.E.

Neighborhood development fights attract all types. If you're lucky, your case will bring out the sharpest, coolest, and wisest among your neighbors. But in all probability, it will also bring out a few members of each of the categories below:

- hot-heads who are just looking for a fight
- lonely people who have nothing better to do with their time, who take the neighborhood organization as a ready-made source of companionship
- people who always want to be at the center of things, who seek any opportunity to take charge (would-be Napoleons)
- people who have a secret agenda (a personal grudge against a business or a neighbor, perhaps), who want to use the organization somehow for their own ends
- people who either missed out on or want to call back the great protest days of the '60s, and who want to charge the barricades, no matter how that might affect the outcome of the case
- people who are not fully connected to planet Earth (who may be paranoid and believe the developer is out to get them personally, or who show some other obvious difficulty in perceiving reality).

I call these people collectively F.O.E.—for flakes, oddballs, and eccentrics. I can say from experience, if more than two or three of them get on the board of your organization, big trouble is on the way. It's just too easy for your whole group to be tagged with a flaky, oddball, and eccentric reputation, based on the unauthorized actions of just one or two of these loonies.

A (perhaps extreme) example makes the point: A group of neighbors in Charles County, Maryland, were opposed to the construction of a $2 billion dollar project along the banks of the Potomac to be known as Riviera. But a self-appointed spokesman of the organization SWORD (Save Wildlife, Oppose Riviera Development) took out ads in the local newspaper describing the project in apocalyptic terms, employing racist and anti-Semitic rhetoric. A front-page expose' by the *Washington Post* revealed the author of the ad to be a supporter of a neo-Nazi organization.* The minute the story appeared, the focus of the case shifted from problems of the development itself, to the motives and credibility of the group opposing it. Any reasonable points the other neighbors may have wanted to make were lost.

Can F.O.E. damage to credibility be avoided? Yes, if you have at least four or five others at the core of the group who are willing to confront the problem

---

* *The Washington Post* April 25, 1988, p. 1.

squarely and take the necessary steps. The minute you first suspect that so-and-so is acting out of step with the goals of the group, you should meet with those you trust and see if you can get agreement on which of several methods you will use to deal with the troublesome member. Kick him off the board? Yes, you may have to, if the person is actually disruptive of your group's stated policies and procedures. But it's generally better not to create an open rift (unless of course he's like the neo-Nazi in the above example, in which case, waste no time—CAN HIM!) You may be able to handle him by telling him how valuable he is, playing to his ego—all the while assigning him to trivial (but importantly labeled) tasks. Set him to doing research on the development company's history back to its founder, for example. Or put him in charge of mailings (it's hard to foul up envelope-sealing and stamp-licking). If he insists on doing something connected to the decision-making process, ask him to prepare a report analyzing the merits of the various options open to the organization and concluding with a recommendation (you can always ignore the result). Do whatever you must to keep him busy and still feeling a member of the team, but out of the limelight.

Not all F.O.E.-types are equally bad. I've seen cases in which individuals with certain weird quirks ended up doing their groups a good deal of service. Someone who had a mania for details, for example, dug around obsessively in the city's archives for evidence about a development deal and ended up discovering a 100–year-old document that muddied the developer's title to his building site—a fact that gave the neighborhood an appealable issue before the court. Others, who at first seemed only interested in making speeches and offering criticisms, were only waiting to be handed a more constructive role to play in the group's effort. Those who strike you as "loose cannons" may only require a little instruction as to when they can spring into action, and where they should aim their fire.

The lonely types, especially, tend to turn out well. These are the ones who showed up at your first meeting just looking for someone to talk to. You might think they have no skills or ideas to contribute. But they are often patient and willing to work at learning whatever task you can find for them. All they need is a chance to feel useful, and when your neighborhood is facing a serious threat, that isn't a bad thing. You could well find them ready to take on the boring but essential sort of administrative chore no one else has volunteered to do. In that event you may find that your flake, oddball, or eccentric has actually become more of a friend than a F.O.E.

Positive Recruitment

You will want to do more than manage the less desirable members of your organization. You'll want to take some positive steps to bring in the people you do want. The initial contacts you made to neighbors and to heads of interested groups (discussed in Chapter 2) got you headed in the right direction; putting on a big public meeting (also described in that chapter) should have produced many other volunteers who are willing to assume a number of start-up tasks. But if you're going to be in this for the long haul, you'll need all the good people you can possibly get. So you'll want to seek out certain individuals known to have special skills and talents as volunteers.

In this regard you've got a decided advantage over the developer. His company may have more money than all the bank accounts of all your neighbors put together, but you're richer in people. You've got hundreds, if not thousands, of potential supporters to draw strength from. You only need some way to draw them in and tap their talents.

Here are some of the neighbors you will have who are likely to agree to put in the time and effort needed to protect the quality of life in the neighborhood.

Full-time Parents. Every community has its share of women (and occasionally men) who choose to stay at home when their children are young. Many of these parents left jobs that paid well for special skills. Now they're working hard to give the next generation the best start in life, which could be threatened if the development occurs as planned. But this at-home job can sometimes seem confining and monotonous when compared to the business world. An interesting and important development fight can provide a chance to use those business or professional skills, without taking too much time away from the needs of the kids at home.

Full-time parents are also likely to have ties to other community organizations, like the PTA, recreational associations, and church groups, whose support your organization might want to solicit.

Home Businesspeople. Many "cottage industries" go on in offices or workshops within the home. Home business-owners may work as consultants, writers, designers, artists, accountants, therapists, or in any of a dozen other occupations. Their schedules are often flexible, allowing them to participate in daytime meetings with the developer or city officials; their volunteered skills are often invaluable; and their business equipment (computers, drafting tools, copying machines, etc.) are sometimes available for your organization's use.

Retired People. Think of the people in your neighborhood who are no longer working. You might find former heads of corporations, former scientists and engineers, and other leaders in their fields. Many retirees don't realize how much they miss public life until they are out of it; yet the younger, more active residents often assume their older neighbors don't have the interest or the energy to devote to a controversial issue. But you won't know for sure until you ask—and most retirees I've met have been very pleased to be asked, and have put in more hours and worked harder for the neighborhood's good than members who are thirty and forty years younger. But when you set meeting times and dates, keep your older members' needs in mind. Many older women (and men, for that matter) are reluctant to go out alone at night. Saturday morning or afternoon meeting dates can help to increase participation of this important segment of your neighborhood.

Younger People/Students. People too young to be full-time members of the work force are often bright and just as interested in what goes on in the neighborhood as long-time residents. They're the ones who will be living the longest with the outcome of the development problem. They're usually attracted to the challenge of a political scrap, and have fresh ideas to offer—as well as strong arms and legs. They'll ring doorbells, stand out in front of the store handing out flyers, deliver newsletters, and take on more specialized work if given good instruction. My neighborhood of Cleveland Park got itself declared a historic district largely based on research done by volunteer student interns, recruited from the Urban Preservation program at George Washington University. They spent long hours down at the city records department, looking up original deeds to the houses and commercial buildings in the district. Without their contribution, demolition crews would likely be at work right now tearing down some of the neighborhood's jazziest Art Deco-designed storefronts.

Experts. It's worth going out of your way to get the participation of neighbors who have certain areas of expertise. The particular development problem you're facing will dictate the kinds of specialists you'll need, though nearly every anti-development group could benefit from having an architect on its Board of Directors. Lawyers, engineers, traffic analysts, economists, statisticians, environmentalists, architectural historians, and geologists all will have something of value to contribute, if you can recruit them to your side. Even if you later conclude it's best to hire outside help, you'll still have the benefit of having a member with the same skill to help choose, supervise, and evaluate the paid expert's work.

But you should exercise some care in your approach to your neighbor/expert. It's no honor to be asked to serve on the Board of an organization if you're only there to provide free labor. Your expert will want to hear first about the development problem just as any other neighbor would. Let him or her be the one to suggest any special services he or she might be willing to contribute. The expert may well hesitate for fear that the effort could take up too much time. Here are some considerations you may want to offer in that case:

- Not every board member needs to come to every meeting. The expert could serve on a subcommittee that will deal with one specific issue, or perhaps, work alone on that aspect of the case. The geologist, for example, might be asked to do one soil survey of the development site, with assurances that he would not be asked to do anything else.

- Work volunteered in aid of the community in a public controversy can often lead to paid assignments. I've seen this happen especially with young architects who are starting out on their own. They do some height and massing studies to help make the neighborhood's case at a public hearing; the neighbors see this well-presented example of the architect's work, and soon he has several new residential commissions. Not only other neighbors, but developers will sometimes hire new talent from among the opposition's experts. (Of course, this can end up being a problem for the neighborhood, when all its brightest experts end up working for the other side. You may find yourself at the next hearing attacking the competence of the neighbor whose work you once praised to the skies. But don't worry about that as you're entering into your first development fight. The important thing now is to get your expert/neighbors to help you when you need it most.)

- The amount of volunteer time and energy to be spent helping to defeat the bad development scheme must be weighed against the time and energy needed to cope with the results of the developer's success. If people understand that they're going to be spending an extra forty or fifty minutes each day sitting in gridlocked traffic caused by a new development, they tend to be more willing to set aside the few hours of their professional time needed to help prevent that outcome. The closer the expert lives to the development site, the easier he will be to persuade. Some experts won't need any of the above reasons and reassurances to volunteer. In many cases I've seen, professionals were pleased to have been asked. It shows them that their neighbors recognize their skills and value their judgment. It also looks good to have "Member, Board of Directors of..." on their resume'. It's nice to be recognized as a "community leader." So as long as your cause seems worthwhile, and your organization looks efficient, with responsibilities to be divided up fairly among the volunteers, you should not find it too difficult to attract good people to your membership list.

Leadership

How leaders emerge is a mysterious process. No book can tell you how to ensure that the best people available serve as your leaders. But there are plenty of books that will tell you how to become an effective manager, or how to negotiate your way through a difficult problem, or how to cope with a crisis (many development plans induce a sense of panic among nearby residents). Some useful how-to books are listed in the Bibliography at the back of this book, and while reading a book is not going to turn a shy, inexperienced person into a leader, it can at least help him or her to sharpen some of the skills that may serve an organization better in the end than a strong personality might do.

It is likely that among those who were the first to recognize the development problem and were willing to face it head on, you will find one person ready to take charge and get the neighborhood fired up to win. You may be that person! If nobody with that kind of spirit seems to be at hand, then you should at least find someone willing to assume the title of organization president, chairperson, or whatever with the assurance that many other neighbors who chair sub-committees will help to share in the responsibilities of leadership.

If no one person has the time or inclination to serve as the organization's chief, you might consider naming two co-chairs. This set-up has worked well for one citizens' association in my area. The two leaders have very different personalities, but they are equally committed to the neighborhood's goals. One co-chair is a take-charge sort of guy, who likes the challenge of a fight; he's the one who makes the calls to the developer, to the politicians, city officials, and the press. The other co-chair is the elder statesman of the neighborhood, a quiet sort, good at bringing opposing parties together to work out an acceptable compromise. He runs the meetings smoothly and efficiently, seeing to it that everyone gets a chance to speak, but that the meetings don't go on for hours. The split leadership has worked because each is clear about the other's sphere of authority, and neither finds the other a threat.

The co-chair solution can be problematic, however, if the two leaders' styles conflict with, rather than complement, each other. In that case the more conventional chair and vice-chair approach is recommended. Another variation is to have a chairperson and two vice-chairs, one with responsibility for administrative and organizational matters (the running of meetings, maintenance of records, fundraising), while the other one is responsible for overseeing the substance of the case (working with the witnesses on testimony and reports, and dealing with the developer, government officials, and the press).

The Executive Committee. There may need to be some shifting around of responsibilities and positions at first, as different people discover by trial and error how much of a leadership role they can handle. Just be sure your by-laws are flexible enough to accommodate a few shuffles. You don't want to have to call all your members in for a formal vote just because one person wants to take a breather for a while and someone else has stepped forward to fill the vacant seat. The way most organizations obtain this flexibility is through the working of an **executive committee.** This is a sub-set of the larger organization that is given authority to make certain decisions (such as interim replacement of board members, or dates and times of general membership meetings, or allocation of funds) as allowed in the organization's by-laws. The executive committee might consist of the four officers (Chair, Vice-Chair, Secretary, and Treasurer), along with the heads of each of the organization's subcommittees. If the organization has formal affiliations with other groups, designated liaisons with those groups could also serve on the executive committee. The total number of executive committee members should be kept small enough (probably under fifteen) so that this core group can get together easily and get to know each other well.

Lawyers (Can't Live with 'Em, Can't Live without 'Em)

Finding a Lawyer

All developers have lawyers (you can take that as a given). And those lawyers are well-paid (another given). But whether or not your community group needs to have one, and if so, whether or not you're going to have to shell out big bucks for the fee, is a complicated question.

In some circumstances (most notably, the process of incorporation, discussed on pages 30–31), you absolutely must have legal advice. Each individual development problem will present different legal issues, and sometimes only a zoning attorney can recognize what they are and figure out how to deal with them effectively; in other cases a preservation law specialist or a tenants' rights attorney will be called for; but in quite a few cases, no special area of expertise is needed—any articulate, well-prepared advocate could put on a competent and successful case. In many jurisdictions, that advocate need not even be a lawyer. The hearing panel may allow your organization to designate any individual to act as its chief presenter, arguer, and cross-examiner.

How can you tell whether you'll need a specialist, or whether any sort of lawyer will do, or whether you can be competently represented by a non-lawyer? This is a Catch–22 sort of question, since you'll need a lawyer, if only to help you determine whether you'll need one or not. Here are some ways you might get one at a minimal cost.

First, look to your own neighborhood for a volunteer. This country has more lawyers than any other in the world (Manhattan alone has more than three times as many as in the whole of Japan). *Some* of them must live near you and have an interest in helping out in the neighborhood's problem.

If you don't find one that way, try checking with foundations and public interest groups such as the Sierra Club's Environmental Defense Fund. There are any number of local and regional organizations who fund or supply **pro bono** legal help when development conflicts with the values they're founded to protect. *The Foundation Directory* and other books cited in the Bibliography list names of sources of aid.

Some private law firms also have a **pro bono** department, and if your neighborhood's plight is likely to make a worthy and legally interesting cause, you may be able to sign on a normally top-dollar attorney at no charge. More commonly, however, you will be asked to pay as much as you can afford; so if your neighborhood has a strong economic base, you may not be getting very much of a reduction in the fee. If incomes are low, however, you may be asked to pay only a fraction of the firm's regular rate. There's no cost to hunting around for free services, so you should always try this route first.

If you aren't able to find a volunteer or reduced-rate lawyer, how do you go about finding a good one who's worth the full fee? Get personal recommendations, call other organizations that have won cases similar to yours, or ask your local bar association for a referral of a land-use specialist.

Then arrange to interview two or three of the lawyers. Ask them to talk about their experiences in cases similar to yours. Have they worked for community groups before? Try to get a sense of how familiar they are with your neighborhood and its special conditions. Check carefully for **conflict of interest.** Have they or their partners ever had the developer or any of his subsidiary companies as a client? If you find out about this fact after your case has started, you could end up with a major problem—your attorney having to take himself off the case midway through the proceedings. And in this increasingly litigious world, the fact of the prior representation could easily slip by unnoticed. So explore the possibilities thoroughly before you sign somebody on.

I know of one neighborhood group that got the brilliant idea of hiring the city's best-known **pro-development attorney**. The neighborhood wanted the best, and this lawyer was supposed to be it. He'd never worked for that particular developer before, so he had no apparent conflict of interest. But still he turned the group down flat, saying he would not like to advance a legal argument in conflict with those he usually makes on behalf of his other clients. In other words, he was not willing to be seen in public saying things he knew would make all his developer-clients wince. It was actually a good thing, in my view, that he declined. I think a group is far better off getting a lawyer who is fully in sympathy with what its members hope to achieve, someone who can plead your case honestly and without reservation. He or she may not be the biggest name in town or have the plushest office, but that shouldn't bother you if the lawyer seems headed in the right direction. (Actually, it can be something of a handicap to have a known "big gun" as your public advocate; the developer might be able to assume the role of the weaker party, and usurp your neighborhood's normal underdog advantage. See *Rich Neighborhood Syndrome*, discussed in Chapter 4.)

Once you think you've got a lawyer who knows the subject, take the time you need to brief him or her fully about your case. Don't be shy about bringing up the fee (the lawyer won't be). After you've settled on the hourly rate, get the lawyer to give you a best estimate of the total cost of seeing the case through each of its likely stages. Do not hire someone who won't give you this! I know of one group that got halfway through a case, and had already piled up so many billable hours that they had to instruct the lawyer to limit his work as the case neared its conclusion. Many years later, that group is still struggling to raise the money to pay off the balance of the lawyer's bill.

Find out how far the lawyer is willing to go for you. If you lose your hearing, will he take it to appeal? If your fund-raising is running behind his billing, will he let that affect the amount of time and effort he's willing to put into your case?

The next most important thing you need to know (after how much it will cost) is who is going to be in charge of supervising what the lawyer does. You need just *one* person to be your legal coordinator. If you have two or three different people calling up the lawyer with instructions, he or she won't know who to listen to, and you'll end up wasting the lawyer's time (and your own money). If you have several members who are lawyers or who have an interest in working with the lawyer, they can form a **legal committee**. The chair of that committee can serve as the one **legal coordinator,** who will report to the whole organization or to the executive committee on the progress the lawyer is making on the case.

The Volunteer Neighborhood Advocate

I've watched a lot of different neighborhood groups seek representation for their cases. Some raised and paid out thousands of dollars for the most expert legal help they could find. Others relied solely on volunteers (either a non-lawyer, or a lawyer not specializing in land-use law) to represent them. Based on ten years of results, I have come to the conclusion that, for most ordinary cases, the non-lawyer or non-specialist from the neighborhood can do a perfectly adequate job representing the neighborhood's position before a zoning commission or land planning board. It's only necessary that the person have some experience with adversary proceedings and be articulate and alert. Some of my reasons for preferring volunteers are as follows:

- No hired lawyer cares as much as you do about the outcome, so no one else is going to argue with the passion and spirit that you'll bring to the case.
- No outsider will be as knowledgeable as you are about what your neighborhood is like and how the development will affect it. You're going to have to do a great deal of the groundwork for your case in any event; it probably won't be that much more effort to learn to handle the filing of documents and other matters that would, in any event, be handled by the secretary or para-legal of the attorney you have hired.
- If you appoint your advocate from within your group, you don't have to worry about whether your representative will be keeping an eye out for future clients or seeking to establish a certain image before the zoning panel, while pursuing your case. Your advocate/neighbor's only concern will be "Is my effort going to help my neighborhood get what it's after?"
- Though every zoning lawyer will argue to the contrary, in most cases the zoning process is just not that complicated. The developer's side comes in with all the facts and arguments it can muster to prove the development is good; your side tries to shoot those arguments down with evidence to the contrary. If you understand the elementary rules of evidence and questioning in any fact-finding proceeding, you will probably feel comfortable with the procedures used by almost any county hearing board in the U.S.
- Development cases tend to drag on for a long time. With paid lawyers, the hours can quickly mount up, and it's very easy for the lawyer's bill to run thousands of dollars ahead of his best up-front estimate of the costs. Developers are usually right if they figure that

the neighborhood will run out of money for lawyers long before they do. This isn't something you'll have to worry about if your own people are your lawyers. (It isn't something to worry about, either, if your neighbors are willing to commit an unlimited amount of money to the cause—though I've never seen that happen yet, even in the very richest neighborhoods.)

To illustrate the above points, I will cite just one example. It was the very first case I ever worked on. My neighborhood organization, though it had plenty of members who were lawyers, concluded it must have a zoning specialist as its chief advocate. So we raised the several thousand it cost for a retainer, and we hired the best. At the same time, a separate group of neighbors who lived in a condominium building next door to the development site, also filed their opposition to the developer's plan. But, being owners of modest apartments, not large houses (as were most of the members of my neighborhood group), they couldn't afford to pay for an attorney. So the president of the condominium association, a mid-level civil servant, took on the job of speaking on his association's behalf.

During the zoning hearing I watched both the paid lawyer and the volunteer non-lawyer as each framed questions designed to bring out points favorable to the neighbors' point of view. Through many hours of testimony and cross-examination, both did an excellent job, the condominium president no less so than the lawyer.

Then came the part of the hearing when the developer's arborist took the witness stand. Without any hesitation he predicted that a 200–year old oak tree on the development site would be preserved. The lawyer for the homeowners had no cross-examination on the issue. But the non-lawyer, whose own apartment overlooked that beautiful tree and who knew it as an intimate friend, had several things he wanted to know. With one short series of yes-or-no questions, he elicited from the arborist the following admissions:

1. The root structure of the 200–year old tree spread as far below ground as its branches did above ground.
2. Four rowhouses were to be sited on top of the root structure of the tree.
3. In the process of creating a foundation for these houses, the roots of the tree would be extensively cut back.
4. If the roots were cut back, it was likely the tree would die.
5. If the tree were left undisturbed, it very likely would still be alive in another 200 years, reaching the same size and splendor as another tree of the same species—the Wye Oak, a state-designated natural landmark that attracts thousands of tourists every year to the Eastern Shore of Maryland to see it.

Months later, when the Zoning Commission finally issued its opinion denying the developer permission to build his plan, chief among the reasons cited was the public's interest in preserving this one tree for future generations of children to behold.

Cost to the community for the advantageous exchange that led to the Zoning Commission's denial: $0.00.

Cost to the community for the paid attorney's handling of the case: $38,000 (in 1982 dollars)!

You can see why I think the condominium owners got a better deal. Of course, you'll be pretty lucky to find a member of your own organization who's as savvy and quick on his feet as the condominium president was. But, drawing on a large enough pool of members, the odds are good that there will be someone up to the job.

Of course, if you aren't able to find a capable volunteer, by all means, hire the best talent you can afford. But do try to use the lawyer's time as sparingly as possible. Those fifteen-minute billable intervals will fly by a lot faster than you can imagine!

Non-Legal Experts

I feel much the same way about other paid professionals as I do about lawyers. If you can manage to find volunteers from your neighborhood who'll do a respectable level of work—grab them! If you can't find resident experts in your own back yard, before you start running up big bills, look for an alternative source of help: Think tanks, community-based grant agencies, universities, and various public service and cause organizations are possible sources of assistance. If it's a soil survey you need, call one of your national or local environmental groups and see if you can get the name of a geologist who might be willing to help you out. If your case involves historic preservation, you might go to your town's historical society for the name of an architectural historian. Your library's reference section might have the directories put out by the various trade and professional associations listing those certified in each field and giving some information about particular sub-specialties. Pick your members' brains, use all the contacts you can think of, be creative...and don't overlook the obvious (for example, the phone book as a source of information).

If you can't get a volunteer expert and can't afford to hire one, consider ways you can use laymen's work as a substitute. Traffic analysis is a good example: It doesn't take a Ph.D. in traffic management to stand out on a corner with a counting device in hand and click once for each car that goes straight, or right or left at the intersection.

Graphic display is another skill that non-professionals can handle competently enough for the purposes of a case. A neighbor who owns a good camera can take most of the pictures you will need of the site and its surroundings; anyone with a decent eye for lay-out can arrange them on a display board, the sort you can buy at any office-supply store. A professional design firm might charge you several hundred dollars for doing a similar display—and the only real difference might be that your captions will be hand-lettered or typed onto adhesive labels and stuck on the board, instead of printed.

What you can't do yourselves you might well be able to prevail on government officials to undertake for you. The planners at the Department of Transportation may not have been thinking of doing a "turning-movement study" on those neighborhood streets that you believe will be overloaded by cars from the development, but they could be persuaded of the need if they hear enough people clamoring for their action. The Fire Department might not have been planning to make public their internal report on the accessibility of fire-engines to a new cluster of townhouses to be sited along a narrow mews, but they might do so if asked. The law in your state may give you the right to demand that an EIS (Environmental Impact Statement) be done before the government can issue permits. Check into the possibility of these and other governmental experts' availability before committing a large portion of your budget to hired assistance.

Of course, there will be circumstances that call specifically for a well-credentialed, indisputable expert, whose report or testimony is only available for a fee. Then, as with lawyers, make sure you get an estimate of the cost, and negotiate for the lowest rate you can. Plead poverty if it helps.

The one type of expert I've generally found to be well worth the cost is an architect. Land-use cases are disputes in three dimensions; all the lawyers' arguments and witnesses' testimony, no matter how eloquent, won't convey the meaning and understanding of the site that a good **model** will. Developers are wise to spend as much money as they do on models—and their version of the future is usually the only one that gets shown. Of course their architects use all their considerable presentation skills to make the development look pleasing in its cardboard-on-plywood form. Seldom is the building profile of the wider neighborhood included in the model, and so the new construction is depicted without context; there's no sense of how it will relate to the nearby structures—unless your side pays to have its own model made, including several blocks all around the new building. No question about it, this will cost you a hefty sum. But based on how I've seen zoning commissioners react to community-generated models, I'd say it's always well worth the price.

Here are three other expert expenditures I've seen put to effective use in public hearings.

1. Aerial Photo. An organization I worked with hired a company to fly over a proposed development site with a helicopter and shoot pictures. The overhead photos did a better job showing problems in the road configurations and scale relationships of the project than any eye-level photos were able to do. The zoning commissioners thanked the neighborhood for having provided them with the visual back-up that proved the points made in witnesses' oral statements.

2. Balloon Measurements. This method was helpful to a group of residents trying to demonstrate that a proposed apartment tower was too tall for the neighborhood. They hired an engineer who marked off where the roof of the new ninety-foot building would stop by flying red helium balloons to that height at each of its four corners. He took photos of the balloons in place, and then sketched in the outlines of the buildings right on the photograph. This also provided a shockingly clear idea of the number and size of the trees that now stood in the proposed development's way.

3. Airline Tickets. When an organization found an expert who was tops in his field, and who was willing to testify in the neighborhood's behalf, it didn't let the fact that he was from out of town stand in the way. Round-trip tickets were sent from Washington, D.C. to the renowned professor of Urban Studies from San Francisco. He not only made an important contribution to the neighborhood's case, but also helped to reassure the zoning authorities that the neighbors' desired zoning relief was in line with the thinking of experts in other parts of the country, and so was not radical or untried.

There must be hundreds of other ways that evidence helpful to your case can be gathered, and you probably won't know what will work for you until you sit down with your neighbors and start throwing ideas around. Some of these, like the three named, will cost you money; others you'll be able to arrange on your own at a minimal cost. Only you can decide how much of your resources it's worthwhile to devote to making a particular point—but in each case, you'll need to have a complete budget in mind for the whole case, so that you can get a sense of what percentage of the total any one expenditure is likely to be.

Six

How to Get Organized

Do you have a copy of *Robert's Rules of Order?* If not, get one; you need not do everything as formally as called for in the book, but you should at least be familiar with the outline of meeting procedures. This will help you to keep your meetings short and on track. Always have an agenda and stick to it. The chair should allow all participants the opportunity to make their points fully, but keep the discussion from wandering off on tangents and irrelevant diversions. A set end-time for meetings may help to keep everyone focused on the business to be covered.

Minutes should be taken, written up, and distributed to everyone at the start of the next meeting. They should be brief, recording only actions and facts, not argument and speculation. Do not put anything in your minutes that you would not be willing to see printed in the public record of your case. It may be possible under certain circumstances for the developer to subpoena your minutes.

I have discussed in Chapter 2 the need for by-laws and incorporation. If you have enough members to support the structure, you should consider dividing up into subcommittees, with a specific task to be handled by each. The heads of the subcommittees can serve on the executive committee, which then oversees the progress of the organization as a whole. Some useful subcommittees might be:

- Legal
- Publicity
- Newsletter
- Membership
- Fundraising & Functions

- Distribution & Flyers
- Political
- Research

If your membership isn't adequate to support distinct committees, you could still cover all these bases by assigning just one person to cover each one. If you don't even have eight members willing to take on the eight tasks listed here, you can do without a few (newsletter, for example) and combine a few of the others (Membership can easily be made part of Fundraising & Functions). The main thing to keep in mind is the need to maintain good communications among the different committees, so that you won't have people duplicating each other's efforts or stepping on each other's toes.

The Legal Committee

The province of this committee is first to determine whether a lawyer is needed, and if so, whether a zoning specialist is called for; second, if one is to be hired, to find a suitable one; third, to work out the costs and responsibilities of the attorney-client relationship; and fourth, to provide the larger organization with progress reports on the legal side of the case as it goes along. The section on lawyers in the preceding chapter discusses these considerations in greater detail.

The Publicity Committee

The members of this committee will work to see to it that your neighborhood's case gets the attention it deserves on your local TV news and in the papers. Good publicity will help you to attract support from all over your town or county and bring out the crowds to your meetings or to the public hearing. Local officials tend to be far more easily swayed in your favor, for some reason, if they see your complaints aired on the evening news, than if they hear it from you in person in their offices.

The media committee ideally should include people who have dealt with the press before—someone who's written press releases, arranged for TV camera crews to cover an event, or had articles or letters published in the newspaper or in magazines—but that's not strictly necessary. Press skills can be quickly picked up in a pinch. A book like Holland Cooke's *How to Keep Your Press Release Out of the Wastebasket* can provide some helpful tips.

Some kinds of good press are a cinch to get. Many localities have what I call "throwaway" newspapers: these are local bi-weeklies or monthlies targeted at a small section of a city, supported mainly by classified advertising for home improvement services, yard sales, and automobiles. The articles are often nothing more than announcements of garden shows, antique fairs, and banquets, in many cases printed verbatim from the sponsoring organization's press release. But don't scoff at these publications—the circulation can easily be in six figures. Some throwaways are distributed to every household in a given area for free. Others are available in stores, cafes, and beauty salons. People read them while waiting for service, and if they chance across an article of interest about the neighborhood, they pay attention.

I discovered the power of the throwaway press in the first development fight I ever got into. Hoping to get a good turnout for a neighborhood rally against a dense development scheme, I sent in an article to my neighborhood bi-weekly describing what the developer was up to, and announcing the date and time of the "Town Meeting" we had planned. When the paper came out about a week later, I was delighted to see my article printed, word for word as I'd written it, on page one. The headline was "Neighbors Oppose Tregaron Plans, Set Rally for May 2." I was even more delighted when hundreds of people packed the community auditorium to hear more about the case.

Though some local papers (as in my example) will print anything you send them, in most cases your chances improve if you can maintain an objective tone in your writing about your case. You don't need to hyperbolize or editorialize to get your case across. Let the facts speak for themselves—but be sure to include the most damaging facts you can think of about the building plan.

I've heard of a situation in which the local editor was unwilling to run a story about a development problem because she thought the tone of the piece would offend some of her regular advertisers in the real estate industry. If you discover that your paper is too timid to print even the straightest sort of reportage on your case, you could still reach the same audience by taking out ad space yourself. A half, quarter, or even an eighth of a page may be all you need to convey the information you want to get out, and you may find the cost per reader reached makes the expenditure seem quite reasonable.

Though the publicity committee will want to concentrate on informing those in the immediate vicinity first, they should also look for ways to influence opinion in the larger community. Mainstream newspapers and TV stations need to be convinced that your case will have implications going beyond your own small area. But editors and TV schedulers also have an ever-present need to fill up space or air time and so are frequently receptive to calls from organizational spokespersons seeking coverage of a particular story. You may not be able to get the editor to see the importance of what's going on in your neighborhood on the first contact, or even the second, but don't give up.

This ad did double duty, informing neighbors of a development crisis and raising good money for the citizens' association.

Sometimes it just takes a while for the notion to settle in the editor's brain; in other cases you'll have to wait for the editor to hear the story-idea repeated from another source; or you may just need a slow news day to get the story into print. If you find you have any input at all into the timing of the story's appearance, do try to get it a few days before your public hearing, to boost attendance and letter-writing from the public. After your case is all over, a news story on it will be too late to do your side any good.

Of course you'll need to provide the media not just with a general topic to talk about, but with a specific event to cover. Development controversies tend to move slowly at first, and you can be sure that no newspaper or TV station will want to follow every plodding, jargon-filled detail of the highly-technical zoning docket. They need (as you probably already know) the quick *sound-bite*: the punchy phrase, the hot quote, the summation in twenty-five words or less of a problem that may have taken months to unfold. So when briefing the press, keep your talk short and your images concrete. Does your development entail the destruction of trees? Arrange to meet the camera crew in front of those trees. Is that skyscraper going to be too tall? Pace out the furthest point of the proposed tower's afternoon shadow (will it fall over the community gardens just when the tomato plants should be getting maximum sunshine?) and give your interview standing on that spot.

Whatever large events you put on—**rallies, "town meetings," demonstrations,** etc.—be sure to invite the press along. But remember that they get asked to cover staged events like yours all the time, and they only have room to deal with a few. What can you do to make yours more newsworthy? The prospect of conflict is a good draw. Is the developer going to be there, explaining his plans to an angry crowd? Fireworks of that sort might make the 6 o'clock show. Have you succeeded in persuading a formerly reluctant, originally pro-development politician to come over to your side? Call a press conference and let the media see that so-and-so has now changed his tune. The unexpected can be just as telegenic (if not more) than the unpleasant.

Though you'll want to think up ways to pique the media's interest, you'll need to be careful not to twist the facts or fabricate events. Not that you'll have to; development stories generate enough real crises on their own. Where people's homes are involved, emotions run high. So you won't have to script your elderly neighbor's lament over the demolition of the little brick school-house where she learned her ABCs—(she's capable of expressing herself quite well on her own)—though you might want to give her name and number to the reporter who's looking for a human-interest angle on the story.

It's neither cynical nor manipulative for your publicity committee to do their best to see to it that your group ends up with the type of public image it wants to project. It's just common sense. Remember, the developer also has his image doctors at work and so the media may already be well aware of the controversy—from the other side. In that case, you're only trying to balance the picture, to correct whatever there is in his version that doesn't square with your view of things. But you don't want to over-react to the developer's publicity. You could end up sounding defensive, or even paranoid. You'll try to be straightforward, open, and able to deal with the economic realities of your town. You'll always seem ready to consider "any fair-minded compromise that may be offered." A dig-in-your-heels stance will only hurt you—unless the developer's already cast himself in that position by refusing to deal with you.

Each side always tries to capture exclusive use of the term "reasonable" to describe itself. Community groups generally are able to get a monopoly on the use of other words with positive associations: home, neighborhood, residential character, charm, small-town, village, family-centered, traditional, quiet, tranquil, tree-lined, natural, and safe are some of the ones that pop up again and again in anti-development press releases. You may think these phrases sound hackneyed and sentimental (and sometimes they do)—but they also work to get the point across.

What works less well, and sometimes backfires, is an attack on the developer. Greed may be, in your opinion, what's behind the developer's scheme, but I wouldn't recommend throwing the word around. Better to come across as calm and cool-headed about the development game. Make it clear that you're not against a businessman's efforts to get a decent return on his investment—but he just shouldn't be allowed to wreck your neighborhood along the way. If your developer is seeking greater density than the zoning allows, you need to keep the press focused on the fact that the developer knew what the zoning allowed when he bought the land. He took a risk, and like any gambler, must be prepared to lose money as well as make it.

Not forgetting that it will be hard to get more than a sentence or two of your position into the paper or on TV, you should also be looking around for longer formats to air your views. Ask about getting bookings into local radio, TV, or cable channel talk-shows, which may devote a half hour or even an hour to a single issue. If you've got a member who's a good debater, you might even suggest setting up a panel with spokespersons from both the developer's side and yours to go head-to-head on the issue, live and on the air. Station managers are often more comfortable covering a controversial issue if they can show they've given equal time to both sides.

The members of your publicity committee may come up with other ideas on their own, perhaps far better than these. This is really the fun part of the neighborhood's work, so you should have no trouble finding people to volunteer for the job. After all, doesn't everyone like to see his name in the paper?

Newsletter Committee

If your development problem is likely to be around for six months or more, you should consider setting up some regular means to keep your members up on the status of the case as it unfolds. A newsletter is a good way to accomplish this. If people are going to be shelling out $25 or $50 or even $100 or more to support an organization, they like to be informed from time to time on how their money's being spent. Newsletters can also be a way to get the news of your cause out beyond your immediate neighborhood and so tap more readers for donations.

A newsletter is not something to undertake, however, if you are running short of funds to deal with the substantive tasks (like filing court documents or processing the photographic evidence) necessary for your side to make your case. Nor should you do it if you're running short of manpower; in that case let your volunteers spend their time on essential parts of the case first.

On the other hand you may well have someone in your group who has editing and layout experience, and possibly even the desktop publishing software and a computer printer capable of producing camera-ready copy. In fact, it's getting to be almost commonplace in some neighborhoods for many residents to be so well equipped. But don't feel stymied if no experienced newsletter-maker steps forward. The skills involved can be acquired relatively quickly (just remember that nearly every high school in America manages to put out a student newspaper). If your committee has just one good writer, and one other person with a good sense of spatial relations, you're in business. Get hold of a guide (like Nancy Brigham's *How to Do Leaflets, Newsletters, and Newspapers*) for any technical advice you might need.

Features. Your organization's newsletter should have

- a logo or heading design that's pleasing and easy to associate with the issue(s) in your case.
- a lead story that tells the latest on what's happening in the case.
- secondary "sidebars" that fill new readers in on the background of the case, or highlight events (such as hearings) that will occur in the next few weeks or months.
- non-news stories that help to provide a broader context to the neighborhood's fight (e.g., you're trying to prevent the demolition of a 1920s tavern, and your newsletter provides a short history of the building, along with a humorous look back by one of your older residents who remembers the place when it was a speakeasy during Prohibition.)
- definitions of any planning, zoning, legal, or architectural jargon, written in simple language any layman can understand.
- photos, maps, graphs, or drawings to help break up the copy, make the newsletter visually exciting, and illustrate the who, what, and where of your case.

- a tear-off coupon on the lower-third of the back page, so that interested readers can apply for membership, make extra contributions, or volunteer to serve on committees.

Before it goes to the printer, the final copy should always be checked over by the chair or other leaders of the group, just to be sure that no misstatements of position or other errors have crept in. A few things to watch for: Are there ongoing negotiations that the newsletter tells too much about? Does it commit the organization to a course of action that might not have been approved? Check the tone: Is it too inflammatory for the group's purposes—or is it too bland and say-nothing? If you're saying anything negative about the developer or his motives, you might also want to have a lawyer read over the copy to be sure there's nothing libelous.

Printers. Once the copy's been gone over by a few pairs of eyes for these problems (and for typos!), you'll need to find a printer. In many cities you'll win support more easily if you stick to a union shop (readers will check to see if there's a little union imprint, or "bug" in the corner). You probably should also try to keep your printing business in the neighborhood. You might even find that the local business owner shares your concerns and so is willing to give your paper a small break in the printing price. If you're going to be putting out issues regularly, establish yourself early as a repeat customer: Open up an account. By saving the heading and knowing ahead of time what paper stock, color of ink, and other printing setup will go into your next issue, the printer will be able to save some money for you on your future print runs.

Mailing. If you've incorporated as a non-profit organization, you're entitled to buy a permit to mail at a lower rate. There are also lesser charges depending on how you bundle and pre-sort your bulk mailing. One of the committee members should call or visit the post office to check into this. If your organization has the money to spend, you could also contract with a mailing-house to handle this part of the newsletter job for you. Mailing-houses maintain targeted lists of addresses that different companies and organizations need to reach. If your mailing is large enough, use of this service could actually be cost-effective in terms of potential donations in return. It costs nothing for you to look into the possibility.

If your geographic area of interest is relatively small, you probably should forget about mailing, and look to having the newsletter hand delivered. The section in this chapter on *Distribution* describes how a hand-delivery system might work.

One segment of your reading public, however, needs to receive mailed copies: That is your local government. Your mayor or county executive should be at the top of your mailing list, and each member of his or her planning staff should receive an individually addressed copy as well. Even if your county or city councilmembers have no official role in the zoning process, you'll still want them to be kept up on your organization's activity, so mail to them as well. And don't forget to send copies to the heads of all the other citizens' organizations around town, whose good wishes and supporting testimony you will want to encourage. In fact, you will want to be sure that any person or individual you can imagine will be helpful to you, now or in the future, is on your mailing list.

When people get your newsletter, and see that it is intelligent, spirited, eye-catching, and persuasive, they also get the impression that your group is strong, well-organized, serious, and ready and able to protect the people of your community.

Membership Committee

Someone is going to have to do the boring bits of running the organization: keeping the records straight, keeping track of who gave how much money and when, sending out the thank-yous for the checks and other support, stuffing the envelopes, and licking the stamps. Though it lacks glamor, this job is more important in the end than working with the press or designing a newsletter, no matter how good it might be.

When I first became active in my neighborhood's battles, I knew very little about the local political scene or the development process, but I was eager to do something, *anything*, to help stop a bad development near my house, and so I took on the administrative chores. I had worked briefly as an office manager before, and so had a little experience at managing files, mailing out notices, making labels, ordering office supplies, and so on. I turned a part of my study into the organization's headquarters and managed its business from there for several years. That was before I had a home computer, and so I kept the names and donation-amounts of all the members on a set of 3 x 5 cards in a recipe file box.

Nowadays, with PCs in every other house, you'll have no trouble finding someone with the hardware and the database and mail-merge software to make the list-keeping a snap. With the right programming, you'll be able to pull out the names and addresses of all your contributors of $100 or more, or target an appeal to the people who live on one side of the development, while sending a different sort of mailing to those who live on the other. You can even get some computer printers to address your envelopes for you.

Even better than finding a person with good quality home equipment is finding a businessperson or professional who is willing to donate the administrative services of his or her office to your cause. The president of one of my neighborhood organizations, who runs his own law office, does this for his

Tenley & Cleveland Park
EMERGENCY COMMITTEE
Joel Odum, President
3941 Van Ness Street, N.W. • Washington, D.C. 20016

4100 WISCONSIN:
Another Building, More Traffic

Residents already worried about traffic from 4000 Wisconsin Avenue should be doubly concerned with the proposal to build another office building at 4100 Wisconsin Avenue—the site of the now-vacant J.T. Ribbs Restaurant.

TACPEC has learned that the project would probably require the widening of Van Ness Street for several hundred feet west of Wisconsin. It may also lead to other commuter-oriented TSM (Transportation System Management) measures to increase traffic capacity (and decrease parking) on the already overburdened Wisconsin Avenue.

Original plans called for a building providing approximately 138,000 sq. ft. of office space (adding parking and "cellar area," the building would total 169,600 sq. ft.) This is equivalent to approximately three Tenley Point buildings—the new office building at Wisconsin & Brandywine, opposite Hechinger's.

The primary occupant will be WUSA TV-9, whose parent company, Gannett Corporation, is designing the plans.

Council Chairman Dave Clarke had provided his good offices last fall in order to bring the parties together over this and related issues. Unfortunately, the parties could not agree.

Last December, Gannett offered to reduce the building size by about 24,000 sq. ft.—still leaving a building substantially over 100,000 sq. ft. TACPEC rejected this offer.

The Comprehensive Plan designates the Wisconsin/Van Ness area as a Local Neighborhood Center which should have "limited office space." Recent developments have already grossly exceeded this. Moreover, TACPEC was informed last summer that WUSA TV-9's current needs are for about 85,000 sq. ft.

TACPEC would like to support WUSA TV-9's continued stay in the area. But TACPEC does not believe the Comprehensive Plan should be sacrificed, or that our neighborhoods should suffer from more office development and related traffic.

Plans Held Up

Late last year, the Mayor's Planning Office agreed with TACPEC and rejected the original plans for 4100 Wisconsin. The city said:

". . . .a project of the type proposed does not meet the spirit and intent of the local neighborhood commercial center of the Comprehsneive Plan.... The applicant may wish to re-evaluate whether the proposed use is appropriate for this area of better suited somewhere else in the city."

TACPEC has learned that the developers have since undertaken negotiations with the city, but the project has yet to be approved.

YOU CAN HELP: if the possibility of another large office building concerns you, write the Mayor and/or the Office of Planning (with copies to TACPEC). Send to: Mayor Marion Barry, the District Building, Washington, D.C. 20004; and/or to Fred Greene, Director, D.C. Office of Planning, 5th Floor, 415 Twelfth Street, N.W., Washington, D.C. 20004.

It's better to object now than to deal with the traffic later.

Write Today & Attend the Hearing

There are two ways you can help to protect the Giant/Murphy's shopping area: write a short one-page letter supporting downzoning to C-1, and attend the April 25 hearing at 7:00 p.m.

Although the Zoning Commission reaches its decisions after independent consideration, letters from the community are enormously helpful. Lots of letters will show the strength of our community's concern for this area.

Please write a letter *today*. Address it to:

Executive Director, Zoning Secretariat
D.C. Zoning Commission
The District Building, Room 11
1350 Pennsylvania Avenue, N.W.
Washington, D.C. 20004

Refer to "Case No. 8 7-27." It is important to send a copy of your letter to the Mayor. He needs to know directly that a great number of people support C-1 zoning.

Simply express your sentiments—that's what we need. Say as much or as little as you like, such as why this shopping center is important to you. Explain why you think it is inappropriate to have so much commercial development bisecting our residential neighborhoods, replacing our neighborhood shops. You might mention our area's numerous schools and churches. Insist that this city abide by its Comprehensive Plan.

If you think our residential side streets are already impacted by traffic, imagine what will happen with even more Wisconsin Avenue Development. *Write today!*

Attend the public hearing if you can. Large attendance is very important to show public support. Standing room only will impress City Hall.

Our greatest weapons in fighting development are numbers and noise: that there are a lot of us in the community opposed to over-development. Ten days after the 1986 Mayoral Primary Election—where 1500 votes were cast in our write-in campaign—Marion Barry reversed his position on development. We need to speak out again. Letters must be received by the Zoning Commission no later than Monday, April 25th. You should include your name and address on your letter.

Whatever you say, please write it today.

Dear TACPEC Supporter:

Thank you for your continued support these two years. I am pleased to say that we have made a difference: downzoning, height overlays and restrictions, and a continued awareness by the city of the problems we face in Ward III with overdevelopment.

I, like you, feel that the D.C. Comprehensive Plan must be enforced; it is one of the greatest protections we have. That is why TACPEC continues to push both our elected officials and the courts to enforce it.

Our community is unique—like the small towns many of us grew up in. We all pitch in to save it in times of crisis, and will continue to do so.

I love this city and want a safe, comfortable environment for all of us. As long as we stick together, we'll win.

Thank you again.

Joel Odum

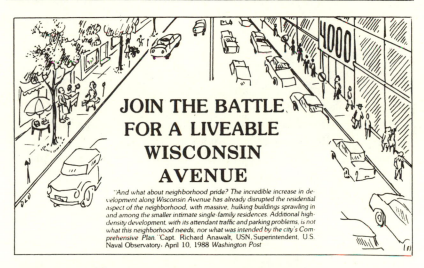

JOIN THE BATTLE FOR A LIVEABLE WISCONSIN AVENUE

"And what about neighborhood pride? The incredible increase in development along Wisconsin Avenue has already disrupted the residential aspect of the neighborhood, with massive, hulking buildings sprawling in and among the smaller intimate single-family residences. Additional high-density development, with its attendant traffic and parking problems, is not what this neighborhood needs, nor what was intended by the city's Comprehensive Plan." Capt. Richard Anawalt, USN, Superintendent, U.S. Naval Observatory, April 10, 1988 Washington Post

Please Contribute to TACPEC

TACPEC is fighting developers who have spent over $1 million on legal fees just for 4000 Wisconsin and its access road. Against this war chest, we are limited in our resources. Yet the generosity of our contributors has brought us far.

City Paper has said that the development uproar started by TACPEC "has turned into Washington's loudest and, in terms of political heat, most important development battle in 25 years." The January, 1988 Regardie's magazine says TACPEC has "fought the city's most intelligent, unremitting, highly publicized, and successful antidevelopment campaign."

We will continue our fight to protect the quality of life in our community. And this will continue to cost money. No contribution is too large or small. Hundreds of neighbors have given from $1 to $1,500. Some have given repeatedly. Please give what you can (both money and time). It will help. Thank you.

JOIN OUR TACPEC RALLY!

Saturday, April 23rd at 10:30am at Wisconsin & Macomb. This one-hour demonstration will show our support for local businesses and our desire to protect them through downzoning.

Tenley & Cleveland Park
EMERGENCY COMMITTEE

☐ My check is made payable to TACPEC so it can be used immediately.

☐ Because tax deductibility is important to me, my contribution is made payable to "Sierra Club Foundation" ($50 minium, please).

Either way, the check is returned:

c/o Joel Odum, President
3941 Van Ness Street, N.W.
Washington, D.C. 20016

☐ YES, I want to help the Tenley and Cleveland Park Emergency Committee (TACPEC). Enclosed is my contribution of:

☐ $50 ☐ $100 ☐ $200 ☐ Other

I can also help in one of these ways: ☐ Letter Writing ☐ Phoning ☐ Petitions ☐ Other

Name

Address

Telephone

cause. He pays his secretary to keep our mailing lists, type correspondence, and notify members of meetings and events. You may have someone in your organization who's willing to do the same, or you may be able to hire the secretary to do the organization's work according to an arrangement that suits the secretary, her boss, and the organization.

With good administrative practices, even a small, inexperienced group will find itself taking on the appearance of a force to be reckoned with. You may not yet be much more than a ragtag group of neighbors who have picked a name and a mailing address, but if your administrative person has ordered sharp-looking letterhead, and can produce a letter to the developer that is grammatically correct and crisply laid out, he'll be much more prone to sit up and take notice. But send him a letter that looks sloppy and amateurish, and he may just dismiss your correspondence as a piece of crank mail.

Despite its real importance, handling the administrative tasks can often seem like a thankless job to the members who are doing it; so after it's all over and your battle is won, be sure to give a special round of applause and thanks to the volunteers on your Membership Committee.

Distribution & Flyers

The fastest, cheapest way to reach the people of your immediate neighborhood is by making and posting (on phone poles and in store windows) single-page flyers. With hand-lettered, typewritten, or computer-composed copy you can inform your neighbors of upcoming hearings, town meetings, rallies or demonstrations; you can urge that letters be written to politicians or to your zoning authorities; you can provide a sketch of what a development proposal will look like (as opposed to the level of development the neighborhood might support); and you can provide quick updates of information on the case and so mobilize the citizenry to react within a deadline.

It was by receiving a photocopied flyer under my door that I first learned of coming intense development of the property across the street from my house, which led me to become active in my first anti-development case. I turned up at a meeting called by one of my neighbors, and on the spot volunteered to do some work for the neighborhood group. I've been doing that same sort of thing ever since.

But a flyer will only get good people to pay attention if (like the flyer I received) it's clear, informative, and of apparent relevance to the reader; otherwise it will most likely be dismissed as just the usual clutter of advertising or junk mail.

To Be Effective a Flyer Should:

- make clear at a glance what it's about. Pictures and maps are the easiest way to let the reader see that the subject will have bearing on his or her future quality of life. Don't assume, just because the development issue may have already been written up in the newspapers, that readers will be familiar with names and street addresses. You'd be surprised how many people only glance at the local news. So if you want to stir people up over a plan to build a hundred townhouses on "The Miller Tract" (2000 Station Street), identify it this way: "The seven-acre meadow that lies between the 7–11 store and the Station Street Post Office."

- be laid out sparingly. Very dense copy, presenting an overabundance of information, can be daunting. Flyers are meant to spark interest and lead the reader to seek further information. They can't cover every issue and shouldn't try. (It's up to your newsletter and/or media committees to try to get the full picture of your case across to the general public.)

- use graphics. Computers can generate many pictures, or you can have one of your artistically talented members do a drawing. Copying onto colored paper is an easy way to make the flyer more attention-grabbing.

- include an identifying line. People need to know where the flyer came from: Is it the work of an organized group, or just some loony neighbor in a snit? Anonymous flyers will rightly be received with skepticism by many residents. All you need is a single typewritten line at the bottom to tell people who the responsible party is. Be sure to include a phone number (which can be connected to an answering machine if you're worried about nut-calls) for those who have questions about anything the flyer states.

Some Do's and Don'ts:

- Avoid technical jargon. Don't describe the building proposal as "4.5 FAR" or "94,000 square feet"; say "the building will be five stories tall and span the entire block." (Better yet, provide a scale drawing of the new building next to a recognizable existing building.)

- If your flyer advertises a meeting or event, give the place, time, and date some prominence (put in larger type, or draw a box around the information). Always give simple directions to get to the meeting place (e.g., "Church at the corner of 34th and Lowell Street. Go down the stairs to the basement meeting room.") If you can find space, include some information on transportation for people without cars (e.g., a number to call for ride-sharing, or the route-numbers of the most convenient buses).

- Watch for language that conveys the impression of a *fait accompli*. Don't say "The development *will* be ten stories high"; say, "The developer wants to build (or has applied to build) a ten-story building." You don't want to give your neighbors the sense that there's nothing they can do to stop the project. Even if the developer's fairly far along toward his permits, you'll want to let neighbors see that they must participate in the process to have any positive impact on the outcome.

Flyers That Worked. The three samples on pages 110–112 each helped to pack a hearing room or meeting with supporters from the neighborhood.

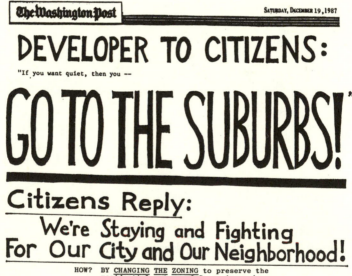

Advisory Neighborhood Commission 3C
sponsors a meeting to discuss

CLEVELAND PARK
AN HISTORIC DISTRICT
TUESDAY JUNE 5 TH – 8 PM
JOHN EATON SCHOOL
34th & LOWELL STS, N.W.

Our neighborhood has been nominated for inclusion on the National Register of Historic Places as an historic district. This will bring important changes in the way development is carried out. Currently, there is no neighborhood or city review of demolition or new construction; that means that a developer is free to buy as many buildings in a block as he can, tear them down, and put up a 65 ft. office building in their place, without any sort of public hearing.

Historic district status will give us the right to participate in development decisions before the city's Historic Preservation Review Board--but it will also affect what a homeowner may do with the facade of his/her house.

Come to this important meeting and learn what historic district status will mean to you and your neighborhood. A panel of six experts in various fields will be present to answer your questions regarding:

- ARCHITECTURE AND DESIGN
- SOCIAL HISTORY
- THE PUBLIC HEARING PROCESS
- COMMERCIAL DEVELOPMENT
- ADDITIONS AND REMODELING
- ZONING AND PRESERVATION LAW

****

FOR MORE INFORMATION CALL

JULY 20

Community Picnic!

4:00 P.M.

PARKS FOR THE PE~~OP~~LE

Developers ?

MAYOR BARRY HAS ISSUED A PERMIT GIVING EXISTING PARKLAND AT THE VAN NESS ENTRY TO GLOVER-ARCHBOLD PARK TO DONOHOE COMPANY AND HOLLADAY CORPORATION TO PAVE AN ACCESS ROAD TO SERVE ITS HUGE DEVELOPMENT AT 4000 WISCONSIN AVENUE.

PLEASE COME TO A COMMUNITY PICNIC IN THE PARK AT VAN NESS STREET (BEHIND ROY ROGERS) TO PROTEST THIS GIVEAWAY OF OUR PUBLIC OPEN SPACE. THE PICNIC WILL BE JULY 20 AT 4:00 P.M. BRING YOUR FOOD, FAMILY AND YOUR FRIENDS.

INFORMATION WILL BE AVAILABLE ON THE COMMUNITY'S CONTINUING EFFORTS TO FORCE 4000 WISCONSIN AVENUE TO SCALE BACK AND TO SAVE ALL OUR PARK. A LARGE TURN-OUT WILL SHOW THE MAYOR HOW THE COMMUNITY FEELS.

For Information Call Joel Odum
President, TACPEC

RAIN DATE JULY 27

PLEASE COME!

Distribution

Once you have your flyers (or newsletter, membership forms, or other literature), you need some means to spread them around the neighborhood. Why else did God make teenagers? Some (fortunate) parents will be able to get them to do this job for free, having properly instilled in their children from an early age the value of service and loyalty to the neighborhood. The rest of us will be able to get their help with the offer of a few dollars' payment for a few hours' easy work.

If your case is likely to require multiple community-wide meetings, you'll be well-advised to set up a dependable network of distributors for all of your blocks. This can be done by dividing the area to be covered into small sections of two or three blocks each and assigning **block captains** to handle the distribution for each area. Most volunteers don't mind being asked to deliver a manageably small number of notices to houses within an easy walk—but nobody likes being asked again and again to have to take on the task for the whole neighborhood. (If your neighborhood is made up of apartment buildings instead of houses, you should look for **building captains** to handle each apartment complex, rather than take on an entire block.)

Though the work is simple enough to be done by kids, there's an advantage to having adults do the walking, if you can get them. When they see an adult neighbor handing out flyers, other neighbors are more likely to stop and chat, ask questions, and learn what the problem's all about. Adults tend to be better at explaining the details; they're also more likely to be able to recruit volunteers and take in on-the-spot donations.

Sending the distributers door-to-door is the surest way to see that everyone who should know receives word about the development problem. You don't need a special permit to call on your own neighbors in most areas—as long as you're not selling anything or actively soliciting donations. But you do need to exercise some thoughtfulness, or the activity may end up generating more hostility than support. Don't send people calling during the dinner hour. If you get a "Not interested" response, take it at face value, and move quickly on to the next neighbor. Persistence is not a virtue in this venture. If you know that the residents are elderly, sick, or disabled and it's trouble to them to answer a knock, just leave your flyer in the mailbox with an invitation for them to call if they'd like to hear more. And don't visit anyone past 9 p.m.

If you're out posting notices, you need to show a different sort of consideration. Use heavy-duty strapping tape or a staplegun to attach your flyers to telephone and utility poles only—never to trees (it hurts the bark, and will make your environmentally minded neighbors very annoyed with you, and probably your cause, too). No matter how securely you try to attach the flyers, some will fall off (or opponents will rip them down); *always* pick up any that have become litter and throw them in a trashcan. And after the meeting or event date has passed, send someone around to remove the outdated papers from public view. Neglect these simple rules and the developer will be able to claim that you really don't care that much about the cleanliness and appearance of your neighborhood streets.

Other Circulation Methods for Flyers. Your grocery store, restaurant, cafe, ice cream parlor, bicycle shop, or other community gathering place may have a bulletin board available for people to post a variety of notices—usually to sell items, to match roommates, or offer lessons, etc.—but your community meeting notice should fit right in. Hundreds, if not thousands, of neighbors may read these boards each week.

Some merchants (typically dry cleaners and video rental stores—places with long counters) allow neighborhood organizations to leave stacks of materials in a corner of the store for customers to pick up and read while waiting. Others may allow you to tape the flyer in a corner of the front window. Of course, many storekeepers might be reluctant to be seen taking sides in a dispute with a developer (who could even be the merchant's landlord). Don't press your case too hard if you receive no for an answer; but you might drop a hint that your members would be more likely to frequent those shops that are helpful in getting the news out about matters of neighborhood importance. If the store owner is not sure whether he wants to let you put up notices in his space, you could take some time to chat with him about the development problem as it touches on his business interests. Big new buildings often have the effect of introducing more competition to the retail market, driving rents up, and forcing the smaller establishments out of business. If that looks to be the case, and you can get your neighborhood merchant to see it, you might not just win his approval for you to leave literature in his shop—he just might offer to lend his business services to your cause.

Leafletting

If you don't have time to deliver flyers door to door, but you want more exposure than you can get simply from tacking the papers up on phone poles, then consider handing out your flyers at highly trafficked areas: at a bus-stop or subway station at rush hour; at the regular Saturday morning farmer's market or flea market; or in front of a major supermarket. You should not need any sort of advance permission for this, unless:

- you're standing on private property. Then you must get the consent of the owner of the parking lot, store, or mall.

- you've brought some furniture or apparatus with you (such as a card-table, a chair, or a free-standing sign). In that case you may be required to have a permit, which you should be able to pick up from your local police station, having given a day or two's notice. The permit is not for the distribution of literature (your right to do that is secured by the First Amendment) but for the placement of objects on public space.
- you and your helpers are out in force. The number of volunteers handing out material is large enough to impede the flow of pedestrians on the sidewalk. The police may then be acting within their authority to tell you to disperse. (You won't want to adopt this tactic in any case—the inconvenience to pedestrians makes it counterproductive.)

A few tips on handing out the flyers:

- The afternoon rush hour is better than the morning. Many people on their way to work are grouchy and in a hurry; on the way home they tend to be more relaxed and receptive to information.
- If it's winter and dark out in the evening rush hour, stand in a well-lit area. People are right to be nervous about being approached by a stranger in the dark.
- Wear a name tag that tells who you are and what organization you're working for. People will be less suspicious if it's clear you're with an established community organization.
- Never try to force a flyer on a reluctant passer-by.
- Don't just shove a flyer into a person's hand; have something short but descriptive to say about it, for example: "This is about a meeting on the South Street development plan." Or ask permission to give the person a handout: "May I give you this information sheet on the Highway Plan for our neighborhood?" Few people will refuse something that sounds relevant to their lives, and they'll feel less put-upon because you've asked them first if they'll take it.
- Make sure there are trash barrels nearby. Many people will just read your flyer and toss it (or toss it unread), and you want to discourage littering. Pick up any copies that miss the trash barrel. You'll leave a bad impression of your cause if people see your flyers blowing around on the ground.
- If a passer-by stops to ask questions or engage you in discussion, be friendly and willing to answer—but not to the point that you have to stop leafletting. While you're arguing with an opponent or chatting amiably with a supporter of your cause, you'll be missing

the chance to reach all the other pedestrians who've walked past. Invite your questioner to call you later to discuss the case in more detail—but only if you think the person might want to volunteer to help.

- Don't leaflet more than a week in advance of the event you're promoting. People have short memories and treat farther-off dates as too remote to worry about. Leaflets attract people to your cause on impulse; you can't rely on a hand-out from a stranger on the street to bring in people who will get heavily involved in the planning and progress or your side's position on the case.

Leaflets are for getting quick bursts of attention or action: getting turnout at a meeting, where people will learn more; telling people where they can write to express an opinion and one or two points they could make; supporting a vote on a referendum or for a candidate that will make a difference in your development battle; and so forth.

Telephone Tree

This is a fast, efficient way to get information out to specific groups of neighbors. It works like a pyramid scheme. The president of your organization has, for example, just concluded a last round of talks with the developer. The developer will not agree to hold off on the destruction of some trees the neighborhood's been trying to save. The whole organization needs to gear up to deal with the looming threat. The executive committee members have decided to stage a press conference in front of the trees. The media committee needs to see to it that the TV camera crews and reporters are there when it starts. The membership committee needs to round up as large a crowd as possible to show the strength of the community's commitment. The political committee will be contacting the heads of other community organizations, as well as all the local politicians.

Through the workings of a telephone tree, the president need only make four phone calls, one to each of the four committee chairs, to get this event rolling. The media committee chair then calls her four of five members, each of whom has assigned TV stations or newspapers to inform. The political committee chair calls his members, who each know which elected officials and community leaders he or she is responsible for contacting. The membership chair calls each of the block captains, who in turn call their own sub-groups of volunteers, and so on and so on. Though each person has only a few calls to make, the multiplication of calls quickly produces a large total of contacts (as those of you who remember your eighth grade math will understand). At five calls apiece, by the fourth go-round of calls, you'll be up to 625 people notified (5 to the 4th power = 625).

Fundraising & Functions

As soon as you have someone who has agreed to act as treasurer, he or she should open a checking account for the group. Now you'll need to have some money to put in it. The initial founders of your group have undoubtedly come up with twenty or thirty dollars out of pocket each, to give you a few hundred dollars to start with. That's sufficient to order some letterhead and photocopy a first round of meeting notices. But to get the organization going anywhere— even with maximum volunteer labor—you'll need to raise much more.

Just how much, and how the money will be apportioned among the various tasks is an integral part of your strategy—the subject of the next chapter. This section just deals with how to get people to give. But raising money—whether a few dollars at a time or by the thousands—is a highly specialized art. You'll be best off to find someone in your community with work experience in this area: if not a professional fundraiser, then someone who knows marketing, sales, direct mail solicitation, or advertising.

There are four basic ways an organization can raise money, and I recommend you try all four. They are:

1. The direct approach—ask people to give.
2. Mailings of fundraising letters to a wide or specially targeted audience.
3. Staging of events—rummage sales, raffles, exhibitions and shows, etc.
4. Applying for grants from foundations or other organizations.

The Direct Request

Many people are shy about asking their neighbors, people they may know only fleetingly, to get out a checkbook and give. Actually, once you start incurring out-of-pocket expenses, you should feel your reluctance fading. Be forthright about the need. Spell out for people all you know about the costs involved in the effort, and assure them that the organization's books will be open and treasurer's reports available for all who are interested.

As soon as you are able to do so, prepare a projected budget to show neighbors when asking for money. Estimate your costs on the high side, to show need, but don't pad them so much that they seem questionable.

Once you have an idea of how much you'll need to raise for each stage, your fundraising committee should sit down and sort out who among the neighbors has the most to lose if the development goes through as planned, and who can most afford to support the fight financially. Make your first approach to neighbors who fit into both categories, and target the members of only one category a little later on.

It's always a plus if you can have friends approach friends, but make sure the approacher is well-briefed on the legal and practical implications of the case. Nobody likes to give money to a case that looks like a sure loser. Many people will need the financial impact of the development spelled out for them. If the development will depress property values, tell them, "Your home will lose x-many thousand dollars in resale value." If the development is likely to boost property values, say, "Your real estate tax assessments are going to skyrocket, costing you maybe another $500–$1000 a year," or "Your landlord will probably want to increase your rent by $100 or more to keep up with the market." (But only use figures you have some evidence are valid. It won't help your cause at all to throw numbers around irresponsibly.)

If you can't figure the financial costs of the development for your prospective giver, then concentrate on the quality-of-life considerations that are harder to reduce to numbers. Will traffic become so much worse that residents will be losing more time everyday sitting in their cars? Will neighborhood stores be forced out, so that people will have to drive a mile or two just to buy a quart of milk? Will parking be a nightmare? Will jackhammering and construction dust make life hell for the next two years? People will figure out what it's worth to them to avoid these grim prospects and support you gladly if they think you've got a chance to prevail.

The first case I worked on taught me well how far some neighbors are willing to go. The families in houses directly bordering on the development site, with very little coaxing and only one or two exceptions, came up with $1000, $2000, and in two cases, $3000 contributions to see the case to its victorious conclusion. All who gave, when they look out their windows and see their woodland views preserved, feel they got their money's worth. Of course, each was able to afford the gift.

You don't want to ask the widow living on social security for a large donation, no matter how great her personal stake may be in the outcome. But the surgeon or corporate lawyer around the corner can certainly be asked for more. You might think you should also hold off on soliciting funds from those who volunteer their time, on the theory that they will respond, "I'm already doing enough for the organization by donating my time." But perhaps surprisingly, I've always found that the people who contribute time are also generous with whatever income they have. And they're seldom if ever offended at being asked to write a check.

But don't keep going back to the same people again and again. Call on as wide a field as possible. Try calling for specific amounts for specific purposes. Say, "Could you help us out with the balance of the printing bill? It's only $50." Or, "We've got an architect drawing alternatives to the developer's plan. He's giving us a discount rate of $60 an hour. Do you think you could pay for an hour of his time?" People often feel better about giving if they know their money has paid for some particular item they can visualize.

They also like to be thanked for their generosity. A standard note typed on a computer that can have the giver's name and other personal information plugged in will do well in most instances. But if the contributor has given more than a certain amount (say, over $200), the president or treasurer should hand-write a genuinely personal thank-you.

People generally like to get something for their gift, if only a title. Labelling your givers as "Sponsor," "Benefactor," or "Patron" can make them feel important members of a team. The designation "Member" should not, however, be reserved only for those who can afford to give a certain amount. To do so will unnecessarily restrict the size of your organization to people with money to spare. You will want to be able to claim all the members you can get, including children who give a quarter and those who have nothing more to give than their signature on a dotted line.

Mail Solicitation

Though it's not the same as a neighbor-to-neighbor request, a good letter appeal can still sound personal and urgent. Don't "Dear Neighbor" the people on your block; take the time to fill in as many names and addresses as you can. Keep the letter short and to the point, telling in one sentence or two the actual harm that will be done to the neighborhood if the development proceeds as planned. Say something about how the money will be used. Make sure the letter is grammatical and cleanly laid out (it helps to reassure donors that their money is going to a competent group with some chance of success). If you can afford it, enclose a return envelope (without a stamp). Response rates are always higher if you take the time to do this simple step for the recipient. If you can't, at the very least have it very apparent in your letter how to make the check out and where to mail it in. Say whether or not the contribution will be tax-deductible. (It will really help you to get donations if your organization can offer tax-deductibility, or is affiliated with an organization that will receive tax-deductible funds on your behalf and distribute the money to you.)

All on your fund-raising committee should sign their names to the letter; that way you increase the chance that any one recipient will recognize someone and be likely to respond to that person's appeal.

You may not want to send out a letter only asking for money. You may find it more worthwhile to combine other tasks with fundraising in your mailing. Your packet might also include a membership form, or a brochure describing the organization's history and purposes, or a flyer announcing a general meeting, or a list of committees looking for volunteers. This helps to get across to your neighbors that you value them for more than their bank accounts.

Some tips on format:

- Use double-sided copying for letters of two pages or more. That way the mailing is less bulky, and recipients are led to think they're being asked to review less material. You can also copy your one-page letter onto one side of the page, and copy your one-page flyer or membership information onto the back side.
- Use legal-sized paper to include a tear-off membership coupon at the bottom of a one-page (8½" x 11") letter. The coupon could have boxes to check off for suggested amounts of donation. Be sure to type in a dotted line between the letter part and the mail-in form!
- Newsletter insert. Instead of mailing your letter to selected potential contributors, insert it inside your newsletter to go out to the better-off houses along the delivery route. When people receive a newsletter for free, they sometimes feel subtly obligated to help share in the costs, and so will be more likely to respond to an enclosure soliciting donations.
- List suggested donation amounts in *descending* order, like so: [] $100 [] $50 [] $25 [] $15 [] other $_____. This arrangement will direct the donor's eyes first to the higher amounts, giving that option a subtle psychological boost—though it by no means rules out a lesser contribution.

Special Functions

By far the most enjoyable way to raise money is to put on some kind of special function or event. Some of these are so simple to organize that kids' groups use them all the time (think of all those boxes of cookies you've bought from Girl Scouts who knocked on your door). Others are more of an effort to put on, but are also more fun for all ages (a block party, with games of chance and skill for adults, clowns and pony rides for kids, etc.) Let all your committee-members put their heads together and see what special events you can offer that will bring your people out and get them to open their pocketbooks gladly.

A few ideas to start you thinking:

Neighborhood-wide Yard Sale. You not only raise a lot of money; you give people a great opportunity to get rid of all that unwanted junk up in the attic and take a tax donation for it.

Bake Sales/Food-tasting Fairs. Particularly good in multi-ethnic neighborhoods as all the volunteer bakers get a chance to show off the cuisines of their cultures. Love of good food is sometimes the common bond that brings together neighbors from different backgrounds.

Sales of Specially Ordered Items. Put your neighborhood's name and logo on T-shirts, sweatshirts, canvas tote-bags, posters, balloons, buttons, notecards, aprons, and/or any other item you think people will buy. If attractively designed, these items can be a big winner for you. Whenever I wear my Cleveland Park T-shirt (it's got a fabulous picture of a Victorian house on the front), total strangers come up to me and offer to buy the shirt off my back—so I know how successful a good design can be!

Costume Ball. Does your cause have to do with preservation of a structure from an earlier era? Make use of the glamor and romance associated with that period by putting on a ball in the style of the time. For an Art Deco cause, you might consider this variation: Rent a '20s or '30s–era movie palace for a benefit showing of a film, and put on a grand premiere in the best Hollywood style. Those who wish to get dressed up like Ginger Rogers and Fred Astaire can do so, and those who don't can dress like ordinary fans going to the movies.

Picnics, Barbeques, Softball Games, Frisbee Throws, and Other Outdoor Events. These are especially appropriate if your cause is centered around an open meadow or other piece of land with recreational or environmental value.

Banquets and Receptions. These can be as formal as a catered affair in a big hotel, or as simple as a gathering with pot-luck food in a neighbor's house. If you are paying a caterer to serve the meal, be sure to sell your tickets for at least double the cost of the dinner; otherwise your members may grumble that they're contributing more toward the caterer's benefit than to the good of your cause.

House-Tours and Garden-Walks. People who are interested in the architecture or landscaped beauty of your neighborhood may be willing to pay $10 or $20 dollars each for a nine- or ten-house tour. In my neighborhood, which is in a registered historic district, we've had good success with our house tours. Owners of chosen homes are usually proud to show off their decorating or gardening skills, and ticket-holders on the tour have an opportunity to learn more about the built and natural environments of your neighborhood, while contributing money to your cause.

Auctions. These may be handled by an auctioneer, or be the "silent" type, where bidders write down how much they're willing to pay on a sign-up sheet that accompanies the photo and caption that describe each item. Neighborhood merchants may be induced to contribute services, such as a haircut and perm by the local salon, or dinner for two at a nearby restaurant. Homeowners should be encouraged to donate more than the usual, standard pieces of clothing or home furnishings. Baby-sitting services, or a weekend of sailing on someone's sloop, or having a picture of one's house done in watercolors and framed—these might provoke some spirited bidding. Keep a watch for donations that are one-of-a-kind or hard-to-find.

Coffees. These are not only a fine way to raise money, but they also tend to make neighbors feel more intimately connected with the success of the effort. If you have the people willing to play host, you can set up one every few blocks, or one per large apartment building. It doesn't call for much effort on the sponsors' part. All the hosting couple (or single) has to do is send out invitations to the neighbors they know (and any others they would like to get to know), inviting them to come over some weekday evening, or weekend late afternoon, to share some refreshments and hear some words about the neighborhood's development problem. A suggested donation of $5 or $10 may be set—though I'd advise making it free to come, and putting in the pitch for checks or cash contributions at the end. That way people will be more likely to show up, and make up their own minds about their level of support once they've asked all their questions and found out what it's all about. The hosts' part can be very simple: They just buy a nice box of cookies from the supermarket, or a cake or pie from a bakery, and serve it along with a pot of coffee and a pot of tea.

No set program needs to be arranged, though it's sometimes helpful to do so. A slideshow of the development site and the houses around it may help to make the problem clearer. If historic preservation is an issue, you might invite an expert to speak briefly on the historic importance of the building to be saved. But don't let programmed parts take over the evening. Coffees are primarily an informal way to reach out to neighbors and contributors. They are more suited to help create a general climate of understanding and support than they are for raising a war-chest. So if you need big money *now*, don't look to a few coffees to raise it for you.

Some Other Events That May Do More to Attract Good Publicity Than They Do Large Contributions: Walk-a-thons (Bike-a-thons, Hike-a-thons, etc.)—good especially if your organization's purpose is to save a trail or bike-path; Camp-ins, ski-ins, canoe-ins, fish-ins (as best suits your particular case), to raise money to fight off a challenge to a wilderness or vacation area; competitions with entry fees/prizes for winners— can work to solicit ideas for solutions to problems posed by coming development. (An example in design: ask for entrants to come up with the best plan to adaptively re-use a historic but outmoded building rather than tear it down; an example in engineering: reward the person who best suggests how to protect neighborhood streets from commuter traffic, without causing gridlock on the major thoroughfare; and in the arts: give out prizes to the photographer or painter who best captures the spirit of the neighborhood in an artistic medium.)

There are an infinite variety of other ideas to raise money. It can be fun to think up ways that are new and different. Get your kids in on it; talk to members of other groups who've done it successfully; or check for books in the libraries on the subject—but get moving!

Outside Sources of Funding

You will want to raise the bulk of your money from inside your own neighborhood. But if your neighborhood's resources are limited, you may have to go looking beyond your own borders for help. There are foundations (local, regional, and national) that exist to fund worthy causes like yours; there are other anti-development organizations that have emergency funds ready for the use of poorer, newer groups; and there are a variety of grant-in-aid programs set up by government agencies and semi-public and private corporations. In some cases the application process is long and tedious, and hardly worth the effort. In other cases, practically all you have to do is ask, and the money is yours. It only remains to you to start looking around and see what you can find.

You might start by getting hold of *The Foundation Directory* (New York: Foundation Center.) It costs $60 to get the book and another $30 for the supplemental updates, but if foundations look to be a major source of your funding, you may find the expenditure worthwhile.

If your battle involves either historic preservation or retention of small businesses in the neighborhood, try writing to the National Trust for Historic Preservation (1785 Massachusetts Avenue, N.W., Washington, D.C. 20036) for further information. The Trust's DeSchweinitz Fund has supported the work of a few neighborhood organizations I've worked on, and its Main Street Center oversees a variety of programs designed to protect the small-scale shopping areas of our cities and towns.

The Bibliography lists other books and pamphlets that discuss granting sources and methods to apply. But it might be faster and more efficient for you to ask around locally first, before you go seeking funding from nationally listed agencies. Try calling your local representative's office. When your local administration is mailing out announcements of grant programs or when a corporation is setting up programs in a politician's constituency, they usually like to let the politician be the first to see what good things they're doing. Of course the politician hardly ever has the time or resources to go out looking for constituents who fit the program's guidelines and should know about the money, but if someone happens to call and inquire, they're very happy to pass the application information along. Through the existence of government grant-funding, one neighborhood group I know of was able to get nearly all of the costs of its zoning fight paid for by the public treasury. That really made the citizens of the neighborhood feel they were getting value for their tax dollars!

Some guidelines in grantsmanship:

- Ask to read a successful application form if one is available. It's always good to see what has worked in the past.
- Find out the range of the grants most often dispensed by the organization; then apply for an amount at the high end of the scale—but not over it. Apply for too little, and it may seem you're too small-potatoes an outfit to be asking for money; ask for too much, and they'll think you've come to the wrong agency for support.
- Try to find a friendly contact at the granting agency. That person shouldn't lobby for you, but should just make sure that your application doesn't get lost in the shuffle, and that the trustees know that they can ask the contact for further information about your funding request if it's necessary.
- If the agency's rules forbid funding for certain purposes (e.g., litigation, or lobbying of politicians), see whether your organization is eligible for funding if the money is specifically earmarked for purposes other than the forbidden ones (such as printing a newsletter or holding meetings on topics of general educational or cultural interest).
- If your application is turned down, find out why. Perhaps you failed to provide some needed information, and can amend the application and be reconsidered. Perhaps the granting agency has given out all its funds for the fiscal period, but may have more to give out later, if only you ask to have your application held over. Perhaps your grant request isn't really the sort of work the agency is designed to support—but the administrator will steer you to another organization that is just what you're looking for. Remember, it costs nothing to ask.

A Final Thought about Fundraising. The need for money will be a constant thing, but don't let it become the overriding thing. As long as you have the bodies willing to work, you can keep going, even if your pockets are empty. Fundraising can usually work on a catch-up basis; but hearing deadlines have to be met. So you don't have the money to pay your printer? Pay what you can, promise more will come later—but keep those flyers rolling off the press! Many businesses know to expect payment problems from non-profit organizations. You'll have expenses cropping up in bunches, and they won't coincide with your big fundraising harvests. Just as long as you can get your creditors to see that you've still got forward momentum, that you're still reaching out to new people (and those people will eventually give), they'll keep faith that the money is coming. Of course, if you can get the businesspeople to donate their services or forgive the debt for the good of the neighborhood, so much the better!

Political Committee

The job of this committee will vary depending on whether land-use decisions in your area are handled in an explicitly political fashion (i.e., by elected county or city councilmembers) or whether authority over zoning rests in the hands of an independent, appointed board of professionals and land-use experts. The whole idea behind the latter set-up was to de-politicize the process, to free the zoning authorities from the pressures that beset politicians—the need to be popular, the need to attract large campaign contributions (often from developers), and the constant lobbying of special interest groups (like, perhaps, your neighborhood's political committee?). The appointed board of experts is then supposed to be free to judge each case solely on the needs of the whole community, allowing development to proceed along rational, thought-out lines, in concert with spread of roads, power capacity, and other essential services, and to prevent too much from going up in one area while nothing is built in another.

That sounds good, doesn't it? With such a system, a political committee should have nothing to do, right? Wrong. Though it sounds ideal, no system works that way—no matter where you are. *Land use is always a political process*. You need to recognize this principle and work with the process—though you may have to do so by more indirect methods in some areas than in others. So your zoning commissioner members who always side with the developers in land-use cases may not have to worry about being voted out of office; but you can arrange to make them worry if the elected officials who put them in office become unhappy with development trends in their district. And the way to make elected officials unhappy is to give them to understand that the greater part of the voting public is unhappy. And that is the job of your organization's political committee.

The committee can show evidence of the community's unhappiness with a development proposal in a number of different ways, or, for maximum impact, by all the methods combined. These are:

- letter-writing campaigns (to the Mayor/Chief Executive; to members of the council; to the Zoning Board; to the head of the planning agency; to other officials who might play a role in the decision-making process)
- petitions
- packing hearing rooms with supporters of your neighborhood's position
- rallies, demonstrations, "town hall meetings"
- briefings or more informal discussion sessions with elected officials to explain your organization's position on an issue.

Your political committee will strive to show that there is an overwhelming consensus of opinion that the development will be bad for everyone except the developer. My neighborhood did this when seeking a downzoning for a small strip of shops along a major thoroughfare. We brought in a petition of so many pages it wouldn't fit into a binder clip; so many neighbors came to hear the case argued that people were standing along the back and sides of the hearing room; we generated hundreds of individually written letters; we lined up testimony from our ward and at-large council representatives; and we had endorsements from every civic, condo, and tenants' association in the area and for miles on all sides of the area.

The developers saw this onslaught coming and tried in vain to protest. "This is zoning by plebescite," their lawyer complained to the press. The independent zoning commission should not base its decision on what the people wanted, he argued, but is bound to do what is in the city's economic interests, what will maximize tax revenues and create more jobs—nothing more.

The zoning commission, however, understood its charge to be broader than that, and voted unanimously to grant the neighborhood's request. They may not have been won over simply by the sheer number of bodies in the hearing hall or the stacks of paper in the petition; they may not have believed in "zoning by plebescite." But they did understand (contrary to what the developers were saying) that zoning decisions can never be based purely on quantifiable, objective evidence. Pleasing the citizenry does matter—if only because residents, when sufficiently displeased with the way their town is developing, can always "vote with their feet"—that is, pick themselves up and move to another town. And the loss of stable, income-earning communities is one of the clearest signs to a professional planner or a politician that development policies have failed. Your political committee will be working, in a sense, to prevent the politicians and planners from failing by showing them what the people want them to do while there's still time for them to listen and respond.

Talking to Politicians

Different politicians need to be approached in different ways, by different contacts. Poorly handled, your request for support could seem like pestering or even threatening behavior. But without knowing your local officials' personalities and the political traditions of your district, I can't be more specific about the kind of approaches that might work. I can only advise that you try to learn how things are done around where you live. Should you send the elected official some background material and a letter describing your neighborhood's case, before you ask for a meeting? Or is that too formal? Is he the type you could just call up on the phone and ask to come out and see the development site for himself? Is he likely to see your point of view only if you link your case to an issue he's known to care deeply about? (Will the development have some special harmful impact on the environment? Will it displace the elderly? Will funds for new roads need to be found? Is there some point of local pride involved?) Is he known to be more responsive to a certain segment of his constituency—say, church groups—and if so, can you get the minister of a neighborhood church to be the one to meet with him and court his support? Is he known to be friendly to developers and/or dependent on developer-donations to his campaign?

Once you decide who will talk to the politician and what to say, you need to give some thought to what his response might be, and how you'll react. You may be told at the start, "My office doesn't get involved in land-use cases. That's for the Zoning Board to decide independently." You should not let your elected leadership get away with this fence-sitting sort of reply. If a tornado hit your neighborhood and destroyed all the houses, you wouldn't expect him to say, "Tornadoes and other natural phenomena are for God to deal with—my office doesn't get involved." Why should it be different when the threat to your home comes from a man-made source? Whatever the official's longstanding policy on the development issue, you must try to get him to see your case as unique. What makes it different from all the other cases is, if he doesn't help out this time around, your neighborhood's not going to put up with it the way other communities did. You're going to see to it that he's replaced by someone who knows what he's been put in office to do.

Of course you're not going to tell him this bluntly. You'll adopt a circumspect tone and phrase all your sentiments in the most polite and respectful terms—but the underlying message should still come across.

To attempt to get the relationship started on a cordial note and start it moving along productive lines, your political committee should keep these few rules in mind.

- When calling on a politician, never send people who have a temper—especially if the politician is known to be a hot-head himself.
- Look for those among your members most used to dealing with people in positions of power, people who are not afraid to push for what they want, people who will recognize when they're being put off with a show of friendly non-answers and vague assurances, but who won't appear pushy and obnoxious when pressing for a substantive response.
- Meet at the politician's convenience, but try to get the meeting place in your neighborhood, so you'll be able to point out to him problems with the development on-site. Few politicians can understand a spatial problem without seeing the space themselves.

The Power of the Ballot-box. What if, after all your polite discussions and carefully guided on-site tours, the politician turns out to be opposed to your group's viewpoint? Then you have no choice but to make good on your unstated threat to work against the politician's re-election. If it's election season, call his opponent and seek a public statement in support of your group's position (if you can't get that, your cause is undoubtedly in deep trouble). In exchange, offer to get your group's endorsement.* But what if the hostile politician is not up for reelection any time soon? Many officeholders will count on the voters' short memories and treat their seats as life-tenancies. Resignation and apathy will work against you, too: Your case may be all over and people will feel it's no use now to try to get the unhelpful official out of office. But you mustn't let this kind of thinking get to you. Then, when your neighborhood faces another development problem (and it could be sooner than you think), you're going to be dealing with that same bad politician all over again, and you'll wish you'd worked against him when you had the chance.

If apathy is widespread enough (and for petty local offices it nearly always is), you may be able to turn that factor to your advantage. The lower the

---

* Please note: If you have incorporated as a charitable, nonprofit 501(c)3 organization, you are banned from direct participation in a partisan politial campaign. Individual members, however, are still free to give their personal endorsements.

turnout in an election, the easier it is for a particular bloc of voters to make an impact. Get just a few heads of citizens' associations to call their members and remind them of the politician's record, and you could have enough votes going to determine the winner.

Still better—if you're really into this—don't wait for a good opponent to materialize and seek your support. Draw up a platform based on your neighborhood's needs and views, get the group endorsements to get a campaign going—and *you be the candidate*. That way you will be absolutely assured that the officeholder is someone who will faithfully represent the neighborhood's interest. This isn't as dramatic or far-fetched a solution as it might sound. Many local politicians run unopposed election after election. They forget any campaign skills they may have had and lose touch with what the people really want. It doesn't dawn on them that their reelection is in jeopardy until they turn on the radio and hear there's been an upset. I've seen this happen to more than a few local "pols." That sneak-in victor could be you!

A Political Checklist. The political committee should be looking to gain the support/get testimony from/establish a working relationship with the following political leaders:

- ward or district representatives (county or city government);
- at-large representatives;
- state assembly delegates (upper and lower houses);
- mayor or county chief executive;
- important staff members in each politician's office;
- Congressman (if case has any federal involvement).

Networking with Other Organizations

The political committee must also reach out to other political entities in your own community and around the region. Each organization that you add to your list increases your base of support by the number of heads in that group's membership. Look for groups that share some common purpose with your own group. Does the neighboring civic association face the same sort of development problems? Does the hiking club use the land that's threatened with development? Does the PTA worry about the safety of school-crossings on the road the developer wants to widen?

Once you know on what basis you will seek support, call the president of the organization and ask for time on the agenda to make a short presentation on your development issue. Prepare a map or visual display so the members can see what you're talking about. Be prepared to answer questions. Make clear what it is you'd like the organization to do. Send someone to testify at your hearing? Mail in a resolution of support? Help to marshall evidence and participate actively in the presentation to the zoning commission? Contribute money? Lend you their mailing list?

Sometimes the members of an organization seem sympathetic but lack the manpower to take on any of the work. In that case you might offer some assistance. Prepare a draft (or final version) of a letter of support from the organization to the zoning commission, which the president can sign. Provide the person who will be testifying in your behalf with an outline of points that could be made. Offer to take care of typing, copying, and mailing of the organization's statement of support. Of course, some organizations are not only quite capable of doing their own position-drafting, but they'll be offended if you look like you're trying to put words in their mouths. You need to know something about the organization's working style before you make any of these suggestions.

Many organizations are only too happy to help out, if someone else will take care of the work. I found this to be true when I was going around Washington, D.C., trying to drum up support for a development case in my neighborhood. Six different citizens' groups were ready to send in a letter on their letterhead—provided I took care of the whole thing, from salutation to stamping the envelope and putting it in the box. I was careful to use different typewriters to compose the six letters, and to make different points in each letter, stressing what each organization's special interest was in seeing that my neighborhood's side prevailed. That way the zoning commission would get the sense that there were all these hundreds of people standing behind the letters (which was true!)—even if only one person was behind the prose.

Though letters are useful, live testimony is nearly always more desirable. When members of other organizations are willing to sit through long hearings in order to say in five minutes what they could have said in a two-page letter, that (for some reason) shows a commitment the zoning authorities respect. Just be warned, however: Organizations that agree to send a member to sit through your hearings may well turn the situation around and ask you to do the same for them. You'd better be willing to oblige. (The same holds true for giving financial support, sharing mailing lists, and other favors.)

Getting support from other organizations is crucial if your own neighborhood is small in population or lacks diversity. Networking with other organizations may be the only way you'll be able to broaden your base. If you come into the zoning hearing alone and push your viewpoint, it could easily look as if your group is the only one in the whole area that objects, and you're only interested in what benefits you. The selfishness looks even worse if your neighbors are generally upper-income, or all of one race. So get your members out talking to organizations in different neighborhoods, tell them your problems and invite them to tell you theirs. Show that your neighborhood is just one piece of the larger quilt of neighborhoods—and we all need to keep the fabric from being torn apart by bad development. If you can establish your common goals and lay the basis for cooperation on future problems, you'll find yourself able to draw on the strengths and talents of people from all over the city. And nobody (not even the developer) can then accuse you of only caring what goes on in your own back yard.

A Networking Checklist. These are some of the different types of organizations whose support you should try to obtain:

- city-wide or regional land-use planning groups (non-governmental);
- citizens' associations of other neighborhoods (and/or the citywide Federation of Neighborhood Associations, if there is one);
- governmentally established neighborhood review boards, such as New York City's *Community Boards*, or Washington, D.C.'s, *Advisory Neighborhood Commissions*;
- historical societies and other preservation groups;
- environmental organizations (local/regional/national);
- PTAs and other school improvement groups;
- school administrations and day-care providers;
- clubs (scouting, gardening, hiking, biking, train enthusiasts—as may suit the particulars of your case);
- unions (as in this example—the developer is building a movie theater that will hire non-union help; the neighbors contact the film projectionists' union for a statement of support);
- church groups and religious organizations;
- business and professional organizations (especially if displacement of small business is an issue);
- civil rights organizations (may be interested if development results in urban displacement of blacks, Hispanics, or other ethnic groups);
- local Democratic and Republican committees.

Petitions

In most development cases a petition is a useful tool; I can't think of a single case where it's hurt. Petitions are not only an excellent index of popular opinion; they are also a good means of mobilizing the neighborhood. Your petition-gatherers are a visible force; as they walk the neighborhood or stand in front of the supermarket requesting signatures, they're also talking to people, explaining the issue, and attracting new volunteers to the cause.

But some petition-drives accomplish these goals better than others. A petition-drive with articulate, well-dressed, non-threatening adults doing the name-collecting will probably fare much better than one where teenagers are sent out with the clipboards and pens.

The right wording will have a lot to do with whether people will stop, read, and sign, or glance, shake their heads, and move on. No one likes to be accosted in the middle of a shopping trip and asked to study a full page of densely typed copy. So keep the wording brief, the meaning clear and the print large and easily legible (no tiny, light, dot-matrix printing!). Don't use technical jargon, as in this example: "We, the undersigned, oppose the proposed rezoning on Lot 807, Square 2086 from R–1/R–2 to C–2–A/R–3." Say instead: "We, the undersigned, oppose the developer's plan to build three office buildings and a condominium complex on the ten-acre tract of land on Spring Street and Pine Place (Lot 807, Square 2086)."

If you can, it's preferable to frame the petition in positive terms. Some people feel more comfortable signing something that stands for something, rather than listing themselves as nay-sayers to an idea. The petition might just as easily read: "We, the undersigned, support keeping residential zoning on the ten-acre tract of land on Spring Street and Pine Place."

Wording also affects how the recipient government agency treats the petition. In some cases the government will not even consider the petition in relation to a case, unless it's worded or marked according to some specified formula (such as, case number must be written on each page in the upper right hand corner). So check with the clerk at the government office where you'll be sending the petition to see if there are any special format requirements.

Once you've stated the basic position you're advancing, you may want to list two or three brief reasons why the signatories are in favor of it; for example:

1. The size of the proposed development will generate an unacceptable increase in traffic on Spring Street.
2. The construction of three large office buildings so near to Spring Elementary School will cause noise, dust, and disruption of class scheduling for the schoolchildren and staff.
3. Spring Elementary School, which is already at capacity, would become overcrowded if it had to accommodate the children of the residents of a new high-density apartment complex.

You need not describe all the potential problems the development poses, or go into detail about any one problem. The hearing will give you the opportunity to present all your evidence in support of all your assertions. You also don't want to include any statements that people are likely to argue about. Remember, a lot of people like to quibble over small points and don't like to sign onto anything that sounds the least bit doubtful. So look for the points of certainty and general consensus to put in your petition, and "when in doubt, leave it out."

Petition-gatherers should be warned not to get involved in arguments with the people they approach. Accept all refusals to sign amicably, and move on to the next person. As explained under *Leafletting* (pp. 114–16), the volunteers should look for well-trafficked, well-lit places to stand, and avoid trespassing on the developer's property or impeding the flow of pedestrians on the sidewalk, or otherwise causing inconvenience.

A tip about length: Although you want to keep your wording short and to the point, you will still want to take up a lot of room on the page. Why? Because you don't want to leave a whole lot of blank space for signature lines. The fewer signature lines per page, the more pages you will need, and the easier it will be to make your petition look as thick as a telephone book. Space can be taken up with the heading, the case number, and your organization's logo—or maybe a sketch of the proposed development (emphasizing its least attractive side)—as well as the statement that the signers will endorse. Space the lines well apart to give adequate room for those with large handwriting and lengthy addresses.

Presenting the Petition. Once you've got a respectably hefty document together, you should make sure that everyone who has any significant role to play in the case receives a copy. So send it, not just to the zoning commission, but to the head of the Department of Public Works, the head of the Traffic Management Bureau, the Director of City Planning, and to all the politicians whose support for your neighborhood would be helpful. The original must go to the zoning authorities (or whatever panel has the deciding vote in your case), but be sure to keep a good photocopied set of all pages for yourself. It may be required (or you may want to do it, just to make the petition look more impressive) for you to attach a notarized statement from each of the petition-circulators to the effect that he or she personally witnessed each of the signatures obtained.

Pages should be numbered only when the petition is complete, so that you'll be able to rearrange them before submission in any order you like. For example, you might want to put a page containing the signature of a prominent person on the top of the pile, and scatter the incompletely filled-out or illegible pages in the middle and toward the ends. Pages that have only one or two names on them should either be dropped, or cut and pasted so as to create a complete page. (If the petition-drive was not done well, and you have only a few dozen names altogether, you had probably better toss the whole thing, rather than turn in something that only makes your level of support look deficient.) Individual lines should not be numbered, and should be added up only after the whole petition process is over. But pencil in the total in the corner of each page, to make it a simple job to add up the page totals when you're done. That way, if you get some last-minute additions scribbled at the bottoms of pages, you won't have to re-tally the whole petition.

Be sure the petition is received (and get a time/date-stamped copy of the front page returned to you as proof) by whatever pre-hearing deadline the regulations may impose!

Tenley & Cleveland Park
EMERGENCY COMMITTEE

WE, THE UNDERSIGNED, URGE CITY OFFICIALS NOT TO ALLOW THE CONSTRUCTION OF A MID-RISE OFFICE BUILDING AT THE CORNER OF WISCONSIN AND VAN NESS STREET (4100 WISCONSIN AVENUE).

We believe the proposed development

● conflicts with the city's Comprehensive Plan, which calls for "limited office space" and "neighborhood-serving retail stores" at this location.

● will have a harmful effect on Glover-Archbold Park, its immediate neighbor to the west.

● will cause an unacceptable increase in commuter traffic on neighborhood streets.

NAME	ADDRESS	DATE

Letter-writing

All politicians pay heed to their mail. People who take the time to write are people who take the time to vote and campaign. Thoughtful, non-abusive letters can influence officials' thinking about a matter, as well as tell which way the wind is blowing. Letters in quantity—whether it is a few dozen or a few thousand—will register more than a few individual appeals.

But how to get people to write? If the issue is truly one close to their hearts, they won't need much urging. When developers proposed to build an enormous shopping mall over the Manassas pastureland where Stonewall Jackson's headquarters stood and where some of the bloodiest days of battle occurred— even before the Save the Battlefield Coalition was geared up, even before the

National Trust was calling for all its members to write— thousands of letters began pouring in from Civil War buffs all over the country, protesting the desecration of hallowed ground. A nerve had been touched. By the time all the various anti-development organizations got into the act, every member of Congress was receiving mail by the sackful. In the end the 307 of them voted to have the Federal government capture the land by **eminent domain.** The oft-described "Third Battle of Manassas" was over, and the developers' plans lay dead on the field of honor, proving once again what a mighty weapon is the writer's pen!

To encourage letter-writing you should provide your potential correspondents with:

- Name and title of the person to whom letters should be sent.
- Address, including department, office or suite number, and zip code.
- Case number and title (if necessary for acceptance of correspondence into the official record to be considered by officials).
- A "cc" list of other officials and political figures who should receive copies of the correspondence, if possible.

You might also want to make some suggestions for both the style and content of the letters. You could suggest a certain length (keeping letters to one page each), or preferred type of paper (heavy stationery, so that the file-folders of letters received will look thicker and feel heavier). You could urge letter-writers to cite some particular problems the neighborhood will face if the development is approved (e.g., traffic, loss of sunshine, or bad precedent for other large tracts in the neighborhood)—but *do not* suggest any particular phrasing, or all the letters will come out sounding alike. That will make the letters seemed like canned responses produced by a machine, not sincere pleas of distressed citizens. The fact that so many individuals took the time to think out their own feelings and write them out in their own words is what makes a letter-writing campaign impressive.

But if your issue is arcane, or not of much impact beyond a small geographic area, you may not be able to get a great many people to take to the mails. In that case, the most you may be able to get from those farther away (no matter how readily they might agree with your position) is a signature on a pre-worded postcard. It might read something like this:

Dear Mr. Chairman [of the Zoning Commission]:

I urge you to deny the application of the XYZ Development Company (Case No. 89–015) to change the zoning on the lot at the corner of Spring Street and Pine Place (Lot 807, Square 2086) from single-family house lots to mixed-use mid-rise office building and apartments (R–1/R–2 to C–2–A/R–3).

Sincerely,

Frankly, most of the politicians I've talked to pay far less attention to postcards than to individually written letters. Postcards are just too easy to generate—anyone, even a developer, can usually get a few hundred off in the mail, and there's no way to be sure that they're signed by real constituents who have some real stake in the issue. Furthermore, it can get expensive to have postcards made up, stamped, and distributed. You might think the effort is better than nothing, but I'm not really sure. If all you're after is something to provide an index of support, I'd say you're better off working on getting a thick petition together, and forget the postcard approach.

Research Committee

You can't win on political clout alone. You need facts: surveys, traffic counts, height and shadow measurements, wind tunnel tests, A.Q.I. (air quality index) reports, geological data, demographic studies, income and property tax figures, and other even more specialized information, depending on the sort of problem your development presents. As with legal help, you may end up paying for the work involved and consider the money well spent—but you'll probably want to look first in your own neighborhood to see if there's a qualified person who will do the job for free, or at a steep discount. (How to get someone to volunteer is discussed under *Non-legal Experts* in Chapter 5.)

Once you have people lined up to study all of the issues, you need to see to it that they have adequate access to the development site. Because the land in question is very likely to be privately owned, the developer will probably be able to keep your researchers out if he so chooses. But he may not want to. More often than not, the developer will wish to avoid seeming secretive and closed-off to reasonable requests of the neighbors. So in most cases I've worked on, my group has been freely given a set of blueprints and other supporting documentation produced by the developer, so that we had accurate site statistics (building measurements, maps showing size and placement of trees, soil data, etc.) to use as a data-base for our own studies and critiques. Developers have been willing to grant, if not free access to their land, then a guided site tour arranged by appointment for selected "community leaders" and government officials, and/or to provide answers to specific requests for information (what degree of slope in a particular area of the site? how many trees over fifty years old? how many lumens of light will outside fixtures produce? and so forth). No matter how obnoxious the developer's plan may seem at first, it's always good to try to establish a cordial talking relationship with him, so that you can request this sort of cooperation from him, and have some hope that he will comply.

However, certain types of information all developers like to guard closely. For example, it can be difficult to impossible to get a sense of what sort of profit margin the developer expects the completed project to produce. Similarly, you may have a hard time finding out other economic facts: how much was paid for the property, who are the real owners behind the corporate veil (if you find yourself dealing only with the company's public relations person, a manager, or some other underling), how much the units or offices will cost, what conditions and restrictions attach to his financing, what interest rate he's paying, what tenants for retail or office space he may already have signed up, etc. If he is, as expected, coy with these answers, you should be able to find out some of what you want to know by searching the public land and tax records, and by reading your local business journals and real estate trade publications.

The Research Committee should first sit down and try to figure out in what areas the developer's information seems faulty, and if so whether in methodology or in conclusion drawn. Then discuss ways to obtain data to counter the developer's points. Consider, too, how the research is likely to be used. If you put all your energies into disproving the developer's claims about his tree-replacement plan, but your zoning panel has no authority over landscaping—you'll have wasted your time. If your case involves review by a landmarks commission, and that commission's authority under the law is sufficiently broad, you might want to spend the bulk of your time and money on your architectural history research, and turn your attention to zoning questions only if you lose your landmark bid.

Before you undertake a major research project, you'll do well to look into any ongoing or previously completed studies of the same subject. If you're lucky, someone will have already done a good portion of the job for you. This was a tremendous time-saver for my own neighborhood in its tangle with McDonald's. The giant fast-food chain had bought a small limestone building a block from my house, and wanted to resurface the facade with plastic in the usual McDonald's colors (bright red and yellow). One of the neighbors thought to contact the head of the historic preservation program at nearby George Washington University. She'd heard there was an ongoing study of Art Deco commercial buildings in Washington, D.C., and thought someone might have already done some research on the building. She was right. A wealth of information was available: when it was built, who the architect was, what other important buildings he designed, where the zig-zag design of the distinctive copper cornice piece originated, and, most importantly, how the limestone was obtained (from a now-defunct Virginia quarry that also produced the stone

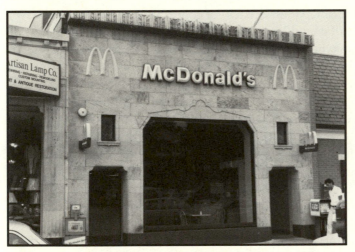

that went into the White House, parts of the Congress, and the National Portrait Gallery. No more of the stone is available from any source). Having all this data available so quickly, our group was able to file a landmark application within two weeks of hearing of McDonald's plans. The filing prompted McDonald's to enter into negotiations with the neighbors over hours of operation, litter-patrols, odor controls, and other problems, as well as to obtain from the corporation a pledge to restore and maintain the historic limestone and Art Deco detailing of the building. That pledge has been kept, and the fast-food stand today is one of the most distinctive, architecturally pleasing McDonald's I've ever seen.

Of course you'll probably have to do a lot more digging on your own to come up with the facts you need to make your case. It's relatively rare that you find a "smoking gun" that allows you to prove the developer's plan is fatally flawed and should be stopped at once. But have your members dig diligently into all troublesome aspects of the development and consult with each other on their findings. Someone just might come up with something that seems small and insignificant at first, but is actually big enough to block a bulldozer. You may remember the story of the Tennessee Valley snail darter—a tiny, homely fish living in a large pond. Someone opposed to the construction of a dam in the area did some research and found out that any development that threatened to cause the extinction of a species, no matter how slimy and un-cuddly the animal, was prohibited by Act of Congress. Though it turned out in the end that snail-darters were in fact plentiful in neighboring streams and rivers, the construction was at least halted long enough to give opponents some negotiating room.

So get your most thoroughminded detail-sifters out looking for those snail-darters, and good hunting to them! (Special types of research will be discussed, problem by problem, in Chapters 9–15.)

S e v e n

WHAT YOU'RE WORKING FOR

Calculating What's Attainable

None of the how-to advice of the preceding two chapters will get you very far unless you've worked out what it is you hope to accomplish with your organization. At the start you probably had no more than a generalized dislike of the developer's plan. That was enough to get you going. Perhaps when talking it over with your immediate neighbors you decided that the new building's height was its most objectionable feature. But when you started talking to people who live further away from the development site, you began hearing that parking was the biggest concern. Later on, when the heads of the area's civic associations got involved, they told you they were for less office development but more retail store space to serve area shoppers. Yet the environmental groups you talked to felt the entire project was an abomination and should be opposed in all of its parts.

And that's just from the citizens' side. As you got further into the case you began hearing many other opinions that mattered: The county's planning office had a ready-made set of criteria to judge the plan, based on its interpretation of the county's **Master Plan**, a law that sets development goals for the area over the next twenty years. The Department of Transportation had its own standards and policy goals to be met, which would cause the developer to rethink the access points and curb-cuts shown on his plan. The Fire Department had problems with the curviness of the driveway, which would make it difficult for the largest firetrucks to reach the rear of the building; and the state's Environmental Protection Divisions had sediment-control standards that could only be met if changes were made to the site-grading of the plan.

You're not only trying to gauge what your neighbors and your local officials want and/or require—you're also trying to figure out how flexible the developer is: what aspects of the plan are negotiable, what parts he's absolutely committed to, and what are the "extras" he never seriously thought he'd be granted in the first place.

And finally, you find yourself looking closely at who the zoning panelists are and what kind of development plans they've approved, turned down, or ordered modified in the past, so that you can get a sense of how the developer's plan measures up against the record.

Only after you have some sense of all the players' roles can you begin to work out what you can reasonably hope to achieve, and to craft the best strategy for action.

This checklist sums up what you should be asking yourself:

- How do the immediate neighbors regard the plan?
- What about the neighbors from further away?
- What is the depth of neighbors' feeling on the issues; how willing are they to volunteer to do the work/put up funds?
- What are the reactions of citizens' organizations, special interest groups?
- How have government agencies evaluated the plan? What special requirements could they impose on the developer?
- What is the developer's attitude toward negotiations? Has he shown some flexibility and willingness to compromise on important points?
- What is the state of the land-use law as it affects your case?
- How does the regulatory process work? Does it seem fair to the citizens?
- What has been the outcome of similar cases by zoning authorities in your area?

Though it takes little time to run down this list of questions, it will take (and should take) a long time for your group to come up with the answers you'll need in order to choose your group's best course of action. These are matters calling for some thorough investigation, and careful analysis of the findings. Yet, with only 45 or 60 days until a hearing, in many cases, you may find yourself having to proceed with less than a complete understanding of many of these issues.

This is just one of the great difficulties you may face. More troublesome may be the division that occurs when some of your members answer some of the questions one way, while others see things in quite a different way. This may happen over substantive issues (such as whether traffic from the development should be routed down one neighborhood street or another); or over strategy decisions (some of your neighbors insist that the developer's offer of compromise is the best outcome the neighborhood can hope to achieve, while others say you're bound to win a complete victory in the public hearing).

When attempting to calculate what's attainable, you need to factor in the pressure of time and the strains caused by disagreement among your members. Though there's little you can do about the former, you will be able to take some steps to minimize the internal divisions, as the next section advises.

Building and Keeping Consensus

It's not enough just to find a position and stick to it; you are going to have to stay flexible enough to respond to whatever changes of plan the developer or city officials throw in along the way. That's where community groups commonly fail. One segment of the neighborhood gets entrenched in its first position; the other segment decides to go forward in support of a modified development plan; both segments of the community start accusing the other of back-stabbing and bad judgment; and the zoning commission is unable to figure out what the citizens really want. Often amid all the clamor and confusion, only one voice manages to sound calm and level-headed, and that's the developer. And so the zoning commission sees things his way and gives him the permits he needs to build his plan.

Developers in some cases have learned to create plans with elements sure to cause discord in the community; knowing that consensus will be difficult if not impossible to achieve, they then sit around, waiting and watching for the community to turn on itself and do its own case in. By the time the zoning hearing is on, they hardly have to do much more than waltz in and pick up all the pieces.

But it doesn't have to be that way. Even if your group seems very diverse in personalities and interests, you are all still citizens who have one basic thing in common: You all want to live in a neighborhood that's pleasant, clean, and safe. And you probably have a second, even more important thing in common: You are all tolerant, fairly reasonable people, capable (with some reminding, as may be necessary) of respecting each other's differences and perspectives.

Now, about those two or three of you who are not tolerant and reasonable—see Chapter 5 for some suggestions for dealing with these **Flakes, Oddballs, and Eccentrics (or F.O.E.s)**. You may feel my recommendations for removing difficult neighbors from positions of authority in the group is a bit harsh, but I've seen more than one neighborhood organization wrecked by these types. Sometimes it's necessary to act unneighborly and impolite to one person, in order to preserve the civil tone of discourse overall. But, assuming that all of your members are essentially people of good will, you should now start to come up with a list of all those things you do agree on. Stick to generalized concepts at first, not specifics—for example, on traffic: You can agree that you want to minimize the development's impact on residential streets (you haven't yet identified which streets are likely to bear the greatest traffic burden, or what measures should be taken to protect them). On density: You know only that you want the building to be low-scale (you haven't yet determined how many stories and how much gross square footage would be acceptable to all). On a proposed change of zoning category: You are sure you want to maintain the residential character of the neighborhood (you still don't know how much and what types of retail and/or office uses would be consistent with that goal).

Once you have identified these broad common goals, you then move on to the more difficult step of considering possible solutions. Let's take traffic as a sample problem. You've agreed that the impact on neighborhood streets should be minimized. But some neighbors think there should be no access to the development from their street, while other neighbors believe, if you prevent the cars from using that street to get to the new building, there will be gridlock on the next street over. If you try to decide the question with a straight majority-vote approach, you will have a very dissatisfied minority on your hands who will feel their legitimate interests have been unfairly overridden by uncaring neighbors. They could even come into the public hearing and attack your neighborhood group as unrepresentative of the citizens.

It's better in that case not to advance a street-specific solution to the problem. Yes, your group will appear to be dodging the issue, to some extent— but at least you'll still be together. At the hearing, however, you should make the point that you did consider the issue. You could handle it something like this: "We've looked at the traffic problem from all sides, and we just don't see a solution that will answer the needs of all the neighbors. But we don't feel the burden should be put on us to come up with all the answers. We're not experts. Traffic engineers have already told us that an increase of thirty cars per hour would cause light-cycle back-up on any of the smaller side streets. We feel the burden should fall on the developer to come up with a plan to ensure that the traffic flow to and from his project remains under twenty cars per hour."

You could also present the view that the extra traffic, whichever street it would use for access, would be an unacceptable burden on the neighborhood. In that case only a reduction in the project's size and use will alleviate the problem. You might be able to agree that a building that's only half the size of the one proposed would produce only half the traffic—an acceptable increase in volume. Or you could ask that certain automobile-attracting elements of the plan, such as a movie theater or a fast-food establishment, be omitted, while the rest of the plan goes forward.

Still another possible way to get consensus on the traffic issue might be to find an acceptable alternative—public transportation, for example. Your group could unite on the principle that a development of the size planned should include incentives to employees and customers for the use of buses and subways. The developer could be required to operate a shuttle bus from the subway stop to his site, or to provide his workers with vouchers to subsidize their bus and subway tickets. Your organization could urge the zoning commission to write such public transportation incentives into the zoning order for the project.

Try though you might to achieve consensus on an approach to a problem, you still could find it elusive. In that case I'd advise you go on to the next issue. You need not comment on every aspect of every case. You do, however, need to define your group's position on the most important features of the proposal in front of you. What's important? Changing the zoning classification from one type to another; increases of 15 percent or more in height or density; taking down an existing building of possible historical or cultural significance; construction of new streets or changing of traffic patterns on existing streets—to name just a few. These are actions, that once taken, will alter the way your neighborhood looks and functions for a great many years to come.

So if you haven't found an approach that everyone can wholeheartedly support, you're going to have to try to come up with one that the majority can support wholeheartedly—and the rest of the group can support half-heartedly, or at least not oppose. How a group might go about finding an acceptable middle ground is illustrated by this story:

A developer has planned a twenty-story apartment tower along a major avenue. The people who live in the low-rise townhouses behind the development site are afraid the new building will cut off their light and air. But the neighbors who live in the large apartment complex across the street from the proposed tower aren't bothered by the height; their building is equally tall. They're mainly concerned that, lacking sufficient garage space, the occupants of the new building will be competing with them for spaces on the street. But members of the neighborhood's civic association want to oppose the height of the proposal, because the site is now zoned to allow only sixteen stories, and they're worried that a four-story variance, if granted, will set a dangerous precedent for development of many other lots in town. However, the association members do not believe, as the immediate neighbors do, that eight stories should be the maximum allowable height. Looking at the building profile for the larger area, they've concluded that twelve stories would be a more practical limit.

What's the best way to resolve these opposing views? The group could do it by giving the greatest weight to the opinion of those most affected by the controversial aspect of the development, which would mean, that those who don't have to live under the building's shadow will yield to the wishes of those who do.

Another way of resolving the conflict would be to have the group favor the most restrictive of the various members' approaches to the problem, on the theory that you never get more than you're asking for, but you often get less. So the group will go into the zoning hearing asking for the building height to be lowered from twenty stories to eight, and will feel victorious if they end up with a building that's twelve or fourteen stories tall.

Taking either approach, the group would end up with the position put forward by the nearest neighbors of the site.

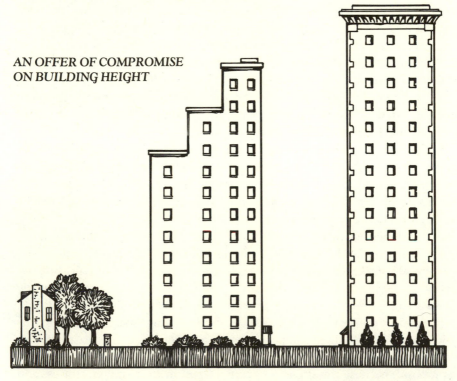

AN OFFER OF COMPROMISE ON BUILDING HEIGHT

A third approach might be based on a hybridization of the various neighbors' points of view. The group takes the arguments made by each group and synthesizes them into one position. So they advance the precedent argument brought up by the citizens' association leadership; they cite the presence of existing buildings as a reason for allowing tall buildings fronting the main avenue; and they cite the light and shadow arguments of the neighbors to the rear as reason not to allow a tall building facing the opposite direction. The result: a recommendation for the new building to vary in height from back to front. It should be limited to eight stories in the rear, nearest the low-rise townhouses, and then "step up," story by story, until it reaches its maximum height of twelve stories fronting the major avenue. All three segments of the neighborhood should be able to support this position.

Yet another approach would be simply to lay out all the ingredients that influence the neighbors' views on height for the zoning panel to consider, and offer a range of solutions that might be acceptable to the neighborhood: say, 8–12 stories in the example above. If your group adopts the "range of options" approach, you should be warned: The developer will almost certainly seize on the maximum figure of your range and claim that it's what your group wants. Any compromise solution worked out by the zoning board could very easily end up being an average between the number of stories the developer wants, and that maximum you've given (in this case, that works out to sixteen stories). If the figure you're likely to end up with will be too disparate from the position put forward by an important segment of your membership, then the range-of-options approach is probably not an appropriate one for your case.

I've spoken above about forming consensus on issues of importance. But what if the members of your group can't agree on what's important? Aesthetic features are commonly controversial in this regard. Some members of your group may feel that the way the development looks has as much impact on the quality of life in the neighborhood as its size and parking capacity. Others will feel that it's all just a lot of quibbling over the color of bricks, and that it's not the function of a neighborhood organization to advise on matters of taste.

But it may be possible for a certain segment of the group to pursue an issue it deems important, without causing disunity or contradicting the policy of the larger organization. Let's say the new building is going to be part of an 1880s block of buildings with a strong Beaux-Arts character (though not part of an officially recognized Historic District). The neighbors who care about style may want to call themselves by a separate name—perhaps the Whatever Avenue Beaux Arts Society—and contact the developer independently to negotiate on adding some design details to relate the building to its surroundings. This action would in no way detract from the position of the main community organization, and members of the design group would continue to participate in that organization as it pursues the other major issues of concern.

Members interested in one special issue, alternatively, could seek to join with an already existing group that may be induced to take a position on that one aspect of the case. The Beaux Arts enthusiasts (to continue the same example) could become members of the City's Historical Society, and then influence the board of that organization to speak up for maintaining a certain design integrity on the block.

In general, the greater the number of separate organizations that criticize a development, the easier it is for the zoning authorities to come to view the plan as flawed, and so deny the developer permission to build.

Six Steps to Consensus-Building

You may want to consider any or all of the following suggestions to achieve and maintain organizational agreement over goals.

1. **Draft a position paper.** This document will spell out what your organization stands for in principle, and will help your members to stay focussed on the major objectives, however the development plan may be revised over time. The position paper should *not* spell out methods for achieving those goals, or even attempt to define each goal in very specific terms (that will just lead to endless arguing over the wording of the document), but it should address general topics of concern, such as: "preserving mature trees," "pedestrian safety," "maintaining the residential character of the neighborhood," and so forth. A soundly conceived position paper will not only keep your members on track during the length of the development case, but it will also be a ready-made response in future cases in your area. A new developer coming on the scene will find an organized community that knows what it wants and has it down on paper to show to him whenever that first meeting occurs.

2. Suppose your disagreement is over the best method for achieving the goals you share. Then you need a **method** for choosing methods. Before you open your discussion of the merits of each course, decide how the decision will be made. If by majority rule, make sure you have the agreement of the losing minority that they will support (or at least abide by) the winning side. Or you may wish to leave the judgment up to the leadership of the organization. In either case, be sure the advocates of opposing views have a full opportunity to express themselves. Otherwise, those whose advice is rejected may feel unfairly treated and consider severing ties to the organization, or still worse, opposing it in public.

3. **Defer to the opinions of experts** or to members with experience on particular issues. If, for example, your lawyer should tell you, "This argument's a weak one—no court has yet accepted it," then even if a

sizable segment of your membership wants to go forward with the argument, you probably shouldn't do it. (Of course, if a great many of you are convinced that your lawyer doesn't know what he's talking about—then it's time to get another lawyer.) Expert opinion can be especially helpful in getting agreement over potentially divisive issues like traffic. Neighbors who might reject a citizens' traffic plan because it seems to protect other neighbors' streets more than theirs are sometimes willing to accept the same plan when it's put forward by someone they know to be a certified professional with no personal stake in the outcome. If your group can't afford to hire outsiders, you could still defer to the opinions of those who work with similar problems in their jobs, or who have been involved in previous development disputes.

4. **"Form follows function."** This is a principle as applicable to consensus-building as it is to the design of buildings. If you want to form an agreement, you need a functioning system through which ideas can be generated and judgments made about them. This means you need to have a set time for people to say what they want to say, and know that others who should hear them are listening with respect and are not distracted with other duties and interruptions. Your agenda should be divided into particular segments, so that the committee reports and recommendations are all heard at one time, and not split up before and after guest speakers or left until late in the evening when everyone is tired and wants to go home. Once a proposal for action has been made, you need a formula for dealing with it: either by referring it to a committee for further study ("tabling"), or modifying it as other members may wish ("amending the motion"), or considering a different approach to the same problem (a "substitute motion"), or bringing it straight to a vote ("calling the question"). The process for handling discussion and proposals for action at meetings is laid out in great detail in *Robert's Rules of Order*—though your neighborhood organization will probably work more easily with a less formal, somewhat abbreviated system of management.

5. Keeping consensus means **continuing consultation.** You are likeliest to lose people when they feel cut off, not valued as a part of the whole, not consulted, and not informed. The only way I can think of to alleviate the sense of exclusion (regrettably) is by holding frequent meetings. Keep your members coming in on a regular basis so they can be updated on any progress that's been made and you can hear what they have to say about it. Make no decisions unless you have a suitably

representative group of members present; otherwise, your organization can quickly come to seem to be the tool of a determined few activists.

In emergencies requiring a decision to be made on a day's notice, you can poll your board members by phone, to be sure the action meets with majority approval. But if a decision can possibly be put off until you can schedule a meeting that most people can attend, then it should be.

6. **Minimizing damage done.** Suppose your best effort to achieve consensus on an issue has failed. You can't even get agreement to set it aside and come back to it later. You're afraid the group will be split apart. Let's say that your group as a whole had agreed at the start to enter into negotiations with the developer. Now he's made an offer to reduce the building to a height that the majority of your members find acceptable. But a substantial minority feel the height reduction is insufficient and they are determined to continue in opposition. You have no choice but to deal with the split that's occurred.

One way of handling it is to keep the fact of the split confidential. You will simply go back to the developer and inform him that the group is unable to accept his compromise offer on height. You may well be able to keep negotiating on the other outstanding issues between you, and still reach an acceptable compromise in those areas. Another way is to acknowledge the split frankly: Let the developer know that a sizable fraction of your membership cannot go along with the deal, and that those who are for it are unwilling to take a public position in conflict with their neighbors. Under no circumstances should your organization agree to support a developer's compromise offer, in the absence of true consensus in its favor.

But what if the minority view is just flat-out wrong? What if the height limit they say they must have is unreasonably low, and there's no basis in the zoning law for their view to prevail? That makes it more difficult, certainly...but they're still your neighbors and you have to live with them, long after the building is finished and the developer has moved on to other projects. So you will do your best to persuade them of the majority view, but if they are still bent on pushing the issue, then let them try to make the best case they can on their own. The larger group should neither help nor oppose their efforts. They may just win, and then you might see that their position wasn't really so far-out after all.

To Negotiate or Not: A True Story

One of the most important questions your group needs to decide early on is whether to oppose the development all out or to try to negotiate a settlement. After you've asked yourselves the series of questions listed in the first section of this chapter, you should have a sense of how strong a case your neighborhood can put together, legally, politically, financially, and morally speaking. If most of you have confidence that you will win your case hands down, then you have very little incentive to negotiate a settlement. However, if the developer seems to hold some very strong cards, you will probably do well to try to work out the best compromise you can before the hearing. His incentive to work with you in this case is that, by obtaining your agreement to support his plan, he will be able to breeze through the public hearing process, and be spared the extra legal expenses and aggravation of fighting your group's legal maneuvering, delaying tactics, and other means of attack.

It's easier for both sides to agree to begin talks when they are not very far apart from the start. Then, with some good will on both sides, an agreement acceptable to all should not be far in the future.

In most of the cases I've worked on, negotiations, even when ultimately unsuccessful, have left the community in a stronger position vis-a-vis the developer. The TACPEC story illustrates how this can be so:

The Tenley and Cleveland Park Emergency Committee (TACPEC) was formed by neighbors in opposition to a developer's plan to build a gargantuan (800,000 square foot) office building right next to a federal park. At the very start of the controversy we met with the developer and city planners to try to negotiate some kind of settlement over the plan. But the sides were always far apart over basic issues like height, density, and traffic access. The development was to be serviced by a roadway that cut across a strip of the park; the neighbors insisted the roadway was illegal and would not give one inch on that point. Because the developer already had his permits in hand, he had little incentive to give up anything, either. After two years the talks had reached utter deadlock—but by then the building was already done.

But also in that time, another corporation had applied to build a building along that same disputed access road. When the developer went to city officials for permits, none were forthcoming. The citizens, having held firm in the first set of talks—though we lost—had impressed upon the city one fact: that there should not be another large-scale building near that park. Before any permits could be issued, the city decreed, plans for the new building needed to be scaled back by half; there should be more open space left on the side facing the park, and the road through the park (which had already been finished and was now in use) had to be torn up, and the park meadow restored. Because the owner of the second building had come on the scene after the TACPEC position had become well known, he could not say he was caught by surprise by the strength of community reaction. Nor was it unexpected that the city would eventually be won over to its citizens' point of view. Grudgingly, the second property-owner complied, and a building that suits all the neighborhood's criteria is now under construction.

In the meantime, several other developers who had eyed property in the area of the park have stayed away, not wanting to tangle with well-organized citizens who have shown they know how to "hang tough."

Five Tips in Summary

To help decide what to fight for and how strongly to fight for it:

1. List your organization's goals, from most important to most dispensable.
2. Figure:
   (a) how many people care deeply about each goal; how they would likely be affected if that goal were to be compromised.
   (b) how much money can be raised overall.
   (c) how long people are likely to be willing to keep working to try to meet their goals.
3. Get informed advice on the legal merits of your side's position.
4. Cash in your political chips (that is, get all the local elected officials and community leaders to say how far they're willing to go in support of your side).
5. Try to project into the future (consider the long-term implications or precedents your neighborhood's position could have on other developments that may be planned for your neighborhood).

I wish there were some set formula I could give you for weighing all these factors. Something like "3 points for each goal times the number of people willing to work on the goal, divided into the total amount of money likely to be available to the group"—and if the answer is below a certain figure, then you'll know that the issue is not worth fighting for.

Developers have it easier in this regard because they usually are able to add up their costs and predict their income, and so figure out, in numerical terms, whether it's worth their while to proceed. (This is called "making the numbers work," and it's discussed at some length in the next chapter.)

But in the end, you, the citizen, are just going to have to rely on your gut reactions and instincts, and just hope that all your neighbors' guts are churning at more or less the same speed!

KNOW THE ENEMY!

A big ingredient—if not the key component—in setting strategy is know-ing what your developer is really after. Naturally, I can't tell you anything about the particular developer you may find across the table from you, but I do know a thing or two about the species in general. I've observed enough of them in nature to have compiled a sort of field guide for beginning developer-watchers.

The Developer (*Terra-voracious Speculatorius*) is a variety of *Homo Sapiens* found widely in all climates and zones, but especially in large urban or ex-urban centers. The male is usually indistinguishable in outward appearance from many other varieties of the species, having no fancy plumage but being seen in the same drab colors (mostly gray or pin-striped) as is the norm for professionals of his sex. The female, spotted far more rarely, may appear equally drab, although a few have been known to take on a more flamboyant coloration (especially in hair and fingernails) and put on adornments of sparkling gemstones and precious metals to attract attention.

The developer's chief characteristic is his extraordinary instinct to build. Evidence of developer activity dates far back into prehistory, and many sites remain marvels to this day: the pyramids of Egypt, the Taj Mahal, and the Los Angeles Freeway System being among the many enduring examples.

Until fairly recent times developers have been cast in a subordinate place in the human hierarchy, doing the bidding of kings, nobles, or other leading figures of society. Though often aspirants to the aristocracy, they were more typically shunned by its members and treated as a higher, more moneyed class of tradesman. This lack of complete acceptance has traditionally led to the assumption of an intensely aggressive and self-promoting stance on the part of the developer, as he strives to win for himself a secure place among his society's power-elite. Though in a great many cases, such acceptance is in fact achieved, many developers continue to exhibit the aggressive behavior patterns that helped them to arrive at their top positions, long after the need for such display has passed.

The Developer now may be found at the very highest levels of privilege. This was demonstrated when George Schultz, the president of the Bechtel Corporation, an international development concern, was named Secretary of State. Hundreds of others have assumed somewhat lesser roles in government, most notably as ambassadors to foreign governments.

Despite their ascension to high places in human society, developers remain closely akin, in many respects, to a far more humbler species: the carpenter ant, as both are known chiefly for the prodigious constructions they leave behind. Sometimes these are fanciful and appealing, of highly sophisticated design—though more often they are no more than massive, block-like structures, pushing upward toward the sky. One can only look at them and wonder what drove the creature to produce such creations. The structures themselves, if found on an isolated plain or nestled in a valley along with others of the same type, may do little damage to the landscape. They may even be beneficial, if properly constructed and maintained against the elements and the natural corrosive effects of time.

However, on occasion the developer seeks to impose his building activity on the landscape in a haphazard, even reckless manner. He builds too close to the habitats of other species, or builds with too little care for the effect that his hole-digging and earth-moving will have on the workings of the environment; he may even take over land occupied by others and end up driving the hapless native dwellers from their homes.

Amateur observers, in looking for an animal parallel for developer behavior, may too easily assume that developers are a predatory species, akin to wolves or jackals. They appear to move in packs, selecting the best territory they can find for their hunting grounds, surveying the game available, and then picking out and isolating the most vulnerable targets, and moving in for the kill.

However, I believe those who study the developer in more depth will find this metaphor less than fitting, chiefly because the wolf, unlike the developer, has the free range of the landscape to explore, and his attacks are largely unrestrained, except by his own capabilities and luck. However, the land available to the developer is usually broken up into specific lots, each "fenced off" in a sense by restrictions and regulations. To understand how the species copes with the landscape so divided, we may rely on yet another animal comparison, this one a near-opposite of the wolf-analogy: Developers are more like sheep. They are a herding animal, contained by natural and man-made features into certain areas and restricted from others. Within their overall range, they are even further restricted by their own preferences and timidities.

Certain land ranges, for reasons that may be hard for the observer to discern, are far more desirable than others, while other areas that look identical in appearance may go completely untouched for years. They are also tremendously affected by the activities of the leader of the herd. If the most prominent of their number should happen upon a range where the feeding prospects seem rich, all the others will soon follow. They will graze until the land is dead—even with other still-green ranges in sight. But developers, like sheep, never want to be the first to try out new ground. What if it doesn't feel like the old ground? What if they must tread more lightly in order to get the benefit from it? What if it's not rich enough to fatten them quickly? They find many reasons to stick with what they know.

It usually takes a strong-minded shepherd—with a lot of prodding and pushing (the sheep kicking and bleating all the way) to make the sheep go where there's enough room for them all, and where the neglected, tall grass could use a bit of trimming and get some fertilizing benefits from what the sheep leave behind.

With developers, this "strong shepherd" *should* be the zoning authority of the government, which is charged with making the rules, not with the developers' wishes in mind, but with the overall good of the land as its purpose. Sound zoning ordinances should work to permit only as much development in one area as its **infrastructure** (i.e., roads, sewerage systems, power supply, school capacity, etc.) can safely accommodate. There should also be a requirement for consistency with the broader aims of public policy (such as the preservation of historic sites, maintenance of sufficient open space, circulation of light and air, retention of neighborhood-serving businesses, and other important amenities). Land-use policies should equally encourage the development of parts of the city that lack a healthy level of new construction—neighborhoods where more housing, more places to shop, and more centers of employment are sorely needed. The authorities should be able to reevaluate sections of the city often enough, and enact zoning changes quickly enough, to prevent development from passing the saturation point in one area, while another, formerly lively area is allowed to fall into neglect and disrepair.

To continue the sheep/shepherd analogy: How can those in charge determine which areas are in danger of being overused, and which need more attention? The way the shepherds traditionally solve this problem is by keeping watch over their flocks day and night. They sleep out on the same ground, and move where the sheep move, and come to have an instinct for where they're headed. But those in charge of planning are seldom so knowledgeable or devoted to the preservation of their land. That would not be a problem, as long as they were willing to follow the advice of those who are (meaning the people who live there). Experts may be brought in to check on conditions not immediately apparent to either the authorities or to the residents, such as the quality of the soil and the pollution levels in the air and water.

But in far too many places the residents and the specialists who are brought in to talk about the land are given much less of a say in the regulatory process than the land-users whose activities the process is intended to control. In other words, all too often, the sheep are in charge of the grazing ranges.

The "Bottom Line"

You probably will not be out to reform the system; you're only looking to deal effectively with the developer you have. But if developers are basically timid, herding animals, you need to keep in mind how they got that way: They saw a few of their number getting fleeced! Development, even in the best of times, is a high-risk proposition. One or two false moves—say, taking a chance on building in a marginal area—and even a strong company can go under. Bankruptcy lays many traps: a few points up in the prime rate, a jump in oil prices, a labor dispute, a small change in the tax code, and the expected profits can suddenly disappear, or turn into huge losses. The variables are endless, and so can never be fully anticipated; the debacles are well known (and every developer will gladly recount them for you if you'll listen). It's their justification for wanting (no, needing!) to make profits of 30, 50, or even 100 percent on a venture. Below 15 percent they'll tell you it's not even worth their while to break ground. ("If I wanted to make less than that," one developer sniffed, "I'd keep my money in CD's.")

You should be thinking, as you read this, "OK...but it's not *my* neighborhood's problem to see that the developer makes some money. *He* bought the land, *he* had the responsibility to learn what the neighborhood was like, *he's* the speculator—now let him assume the risk." (If you're not thinking these thoughts at this point, the developers are probably going to find you a very easy mark.)

But you don't have to be persuaded that the developer's need for profit supersedes your own need for a livable neighborhood; you just have to recognize that this is his motivating logic (just as he certainly will recognize that it's your motivating logic to try to stop him). Only by discovering, in hard numerical terms, just what his needs are, will you be able to negotiate with him effectively. Of course, a large part of his strategy may be to keep you in the dark as to his capital outlay, his construction costs, and his projected income from the completed building. But much of this information will be accessible (or at least guessable), either from the public records (in the

Recorder of Deeds Office), or from various other sources in the real estate industry (it's generally very difficult to keep multi-million dollar deals a secret), or just by finding out the average cost and rental-return per square foot for new construction in your area.

Take, for example, a piece of land that sold for $500,000, on which a developer intends to construct a new building of 100,000 square feet. Just to use round numbers, let's say construction costs $50 a square foot.* Office rents go for around $20 a square foot. The interest rate is at 10 percent. You can figure it roughly this way:

100,000 x $50 = $5 million cost of construction
             + .5 million cost of land
───
             $5.5 million borrowed at 10%=$550,000 year in simple
             interest
100,000 x $20 = $2 million per year in rental income

Rough estimate of the "bottom line"—a net income of $1,450,000 per year. That return, divided by the amount of money used to produce it ($1,450,000 ÷ 5,500,000 = .26) works out to a rate of return of 26 percent. When you consider that the developer may have had to pay only one-fifth or so of the total costs upfront, he may actually be earning nearly 150 percent on his invested principle.

Performing a calculation like this should give you some idea of how much "give" there is in the developer's plan. And if your data on the breakdown of costs is fairly reliable, you should even be able to figure out where that "give" is. You will also benefit by knowing the specific market conditions in your area. Is the office market "soft" (vacancy rates above 10 percent) right now? Is the market for upscale housing still strong? Then perhaps you can negotiate down the number of commercial floors in a mixed-use complex, to be compensated by an increase on the residential side. Are you looking at a plan you think lacks adequate parking for the retail component? You might be able to work up some figures showing that retail space can command considerably more per square foot if it includes abundant parking. Is your developer planning to tear down a historic building? Then you'll try to prove with figures that a beautifully restored landmark building can bring in as much, or (because of its prestige appeal) even more income, than the typical new construction can provide. Such calculations, in the developer's vocabulary, are called "making the

* To keep this example simple, let's say the $50/sq. ft. cost includes such expenses as lawyers' and architects' fees, brokers' commissions, taxes, insurance, and other expenses. But if you're able to figure these costs separately, for greater accuracy, you should do so.

numbers work." And if you can show to his satisfaction that they really do work, you may well be able to persuade him to modify his plans according to your wishes—and so avoid a costly and time-consuming zoning fight.

This is exactly what my neighborhood did in dealing with McDonald's. The fast-food giant wanted to paste on a plastic facade over a lovely little limestone building to make it look like the usual burger-shop. My neighbors and I did some quick research on the building and concluded it was of enough historical interest to support the filing of a landmark application. McDonald's didn't want the expense and delay of fighting the neighbors in the public hearing process, but neither did they want to accept the potentially heavy costs of architectural restoration. But my neighborhood found a volunteer architect and stone specialist to examine the building and report on its condition. They were able to prove to McDonald's satisfaction that the cost of keeping and repairing the existing structure was considerably less than the cost of creating a whole new facade. McDonald's was then willing to sign a letter of agreement with the community, in which they promised to leave the stone intact, and we promised not to oppose the installation of two small projecting "golden arches" near the edges of the building. (These elements are removable, should the building ever convert to another use.) The result is not just an acceptable building, but something McDonald's has been proud to show others as an example of their corporate cooperativeness with their neighbors. See photo on page 138.

When Money Isn't Everything

Understanding the "bottom line" always helps you to deal with your developer. But in some special cases, the developer's response can involve a bit more than simple profit and loss. He may also feel that his pride, judgment, or design sense is on the line, and if his ego is big enough, he may even place his personal feelings above his economic welfare.

I found this especially true in cases where the developer was also the architect. In the usual sort of bargaining sessions with developers, I've observed that building style tends to be the most negotiable item. The typical developer will say, "You don't like those red bricks? Fine, I'll make 'em beige....You want to lose that cupola on top? No, problem, let's take it off." Then he'll direct his hired designer to redraft the blueprints. But it's not so easy when the drawings you're criticizing are the creative work of the person you're facing across the bargaining table. Then it's necessary to speak more gently about the development's appearance, and consider the impact your words could have on

his artistic sensibility. You may also need to find another architect or professional with design credentials to put your views across in terms your
developer/architect will be more likely to respect. (But be warned: It can be
very difficult to find an architect who will agree to criticize a colleague's work.)

Corporate ego can be a problem just as easily as individual ego can be. I
discovered this when negotiating with a developer over the construction of
the headquarters of a major telecommunications conglomerate. The chairman
of the international enterprise had instructed the architectural firm to design
what he called a "signature building"—meaning one that would stand apart
from other buildings on the block and attract the notice of the architectural
community. The corporate logo was to be carved into a tall, separate monolith
to stand in front of the building, like a three-dimensional billboard for the
firm.

The neighbors in the houses immediately behind the site hated the plan
from the start, but the company hardly thought to consider how they felt. Nor
was there much concern about cost. The main thing the executives wanted
was to have their offices completed quickly, so that they could vacate the
insufficiently impressive little building that had housed them for so long. In
the end, the only thing that kept them from accomplishing this goal was a
change in the political climate for development. The Mayor had recently been
given the power to review all proposed construction over 50,000 square feet
and to deny permits or order modifications for those projects found to conflict
with the city's Master Plan. When the Mayor's top planning appointee said
he hated the design, that's when it had to change.

But that case was a bit unusual. Far more frequently, the neighbors find
themselves fighting alone against the ego-driven developer. And when profits
matter less to the developer than winning, and winning means imposing your
will on others, getting your name carved on a building, or owning the tallest,
glitziest building ever built, then the objections of a few troublesome citizens
hardly matter at all. And if those citizens become so well organized that they
can force the developer to sit up and take notice...well, then that just adds to
the challenge and to the thrill he'll feel if he is able to beat them in the end.

A shockingly large part of the public, I've found, actually admires the
"stick it to 'em" attitude that some developers exhibit (as long as they're not
doing it, of course, in the admirers' own back yards). They see in the developer

a heroic quality—and if he's got the right public relations people working for him, a developer can do a lot to play off this image. New York developer Donald Trump is the supreme example of this. He happily flaunts his billions, and writes in the most self-congratulatory tones of his dealings to make still more.* When dealing with an ego of such proportions, your best chance is to find a champion with an equally enormous sense of power and pride. In Trump's case, that meant Mayor Ed Koch, who was able to call the developer's bluff when Trump threatened to move the NBC headquarters building from Manhattan to New Jersey.

But if you can't find the political muscle willing to take on the big guy for you, your next best hope for a champion may come from the legal arena. You may find a strong-minded planning department head or zoning board chairman who refuses to be bullied; if not, you may have to look to a higher power for help. In the development world, that's a judge, and in a contest of egos between a judge and a developer, the judge nearly always wins.

Seven Common Developer Strategies

What if you tried your best to work with the developer on a solution? What if you considered his bottom line, came up with a reasonable offer, which he rejected, and you don't feel you can offer any more without violating the neighborhood's integrity? It's often the case, when the two sides start too far apart, that no compromise is possible. The developer wants 400,000 square feet, while your side believes that even a 40,000 square foot building would be an intrusion in your sleepy little village. You still haven't lost anything by sitting down with him and talking. And you've gained at least one thing of value: You've come to know him better. You've seen up close how he talks, how he presents himself, and how much or how little he relies on his advisers and associates.

What may have come as a surprise to you is how personable and mild-mannered you've found him. Many citizens who become involved in a development problem come in expecting the developer to look and act like a Hollywood heavy. Instead, they're often struck by what a regular sort of guy they're dealing with—someone who grew up in a neighborhood just like theirs, who likes to talk about his kids and the local sports teams, someone who says

---

* His book, *The Art of the Deal*, will be of interest to anyone who would like to read about the subject from the developer's point of view. Though in no way intended to be helpful to citizen-activists (quite the opposite!), it's full of instructive anecdotes, as the author explains his clever techniques for evicting tenants, strong-arming officials, manipulating numbers, and staring down angry residents at meetings.

he cares about what the neighbors think and sounds like he means it. It's easy to be charmed and take his words to heart.

If you find your developer fits this description, just remember, it's not his personality you'll have to live with for the next twenty or thirty years—it's the development he leaves behind. So concentrate on what *that's* like, in cold, practical terms, and frame your own actions in response to the thing, not the person presenting it.

If, after all the sweet-sounding rhetoric is stripped away, you still find the proposal unacceptable in its basic parts and no further modification is forthcoming, then you'll have no choice but to fight. So you'll start your volunteers moving on all the political, organizational, and legal fronts necessary to prepare the strongest attack. You'll be out there knocking on doors, holding rallies, explaining your side to the press, marshalling evidence, and much, much more. And what do you think the developer will be doing all this time...holding his breath?

Not very likely. He will also be out wooing the media, meeting with politicians and planners, soliciting organizational backing, advertising...doing everything your side's doing with volunteer labor, except that his people are at it full time, with professional expertise, and slick production values. So you're not only going to have to put on the best campaign you know how— you're also going to have to work at countering what the developer is putting out at the same time.

Here is a short list of the more common strategies you might want to prepare yourself against:

1. The Divide-and-Conquer Ploy
2. The Phoney Agreement
3. The Good Guy Pose
4. The Balancing Act
5. The Hit Squad
6. The Scary Decoy
7. The Free Enterprise Appeal

The Divide-and-Conquer Ploy

I list this strategy first because it's so commonly employed by hard-nosed developers. They look over the community to discover any natural antagonisms, which they try to exploit so as to split the disagreeing factions into harshly opposing camps. The split may be rich vs. poor, or homeowners vs. renters; it could be black vs. white, or whatever other ethnic divisions may be present in the neighborhood; or it could be geographic: residents of the north side of the development site vs. residents to the south. Almost any factor or condition present in the neighborhood could be manipulated to create or exacerbate tensions among your neighbors...unless you are alert and working to stop it at an early stage.

Let's say the new building will include a day-care center. The developer may be able to win support from parents of young children in the neighborhood, creating a split between them and their older, childless neighbors. If movie theaters, discos, or taverns are at issue, those who like nightlife may be fighting those who love quiet. Whenever new traffic measures enter into a plan, the interests of car-owners and users of public transportation are likely to diverge. Even as private a matter as religious belief can become the source of conflict when the development of church land is at issue. A neighborhood may find itself split between those who believe that a church should maintain a beautiful physical presence and those who believe it should not hold onto a valuable asset like a developable piece of land, but should sell for the highest price and use the proceeds to benefit the poor.

When a developer succeeds in causing a split, he gives himself a tremendous advantage—and sometimes an insurmountable one. Here's how it happened in one case: A developer was seeking permission to build a huge new office/retail project near an inner city school. In the beginning, few of the residents thought the building would fit in with their neighborhood. Then the developer threw in the offer to fix up the school's deteriorating track and playing field. That won over most of the parents whose children attended the school. The neighborhood was now split. Two different community organizations came to speak at the zoning hearing, one pro-development, the other con. Because the pro-development group had the developer's assistance in preparing and presenting testimony, it came across as knowledgeable about the site and the planning process. The opposition group was not so well-advised or represented. It wasn't surprising, given those circumstances, that the zoning commission found those neighbors who sided with the developer more persuasive, and so granted the developer's request.

Bridge-building Strategies in Response. When the developer starts digging trenches between sides of the community, your response should be to look for ways to build bridges. Here are some examples of how you might do it:

- **Make your board representative.** Ask members of all organized groups present in your community to serve on your board—*before* the developer asks them to start working along with him.
- **Match the developer's offer of help.** Suppose the developer is holding out some benefit desired by a certain segment of the community—let's take the example just cited about the need for a new track and playing field. The developer comes along offering

to pay for the project, in exchange for which the parents' group will support his development plan. Your group should get together with the parents and see if you can do as much or better for their cause. You may not be able to come up with the same dollar amount up front, but you might offer to supplement their fund-raising efforts with some of your own, and so do as much for them in the long run—and *without* asking them to put up with an over-scaled building.

- **Make up for past mistakes.** Suppose the developer is wooing a church group with offers to support their special charitable project in the neighborhood. When you approach them attempting to show equal concern, they rebuff your interest as belated, patronizing, and self-interested. Why did it take a developer's involvement to get you to give a damn? That's a reasonable question, and if you don't have a good answer for it, you may have to do some apologizing to the project-leaders. But though you may have waited a bit too long to demonstrate your neighborliness, point out that you still have more in common with them than the developer. You're going to be around to work with them in the future, which should help (you hope) make up for any neglect in the past. But once the developer gets their support, and gets his project approved, his use for them will be at an end, and his favors, consequently, can be expected to disappear.

- **Seek racial/ethnic diversification.** Unless your city is completely homogeneous, you absolutely must make sure that your organization is not all of one race. Especially if the members are all white, some affirmative action will be in order. Otherwise, you can be sure your developer will find someone to accuse you of racism. Such charges can sink any community group's efforts! So get on the phone and start calling the heads of other organizations in your community, whether they've shown interest in your development problem before or not. Invite them to hold a joint meeting with you, at which you're prepared to discuss your common interests. Make sure, too, that you're willing to listen to their perceptions of their interests and see what support you can give for their problems. Only then can the bridge between you be strong enough to withstand the developer's attempts to bring it down.

The Phoney Agreement

This strategy has the developer presenting himself to your community as being entirely agreeable to all your goals. So you're for maintaining the trees; well, so is he. You want the development to be of low density; that's just what he had in mind. You're set on preserving that old stone bridge; he'd never dream of tearing it down. In fact, he's so enamored of it, he's calling his development plan "Old Stone Bridge Estates." You're working to keep traffic to a minimum on your neighborhood streets; he wants to help you accomplish this. At every step of the way he seems to agree with your views and promises to incorporate them into his plans. He echoes the rhetoric you use, sometimes word for word.

It's not until you see the actual plan that you realize that what the developer means by "low density" and what you mean are two different things. He's got 200 little boxes packed into a tract of land you thought would be suitable for maybe fifty or sixty. He's saving that stone bridge, all right—but he'll have five houses cantilevered above it, turning it into nothing more than a ramp leading to an underground garage. He's not planning to cut down any big trees (at least not on paper), but with all the construction and paving that's to occur on top of the root structures, it will be a miracle if any one of them survives. And his way to help you get that traffic off your neighborhood street is to build a four-lane expressway connecting straight to the development's front gate.

And because he's using your words and phrases to describe what he's planning to the public and to government officials, people are getting the impression that you have an understanding with him that just isn't there.

The only way I know to guard against this tactic is to keep very close tabs on what the developer tells people. Check often with your city planning officials and ask them to let you know what account they're hearing from the developer of your reactions to the plan. If it doesn't square with your own version of the state of relations between you, then waste no time in setting the record straight. And don't rely on a phone call or two to make your point. *Always put these corrections in writing.* This is what lawyers refer to as "papering the record," and it's essential to do this, so that if your case later ends up in the courts, you will be able to produce some real evidence that you raised objections to the developer's plans. Under our laws, silence (or lack of proof that you spoke up) nearly always indicates consent.

Here's how one developer might try to craft a "phoney agreement," and how one community might respond.

After a meeting with members of the community, the developer writes this letter to the neighbor who organized the get-together:

Dear Ms. Homebody:

My colleagues and I of the Old Stone Bridge Estates Limited Partnership were so glad to meet with you yesterday evening at your home. We are pleased to be in agreement with you on so many points regarding our plan to develop the property we purchased in your neighborhood. As you know, we are committed to:

- Building a low-density residential project of the highest quality.
- Preserving and structurally enhancing the Old Stone Bridge.
- Saving all mature and healthy trees over 10" caliper.
- Routing vehicular traffic from the site away from existing neighborhood streets and onto a roadway to be constructed at our expense.

Thank you again for your gracious hospitality. I look forward to bringing this project to completion with the helpful cooperation of you and your neighbors.

Sincerely,
Joe Urbansprawl
President and CEO
OSBE Ltd. Partnership

To which Ms. Homebody immediately replies:

Dear Mr. Urbansprawl:

The Neighbors of Old Stone Bridge, Inc. are in receipt of your letter dated August 1, and I have been authorized to reply on behalf of this organization, to correct your statements as to the nature of our meeting at my home on Wednesday night. No agreement exists between the Neighbors and your company. Various members raised concerns about your project that you promised to "study," and if feasible, incorporate into a subsequent design. At the end of the meeting we made four specific requests:

1. That the density of the project be reduced to a level consistent with the level of the surrounding neighborhood. That would be about four houses per acre, not ten, as shown in your plan.

2. That the stone bridge be preserved unbroken in its entirety, and that any new construction be kept at least ten feet away from it.

3. That a building restriction line be established around all mature trees over 8" in caliper, such that no construction shall impinge upon the root structure of a tree.

4. That any new connecting roads be no wider than Woodland Parkway, a two-lane road.

We believe that these differences between your company and our organization can be worked out and we remain open to further discussions with you. After you have completed your study of the feasibility of our requests and done any redesign work that may follow, we would be pleased to meet with you again to review the plans.

Very truly yours,
Susan Homebody

The Good Guy Pose

This strategy works a little like the phoney agreement, but it's a more generalized approach. Rather than claiming that he and you have identical views about development, the developer allows that his interests may be different, but they're just as good, and maybe better than yours. He stresses how *needed* the development is: how it will add to the housing stock, or spruce up an unsightly area with a dazzling design; how it will boost the city's treasury, create jobs, bring more life to the street, and more variety and quality of goods to consumers. He talks as if he's doing all this out of his deep sense of civic responsibility—as if any monetary gain that might happen to flow from the project is just happenstance, and irrelevant.

Then the developer goes on at even greater length about his company's (unrelated) charitable endeavors: the special education foundation he's set up, and the money he's given to libraries and museums; the sponsorship of the high school band's long-awaited trip to Europe; and any number of other good works. I think of this approach as "the McDonald's refrain" because I first encountered it when dealing with the national fast-food chain. When company executives began writing letters to my community group trying to win our support for their plans for a small storefront in our area, I noticed that *every single piece of correspondence* we got from them contained at least three paragraphs devoted to their corporate big-heartedness: their establishment of Ronald McDonald houses for the families of hospitalized kids; their sponsorship of the Special Olympics; and the contribution they'd made to more localized charitable projects. All very worthy, but none of it having to do with the neighborhood problems we were asking McDonald's to address.

If corporate generosity is not enough to win you over to the developer's point of view, then a more personal attempt may be launched to get you to view the people behind the plan as good guys. The developer will invite you to his office, where he can show you all his plaques for civic achievement and give you an autographed copy of himself shaking hands with Mother Theresa and a leper. This is all to plant in your brain a nagging doubt, which should run something like this: "A man like this, who spends his free time rescuing abandoned puppies from the pound, who leads a scout troop on a hike every weekend in the woods... couldn't *really* be out to bulldoze all those trees and savage the landscape around my house...could he?"

Damn straight, he could—it's his job. And none of those others things he does on the side, however wonderful they may be, has any bearing on what he does as a developer. If you can just keep that fact in front of you, you shouldn't have too much trouble dealing with the "good guy pose." You'll just accept it when you find it as a standard part of the hype and self-promotion most developers learn to deploy. You can then safely ignore it, or quietly point out the obvious: that you and your neighbors are all good guys, too—but you neither want nor expect to be given public gratitude, and certainly not land-use favors, just because you give what you can to charity.

However, there is one set of circumstances that might lead you to adopt a more active counter-strategy—that is if your part of town is vulnerable to *Rich Neighborhood Syndrome* (see Chapter 4 for a description). In that case you might want to make a more visible showing of your own philanthropic qualities, in comparison to the developer's. In other words, fight fire with fire. If he gives to the symphony, you raise some money and donate it to provide music lessons for inner city youth. If he has his name on the library at the university, you start collecting books to be given to public schoolchildren to encourage reading. If he shows up at a ball to raise money for victims of whatever diseases, you and other volunteers from your organization show up at the hospital door prepared to do some volunteer work.

You might also try to pick causes that bear some relationship to the type of development he's building. Suppose his project involves the demolition of a house once inhabited by a famous abolitionist. You learn that the abolitionist's papers are owned by a local black college, but the library lacks the money to put the papers on display or print information about the collection. Your neighborhood could raise funds especially for this purpose, and give some good publicity for your own cause at the same time.

Or you might try to find out what worthy efforts are especially dear to the hearts of your local officials. Would support of the local volunteer fire department's drive to buy a new firetruck help to establish your community's civic-mindedness? Could you show how much you care about maintaining the livability of the city if you all turned out in force for your annual tree-planting festival? Public identification of your group with one or two such events might be all you'll need to prevent the developer from one-upping you in the good-guy department.

More of a problem is the developer's assertion that his *development* is nice—that it will bring jobs, taxes, services, and all manner of other good things to your town. This you can only try to refute with cold, hard figures. So set your research committee to examining each of his specific claims as closely as possible. If it's jobs he's talking about, find out how many of them are in skilled trades or specialties. Then check with your labor bureau: Are there workers now unemployed who will be vying for those positions? Or will personnel have to be brought in from out of state to do the work? How many of them are likely to commute by car, and what cost does the additional traffic entail for the city in terms of road-wear, pollution, and lost time? If the developer's claiming that your area is run down, you might want to obtain comparison figures on projects in other cities that have worked, with neighborhood cooperation, to restore old buildings and erect new ones of compatible scale and style. That way you will be able to assert that his "offer to help" by developing the area is not the only way it can be done.

In figuring benefits and costs, don't forget to list intangibles, such as "loss of sense of place," "neighborhood spirit," and "feeling of spaciousness." You may not be able to fix a firm dollar amount on these things, but you should try to work up some plausible-sounding statistics for how real people are likely to react when faced with the loss of these important qualities. If X-many families move out because they don't want to live next to a big development, for example, that's XXX-many dollars lost per year in income taxes, in sales taxes, property taxes, etc.

If it begins to looks as if the developer's got the statistical edge in added-up benefits his project will bring to the city, then you might be better advised not to try to compete on that level, but instead seek an emotional edge. Let the neighbors use their hurt and outrage at what the developer plans to do to show the zoning authorities how all those "benefits" are perceived by the people who will have to live with the development that produces them. The residents, after all, are a better judge than anyone of whether a proposal is a net plus or minus for your area. So encourage the people to come in and testify—the mothers with toddlers in tow, the older people who have spent all their lives on the block, and the young couples who have been forced out by demolitions of older buildings to make way for those new luxury condo towers. Zoning hearings can be very emotional, and the impact of those heartfelt appeals can be as important to your side's case as the developer's figures and cost/benefit ratios are for his—or even more important, since his are projections for future benefits to come, and your people are here in the present, talking of the reality that they experience every day.

The Balancing Act

With this strategy the developer cheerfully acknowledges that the neighborhood is going to be unhappy with some aspects of the development. Maybe two or three things about it really will cause some discomfort to the surrounding community. Maybe thirty trees *will* come down.... It's a shame, yes, but it's all part of a "balancing act" society must perform in order to achieve what's best for the greater whole. Development (the developers tell you all the time) always involves **trade-offs**. It might be nice if we could all live on quiet, tree-lined streets with no traffic, as they did in the villages of our grandparents' day...but society can no longer afford that slow, uncrowded lifestyle. Our growing economy requires space to expand, and that expansion always brings some problems along with the good it does. The automobile is the oft-cited example: It has brought us air pollution and high accident rates, and yet no one would ever propose going back to the days of the horsedrawn carriage. The speed, convenience, and freedom of movement it has meant for us all has more than made up for the damage it does to some of us every year. Though new development, too, has its disadvantages, when it comes to meeting the needs of today's office-seekers and homebuyers, a modern office building or new house is to an older building as a horsedrawn carriage is to a BMW (so a developer would argue).

Developers have gone so far in establishing the merit of the trade-off principle that most city governments have now encoded some version of it into zoning law. The code will encourage a developer to add some particular sort of public benefit to his project—say, a sculpture plaza in front of an office building, or some low-income units in an expensive new residential complex— and in exchange for the benefit he may be allowed a "bonus" of, say, 15 or 20 percent extra density, above what the zoning allows.

The public benefits are usually called **amenities.** In some cities they are required to be physically part of the development that's being built ("on-site amenities"). A few cities, though, will allow a developer an increase in building-size in exchange for providing the amenity in some other part of town—e.g., building low-income housing units several miles away—or per-forming some other act that serves the public interest (he could make a monetary contribution to a city-run fund for subsidized housing, or to pay for road improvements, or some other essential service). This connection between a particular project and an off-site benefit to be performed is called **linkage.**

In cities like Washington, D.C., and New York the developer initiates the trade-off, choosing the benefits he will include in his package in exchange for whatever bonus the law allows. In other cities (Boston, San Francisco), the city planning department may decide what benefits are to be included as a prerequisite for approval of a project. In general, developers like the voluntary system, because it offers them a cheap way to get bigger buildings (the cost to construct the amenities typically being only a small percentage of the value of the rentable extra floor space). City planners prefer the mandatory approach because it gives them more control over the end-product and makes long-term planning easier.

Either way, the neighbors usually hate the trade-off system, because the only "amenity" they typically want is to have a smaller building. They may complain about "zoning for sale," and feel their desire for lower density has been unfairly regulated out of the bargaining process.

The trade-off system itself may go by different names in different cities, but these are some of the terms in common use: *Planned Unit Development*

(PUD); Planned Development Area (PDA); Planned Mixed Use Development (PMUD); Mixed-Use Development Area (MUDA).

The PUD (or MUD or other alphabet-combination) is generally designed to encourage the clustering of apartments, offices, and stores one on top of the other, or side by side in the same complex. Plazas, fountains, benches, and artworks are all supposed to make the public area of the development into a "people place" where the office-workers will go to eat lunch on nice days, where retirees will set up their checkerboards on outdoor tables, where parents will stroll with their babies in carriages, and browsers will pop in and out of stores looking for bargains.

The idea originated and gained favor in university planning departments from the early '60s to late '70s, but now, after a couple of decades of implementation, we may find that actual developments built under the system do not produce quite so happy a result. In neighborhoods bordering on our downtowns, especially, we see bigger and bigger office buildings approved as PUDs, perhaps with a few apartment units stuck on at the back, almost as an afterthought. The ground floor shopping space found in these buildings is typically taken up by purveyors of designer chocolates, designer ice cream,

designer sunglasses, and other little indulgences. It's rare to find a grocery store or drug store or any other place for people who live in the neighborhood to go and buy the necessities of life.

To see the phenomenon brought to its apogee (or nadir, depending on your point of view), consider Trump Tower in New York. (see photo) Perpetual limit-stretcher Donald Trump showed just how far the definition of "public benefit" could be taken when he won the right to build a project 20 percent larger than the zoning allowed, in exchange for construction of housing that no one but an oil-sheik could afford. The retail component (intended by code to help neighborhood businesses find store-space in the city) is a super-glitzy shopping mall, completely enclosed in salmon-colored marble—the perfect place to shop if you're looking for a talking tie-rack for the executive-who-has-everything, but not someplace you could expect to find a quart of milk and a dozen eggs.

Frustratingly, it has often been difficult for neighborhood activists to get planners to see that some of the innovative theories they studied in the universities have not always worked out as anticipated. Developers have generally been much better attuned to trendy concepts of the day and have learned what buzzwords will work to make their buildings seem the most beneficial. This is not surprising, since they work at it full-time.

But just in the past five years or so, eminent social theorists have slowly been turning away from what was once the "gospel of mixed-use." *New York Times* architecture critic Paul Goldberger has written so strongly in his weekly column against a few massive new mixed-use projects (most notably Moshe Safde's twin-towered plan for Columbus Circle) that he's helped to turn thinking around. And urban sociologist William H. Whyte, in his 1988 book, *City*, effectively shows the flaws behind much of mixed-use theorizing.* This trend should be heartening to you if you find yourself fighting against a PUD.

Taking on the PUD. In looking at cases in which neighborhood groups have successfully defeated dense PUD schemes, I have found three basic arguments repeatedly employed to advantage:

1. The PUD doesn't meet the standards set forth in the zoning regulations.
2. The standards and definitions laid out in the zoning regulations are illegally vague.
3. The developer (and/or the city's zoning enforcement department) cannot be counted upon to implement all the terms in the PUD plan, if approved.

The first argument will require you to study your local zoning rules carefully. What are the general purposes of the PUD as described in the code? How does the developer's plan fit in? How is "public benefit" or "amenity" defined? What distinctions are made between development done under the normal process and that done as a PUD? Does the PUD building have to be "clearly superior" to matter-of-right development, or held to some other definition of a higher standard? Must the developer also show that the PUD process is not being used to "circumvent the underlying zoning"? (This is a

* New York: Doubleday, 1988, 386 pages.

phrase used in the Washington, D.C., zoning code meaning that the plan should still be consistent with density levels and other zoning limits in the area as a whole). What procedures are laid out to guide the zoning authorities in judging the PUD? Are organized community associations given any recognized role? Is the recommendation of the planning office accorded special weight in the approval process?

Once you start stacking the pieces of the developer's proposal up against the specific requirements of your zoning code, you may find that what's being proposed is not really the sort of development contemplated by the drafters of the PUD regulations. Developers have seen that they can get lucrative increases in density, not just for extraordinary projects, but sometimes even for the most pedestrian and imitative designs. It doesn't cost that much to try for it, either—and if the project loses, they can still go ahead and build at the matter-of-right level, regardless. If there isn't anyone to hold them to the strictest standards of the law, they may get lucky, and get the extra density without anything in the way of extra effort in the design. You can't be assured, either, that your average zoning commissioner is fully cognizant of the standards he or she is appointed to enforce. They're often laymen and part-timers, political appointees who like the prestige of the title, Commissioner, and they don't always take the time to do their homework. By quoting the relevant sections of the code at the hearing, and stating clearly how each offered "amenity" should be considered under the law, you could give them solid legal grounds to deny the case, and save them the trouble of having to go back and look up the code citations themselves.

The second argument, that the PUD standards are too vague to be meaningfully applied, is a legal argument to be made in the courts—so, if you are considering going this route, get a good lawyer. Why would you pursue this course? Let's say you've been looking at the PUD process in your area. All kinds of disastrously huge and incompatible constructions have been approved by your local zoning board. Community groups come in time after time, raising what seem to you to be solid objections, and yet they always lose. The Zoning Board seems to find everything and anything in keeping with the requirements of the code. Then, you find yourself thinking, there must be something wrong with the way the code is written. Its definitions are not tight enough; or its wording does not provide the zoning authorities with intelligible direction, in keeping with public policy goals as defined by your city's charter, state law, or the Constitution of the United States. The citizens are thus denied the protection of their health, welfare, and property rights that the zoning code is supposed to be designed to ensure.

If your zoning codes seem vulnerable to the charge of vagueness, however, be warned—you will find this sort of legal challenge both time-consuming and expensive (unless you get **pro bono** help). By the time you get a favorable court decision (assuming you win), the PUD you were trying to fight could well be completed, and you may be told the remedy of pulling it down is too harsh on the developer to be allowed. However, if there are several community groups that in the past have been burned by application of vague laws, you should consider banding together and mounting a challenge as a preventive strike. If you succeed in having the harmful sections of the code set aside, and force the drafting of more stringent regulations, you could end up doing a great service not just to your own neighborhood, but to residents all over your city.

The third argument, about enforceability (or lack of it) is one that has worked well in cities where, in the past, PUDs have gone up that did not fulfill all the requirements of the zoning approval order. Promised amenities never materialized, or when set down in real life were not usable by the public in the manner intended.

The great discrepancy between what gets promised and what actually gets built was the subject of a front-page article in the *New York Times* on August 8, 1988. Investigative reporter David W. Dunlop found that:

"Beginning in the 1960s developers were granted enormously valuable extra floor space in exchange for building plazas, arcades and atriums.... Some are not built to specifications...or are unusable...and some are closed off by their owners." He then cites the case of 2 Lincoln Square, where the developer had pledged to construct a cross-shaped arcade, in the style of a European galleria, enlivened by storefronts. "The plaza turned out to be no more than a dark pit, and the mall [which had attracted no stores] became an oil-slicked, garbage strewn alleyway." (See photo.) It has now taken the city of New York

Dith Pran/The New York Times

fifteen years to work out a settlement whereby the developer will return the space to a use with a public purpose (it will become the site of the future Museum of American Folk Art). All this time the developer has had the use of and income from 63,000 extra square feet of space.

Dunlop goes on to cite the case of the plaza that was built but then barricaded off, and another case in which the plaza was actually sold off to another developer who built a building on it! The record in New York, as the article makes clear, is shameful, and it has become so apparent, even to the most ardent champions of the PUD process, that reforms are in the works. If you find the record where you live is no better, you may be able to use it to push for a similar reevaluation of the PUD concept.

This mixed-use project in downtown Bethesda, Maryland, was approved with a density bonus, contingent in part on the developer's promise to "soften" the facade by planting greenery along each of the levels facing the plaza. The effect was promised to be along the lines of the legendary Hanging Gardens of Babylon. Though the project has been completed for several years, still no planting has ever been undertaken. Where are the Hanging Gardens of Bethesda?

Compliance Standards for PUDs. If your zoning board is determined to approve density increases based on certain public benefits to be included, at the very least you should insist that all such benefits be spelled out in the zoning order in detail, and that their satisfactory completion be made a requirement for occupancy of the building.

If for some reason it turns out that the amenity cannot be built as specified, there should be a set penalty, known in advance, that will be assessed against the developer. The penalty should not be monetary damages paid to the government treasury. That is of no help whatsoever to the citizens who are now living near the higher-density building, without the compensating benefit that the building was to provide. Ideally, the developer should have to remove a certain portion of the extra floor-space he has been granted—though that's not likely to occur. But you could successfully argue that that portion of the floor-space should be made available for a community-selected use. At the PUD hearing ask your zoning board members to consider such "what if?" scenarios and to include in their final order specific compliance standards by which the amenities will be judged.

On the "Amenity-Watch." Developers have no trouble finding reasons why they cannot provide the amenities they have promised. If the zoning order is properly written in strong, enforceable language, you should be able to get compliance, eventually. But you will be far better off watching out for dubious "amenities" before a PUD is approved than you will be trying to get enforcement for unrealistic features after the fact.

The following list is of some amenities commonly promised, followed by some of the reasons they might not be built. If your developer is proposing any of these as a trade-off for greater density of his project, you would do well to raise some of these issues before your zoning board.

- **Low- and moderate-income housing.** Is it clear where the funding will be coming from? Watch for any fine print indicating that approval under federal programs is a condition for completion of this aspect of the project. The developer may come back later saying that, because of budget cuts, the federal support has been withdrawn, and that's the end of that part of the plan.
- **Shuttle buses.** The developer may offer to operate these to take employees to and from subway stations or bus-stops. However, once the building's in use, the employees may find that the shuttles do not run frequently enough, or that shuttle-to-bus transfers are so time-consuming, that most prefer to continue to commute in their private cars, which they can park on neighborhood streets. The developer, then having low ridership figures to cite as justification, will ask to be allowed to terminate the shuttle-bus program.
- **Specific retail tenants.** If your developer promises to provide a grocery store, a health club, a hardware store, or any other particular store you have requested, ask to see some proof that a lease has been signed and that a specific tenant is actually available. Don't accept vague language, such as a "good faith effort" to find the desired tenant; such phrases have no enforceable meaning. It will be too easy for the developer to show that he looked for such

a tenant, but couldn't find one to lease the space at the price he's asking. The space then gets turned into more offices, or goes to an undesirable retail tenant, and the neighbors have no recourse.

- **Set-aside of space for non-profit use** (senior citizens' center, day-care program, libraries, museums, etc.). Make sure the constituent group to be served by the center will be informed of its existence and have easy access to it. If, for example, a senior citizens' center is included in a suburban office park, far from mass transit lines, it may not be possible for many older people who can no longer drive to make use of the facility. Or if the availability of exhibit space is not made known to area artists, no one may apply to have his or her works shown there. Lack of use then becomes a convenient excuse for the developer to shut down the amenity and convert the space to private commercial use.

- **Special design features** (artworks, plazas, fountains, landscaping, etc.). Some typical developer reasons for failing to provide these might be as follows:

    — Sculpture: "We found the public disapproved of the nudity of the figures, so we decided not to install the work."
    — Fountains: "The waterjets didn't function well in the space. The wind kept blowing the water over the sidewalk cafe, soaking the people who were out having lunch—so naturally we shut it off."
    — Landscaping: "The pear trees wouldn't get enough sun on that side; our arborist advised us to put the boxwood hedge there in its place."
    —Street furnishings: "The Parisian-style park benches we put down were attracting homeless people, and the shopkeepers were complaining, so we removed them at their request. Then the homeless started sitting on the edge of the balustrade we built around the plaza, so we had to install a set of small spikes to keep them away."
    —Plazas: "The terra cotta tilework we promised was to come from a particular family-run factory in Italy, but the patriarch of the family just retired, and no one else knows how to cast that particular type of tile. So we decided to substitute brick pavers instead."

—Underground parking: "When the borings were done, we found there was solid rock beneath the surface. It would just be too expensive to dig down more than two levels."

—Stairways: "We found that the marble we had planned to use gets too slick in the rain, so our insurance company insisted we switch to concrete."

Any or all these reasons may be valid, to a degree. But you don't want to put yourself in a position of having to judge in every case. Better to know ahead of time what compensation you will receive for any defaulted part of the plan, whatever the cause.

Remember to keep one thing in mind above all—no matter how good the amenities offered as extras, if you're giving up something basic (like light and air) to get them, it's not a good deal for your neighborhood. Don't let yourself get sidetracked by questions like how many benches go in the plaza, or what color the marble on  the balustrade should be, when it's the project as a whole that is the problem.

The Scary Decoy

This tactic is explained to perfection by Donald Trump in his book-length exercise in self-congratulation, *The Art of the Deal.* As he tells it, he was proposing to build a mixed-use project (to be named, like all his major developments, after himself: Trump Tower) with an FAR of 20 on a midtown Manhattan site zoned for an FAR of 8.5. Part of the extra density he had obtained through purchase of the **air rights** of an adjoining low-rise building; the other part he was seeking through a New York City bonus program which grants the increase in exchange for various amenities. By including a large retail and residential component, and building around a publicly accessible indoor plaza (or *atrium*), Trump felt that he had qualified for the increase in the zoning; but he knew that city planners were still likely to balk at a building of such height and density along a stretch of Fifth Avenue characterized (in his own words) by "short, old limestone and brick buildings." So he threw into the picture a scary decoy, which he describes this way:

"I had Der* prepare a model of the 'as-of-right' building to show city planning. It was hideous: a thin little four-sided box going straight up eighty stories, cantilevering over Tiffany's. We took the position that if the city wouldn't approve the building we wanted, we were prepared to build 'as of right'—and we showed them the model and the renderings. Naturally, they were horrified.**"

Unwilling to call his bluff, the city planners folded, and Trump got almost exactly the increase he was seeking.

I saw the same ploy used in a case in Washington, D.C., but this time with a different result. A developer had acquired a tract of land next door to the Naval Observatory, a federal scientific institution, the centerpiece of which is a huge and highly sensitive telescope for observing the movements of stars. The measurements are then compiled in an almanac given to the commanders of ships at sea, to be used in case of instrument failure. The telescope's degree of accuracy is affected by the amount of excess artificial light and heat in the atmosphere, a random variable that cannot be corrected. Naval astronomers spelled out their problem for the D.C. Zoning Commissioners in terms any layman could comprehend: If the developer were allowed an increase in height and density on the lot bordering the Observatory, the amount of light and heat put out would rise dramatically. The increase could be enough to cause inaccuracies in the almanac; and a miss of a fraction of a degree in space could lead to a miss of several hundred feet on earth—a significant figure if you're the sailor responsible for aiming the missiles at an enemy.

After failing to refute the scientific evidence, the developer turned to the scary decoy to try to win his case. He described plans for a matter-of-right building that would be designed to produce as much light and heat as possible, while the PUD was designed to contain both to the maximum extent. Where the PUD would be roofed in a light-colored material to minimize absorption of the sun's rays, the matter-of-right building's roof would be made of black tar; where the PUD would have minimal *fenestration* (that is, the number and size of windows would be small) on the side facing the telescope, the matter-of-right building would feature picture windows and balconies on all the units. Where outside lighting would be carefully set and shaded on the PUD, no such

---

* Trump's architect, Der Scutt, whose flippant way of dealing with neighborhood criticism Trump clearly admires. He writes of Der: "When someone complained at the Community Board hearing that the building we had in mind was too tall and would block too much light, Der answered, only half kidding, 'If you want sunlight, move to Kansas.'"

**The Art of the Deal*, p. 168

efforts would be made on the matter-of-right building; and so on, down the line, for every heat and light-producing feature found on buildings.

But frightening though the decoy was, the Zoning Commission refused to be moved. In denying the PUD approval they noted this fact: The alternative, bad as it was, was not yet a reality—and there was no guarantee that it ever would be. The city permits office was not absolutely bound to approve the building. "Matter-of-right" exists only after certain other conditions and certifications have been made. In this case, the Federal government would play a role in the process, because it is an adjoining landowner. The PUD regulations were meant to encourage projects that were, in some way, superior to the matter-of-right—not those which were merely acceptable, in comparison to an abysmal alternative (which, in all likelihood, not even the developer really wants to see built).

Donald Trump conceded as much in his conclusion to the Trump Tower story. "I'm not sure they [the city planners] believed we'd ever build it [the as-of-right building] or even that it was buildable, but there was no way they could be sure."* But city planners aren't supposed to be playing a guessing game; it's not up to them to predict just how far the developer's willing to go to make good his threats. They're supposed to judge each case that's before them on its own merits—and one of those merits generally supposed to be included in an application is some evidence that the plan's been done in consultation with members of the surrounding community, and that it somehow serves (or at least does not conflict with) their interests. But if those members of the community are being threatened with deliberately bad planning, that hardly goes to show merit on the developer's side. If your developer has tried a scary decoy threat on you, don't hesitate to point it out to your zoning board.

As for the chance of actually ending up with that awful alternative design...don't worry about that before it happens. Few developers are likely to go ahead, out of spite, with something even they must admit will be of poor design. But if they do, then vow to fight it every step of the way. "Matter of right" doesn't mean a community gives up all of *its* rights to protest. You will most likely be able to get some modifications in the plan—and aren't you better off fighting for improvements in a bad but smaller plan, than simply acquiescing to a plan that you know is too big but may be (marginally) better-designed?

---

* *The Art of the Deal*, p. 168.

The Hit Squad

Most of the developers I've seen in action have tried to come across as "Good Guys." If not everyone is willing to support what they do, then they'll seek support from whatever segment of the community they can get ("Divide and Conquer"); if there is still a large majority opposing them, then they may try to downplay whatever the disagreements are about (the "Phoney Agreement" Ploy), or suggest that the advantages of the development plan far outweigh the disadvantages (the "Balancing Act"). Or they may try some mix-and-match of these techniques.

But on rare occasions you will encounter a developer who disdains these gentler approaches, one who plays hardball, who goes right after you and your neighbors with a direct attack. This guy's not out to win you over, be your buddy, or rack up points for style. He's out to win, and you're standing in his way. So he hits you with everything he has: He attacks your motives, he impugns your civic virtue, he may even assault your character and try to dredge up dirt from your past. He's out to discredit everyone who's a part of your group in every way he can, and will make sure that anyone, elected or appointed, who has anything to do with the zoning case, hears what he has to say.

Now let's look at some of the charges he may bring:

1. You and your neighbors are **anti-progress.** You're just a bunch of "No-Growth" ninnies, like the "Know-Nothings" and the Luddites of history. If people like you had been around in Columbus's day, America would still be a vast, empty space.

2. You are narrow-minded **turf-protectors**. You're against the development because of the impact you think it will have on your own back yard. You're not interested in all the good it will bring to the city—how many jobs it will create, how much new housing it will provide for young families. You're all white-collar people with good homes, and you're not willing to give up an inch of ground for the good of others. Your group will be especially vulnerable to this charge if the development that's being proposed is a public institution, such as a school, hospital, or prison, or if it's a smaller project with a social purpose, such as a drug-treatment clinic, a group home for the mentally ill, or a half-way house for juvenile offenders. (These types of cases are known by the acronym NIMBY, short for the phrase commonly attributed to objecting neighbors, "Not In My Back Yard"—and they're discussed in some detail in Chapter 15.)

3. You're **racist, ageist,** etc. The developer can and will make this accusation if your neighborhood is homogeneous and the development will be likely to break up that homogeneity. Let's say there's a proposal

for a high-rise build-
ing to be added to a
neighborhood com-
posed completely of
detached houses in-
habited by middle-
class families. If the
new building will
feature twenty-four-
hour staffing and at-
tendant services to
attract the elderly,
any opposition from
the owners of the

*Developments that serve a useful social purpose, such as this one
for the elderly, can be difficult to fight.*

houses may be cast as ageism. If the new building will provide subsidized
housing for the poor, and most of the poor in your area are black, then
any objection to the height or density of the building might be
portrayed as a veil for white racism. The racism charge may also be
levied if the objectionable development is to be carried out by a
minority-owned contractor under an affirmative action or set-aside
program of the government, or if the white-owned development company has entered into a temporary partnership with a black-owned
enterprise.

4. You are **elitist** snobs. This charge sometimes crops up when the
   development you don't want is a bowling alley, a car wash, a roller rink,
   a fast-foot restaurant, or any other stereotypically blue-collar use. The
   developer may attempt to characterize those who object as members
   of the brie-and-chablis set, people who are out of touch with
   mainstream, workaday America.

5. You're **fuzzy-headed idealists,** who don't know the first thing about
   economic reality. You expect the developer to give you impossible
   things (more landscaping, more underground parking, more open
   space, etc.). If he's made to provide them, it could bankrupt him and
   probably wreck the whole local economy in the process. Developers
   love to bring in experts and show multi-colored graphs to prove their
   economic points. "We must tear down the mansion. We studied your
   idea of turning it into an inn, but the numbers just didn't work." Or:
   "Our market survey clearly indicates that travellers to this area want
   large modern hotels with all the conveniences. They wouldn't use an
   inn." And the perennial favorite: "We've looked over the opposition's
   figures. If they think an inn will work, why don't they put up the money

and buy it from us?" (Of course, if the developer would sell it for its real value, rather than its purely speculative, upzoned value, maybe they would!)

6. You're **purists, intransigents, fanatics**. These charges often figure in historic preservation battles. As in "Only purists think the original wooden beams are important to the building. We can make some copies in painted styrofoam so real that nobody'll know the difference." And if you won't accept their first offer of compromise: "You people are intransigent, and you never intended to negotiate in good faith." Then the developer goes off telling all the city officials he meets, "I tried and tried to get through to those people, but they're fanatics, and just wouldn't listen to reason."

7. You're **misrepresenting your community.** You're just a vocal few who have taken advantage of the apathy of the general public to pass yourselves off as spokesmen for the neighborhood. Most of the people, if they could hear the facts fairly, would support the new construction, but you're concealing the facts and deceitfully claiming otherwise.

8. You're **two-faced**, making offers and then revoking them. You've tried to up the ante in negotiations, and now are not to be trusted. The developer may never have dealt directly with your neighborhood before when he makes this charge, but may be citing what he's heard from some previous developer, who tried and failed to win your neighborhood's approval for a project.

9. You're **"aesthetes,"** who care more about the design of a building than the welfare of the people within it. This is a useful charge to hurl whenever subjective design questions are at issue. Is the style of a proposed addition compatible with its architect's original conception, or is it in fact a terrible assault on the designer's finest work? If you don't agree with the way the developer answers the question, you're accused of trying to dictate taste. Again, a touchy subject if the ugly addition has social utility (it's a new wing of a library, museum, or university, for example).

10. The flip-side of 9, above: You're not aesthetes, you're **philistines.** The trustees of an art museum or university are most likely to engage in this sort of name-calling. They hire a radical designer who proposes something startling, obtrusive, and completely out of character with the surrounding neighborhood. The resultant public outcry against the plan is then dismissed as "mass-market opinion." The people "don't understand" the design. They just aren't "ready" to recognize the "brilliance" of the artist who created it. The architect, in some cases,

may deign to explain the work; in most cases, however, he figures you're just too dumb to get it.

11. You're a **crook, a liar, a cheat,** or other terms of direct, personal abuse. The developer singles out an individual in your group instead of taking you on all together. Any citizens' group may find itself vulnerable in this regard, if it does not have a way to rid itself of the flakes and oddballs it may attract. Should the developer find out about the loony or unprincipled past behavior of one of your leaders, he may legitimately use it against you. Say, for example that your Vice-President was once a member of the Ku Klux Klan, or your treasurer has served time for tax-fraud—you may have some fast explaining to do on behalf of your organization! You may not even know who your liabilities will turn out to be, until your developer uncovers them for you. The attack may or may not have relevance to your group's position on the issues: For example, it would certainly be pertinent if your chairman were to be charged with secretly bidding on the developer's property; his opposition to the current owner's building proposal could be seen as a means to lower the land's value and so acquire it at an unfair advantage. But it would *not* be relevant if the developer uncovered the fact that he's also a divorced father who has never paid a penny in court-ordered child-support. But the difficulty for you is, you may not have any way to find out any of these things, relevant or irrelevant, true or purely slanderous.

The Rebuttals. Before you consider what you will say in response, give some thought to who is best suited to answering the charge. If, for example, you find yourselves tagged with the elitist label, you should *not* ask your distinguished elder stateswoman, with her three-strand pearl choker and her tailored suit, to deny the charge in her gentle Bryn Mawr tones. Get your Brooklyn-born-and-raised retired Marine Corps sergeant out there and let him say a thing or two!

Before you unleash whatever righteous anger you're feeling, it's always a good idea to have a few cooler heads (usually the leaders of your group) take a look at your statement, or at least get some general idea of what your response will be like. You'll especially want to watch for any tendency to adopt the same nasty tone as the developer. That nearly always turns the public off, invoking the Shakespearean response: "A plague on both their houses!" But if you can respond promptly and firmly to the developer's offensive, without becoming offensive yourself, you'll do yourself some good.

Here are some ideas for dealing with developer attacks you may find helpful.

1. **"Anti-progress."** You must make clear that you are not against *all* development, but just this project, and for reasons X, Y, and Z. Cite them frequently. Come up with *alternatives:* These will prove that the developer's approach isn't the only way to go, and that you are willing to support development if it's done sensitively, in tune with the special nature of the site and the needs of the residents of the neighborhood.

2. **"Turf-protectors."** Build bridges to other communities (see section on Networking, in Chapter 5). Speak about the impact your case will have on other neighborhoods. If the proposed development will have social value, think of ways the same values could be served, but without the ill effects of the current plan. Example: Instead of building a 600–bed nursing home, the city could spend the same amount of money to provide in-home nursing care to the sick and elderly, who would not have to give up their homes.

3. **"Racist/ageist,"** etc. The only truly valuable counter to the charge is to show that members of the other race/category are active in your organization. If it's not so now, then work to make it so. Once you've accomplished that, you may be in a position to criticize the lack of diversity in the developer's corporate structure. Are the people at the top all white, young-to-middle-aged males? (I wouldn't be surprised.)

4. **"Elitist."** The kind of functions and public meetings you put on can do a lot to counter harmful images of wealth and privilege. Don't put on a black-tie gala, for heaven's sake! Throw a picnic/protest, and invite the press. On the other hand, you don't want to look as if you're trying too hard. If your group really *is* the Fifth Avenue limousine set, it's no good pretending not to be. But you mustn't let yourself get tagged that way if you're really more diverse than that. Don't let celebrities (if you have any) become your main spokespersons when there are more knowledgeable and articulate though lesser-known figures available. A famous face may help you to attract some initial attention—and that's to your advantage—but if he or she should become the center of attention at every appearance, then people may begin to think of your group more as the celebrity's latest hobby than as a genuine cause.

5. **"Idealists."** Real facts and figures are what you need to show you aren't dreamers. If necessary to make your case, hire an economic analyst, a marketing specialist, a demographer, whatever. *Prove* that a smaller development is economically feasible, or that renovation is a practical alternative to demolition. In your calculations, be sure to factor in all the little savings your developer may have ignored; for example, the cost of lawyers and experts to battle neighborhood opposition, which will be avoided when developing in accord with residents' ideas; or, in

renovations of historic properties, the 20 percent Federal tax credit available for commercial projects; or, if a certain percentage of the land is to be kept as open space, the tax write-off value of a donated "scenic easement." Find another developer to come up with a bid on the project the way *you* would like to see it done. (The tenants of a large apartment building near me tried that, and the alternate development plan looked so good to them, they raised the money, made the owner an offer, and ended up buying and renovating their building themselves!)

Alternatively, you could try to show that the developer is the one not attuned to economic reality. If he wants to build a twenty-story office building, look up the vacancy rates in your area, and quote them, if they're high. Nobody wants to see a huge building go up if it's likely to sit unrented for years.

6. **"Purists,"** etc. It will help if you can find others, known to be sensible, reasonable voices in your city or region, who see the situation much as you do. If you say the wooden beams on a historic building should be saved, you'll try to find a reputable, unbiased expert who will sign a letter to that effect. Once you can show that your view is soundly based, you should be able to educate others in your community as to its merits and win their support. The position that at first seems far-out or obscure may turn out to be something that everyone later comes to understand.

This was proved in my own neighborhood when a few of us set out to preserve one of the first automobile-oriented shopping centers ever built in the world. The homely, shabby little building was slated to be torn down to make way for an eleven-story office/residential tower. When we first started talking of the historic value of the building, nearly everybody laughed. "Oh, no, not that ratty old brick thing!" they'd say. But our historian tracked down the original plans, and discovered in the news archives the stories covering the center's "grand opening" in 1929. "Park & Shop" was hailed by the architectural critics of its day as a revolutionary concept, a marvel of design innovation (and so it was!). The accompanying photograph, showing the building as it was, clean and new, with rows of Model-A's parked out front, was priceless. The skeptical neighbors were charmed and impressed. Suddenly, they saw what a shame it would be to lose this reminder of a more innocent time. They saw, too, that if repaired and remodelled by a sympathetic owner, it could well be grand again. So we began to win support for our landmark application. Money was raised, publicity increased, and many more experts turned up to support our cause. No longer were we a small band of arcane history-buffs, now we were a neighborhood united. With strength through numbers, we were able to persuade the city government to back our view, and so saved the building from the wrecking ball. (See photo below.)

7. **"Misrepresenting."** You can shoot this one down any number of ways. Get up a huge petition. Nothing shows community sentiment like a hefty stack of signatures. Or generate a lot of mail for your side. (For a touch of drama, instruct your correspondents to send their letters to the Zoning Board in care of your organization. Collect them all in a large burlap mail sack, bring them to the hearing, where you will open the sack and spill them all out onto a table, as you make your request to have them entered into the record of your case). Or if you have the time and resources, you can conduct a survey of residents' views on the issue (by telephone polling, street interviews, or hand-delivered questionnaire).

8. **"Two-faced."** How you handle this charge depends on how much truth there may be to it. If the developer is refusing to negotiate with your group because you previously reneged on a deal with him or with some earlier developer, you have a problem. Your most workable solution may seem rather drastic: Disband the discredited organization

and form a new one, with a new name and cast of characters. Only this way can you hope to keep your side's image untarnished by the past.

If the charge is false, and you've always played it straight with the developer, you may want to publish a *chronology*, outlining the history of talks between your side and his, giving your version of what was offered and counter-offered by each side, and showing that you've broken no promises (or perhaps never made any). If the developer protests that the content of the talks was meant to be kept confidential, you need only point out that it was he who first went public with his charges against your side's conduct in the process.

If you are able to come to an agreement with the developer, see that it's written out in clear, understandable language which both sides are reading the same way. Never rely on a handshake deal, or "My word is all you need." It's just too easy for the developer to say later that you pledged to undertake certain actions you never meant to do. "Put it in writing" is the way to protect your own reputation for honesty, as well as hold the developer to his side of the bargain.

9. **"Aesthetes"** who care about appearances, not people. This one burns me up. The illogic of it should be so obvious! There is no "either-or" about it: You can care about what a building looks like and *also* care about the people in it. In fact, the two usually go hand in hand. The way our buildings look, the way they fit into the landscape around them has a great deal to do with how well they serve the people who use them. When buildings are designed without care, they make the whole area seem depressing and unworthy of attention, and the people in them get the message that they themselves are unworthy of a better life.

On the other hand, when buildings are treated with respect, their design integrity is maintained, and their ornamental as well as functional parts are kept up, the quality of life improves for everyone. I can think of no better example for this fact than the Art Deco district of Miami Beach. By the '60s and early '70s the once-resplendent pastel-and-neon decorated buildings in the popular '20s and '30s–era style had deteriorated so badly that developers were pushing for wholesale demolition of the area. The neighborhood had become so run-down and crime-infested, they argued, it had lost all its tourist-attracting powers, and so should be redeveloped for office use. This might well have occurred, but for a dedicated band of Art Deco enthusiasts, who campaigned relentlessly for historic designation of the area and wouldn't go away until they got it. All the while the developers were blasting them as "aesthetes" who cared only about glass blocks and aluminum trim. But once those features were ordered preserved, and demolition was no longer an option, the owners had economic incentive to spruce up the buildings they had neglected for so long. As more and more were restored to their glorious original condition, the appeal of the style was rediscovered, and that spurred further renovation. When the producers of Miami Vice went looking for colorful, interesting areas to shoot, the neighborhood was a natural. Once featured on a hit TV series, the style just took off, and now the area is one of the highest-priced in the Miami real estate market. So much for "mere aesthetics"!

10. **"Philistines."** You can deal with this one just the opposite way you'd deal with the "elitist" tag. Have the cultured neighbor with her Bryn Mawr accent explain your neighborhood's position in the loftiest high-Art terms in her vocabulary. Or if you can get one, find a respected art or architecture critic to act as your spokesperson (admittedly, that can be as difficult as finding a doctor to testify against a colleague in a malpractice case). But I've seen it done. Your city newspaper may have an architecture critic who is unafraid to take on the biggest names in the field. Paul Goldberger, architecture critic of the *New York Times*, has caused developers to redesign more than a few projects with his blistering attacks through his weekly column.

   To answer the charge that your community is trying to impose its "mass market tastes" on a particular artist or designer, you may point out that a building which is standing in prominent view is a presence that its neighbors will have to live with for half a century or more; it is therefore quite unlike a work in a gallery or private art collection. Because its looks affect the public, it is appropriate to let the public have some say in the matter. This principle was well established by the outcome of the famous "Tilted Arc" case. On a large, government-owned plaza in New York, a sculptor was commissioned to create a public artwork. The piece he designed was a single abstract shape, a massive "brutalist" sheet of steel, tilted (as the name so helpfully tells us) in the shape of an arc. From the moment of its installation the people who frequented the plaza, almost without exception, hated it. It took them a few years of intense campaigning and petitioning before they were even permitted a hearing on the piece. In the meantime the metal form had rusted to a hideous, peeling, orangey-brown mass. Even so, its defenders were calling the anti-sculpture side philistines and accusing them of artistic censorship. Fortunately for the public, the hearing officers didn't see the public movement in this light and ruled that the offensive work could be removed. It was a good day for citizens' rights when the plaza was finally relieved of the massive and oppressive design. (See photo below.)

Jack Manning/The New York Times

11. **Personal attack** on you or other members of your group. The temptation is, of course, to attack back, to call the developer a "greedy pig" and find a few choice words to describe his parentage, too. But let your better judgment prevail, no matter how angry you might be at first. You will seem the calmer, wiser party for rising above such pettiness.

But what if the attack goes beyond mere insult, and into slander or libel? He's not just saying you're a pin-headed idiot—he's saying you flunked out of college, and that's why you don't understand the economics involved in development questions. But the truth is, you didn't flunk out at all. You withdrew for a year because of illness, then transferred to another school, from which you eventually got a Ph.D. His attack on you is hurting your reputation and causing your business to lose customers. In such a situation you should certainly see a lawyer. You may well be able to collect damages for the developer's unwarranted abuse.

But if the developer's words are not so easy to disprove, or if the harm done will be hard to show in real terms, you might be well advised just to issue a denial, and move on. It's all too easy for a case to become sidetracked when members of the organization become involved in personal litigation. Nor do you want the financial and emotional costs of taking on the developer to escalate beyond control.

But what if the attack on a member happens to be both true and relevant to the case? Then you have no choice but to purge that member, fast! If the charge isn't true, don't dwell on it at any length (that only calls more attention to the allegation). Denounce it briefly, and wonder aloud (on TV, if possible) what the developer, who had once struck you as honorable, thinks he'll gain by spreading such garbage around.

But if the charge is true, but irrelevant to the case, approach it this way: Ask, "What does that have to do with whether or not he gets to stick his big building in the middle of our neighborhood?" You could add, "This seems like a feeble attempt to draw attention from the real issues in this case, but I think it's backfired on him."

In fact, in most of the cases I've seen, when developers adopt the brass-knuckles approach, it really does backfire, and the public and officials become all the more sympathetic to the neighbors who are being bullied.

The Free Enterprise Appeal

Do you remember that old movie *The Fountainhead*, based on the novel by Ayn Rand? It starred Gary Cooper as the brilliant young architect and "rugged individualist" who is so committed to the idea of free enterprise and the absolute right of an owner to do what he likes with his property, that he blows up his own building, rather than let others tamper with his design. Millions of Americans who saw the movie admired the act, extreme though it may have been, because they saw in the hero a man willing to fight for his independence, unwilling to compromise his principles or bow to the trends of his time.

Developers, not surprisingly, have been among those most moved by *The Fountainhead* story, and more than a few of them have tried to cast themselves in the Gary Cooper part. They see themselves as the embattled defenders of liberty—though, ironically, in the story the architect's developer/client is really more of a villain. Still, they adopt a cinematically defiant pose: "That's my property, damn it, and nobody's going to tell me what to do with it!" Anyone who tries is painted as the enemy: If it's the government, the image used is of Big Brother; if it's a citizens' group, they're portrayed as a legion of busybodies, who have nothing better to do with their time. To try to win sympathy from the ordinary homeowners, developers often use the single-house analogy. "How would you like it if some people came along and said to you, 'You can't build a new deck on your house,' or 'We think the fireplace has got to go here, in the bathroom, and the new kitchen's got to go down there, in the basement.'"

Of course, on reflection, you can see that there's little comparison between what one does with a small property like a house and what one does with a multi-storied, multi-million dollar project. The former affects only the homeowner and his immediate neighbors; the latter affects hundreds, even thousands of people for miles around, and can change forever the way a city looks and functions.

Much of your response to the developer's free enterprise rhetoric will simply be common sense. But you may want to back up your common sense with philosophical, legal, or political language. Here, then, are three different perspectives you could bring to the question.

1. The **philosophical** response is this: "Your freedom to swing your fist ends where my nose begins." This old saw is easily translatable to neighborhood terms. The developer's fists are his bulldozers and his crane, and the damages he inflicts with them (the loss of light and air, the increase in traffic, the run-off and erosion problems, etc.) can be felt and seen in neighborhoods so assaulted, just as black eyes and bent noses are painfully obvious to those who have suffered them. So keep focusing on the measurable harm the developer's plan is going to bring, both to individual property-owners and to the individual taxpayers (whether in the form of increased real estate assessments or public expenditures for more roads, sewage treatment plants, landfills, etc.), and he will not be able to say that you are meddling in his private affairs.

2. The basic **legal** question was settled by the Supreme Court the first time it upheld a local government's right to zone land. Construction may be regulated to protect the general welfare, so long as an owner is not deprived of "fair use" of his property (meaning that you cannot regulate him out of the right to do *anything* with his land). He has to be able to get some value from it. How much is enough and how far restrictions may go are always troublesome issues.

A 1988 Supreme Court case illustrates the state of the law today. A church owned a structure on a piece of land in a flood plain. When it burned down, the church sought permission to rebuild it. However, the state, acting in the public's interest to limit flood damage, had enacted a zoning regulation prohibiting *any* building on the land. If the old structure had not been destroyed, it could have stood where it was indefinitely because it would have been **grandfathered**—that is, exempted from the law because it was there before the law was made. But the state held that the law covered all new construction, and so turned down the church's application for a replacement building. The church sued, saying that the regulations went too far; because the church now had no benefit from its property, there had, in effect, been a **taking** by the state. The U.S. Constitution does permit **takings** in the public interest (and flood control is a legitimate public purpose), but only through the legislative process of **eminent domain,** which involves setting a fair price, usually determined by the courts, based on market values of comparable properties in the area, to be paid to the owner. Since the new law deprived the church of the use of the land without compensation of any kind, the Supreme Court struck it down as unconstitutional.

Because a person may not be denied "fair use" of his land, does that mean whenever you buy a piece of land, you're guaranteed the right to build as much as it was zoned to hold at the time you bought it? Although most developers will make this argument, the legal answer is a definitive "no." The courts have held an owner has *no right* to **zoning.** The government may change it, up or down, (that is, allowing more or less density) in order to accomplish certain well-established goals of public policy (the need to keep growth supportable by the **infrastructure;** the desire to preserve open space; the needs of residents for adequate light and air; among others).

What this means in practical terms is this: If you buy a house on a large lot that is zoned to permit a ten-story office building, and you pay a price for the land based on how much rental you hope to take in after your ten-story building is constructed—all you still can count on absolutely is that you own a house on a lot. What you paid for the property, over and above its value for what it is right now, is **speculative.** You *think* and *hope* you will be able to get a permit to build at such a height and density, but *you have no incontrovertible right to do so*.

This concept may be summed up by an acronym borrowed from computer-programmers: WYSIWYG, or "What You See Is What You Get." But most developers either fail to understand this principle, or else they deliberately pretend not to. You will hear them talking all the time as if the fact of high-rise zoning confers on them some sort of guarantee of high-rise profits. So your developer may come into your neighborhood talking about the vacant lot around the corner from you, which is zoned for ten stories, as if it is a ten-story building already. If you then tell him that your neighborhood has petitioned to have the lot **downzoned** to six stories, he'll start yelling that he's having four stories "taken" from him—even though all the stories (whether ten, six, or one) exist only in his speculative dreams. When you go out seeking public support for your downzoning petition, you may need to explain that you are not seeking to take anything real away from anyone. Zoning for more than what exists is a conferring of **future value,** and as any experienced investor can tell you, the futures market is the riskiest way to make a buck.

But just because zoning may be changed doesn't mean it has to be. The owner is guaranteed the right to a fair hearing on how his property will be classified for regulatory purposes. The government can't just change the zoning for frivolous reasons. It must establish that legitimate public purposes are being served by the change, and that the owner's land is being treated with **uniformity** by the panel (that is, it's not being singled out for different zoning, while the lots around it, having identical or similar characteristics, go unchanged). That practice is called **spot zoning** and will generally be overturned on appeal. After hearing all the evidence, the authorities conducting the hearing may assign whatever zoning classification they believe has been legally supported by the facts brought out in the case.

About "Vesting." Though I've stated flatly that there is no absolute right to zoning, that's not quite the end of the discussion. There does have to be some way to assure developers that they can get permits to put up buildings of a certain size and height; otherwise, they could never get financing for their projects and nothing would ever get built. When a developer establishes that right to build, he is said to be *"vested."* Although governments (or citizens' groups or individuals having a stake in the property) may apply to change the zoning on a piece of land at any time—regardless of whether it's got buildings on it or not—if the developer has already managed to achieve vesting of his rights, he will get to build the building according to the old zoning, even if new, lower zoning is ultimately imposed.

How developers vest (or establish) their right to build differs from jurisdiction to jurisdiction. In some places, when a developer completes a building permit application form and files a set of plans, he will be considered vested to build to the extent allowed by zoning. In other places, vesting will not occur until after his application has been thoroughly reviewed and found consistent with public policy in many areas—not only zoning and building safety codes, but also transportation and environmental policy and any specialized areas (such as health or historic preservation) that may be relevant to the application. In a few jurisdictions, a developer will not be considered vested even then; his right to build is not absolutely guaranteed until he has broken ground and actually started work on the building he described in his application.

Whether vesting occurs early in the process (upon the mere filing of papers) or late (not until ground is broken) tells you whether the development process in your area is more favorable to the citizen's or the developer's interests. The earlier the developer is able to achieve vesting for his project, the less you, the citizen, will be able to do about the project if it's objectionable in any way. If he can vest his rights to a building simply by completing some government forms, and you don't receive direct notice that those forms have been requested, then you probably won't even know a project is in the works until after vesting has occurred. By then it will be too late for you to do anything about it. Even if you filed to downzone the property and won the case, the developer would still have the right to build the building he applied to build under the older, denser zoning.

So you can see, in some cases (nearly all of them involving "matter-of-right" zoning), knowing when vesting occurs is of paramount importance. To find out what the rule is for vesting in your area, call your local zoning board and ask. If it is settled in a manner too favorable to the developer, you may want to devote your energies to changing this aspect of the law. Only that way can you save your neighborhood from losing cases over this small, often overlooked question of timing.

If you do decide to examine the vesting issue, be warned: It's an abstruse and highly technical matter, seldom understood, except by a few legal specialists in the field. The subject matter is also dry as dust and guaranteed to make all your neighbors' eyes glaze over within the first five minutes of your explanation of what the argument is about. Maybe that's one reason why developers' attorneys are usually so successful in pressing their side's views of vesting of rights—nobody else can stay awake long enough to make a counter-argument, and so, by default, their views prevail. Despite the total lack of glamor or fun, I do think the effort is worthwhile. When vesting rules change to favor the citizens over the developers, it's like the shifting of the balance of powers between nations. A small, helpless entity (your neighborhood) suddenly acquires an unbeatable ally, the Law, and the developer can no longer count on having his will imposed.

The Political Argument. In the battle for the hearts and minds of your neighbors and citizens at large, the developer may try to attach his cause to the prevailing political sentiment of the times. In our third term of a conservative Republican presidential administration, in most parts of the country a developer will feel confident that nobody wants to be known by the dreaded "L-word,"* so he will use that term to characterize the politics of his opposition. He will say, because you are counting on the government to restrict his private business interests, that you must favor more government regulation, a bigger bureaucracy, and higher taxes.

You need to answer this charge, to make clear to all your neighbors, whether conservative or liberal, that your position on the development is not taken for ideological reasons. Citizens of every political stripe are welcome in your organization, and can unite over their common desire to protect the neighborhood from certain demonstrably negative effects.

People, no matter what their politics, want to keep their streets free of excess traffic and see to it that their children have a safe, attractive place to

---

* Liberal

play. If they're conservatives, they may say they support the anti-development organization because it seeks to *conserve* their traditional neighborhood life, with all the old values that seem so often under assault in our modern urban life. If they're liberals, they may also think it's important to stand up for the "little guy" against the powerful, profit-driven development corporation. Either way, they are willing to work together to press their elected and appointed officials to carry out the wishes of the majority of residents of the neighborhood.

If your developer has managed, nonetheless, to portray your group as ideologically to the left, you should ask your most conservative member to issue your response. Point out whatever government hand-outs (tax abatements, federal or local subsidies, bond issues, road construction, or other forms of support) have helped your developer to complete his other ventures, or will be necessary to complete the one now proposed. You might also want to approach your most conservative political figures (especially any retired, elder statesmen you might have) and court their support, and if at all possible, get them to issue a joint statement in your favor together with other centrist and left-leaning politicians. That way you will show the public that your neighborhood's cause is above all petty partisan considerations.

With a little thoughtful campaigning and image-tending on your part, you will not only be able to deprive the developer of his Champion-of-Free-Enterprise appeal; but you'll manage to substitute yourselves as Champions-of-Home-Family-Democracy-and-the-American-Way.

PART III

DEVELOPMENT CASES

Introductory Note to Chapters 9–15

It's now time to get down to cases. In the following seven chapters, it will be assumed that you know all about the specific development that threatens your neighborhood; that you've got some kind of group organized to deal with the problem; that you're familiar with the process your local government will use to evaluate the development; and that you're aware of what your developer is doing to try to win the case.

You are now ready to start preparing the specific arguments to bolster your side's contentions before the zoning panel or other decision-making body in your case. But each type of case calls for a different type of argument, and so I have addressed each one differently, in separate chapters.

Chapter 9 is about **zoning.** The major issue in this type of case is typically size: The proposed development is too big, too tall, too spread out on its lot; you want it smaller, shorter, pulled back—or not there at all.

Chapter 10 is about **preservation.** The developer wants to take down an old building you value. You're fighting to keep it standing, in part or in its entirety.

Chapter 11 deals with the **government as developer.** When the unwanted development is a highway, a bridge, a tunnel, a freeway ramp, a municipal parking garage, or a government office building, a different set of rules may apply and a different citizen strategy will be in order.

Chapter 12 deals with **suburban development.** Subdivisions and covenant enforcement cases, misrepresentation by builders, public easements, farmland and open space retention are considered.

Chapter 13 looks at **commercial use.** How can neighborhoods retain their small businesses and services in the face of competition from chain stores, offices, and other high-rent payers? The role of taxation and government incentive programs is discussed.

Chapter 14 considers the **non-profit institution** as developer. Hospitals, churches, universities, libraries, and museums are among the special cases discussed.

Chapter 15 is about the difficult **social issues,** the "NIMBY" ("Not In My Back Yard") cases, such as homeless shelters, halfway houses, drug treatment clinics, etc., that have been known to tear neighborhoods apart.

Any real case may, of course, mix issues discussed here in separate chapters—for example, a project to build a new nursing home, which first calls for the demolition of an 1890s building of historic significance, followed by an application for a density bonus (a zoning issue), also involving the use of public funds to widen a road so that ambulances can have access to the rear of the building. You may find some helpful material in Chapters 9, 10, 11, and 14 for such a case.

But if you have the time, I recommend taking a look at chapters on other issues as well. You never know what interesting or novel approach created by some neighborhood group to solve one type of development problem could be adapted by your group to help solve your problem. There is no set formula for success, and flexibility and creativity are always a plus for your side.

SAVING YOUR LIGHT AND AIR

The Density Bonus

It's the classic zoning case: A developer has bought a vacant city lot. On its south and east sides it borders on downtown; on the other two sides it faces densely populated neighborhood streets. The residents *want* to see some development. They're tired of looking at that trashy empty lot. There's a noisy disco next door, and the patrons spill out into the lot late at night, dropping beer bottles, fighting, and sometimes passing out on the pavement.

On the other hand, they're worried. Development has been booming in this part of town. Some apartment buildings have already been converted to all-office use, rents are skyrocketing, and tenants are slowly being squeezed out. If the trend of creeping commercialism isn't stopped somewhere, the neighborhood will be engulfed by downtown, and cease to be a neighborhood at all.

The city's officials don't seem bothered by the prospect. They're happy with the revitalized city center, and love to showcase the new buildings for out-of-town investors, to encourage more building of larger and larger projects. As an inducement to further growth, they're offering a bonus of 20 percent extra floor space for development "of superior quality," provided it includes a retail and residential component, as well as "significant public amenities."

A developer for the vacant lot has come up with a scheme he believes will qualify for the bonus. Before anyone from the neighborhood has heard about his plans, he's already gone over them with city officials and won their blessing. His "Mixed-Use Development Plan" or MUDP (which some residents will insist on pronouncing "mudpie") calls for the construction of twin towers: one to be all office space, the other all condominium—and *each* will be 20 percent taller than what the current zoning allows. Connected to both towers will be a glass-covered courtyard, which is described in the developer's literature as the project's chief amenity. The ground floors of both buildings will be devoted to retail use, creating an arcade of shops on all four sides of the courtyard. There will be cafes, florist stalls, craft galleries, boutiques...intended, as the MUDP application puts it "to create a lively pedestrian environment." As an additional amenity, the developer will set aside some of the retail space in the second, underground level as a community auditorium for use by neighborhood groups, amateur theater companies, aerobics classes, senior citizens' gatherings, or "whatever the community wants to see there" (in the developer's words).

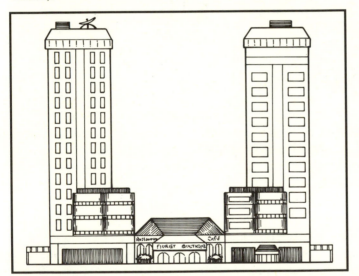

An internationally known architecture firm has produced a stunning-looking model of the new buildings on the site. But they haven't filled in the buildings all around. When residents of the adjacent apartment buildings first see the design, all they can think is, "Goodbye, light and air." No more views of the city lights at night. No view of anything except the venetian blinds of the office windows across the way.

When residents of the blocks of rowhouses toward the back of the site look at the project, all they can think is "How far will those towers throw shadows? Will our houses be kept in darkness half the day? Will that mean no more window boxes blooming in the spring?"

Residents of streets further away have their own misgivings. If the developer is allowed to build an office tower at this end of the residential zone, why couldn't others use that precedent to build more offices right in the middle of the neighborhood? Once you let one in, it's hard to deny others, and soon you could end up with a canyon of glass-curtain walls lining the avenue. The side streets would just become parking lanes for delivery vans, and the major streets—already backed up at rush hours—would become unnavigable. All these worries were expressed by neighbors at the first community meeting called on the subject.

On further reflection more objections surface. The neighbors form a study group to analyze each of the issues with a view toward formulation of a coherent presentation against the MUDP before the Zoning Board—set for just forty-five days away.

They're also working at fostering a political climate unfavorable to the MUDP proposal. They're lucky in the timing in this respect: The recent rash of office construction in the city has left some unhappy voters in many parts of town. Politicians are now hearing many more of these citizen appeals, and they're starting to reevaluate their generally pro-growth views. They remember, too, what happened to one councilwoman who sided with the developer in one of last year's biggest cases. Despite a massive infusion of developer money to her campaign, she still managed to get only 23 percent of the vote in her ward.

The neighbors are further helped by the fact that the developer's an outsider who has never done a project in this city before. He's got no strong ties to any local politician, and his last-minute efforts to make friends aren't going over so well. Even the head of the city planning department, who went out to many dinners and cocktail receptions at the developer's invitation, is now beginning to distance himself and sound cooler to the proposal.

While courting political support, the neighbors also see if it's possible to negotiate a settlement with the developer, and prevent the case from becoming an all-out fight. However, it becomes obvious early on that the sides are just too far apart to find a middle ground. The developer's bottom line is his 20 percent density bonus. The neighbors are set on holding the line at the current height and density limits in the residential zone.

So both sides are looking to the hearing to settle their dispute. Each studies the past records of the individual board members, to see what types of arguments have swayed them in other cases. Both sides prepare their witness lists and other pre-hearing submissions by the deadlines they've been given. Both sides brief their witnesses and run through some rehearsals of potential cross-examination. Neither side wants to lose because of preventable error, but for the neighbors, the case is practically a do-or-die effort. They feel their homes stand in the balance.

The Hearing

The developer puts on the expected, highly professional show, with beautiful slides, plenty of charts and display boards, and that stunning model.

His architect, a world-renowned figure, has flown in from Rome to explain the design (which, in fact, was created by a junior associate. But the developer knows it boosts his case to have the more prestigious, senior member of the firm take the credit.)

The architect is followed by other certified experts to praise each aspect of the plan. The engineer explains how it not only meets but exceeds all government safety codes. The traffic consultant asserts that the new development with its carefully planned exits and entrances will not merely avoid adding to congestion in the area—it will actually help to relieve it. A market research expert reels off statistics showing the need for more office space and more apartment units of the size and style to be created.

As his next to last witness, the developer introduces the chairman of the urban studies department of a major university. He presents a study showing that the area to be developed is suffering now from a variety of urban ills: vandalism, graffiti, muggings, prostitution, public drunkenness, and drug-dealing. Then he shows examples of how new development has transformed similarly blighted areas in other cities, and concludes that approval of this development proposal would likely produce the same positive results.

The developer's final witness is one of the neighbors, a retired schoolteacher, who lives next door to the disco on the same block as the development site. These days she's afraid to walk her dogs at night past the vacant lot where the development would go, and she'd much prefer to see a clean, new building go up in the space. She's especially pleased that the developer will be paying for new street lighting as part of the plan, because the city-owned fixtures there now are too dim, and often broken. She hopes the Zoning Board members will give their speedy approval to the project so that the work can commence as soon as possible.

After a closing statement from the developer's attorney, the applicant's case is concluded.

Though the neighborhood opponents have yet to introduce a single witness, through cross-examination of each of the development proponents, they have already laid out most of the basic points of their attack. Several weaknesses in the developer's proposal are now evident:

- That the "residential component" of the project may also serve a commercial purpose. Some 30 percent of the condominium units have already been sold to businesses and associations which will use them as year-round hotel rooms for visiting clients or as "hospitality suites" for business entertaining and promotional events.

- That the "community center" in the underground level of the apartment building may also be used as a conference or meeting room for businesses in the office building.
- That the traffic counts done by the traffic engineering firm were made in August, when many residents are away on vacation and the streets are at their least congested.
- That the urban studies professor did not compile the crime statistics he quoted. The entire study was funded and carried out by the developer's public relations department; the professor merely agreed to present the findings at the hearing. He has not verified the source of the figures, nor is he familiar with the methodology of those who actually did the research.

Though the attorney for the neighbors has brought out this information through dogged, and sometimes sharp, questioning of the developer's experts, he is gentle with the retired schoolteacher who spoke on the developer's behalf. He doesn't wish to appear to be attacking a longtime resident. Besides, the direct testimony of other neighbors will make it abundantly clear that almost no one else in the area shares her view of the proposal. He simply asks her one question: "Mrs. G., how did you arrive here this evening?"—to which the witness responds: "Why, that very nice Mr. D. [the developer] sent his car around to pick me up." (In soliciting this reply, the attorney has followed the time-honored legal principle, "Never ask a question to which you don't already know the answer." Neighbors had seen the chauffeured limousine stopping in front of the schoolteacher's door, and had figured out who had made the arrangements.)

When the city's planning officials testify, however, the neighbors' counsel returns to a more aggressive mode. "How many consultations did you have with neighborhood organizations before giving the developer advice to apply for the zoning bonus?" The official must admit that no meetings took place until after the filings were already complete. Through his questioning of the Department of Transportation's spokesman, the lawyer is able to show that the city has never done a thorough traffic analysis of neighborhood problems and has accepted at face value the developer's representations about traffic flow. The neighbors will get the chance to present their own conclusions about traffic shortly, when it is their turn at direct testimony.

The Neighborhood's Case

The President of the neighborhood association goes on first, telling how many *families* (not individuals) her organization represents. Then, with two high school students as helpers, she brings forward the stacks of petition pages the neighbors have collected in opposition to the development plan. The Zoning Board is already in receipt of several hundred individually composed letters of opposition. There can now be no question as to where the majority stands.

The next segment of her testimony describes the neighborhood itself: a successful, vital in-town community—not the dangerous, decaying place of the developer's brief. But though it's in relatively good shape now, it's still a fragile thing, and if it changes at all for the worse—if parking gets any harder, if the streets become still noisier and more congested with cars, if there's less of a sense of neighborhood to the place—then the families who like urban living, for all its problems, may feel the hassles now outweigh the advantages, and may pick up and move to the suburbs. Should the city approve a commercial project of this size, it will be sending a signal to the people of urban neighborhoods that that's what it wants: more office workers, fewer residents. She describes this transformation in rather emotional language: "And the city will go from being a *living* city to being a work-day place, a place people come to because it's their job. Not a place where people put down roots, not a place where parents work to improve the schools. Not a place where people know each other and look out for each other in the street. But a place of strangers, a place with no heart."

A few statistics on the decline of the school-age population in increasingly commercialized near-downtown neighborhoods bear out her thesis, and contrast with the developer's chief argument. He measures decline in dollars of taxes not added to the city's coffers. She measures it in the contribution that its people could have given it with their loyalty, their liveliness, and their spirit. "Which," she asks rhetorically, "is the more valuable commodity for the future?"

The next witness is an architect who lives in the neighborhood. He's made a model which takes in a lot more territory than the developer's site study does. This one shows the buildings on the streets for three blocks on all sides. The developer's twin towers are shown as tall rectangles of white cardboard. The shadows they will throw by early evening are painted in black water-color onto the representations of the nearby rowhouses.

He now removes from the model the two boxes representing the towers and substitutes a model showing an *alternative* design. This cardboard representation is closer in scale to the surrounding buildings, starting off low on the side that faces the rowhouses, and "stepping up" in stories to a height equal to that of the tall apartment buildings on the opposite side. The neighborhood architect explains that he is not putting forward a finished design, but merely wishes to show that another approach is feasible. His scheme is 80 percent residential, which he says is consistent with his professional analysis of area demand (the office vacancy rate having suddenly climbed to above 10 percent). The other 20 percent would be retail space, but unlike the developer's plan, the stores in the alternative version would not be enclosed, but would have entrances facing the street. An interior courtyard would be used for additional cafe space, centered around a bandshell and a gazebo.

Next, a neighborhood activist, who is also a physicist, uses the same model to explain how he calculated wind velocity through the twin towers and along the street. Using data from the National Weather Service, he counted how many days per year the neighborhood now experiences winds in excess of 15, 25, and 35 miles per hour. Using wind data that came out of a 1982 lawsuit in New York City,* he was able to project that there would be some 15–20 days per year when the wind velocity would threaten injury to property, children, small adults, and pets.

A cost accountant has volunteered to prepare an economic analysis of the plan from the neighborhood's point of view. His report looks nothing like the developer's economic data. Although he's given the developer all the credit claimed for tax revenues generated, he has also figured in a decline in property values of the houses and apartments which have lost light and air circulation due to presence of their towering neighbor. When these reductions are figured in, along with a few other costs the developer has ignored, the figures show that the costs to the city slightly exceed the return.

The chairman of the neighborhood traffic committee follows with more data in contradiction to the developer's experts. The members counted cars going in and out of a development of a similar size and use. They found that 72 percent of those arriving (not 40 percent, as the traffic consultant had it) came in single-occupant cars. Car ownership patterns of the residents of the luxury condominiums in the comparison project worked out to four cars for every three units—not one car for every two units, as the traffic consultant has predicted.

The last witness for the neighborhood is the pastor of a local church. He is dismayed by one element of the plan: the supposed "amenity" of the community meeting room. His church has always made its basement meeting hall available for a modest fee to any neighborhood group, regardless of religious affiliation, that wanted to use it. For years, the local dramatic society has used the room to stage their plays. The Scouting organizations hold their Den Meetings there. The gardening club does their annual Flower Day show, a guru teaches his weekly meditation classes, and the square dancers put on a

---

* in which a pedestrian named Rose Spielvogel was swept off the ground by a gust of wind diving down between the skyscrapers and smashed into a concrete planter, breaking her collarbone. She sued the owners and architects of the building for damages and won a judgment of 6.5 million dollars.

monthly hootenanny, all according to a convenient schedule. If a new meeting space were to open up in the building, it would only compete with the church's space, and possibly take away this small but important source of income. The church already has difficulties raising enough money to keep up its soup kitchen and other social programs in the neighborhood. Had the developer consulted with the neighbors before incorporating the community center in his plans, he might have found out about the church's role—but of course, he never did.

There follows a brief summation by the neighborhood's attorney, who cites the text of the MUDP regulations to remind the Zoning Board members of the heavy burden of proof required before a density bonus may be granted. Since the developer has clearly failed in at least one aspect, the need to show "clear and lasting benefit to the surrounding community," he urges that the application be denied.

The very last part of the hearing is taken up with the testimony of other opponents of the plan, who were not formally part of the neighborhood's presentation. There are no less than eleven of these, speaking for an average of three minutes each. There are prominent political figures, heads of neighboring civic associations, heads of the tenants' associations of nearby rental buildings, and authorized representatives from some city-wide and national organizations. Having prepared their testimony in consultation with the neighborhood's committee, each is careful not to repeat the other's points, but to offer new reasons why approval for the development should not be granted. Neither side spends any time cross-examining these witnesses.

After they're done, the zoning chairman sets an end-date for receiving additional information, and schedules a meeting a week after that, at which the board will vote.

The Outcome

When the board reconvenes, the zoning panelists discuss the case briefly among themselves. For the first time since the process began, the neighbors get some direct clues as to the thinking of the judges. The first one comments, "You know, before this case began, I would have said this neighborhood, so close to downtown, was really the perfect place for a mixed-use development of this type. But the citizens' testimony about their neighborhood brought up a lot of things I hadn't realized. And they had the data to back up every point. I have to say, I was impressed. I'm now convinced that a density bonus isn't needed to revitalize this area. There are other parts of the city that would do better to have construction of this type."

The next member to speak echoes the sentiment and adds, "It seems, rather than increased density, what this neighborhood could use is a little downzoning. Perhaps the city planning agency would like to look into that."

A third member picks up on the point. "What bothers me," she remarks, "is why the city planners didn't reach that conclusion when they had the area under study, during the evaluation period on the MUDP application. What kind of analysis did they do? We heard that they never met with the neighbors, never did traffic counts, and never did any impact studies for wind and shadows caused by the twin towers. They just gave the project a green light, and put it on our hearing calendar, leaving it up to us to hear days of testimony, taking up both the developer's and the citizens' time. And in the end, it seems to me, there will be nothing to show for it, because I, for one, could not see this thing go through." With that, she made a resolution to disapprove the application, which was immediately seconded, and passed by a unanimous vote.

So the neighbors could keep their light and air—which, as the zoning panelist noted, was only as much as they had to begin with. This case, as you may now discover, could be well summed up by the remark of the Red Queen in *Through the Looking Glass*: "Now, here, you see, it takes all the running you can do to keep in the same place."

Matter-of-Right Problems

Fixing the Problem Before It Starts

Now suppose that the tower that's going to blot out your sunshine does not involve any zoning bonuses; it's completely consistent with the zoning on the site. Your best defense is prior knowledge. If you live in an area where the zoning allows tall, dense structures to go up next to your home, and you don't want to see that happen, you *must act before any building plans are filed.* You and your neighbors can initiate a **zoning map case**—and just like a developer, fill out an application, prepare arguments, and go in to see city officials seeking the needed relief. You don't have to own the property to have a legitimate stake in its disposal under zoning. If you wait until a building permit is pending, the developer's rights may have vested, and you will be too late.

If you're not sure how much development is allowed right now as-of-right, you need to get a copy of your city's zoning map. Your local government planning or zoning administrator's office should be able to give (or sell) you a copy. Locate your house on the map, find out what "zone classification" you're in, and look up the definitions for the building limits listed under that zone. Look also at what zone classifications are within a short walk of your house, and find out what building limits apply there. If the existing buildings are considerably smaller than those permitted under zoning, and you would not want to see developers moving in to "fill the envelope" (build up to the limits allowed), then you should consider your area **over-zoned**. To bring the zoning into line with the maximum amount of development you consider desirable, you should apply to have the land **downzoned**. (Actually, you will be far better off if you can get the city government itself to initiate the case. You and your neighbors, through your recognized citizens' organization, will have the standing to be the applicant, but your chances of getting the change approved will rise dramatically if the sponsor of the move is an instrument of official policy, like the county or city planning department.)

When you apply for any change in land use, you, as the initiator of the change, assume the burden of proof. You must first show that there is a good reason why the Zoning Board should consider holding hearings on your request. Some reasons might be:

- to prevent the street-system and other city services from being strained by excessive development;
- to preserve and strengthen the stability of the residential part of the neighborhood;
- to prevent displacement of neighborhood-oriented commercial establishments (drug stores, grocery stores) by offices and other higher-density, higher-rent commercial uses;
- to ensure consistency with the city's Master Plan (if your city has one).

Although you may be immediately concerned only about one vacant parcel of land, your application needs to cover a wider area. Otherwise, you could be accused of singling out one land-owner unfairly, in violation of the "uniformity" concept that is key to zoning legality.

You must also make sure that the amount of reduction requested still allows the landowner "fair use" of his property. If, for example, the land in question is now zoned to allow ten-story office buildings, but most of the buildings in the area are six to eight stories, it would be unfair to seek a downzoning to four stories. Too severe a drop would penalize those owners who let their land sit unimproved, and for that reason most likely would be denied. To increase your chances of getting the request approved, you should probably seek no more than a one- or two-level drop in the zoning classification. That is, if the zone category is now C–5, ask that it be reduced to C–4, or possibly ask for as low as C–3. A change to C–2 or C–1 is asking too much. An experienced zoning attorney should probably be called to find out how such applications are viewed by your local authorities.

Once your application is filed, and your local zoning panel has found it has sufficient merit to warrant scheduling a hearing, you will probably be required to post placards giving the public notice of the date, time, and place. After you've met this legal requirement, your work has just begun. You will want to do far more than put up a few official signs announcing that the case is on. You'll want to show the Zoning Board that nearly every citizen in the area is in favor of the change, the same as you would do if you were working against a particular development. So you'll:

- hold public meetings to inform residents of the case and how the rezoning will protect the area from excessive development;
- put out informational flyers or brochures;
- seek the political support of elected and appointed officials;
- prepare witnesses to testify;
- prepare graphics, reports, and other evidence for the hearing and submit them according to legal deadlines;
- get neighborhood turnout at the hearings and generate letters and/or petitions in support.

Of course, once developers realize that their development options are about to be curtailed, they'll all get moving, too. Unlike fighting off a specific development plan, you won't have just one adversary to deal with—you'll have five or six or twenty or however many landowners hold property in the area to be downzoned. They'll all come in with their lawyers and experts and consultants and argue at length as to how the downzoning hurts their interests. Fortunately for you, *their interest* is of secondary importance in the zoning decision process. The system is designed to give primacy to the *general welfare*, and when property owners fail to focus on that topic in their objections to any changes, they leave you holding the legally superior position. Provided the process is run fairly and honestly in your area, and your evidence is sound, you should win the relief you are seeking. My neighbors and I have done this (in a city reputed to be one of the most biased in favor of developers) and we have come out ahead in each of the five cases we have filed.

When It's Too Late for a Zoning Fix

What happens when you don't find out about that high-rise plan until after the developer already has his permits in hand? What if you missed all the signs of the coming development, and are only made aware of the project when a giant construction crane suddenly appears on the horizon? Is there anything you can do?

Possibly—though it will be tough. You'll need to be a dogged investigator and complainer, but you could just get some results.

The first thing you'll need to do is examine all the city's files on the case. Did the developer proceed exactly by the book? Were all his plans and applications in on time, with all i's dotted and t's crossed? Are all the signatures on the right lines? Were all notice requirements met? Have all existing covenants and easement lines been observed? Have environmental standards been met? Was an EIS required, and if so, was it adequate and on time? Check through carefully for every little flaw. Any one missing or misperformed step may bring the project to a halt.

The minute you find one, you will of course want to go to court for an **injunction** or a **TRO** (temporary restraining order). But not so fast. Unless something nefarious and demonstrably irrevocable is going on (and that means more than digging a big hole in the ground), the court will almost certainly deny your request. First, you will be told, you need to "exhaust your administrative remedy." That is, you must complain to the proper city agency or enforcement department and give it the opportunity to evaluate your claim, and if it finds a problem, allow it time to act on it.

If the administrative body disagrees with you that the government issued the construction permits in error (as is likely, since most bureaucrats are prone to stand by the decisions taken by other bureaucrats), then you may be able to get the court to review the evidence that you have. But don't expect this to happen quickly. The way the courts are backed up in most parts of the country, you can expect the whole building to be finished by the time you get a hearing. And once the object of controversy is standing there, all complete and representing millions of invested dollars, you will find very few courts willing to order so drastic a step as modification or demolition—even if the permits were found to have been improperly obtained.

But, on rare occasions, court-ordered demolition has been known to happen. In February, 1988, a New York court found that the city had allowed the construction of a thirty-one-story building in an area zoned for nineteen stories. (See photo next page.) Though the building was already finished by the time the case came up for a decision, the court ruled that the top twelve stories should be razed. But it did not say that they *must* be razed, and the city then entered into negotiations with the developer to provide the city with some other form of compensation (such as free public housing units) to make up for the excessive height. The neighbors, who were only seeking a less oppressive structure next door, are far from satisfied with their "victory," and are still battling for demolition.

So it seems clear that a court challenge is a long-shot way to stop development. But there may be other types of legal challenges that will help slow the process down, if not bring it to a halt. Here are three suggestions for courses of action to consider.

1. Check to see if any **federal laws** have been bypassed or broken. The U.S. Congress has passed thousands of laws, covering almost any subject you can think of. Many have to do with development, and if you're lucky, your developer has run afoul of one of them. Some general areas to watch out for: endangered species; wetlands; asbestos removal (may figure into the demolition of an old

The New York Times

building); access points or interchanges to interstate highways; discrimination against the handicapped (if the new building will be public and will lack wheelchair ramps or elevators); discrimination on the basis of age, race, or ethnic group (in the employment practices of the development or construction company, or in the rental application process for tenants of the new building). Consult with a specialist in the field of law you believe may have been violated before you file any complaints.

2. Check to see if the project's completion is **contingent on any action of local or state government,** which you might be able to hold up or block altogether. For example, if the plan involves construction on a "paper street," the legislature may have to act to declare the street officially closed, and removed from the city's register of streets. I know of a case where activists successfully held up a developer's plans to build a large-scale hotel/office/shopping center by just such a means. In order to get the city council to approve what was expected to be a routine alley closing, the developer had to agree to grant the citizens substantial

concessions not required by any zoning authority. Other contingencies that might function as leverage on the developer include: government backing for private bonds; approval for sidewalk cafes or other intrusions into the public space; lane widening, new traffic lights, or any other changes to traffic patterns; parking regulations or the placement (or removal) of parking meters; certificates of occupancy for commercial tenants; and liquor licenses for any bars or restaurants in the project.

3. Check to see if **construction is being carried out according to all applicable building codes and safety regulations.** You will not be able to keep the building from going up this way, but you can almost certainly slow the work down a good deal. If you have no other leverage over the project, you should at the very least be able to get the developer to pay attention with this approach. I guarantee this: Every building put up in America today is built in violation of some written rules from somewhere. You need only study the codes closely and wait patiently for the violations to begin.

Does the construction work begin in the morning before the permitted start time? Does it go on past the time it's supposed to end by law? Is there construction activity on Sundays, when the noise statutes call for quiet? Does the decibel level during the workday exceed permitted limits? Are the workmen wearing the required safety helmets? goggles? gloves? boots? earphones? Are they parking their cars where they're not allowed to park all day? Are construction trucks using any weight-restricted streets? Have they blocked off a lane of traffic without a permit? Is the work kicking up too much dust, exceeding local air quality standards? Do they leave sawhorses in the street without safety reflectors? Is hazardous debris left out overnight where people could trip over it? Are there any holes in the chain link fence a child could crawl through? Are the construction workers sexually harassing female passersby?

For these infractions and any others you may note, you should call the building inspector to the site at once. Demand that the company be cited for each violation. If you have trouble getting enforcement for your complaints, ask your ward representative to check into the matter and get an explanation for why citations have not been issued. If blatant problems are being ignored (and this is sometimes the case in cities where the building inspectors are corrupt), call the press and have them listen while you talk to city officials. Let them videotape or photograph the violations themselves and see if they can get action. That will either result in a good story for them, or in a spurt of action by the agency responsible for enforcement.

If you can just keep at this long enough and hard enough (and you will need a small army of neighbors to assist you in your task), the developer will want you off his back so badly, he will be willing to make concessions on the project. You may not be able to get the overall size of the project scaled back, but you should at least be able to win some palliative measures: perhaps some landscaping to "screen" a blank side of the building from view; some ornamentation to help the building blend in better with the style of the neighborhood; additional space in the parking garage; shorter hours for noise-producing bars or restaurants; whatever you think will help offset problems caused by the operation of the new development. After you've done your best job of negotiating a deal, be sure to put any promises you extract in writing, lest your developer claim to have "forgotten" anything, once the building's done and there are no more construction violations left to catch.

Special Zones

Yes, dear citizen, there is more to zoning than bonuses, variances, and matter-of-right alone. Different cities, different counties enact their own special zoning classifications, tailored to achieve their own particular ends. Collectively, these are known as **special zones** (or sometimes, "Special Purpose Zones"—S-P zones, or **overlays**). There is an almost infinite variety of these things, and in much the same way that doctors, facing an infinite variety of viruses, are unable to cure the common cold, so no single zoning expert can advise you how to cope with the difficulties resulting from every variety of zone.

But I can describe some of the more widely seen types, after which I will offer up a few ideas for containing some of their more problematic effects.

The Central Business District. The CBD, as planners commonly call it, is what you would call "downtown." It is typically the highest-density zoning that your local regulations allow. In many places, the CBD rules were written in the late '60s, when companies were fleeing to the safety and tranquility of the suburbs, and planners feared that the city was dying. Though most city centers had rebounded by the late 1970s, the enticements to big developers to build taller and denser buildings in the CDB are generally still in place.

The Waterfront Zone. Intended to promote a certain style or quality of development along a city's riverfront, lakeside, or bay or ocean shoreline. Certain restrictions on development may be imposed for environmental reasons (to protect fisheries from toxic run-off, for example). In older, former manufacturing centers, abandoned warehouses and docking facilities along the waterfront tend to be rezoned for retail, residential, or office use, to encourage their rehabilitation, rather than demolition. New York's South Street Seaport

is a prominent example. Developers may receive a density bonus as an incentive to create "people places" along the water, such as promenades, plazas, outdoor markets, and scenic overlooks. (See photo.) Some space may also be set aside for parkland, monuments, or maritime history exhibits.

Enterprise Zone (or "Economic Development Opportunity Area" or "Incentive Zone," etc.). This concept is in use in thirty-seven states and the District of Columbia, and, by act of Congress, the federal government will soon establish one hundred federal enterprise zones. When a part of a city or county is economically depressed, and at least 20 percent of its residents live below the national poverty level, and the unemployment rate is at least one and a half times the national average, the area may be designated an Enterprise Zone, and any qualifying business or development that goes into that area may have the benefit of tax abatements, job training programs, marketing advice, and a host of other incentives to further development.

Arts and/or Theater Zone. The idea behind this zone is to stimulate the cultural life of the city by concentrating all the cultural attractions in one place. The zone may give special zoning consideration to art galleries, theaters, movie houses, workshops and studios, concert halls, opera and ballet centers, and possibly jazz clubs and smaller performance venues. By including space for these typically subsidy-hungry pursuits in a commercial building, a developer may be rewarded with a density bonus to be used on-site or transferred to a project in another part of town (**"transfer development rights"** or TDR's).

Tourist Zone. To promote tourism, a locality may require all buildings within a certain distance from a tourist attraction to be finished in a certain style (e.g., Indian adobe, Spanish Mission, or Western Saloon style). The zone may also permit more sidewalk vending or souvenir stands than is the case in other commercial zones. Public bathrooms may be required.

Adult Entertainment Zone (also Sexually-Oriented-Business Zone, or S-O-B zone). Some cities believe the way to handle prostitution and pornography is to declare one area of the city a sort of no-man's land, and allow all the peep-shows, strip-joints, nude wrestling arenas, and XXX-rated movie theaters to locate their businesses there. The local name for this zone may be "The Tenderloin," or the "Red Light District," "The Strip," or "The Combat

Zone." Traditionally, such areas have been located near ports, railyards, or factories, but these days they may also be found near freeway ramps, on the fringes of downtown, or in other areas where there are few if any residences. However, in some cities the trend toward "gentrification" of inner city areas will lead to the development of a middle-class neighborhood bordering on the zone—and when that happens, conflict over the zoning classification is sure to follow.

Convention Center Area. The city may build (or plan to build) a convention center. This is usually an enormous, cavernous hall that takes up several city blocks. The outside tends to be done in poured concrete, with windows or other decoration spurned as a frivolous expense. The later the center is built, the bigger it will be, as each successive city tries to woo away from other convention-center cities the largest of the annual association gatherings (the ABA, the APA, the AMA, and other high-density alphabetic assemblies). The zoning in the area may be changed, not only to permit this single, megastructure use, but also to encourage the development of the surrounding blocks by large hotels, restaurants, bars, and other amenities for the business traveller.

Mass Transit Corridor Incentive Zones. The introduction of a subway system, light rail, trolleys, trams, bus lines, or other means of mass transit may result in special zoning around designated stations or transfer points. Typically, the regulations affect parking and automobile access. Where normal zones might require a certain ratio of parking spaces per square feet of new construction, and mandate certain traffic circulation patterns, a development within a transit incentive zone will not be held to the same requirements. The theory goes, if you make it easier for people to get to work by subway, bus, train, etc., you won't need all those parking spaces. Density bonuses may also be available for developers who donate land as easements for the placement of train switching equipment or lay-bys, or who can provide direct access to stations through their buildings. There may also be incentives for developers to set up private shuttle buses to take employees to bus or subway lines or adopt some other measures to discourage commuting by private car.

Diplomatic Zone. Washington, D.C., with all its embassies and chanceries, and New York City, with its U.N. missions, both make use of diplomatic zoning, appended to the regular zoning in the form of an "overlay." The purpose of the special zone is to encourage foreign governments to establish their offices and residences in the areas so designated. By concentrating the diplomatic community in a few parts of town, the State Department is supposedly better able to deal with the building requirements and security needs of the representatives of the sovereign states recognized by our government. But because the State Department is generally more concerned with getting the reciprocal right to build larger and more fortress-like buildings for its diplomats abroad than it is about pleasing U.S. citizens, the State Department nearly always will support the efforts of foreign governments to build huge new office buildings in low-scale residential neighborhoods. This will come as a shock to many Americans, who had naturally assumed that their welfare would rate ahead of that of some obscure, shaky, and oppressive foreign regime.

Site Specific Control. In some cities (Baltimore is an example), rather than create a special zone to cover an entire part of town, the legislature empowers the planning department to tailor zoning regulations to suit the conditions of specific parcels of land that meet certain criteria. All development proposals for lots near Baltimore's Inner Harbor must first be submitted to the city's planning agency, where they are reviewed on a case-by-case basis. The city may require certain concessions or amenities, over and above what the zoning calls for, without giving away square footage as an inducement. Site plan review procedures may also permit public comments, either by letter or through hearings, to be taken into account by the planners before any approvals may be granted. In Washington, D.C., there is a minimum development size of 50,000 square feet before a project is eligible for site-specific review, and the process goes by the name, "Large Tract Review." Citizens who live in jurisdictions without this added check on excessive development may find it a concept worth exploring.

Ideas for Special Zone Problem-Solving

Citizen activists in many cities and towns have grappled with the different problems of living in a neighborhood bordered by a special zone. The following are seven different approaches citizens have tried that have helped to solve, or at least alleviate, some of the harmful effects of the zone. You may find a few applicable in your case.

1. **Establish a Buffer Zone.** When the Central Business District, the adult entertainment zone, or the tourist zone are too close to your residentially zoned neighborhood, you will surely experience some or all of the following: traffic, noise, litter, crime, drugs, and displacement of neighborhood services. One way of dealing with this is to create a buffer zone between you, by taking some area out of the special zone (do not let any territory be taken from your own neighborhood zone!) and designating it for transitional zoning.

   This new buffer area could have some characteristics of the residential area but also allow some of the higher density uses found in the special zone area—for example, in the area between the tourist zone and the residential part of the neighborhood, allow construction of low-scale hotels, bed-and-breakfasts, and inns, which serve visitors but which also create a lower-scale streetscape that is residential in appearance, like the townhouses on the adjacent streets.

A buffer zone might have prevented this clash between houses and office buildings.

The buffer zone might come about by means of mixed-use (residential/commercial) zoning, with some incentives for developers to build the housing component. This technique has worked in some cities to ease the transition between the Central Business District and surrounding neighborhoods. Developers are permitted to build office buildings facing the commercial zones, but the backs of the buildings, which border on the residential areas, must be apartment units—which may receive some property tax abatements to keep them affordable.

If suitably buffered, even adult entertainment zones may make tolerable (if not welcome) neighbors. Restaurants, cafes, taverns, jazz, dance or comedy clubs may be patronized by both the residents of the area and visitors to "The Strip." Owners of these dual-clientele businesses are likely to want to keep peace and please both the regulars and the out-of-towners. The city often welcomes a practical zoning solution to solve conflicts between two adjacent but incompatible zoning districts.

Big institutions may also fulfill the buffering function of a transition zone. A hospital, school, or government building may mark the edge of the special zone, and still be a welcome neighbor to the residents of the adjacent zone. In a neighborhood in one of the poorer parts of Washington, D.C., residents were looking for some kind of institutional use to create such a transition between the commercial zone (where drug dealing in the parking lots of stores was rampant) and their residential blocks. The city came to the rescue with the perfect institutional answer: It built a police station at the end of the shopping strip, connected to the line of stores and sharing the same parking lot.

The drug dealers have moved away, and the residents, for the first time, feel safe when going out at night to do a little shopping.

2. **Demarcation of Zones.** The opposite approach is to insist on a clear separation of the incompatible zones, to limit contact between them by physical means: by plantings—trees, bushes, vines, or a landscaped berm; or by structures—fences, walls, waterworks, murals; or by traffic patterns—traffic diverters, or a system of one-way streets or a maze of cul-de-sacs to keep visitors to the special zone from straying into the residential area. This approach is often used in fast-growing suburbs where new "city centers" have sprung up in what used to be purely "bedroom communities." The difficulty with this technique often comes in deciding where the separating elements or barriers should be built. With traffic diverters, for example, those living on designated through-streets, which continue to provide access to the neighborhood from the special zone, often feel left out, or even betrayed. For the demarcation idea to work for the whole community, such planning must come as a result of consultation with all residents, and with advice from traffic experts. To respond with barriers only for the block with the loudest-complaining residents is to invite trouble.

3. **Re-Mix the Mix.** Special zones are intended, naturally enough, to serve special interests. In the course of working out the zoning that pleases, say, the arts community, or the tourist industry, the desires of the average citizen are sometimes overlooked. It may only be necessary to modify some of the special zone's guidelines to recognize the residents' legitimate interests. So, if a tourist zone is given over totally to "touristy" uses (it's all vendors and hotels and souvenir shops), it should be modified to include zoning incentives for other types of businesses, too. This formula might go something like this: A separate use classification is created for "Tourist-Oriented Businesses" (the list of such T-O-B uses to be defined in the regulations), and then a cap is set of, say, 50 percent for those businesses in the zone. That means at least 50 percent of the stores in the zone will have to be "real-life" operations, which sell things the neighbors want to buy.

My own neighborhood zoning committee worked out a formula of this sort with city officials. I live on a block between the National Zoo and one of the biggest movie theaters in the country. The neighborhood shopping area was in danger of losing all the ordinary service establishments—the dry cleaners, the drug store, the grocery store, and so on—and new bars and restaurants seemed to be the only businesses moving in. The solution (which is working out very nicely) was to place a 25 percent limit on the number of bars and restaurants located in buildings fronting the major avenue. The occupancy rate for this type of use was already at 23 percent when the limit was announced. Since the new regulations have been in effect, several storefronts have turned over, and the new tenants include a health-food store, a fish market, and a bookstore.

4. **Reorder the Priorities.** In some cases you may not be able to reconcile conflicting interests. The operation of the special zone—especially if it's an adult entertainment zone —may be absolutely inimical to the safety and livability of the residents of the adjoining neighborhood. When that happens, it will be necessary to force city officials to choose which side they're on. But when pressing for a choice, a neighborhood should first make sure that it has the voting strength and political clout to ensure that the government comes down on the right side. When city officials put the needs of local residents above the business interests of property owners in the special zone, they take steps, either to limit the number of blocks in the special zone, or to remove it altogether from the residential part of the city, and reestablish it far from any inhabited ground.

5. **The Band-Aid Approach.** Most city administrations react to neighborhood complaints with patch-up or cosmetic cures. Rather than take the time to discover the underlying causes and the long-term solution, politicians oftentimes go for the fastest, cheapest way to get the troublesome citizens off their backs (and out of the headlines). Let's say you have a special waterfront zone, developed in the "festival marketplace" style of Baltimore's Inner Harbor, or New Orleans' Riverwalk. To keep the tourists coming back, the developer puts on different weekend events: fireworks displays, band concerts, street acrobatics, and other performances that can draw tens of thousands of spectators—most of them arriving by car. People park illegally all over neighborhood streets and sidewalks, they laugh and chat loudly as they return to their cars at 3 a.m., and they

"Festival marketplaces" are great tourist draws, but they also bring problems that need "band-aid" solutions.

leave litter all over your lawn for you to pick up on Sunday morning. You and your neighbors want to see some restrictions on the outdoor festivities, but city officials find it a lot easier just to promise to send in some tow-trucks, a few extra street-sweepers, and some policemen on overtime to deal with the fall-out from the commercial activity, rather than tackle the issue head on. But in most cases, where full development has already occurred and it's too late to unbuild it, this "after-the-fact fix-up" approach may be the most help you can get.

6. **The Voluntary Solution**. When the city is committed to promote the purposes served by the special zone above the neighborhood's interests, and the residents have been unsuccessful in their attempts to have the rules of the zone modified to suit their needs, they may have to turn to their own resources to take on the problem. The neighborhood may form a committee to decide what action is needed, what it will cost, and how to pay for it. Is a line of evergreen trees desired to demarcate the zones? Then hire a landscape firm to come up with a design, raise the money to buy the trees, and apply for a permit to sink some tree boxes in the sidewalk.

A coalition of neighborhood merchants around the National Zoo have done exactly that. The street their stores face is zoned to allow sidewalk vendors with carts placed every few feet. For years the vendors have fought one another for the spaces available, slept all night in their carts, and used the gutters as their toilet. After pressure from neighborhood merchants failed to reduce the number of vendor-licenses permitted in the area, somewhat sneakily, but cleverly, they hit upon the idea of using landscaping to accomplish the same end. They raised the money to plant large spreading trees and got permission to set down benches every few feet. City officials saw the benches and trees only as a pleasant way to increase tourist comfort. They never stopped to think that each tree-box removed one vendor cart-space from the public sidewalk. Each bench cluster removed another. The small businessmen, working together with the citizens' organization, achieved their goal by their own expenditure and effort, when constant meetings and complaints to the planning department to restrict the vending zone had failed.

Other voluntary techniques might include:
- Closing or redesigning privately owned alleys and walkways to demarcate residential areas from commercial zones.
- Meeting with owners of businesses in the special zone and seeking their cooperation to:

— curtail public drunkenness;

— lower the sound levels of amplified music; or

— make parking arrangements for patrons on private lots rather than on residential streets.

- Proposing alternatives that suit the needs of both the neighborhood and the owners in the special zone; for example, if the regulations in the Arts and Theater District encourage brightly lit neon signs, but some residents are disturbed by lights that blink in their windows at night, the sign-owners could be asked to redirect the light-output so that it is visible only within the designated theater-zone. Or the owner might be amenable to installing a shield to prevent the light from shining in the unwanted direction. Or at the very least, the owner might offer to pay for black-out curtains for the residents of apartment units that face the theater-zoned street. It could well be worth the expenditure to defuse the neighbors' discontent.

Any such concessions are easier to get if the neighborhood unites to ask for them in an organized way, rather than leaving it up to the individuals who live closest to the problem zone.

7. **The Solution Before the Problem Begins**. Conflicts between residential zones and special zones can be minimized or eliminated altogether if the neighbors are made full partners in the process whereby adjacent streets are rezoned for special purposes. Planners should be required to give direct notification to all residents who live a specified distance from the zone, while the rules governing its function are still in the drafting stage. They should actively solicit the neighbors' ideas, and establish a working citizens/city-planners special zone committee, and let that group together come up with a formula for mix of uses, design guidelines, traffic and parking measures, whatever else is needed—to achieve the sort of development the special zone is meant to bring about, without taking anything away from the quality of life in adjacent areas. Compromises that are necessary for both sides can thus be weighed, problems anticipated, and solutions studied, before any development occurs and the two sides become incontrovertible enemies.

This cooperative planning arrangement should be mandated by your city planning department's operating procedures; if it isn't, you might want to work for some reform.

SAVING AN OLD BUILDING

The Historic Preservation Movement Today

Do you think of historic preservation as one of those quaint hobbies like genealogy or antique-collecting taken up by blue-haired dowagers? I used to. The same people who like to talk about their ancestry and tell you how far back their lines can be traced are the ones interested in old buildings, or so I thought. It just wasn't a topic for people like me, whose grandparents came over from Eastern Europe in steerage. But that was before I got involved in a zoning battle with a developer who wanted to surround a landmark mansion with a ring of ugly, little townhouses. Suddenly, I began to see the subject in a new light.

In this I was aided by the architectural historian who defended the property from the developer's plan. She spoke so vividly, so passionately about the people who had built the mansion, the place it held in our history, the values its presence still embodied for us today, that I was won over to her view. Before, I had just seen historic preservation as a tactic to be used in negotiations with the developer—a way to force him to scale back his townhouse scheme. After her testimony I was resolved to work to keep the mansion unobstructed for its own sake.

My conversion from anti-development activist to preservationist was not greeted everywhere with approval. My own mother, a veteran of the civil rights movement in the South of the 1960s, was less than understanding. "You're marching to save the home of the Post Cereal heiress?" she asked, incredulous. She thought she'd raised me to fight for the rights of the underprivileged against the rich and powerful. But the assignment of roles in this case wasn't so obvious. The heiress was long gone and her formerly grand estate had been let to go to brambles. A rich development corporation now wanted to transform it into tract lots for a profit. The residents of the area, who were scrambling to raise money, had the clearest claim to the role of the underdog.

But my mother's initial reaction, and my own former attitude, are what you'll commonly encounter if historic preservation becomes an issue in your case. You can take heart, however, because the current trend is on your side. Over the past decade the historic preservation movement has been shedding its elitist associations and working up some populist momentum, the diversity of its supporters growing as the definition of the word "historic" continues to expand. It used to be that the preservation movement was focused almost entirely on buildings fitting one or more of the following limited criteria:

- They were the works of great architects—Benjamin Latrobe, Stanford White, Louis Sullivan, Frank Lloyd Wright, and others of similar august stature.
- They are grand or imposing in scale, such as the stately homes of the Astors and Vanderbilts, or government buildings like courthouses and state capitols, or towering symbols of corporate strength, like the Chrysler Building, the Woolworth Building, and the Empire State Building.
- They form an ensemble of buildings exemplifying a certain style, like the French Quarter in New Orleans, the whaling ports of Mystic and Old Saybrook, Connecticut, and the Spanish-style buildings of San Francisco's Mission District.

But after battles were fought and won to save these and other easily recognizable examples of architectural merit from the wrecking ball, preservationists began to look at some of the less-obvious, less monumental buildings and districts that were being threatened with destruction. They began to consider the architectural heritage left behind, not just by the rich and famous, but by ordinary workers and farmers. As a result one can now find historic marker plaques on many factories, warehouses, shipyards, farmhouses, and barns.

As blacks and other minorities have struggled through the years to claim an equal share in our society, so, too, have they been working to see that the artifacts of their presence in this country are not swept aside. The television series "Roots" played a substantial role in the rediscovery and landmarking of places of significance in black history: Slave cabins, auction blocks, sites of slave uprisings—places that had once been seen as an embarrassment to be forgotten—have been included in our inventory of historic places and so preserved as a chilling reminder of the lessons of our past.

It used to be that only structures built more than fifty years ago were eligible for landmark recognition. But that has changed, too, as developers have attempted to take down some of the most distinctive of buildings in the modern style. When the Lever House (of 1952) was saved from demolition by the New York Landmarks Commission in 1982, the rigid criterion of age was the only thing that came down. Now future generations will be able to perceive the building as an important indicator of the aesthetic ideals of its time and place.

Great size, as well as age, has lost out as a qualifying factor. Where landmarks of the past nearly all stood out from afar (whether skyscrapers, cathedrals, lighthouses, bridges, or monuments), now objects as small as street lamps, neon signs, park benches, and garden gazebos have been deemed worthy of landmark protection.

Where many landmarks used to be temples of "High Culture" —opera houses, museums, theaters, libraries, etc.—now we see merit in saving buildings exemplifying some of the mass-culture habits that make us what we are. That is why the first golden-arched McDonald's in California has been landmarked. And it's why diners, gas stations, movie palaces, and even roller coasters (like the Cyclone at Coney Island) have been taken in under the umbrella of our preservation laws across the country.

Nor does the architecture have to be solemn, nor the engineering complex, for a building to be deemed important by our landmark commissions today. Something as whimsical as a hot dog stand built in the shape of a giant dachshund, or a souvenir stand contained in a sixty-foot wigwam can be accorded designation if it is truly one of a kind. Or the building might be the last of its kind, like the only log cabin left in the state. Or it could even be something existing by the thousands—like one of the Sears houses, ordered from the company's 1920 catalog and shipped in pieces for assembly on a lot—as long as it is a particularly well-preserved example of its type and style. Or just the opposite—the building may be a rare example in one area of something quite

Historic landmarks can come in all shapes and sizes. This Chinese pagoda, a national landmark, is actually Army housing in Forest Glen, Maryland.

commonplace in another; for example, the only prairie-style sod-house found east of the Mississippi.

With so many types of buildings being recognized as historic, these days it might be simpler to define what historic preservation is *not*. It is *not* preservation of the beautiful: A building can be homely, drab, even an eyesore in its present shape, and still convey meaning from the past (though people are generally quicker to grasp the meaning if they find the object's appearance pleasing to contemplate). Beauty and historic value are unrelated qualities; only the latter cannot be copied.

Though a developer may propose to rebuild, brick for brick, an exact replica of a building that was lost, it isn't the same thing, and can never be, because it doesn't reflect the outlook, habits, and aspirations of the people who built the original design. When a developer is denied permission to replace an old building with a new one in a "historical" style, he may well seek to move the old building to a different site, so that the old site is free for new construction. Under certain circumstances, such relocation may be acceptable. For example, if the old building to be saved is a tavern in a Pennsylvania farming village, and the developer wants to move it from one street to another one just like it a few blocks away, the relationship of the tavern to the town will still be apparent, visitors will still be able to understand who frequented the place, and their experience of drinking there will not be substantially different from that of the farmworkers who were its patrons a hundred years ago.

But if the tavern was one where Lincoln dined on his way to Gettysburg, and the developer is proposing to move it away from the rail line, then visitors to the tavern won't be able to approach it as Lincoln did, and its value as a preserved moment in Civil War history will have vanished along with its physical setting.

When and if a building can be moved is something for architectural historians to debate—and they do, they do! It's not at all unusual for different experts to view the same case and come out with diametrically opposite evaluations of a building's historical significance, its architectural merits, and the impact of proposed changes. A well-heeled developer seldom has any trouble finding a highly reputable authority to approve of the way he wishes to dispose of his landmarked property. Nor is it difficult for the dissenting neighbors to find an eminent name to attack the developer's plan as a travesty. What often results is a case of "duelling experts," and the side with the sharpest combat skills usually wins.

Cases may be interpreted differently, not only by the individuals hired to examine them, but also according to regional variations in the strength of the preservation movement. In the fast-expanding economies of the New South, for example, the trend is to favor what's new, modern, efficient, and good for business, above what is old, unglamorous, and hard to adapt for today's commercial needs. So in cities like Atlanta, Richmond, and Dallas, sleek glass towers have gone up, virtually unchallenged, in the place of the smaller, more gracious buildings of the pre-boom years. In more staid, tradition-bound New England, on the other hand, townspeople will sometimes fight to keep property-owners from changing the color of paint on their shutters or putting up a chain-link rather than a white picket fence.

Beyond regional differences, there has also developed something of an ideological schism in the historic preservation movement today. One side views preservation as a shield, to be used only in defense of the most historic properties that are threatened by demolition, while the other views it as a sword, to be wielded aggressively to keep developers on the defensive. Those of the shield-faction hold that overuse of historic designation is diluting its purpose and causing the public to be skeptical that landmarked buildings are really important; but the sword-faction argues that in previous years when the more passive view of preservation held sway, thousands of marvelous old buildings were lost, and that militancy is necessary to preserve what remains of our architectural heritage.

How your area fits into the preservation picture, regionally and ideologically, will have much effect on your chances of saving an old building now threatened with demolition. The only way to find out is to get out and start asking questions.

About Preservation Law

The first thing you'll need to know is who handles historic landmarks in your local government. Call the general information line and find out the exact name of the agency responsible, and get the phone number and address.

Once you know who to call, you should set up an appointment to visit the landmarks office and talk to a staff member who can "walk you through" your local landmark laws. The legislation is often complex, covering a wide range of situations and "what if's" for different scenarios, and you will want to take the time you need to understand how it works. Failure to meet any of the legal requirements in a case all too often results in the loss of the building the neighborhood was trying to save.

The following are some questions you'll need to have answered:

What makes a building worthy of landmark protection under the law? Does it have to be X-many years old? Must a complete history be done (must every one of its past owners be researched and described?) Must the architect have been prominent? Must the building be intact, or is an altered building acceptable? What about cultural importance? What other criteria have been used to justify landmark designation?

If a building seems to fit the criteria, who may apply to have it designated? A historical society? A citizens' association? Must the organization have preservation listed among the purposes in its charter? What materials must be submitted along with the application in order to show standing to file?

Who prepares the text of the application? Must the writer be a credentialed architectural historian? Are photographs required in the application? How many, and what size? (It might be helpful if you could take a look at an example of a successful filing in a case similar to yours.)

Does a completed application block the issuance of demolition permits? What about permits for additional construction? Is there a time limit in which the hearing must be held? Who notifies the developer that the application has been filed? How does the public find out? If by newspaper advertisement, who pays for the printing?

Who judges the case? How many are on the panel, and what constitutes a quorum? How often do they meet? How many are architects? Historians? From other fields of expertise?

How are hearings handled? Is there cross-examination by parties? Are lawyers usually engaged? How far in advance must one sign up to testify? Must requests be in writing? What kind of evidence is considered? Is a slide-show helpful? What about a videotape? Is there a time limit on the presentation? What supporting witnesses may be heard: neighbors? other laymen who have a stake in the outcome? Are letters by out-of-state experts given much weight, or is live testimony preferred?

What kind of opposing evidence is admissible? Must all testimony be strictly centered on the historic or architectural merit of the building at issue? Or will the owner's economic considerations be judged relevant? What other arguments may the owner advance to oppose designation of his property?

How does the landmark panel arrive at a decision? By debate in a public forum? Will they make a site inspection? Can they be accompanied by the parties if they do? Must their decision come within a certain time frame of the hearing?

If they vote to designate, what impact does that have? Is just the exterior protected by the law, or can interiors be landmarked, too (and is that a separate process)? Are there different levels of designation? (For example: a Category I landmark, which prohibits demolition or alteration; a Category II, which prohibits demolition but allows alteration or addition, provided it is done in a style compatible with the landmarked structure; and a Category III, in which demolition or alteration will be discouraged, but still allowed under a variety of special circumstances.)

Very important to understand: After landmark status is conferred, what are the special exceptions enumerated in the law under which the structure can be demolished, altered, or added to? A developer intent on getting around a landmark designation will look for any loopholes that exist, and exploit them to the fullest. If the law in your area permits a wide variety of exceptions, or if the rules to get the exceptions are so vaguely worded that almost anyone who applies for one can qualify, then your landmark law is weak, and possibly of little use, ultimately, in your battle to save the building.

The following are some common exceptions allowed by state and local landmark laws:

Economic Hardship. If the owner of a landmark building can show that maintaining the building as is does not provide him with a reasonable return, he may seek to have it demolished and replaced by a new structure, or altered to increase its income-earning potential. Economic hardship exceptions are intended to be used by small businessmen or nonprofit institutions in land-marked commercial buildings, or by owners of houses in historic districts, who, if held to the strictest standards of the landmark law, might have to sell their property and leave the neighborhood. These days, however, many big developers will buy a landmarked property that has been allowed to deteriorate, and argue that the cost of restoring it for modern commercial use is too high, and therefore request demolition under the economic hardship provisions of the law. (If an owner buys a landmarked property in good condition, and intentionally allows it to deteriorate beyond his ability to repair it, so as to qualify for demolition under the economic hardship exception, he can be accused of "demolition by neglect"—an abuse of the law most jurisdictions will not tolerate.)

Replacement Project of "Special Merit." Some laws recognize that new projects may be of outstanding design quality and offer amenities far superior to those found in a building within a historic district or having a landmark designation. If a proposal for a new building meets the standards set in the law, it may be recognized as a "project of special merit" and be permitted to go up on the site of an existing historic landmark, which would first be demolished. Recognition of special merit may be more easily obtained if the new building serves some identified social purpose, such as housing for the poor. A developer may argue that the historic building now occupying the site cannot be adapted to create apartment units, and that only a new design can fulfill the project's meritorious intent. A well-written "special merit" exception should require the developer to prove that there is a true public benefit in what he proposes (not just benefit to himself) and that the same benefit cannot be achieved through an adaptive reuse of the existing landmarked building.

"Practical Difficulty." The owner of a historic building may be able to prove that the landmarked building is impractical for modern use, and so must be altered or demolished for a new building. A blacksmith's shop, to pick a clear case, would be of little use to most owners today, and a significant amount of redesign might be necessary to turn it into a restaurant or some other more marketable venture. Historic downtown churches, whose supporting members have moved out to the suburbs, are frequently the subject of "practical difficulty" applications. Since there is no congregation willing to buy the church for religious purposes, its greatest dollar value rests in the underlying land, which can be sold for office development—provided demolition permits can be obtained. In Chicago in the last few years the Catholic archdiocese has announced plans to seek demolition for several of its grander, older inner city cathedrals, using the "practical difficulty" exception.

Fulfillment of Code Requirements. Historic buildings constructed with the technology of an earlier age seldom meet all the building code requirements of our time. They are rarely handicapped-accessible. Often they lack the elevators, parking spaces, garbage disposals, dishwashers, air-conditioning, high-capacity electrical wiring, and other features prescribed by modern building codes. Fire safety systems such as sprinklers and standpipes cannot be retrofitted, in many cases, without gutting the interior of the building. Many state laws exempt designated historic landmarks from meeting the same code requirements mandated for new constructions. But in other states, the "low-tech" nature of older buildings can be used as a reason to seek demolition or alteration. Sometimes the developer must first show that retrofitting has been studied and rejected as impossible or prohibitively expensive; but in states with weak landmark laws, no such burden may be placed on the owner of a landmark building before demolition is approved.

Other exceptions may be possible under the law in your state, and you need to get a staff person from your local landmarks commission to explain to you, in simple English, what they are and how they work. You will also need to know what type of hearing process is followed for the consideration of such exception requests. (Ask the same type of questions you asked about the landmark designation process: Who hears the case, who can apply for exceptions, how can the neighbors participate, how often do owners get the exceptions they apply for?)

Now suppose that a developer loses his case against designation of his property, and fails to qualify for any of the allowable exceptions to the law: How does the appeal process work? Who hears the case, and what are appealable issues? How often have designations been overturned? Does the

city defend the designation, or is it largely up to the private historic preservation organization to put together a brief? What happens to the development
plans for the historic site during the time that the appeal is pending?

Once you know the answers to these last few questions, you should have
a fairly good sense of how helpful the historic preservation process will be in
your case. But no matter how well you understand the workings of the law,
unless you are a certified architectural historian, you are still going to need
some expert advice. If you can afford it, you will benefit from consulting a
lawyer who specializes in historic preservation law. Your local historical society
or your local bar association can give you a referral.

If you can't afford a
preservation lawyer,
you should at least talk
to other citizens who
have worked with the
preservation process in
your area. Ask your
government officials
for the names of those
involved in the most
recent case that sounds
similar to yours and
call, introduce yourself,
and ask for some ad-
vice. You probably will
be given a wealth of in-
formation: names of ar-
chitectural historians
who might be willing to
research your historic

*Another one
bites the
dust—worthy
old Baltimore
building dies
a slow death,
Could this
have been
prevented?*

building; how much they charge; names of university students who might do
some of the legwork for class credit; what sort of displays and testimony are
likely to impress which landmark commissioners the most; and tips about the
political mix of the commission, which could be the key to understanding their
votes on the cases they've heard.

As with zoning cases, if you have volunteers who are diligent, well-organized, and politically savvy, you can probably handle nearly all of the work
involved in the filing and preparation for the landmark designation case,
without paying out a lot of money to lawyers and other experts. Just be sure,
before you file the application in final form, that you've had it checked over
by someone familiar with the legal requirements for acceptance (that person

doesn't have to be a lawyer). That way, you can avoid the omissions or technical errors. More than a few historic buildings have fallen through such slips.

Negotiating Preservation

Let's say that you've just finished investigating your local landmark process, and you've discovered, to your dismay, that your state's laws are weak, that few landmark applications are successful, and that even when landmarks are designated, the developers still qualify for all sorts of exceptions, and so are able to knock their buildings down. Don't give up yet. You may still have a good chance to save that building—but through the bargaining process rather than the public hearing route.

File that landmark application anyway, and don't be surprised if the developer asks you to sit down with him and try to work things out. Since all developers know the meaning of the phrase "time is money," and since landmark hearings nearly always cause the developer a long delay in his plans, he'll be calculating the dollars it will cost him each day he's unable to break ground. But if he can get your agreement to withdraw the landmark application, in exchange for his promise to you to preserve the building (perhaps adding onto it in a way that gives him the square footage he's seeking but which still respects the integrity of the original design)—you may have a deal all of you can live with.

The key to working out such a deal is getting a true picture of the costs and returns involved for what each side hopes to accomplish. You should both be trying to "make the numbers work." Your side should be looking to show that preservation of an existing building (with compatibly scaled additions, if necessary) can bring in about the same return for the developer as tearing the building down and starting again from scratch.

You may want to consider the following factors in working out your calculations:

1. Renovation of an existing building saves the developer many costs: of demolition, of architect's fees for a new design, of excavation and laying of new foundations, and of all the materials for the new building. Unless the old building is a complete disaster on the inside, many of its structural and ornamental elements may be reused, for additional savings on interior design.

2. If the developer will support landmark designation and if the property is then listed on the National Register of Historic Places, he can qualify for a 20 percent federal tax credit for the money spent on rehabilitation

work in excess of the cost-basis of the building. This 20 percent tax credit is a powerful incentive for preservation, and it may well make the "bottom line" on the restored building end up better than or equal to that for the replacement design.

3. The developer may also be able to donate a "facade easement" to the National Trust for Historic Preservation or some other recognized conservancy, bringing with it additional tax advantages. This means that the developer gives to the preservation organization a kind of guardianship over the outward appearance of his property; he can then deduct from his taxes the fair market value of the property-right he has transferred to that organization. An experienced real estate or tax attorney is essential for drawing up the facade easement agreement and figuring the best deduction that will withstand IRS scrutiny.

4. Beautifully restored older buildings can attract the highest quality tenants, who, in order to project a prestige image, are willing to pay prestige-rate rents. Look over the commercial real estate ads in your city and find examples of this close by, if you can. If not, pick up the real estate trade journals for other cities (New York, Boston, Washington, D.C., San Francisco) to find numerous examples of the "prestige factor" at work.

5. On the column for the cost of the demolish-and-replace option for the site, be sure to tack on the expenditure for at least two years' worth of hearings, public relations work, legal motions, appeals, political lobbying, and incidental costs, in addition to the cost of interest and property tax while the land sits idle all the while. Don't forget, too, that a lengthy battle with the neighborhood leaves deep scars and memories; even if he wins his fight, the next time the same developer is thinking of doing a project in the neighborhood, he'll be met with bitterness and redoubled opposition. By working out a settlement with the neighborhood, he will not only avoid present costs but will earn a bonus of goodwill redeemable in future projects.

6. In exchange for his offer to preserve an old building, the developer may get concessions from the neighbors on other aspects of the development. Example: In the small 1929 commercial center in my neighborhood, the developer needed zoning approval to close the alley behind his building and build over it, out to his property line. The organized neighbors offered to support his request for a variance as part of a deal in which he would agree to renovate and compatibly add onto the existing building, rather than tear it down.

7. Property values increase when a building is landmarked. Caution: This can be a sticky issue. You will want to persuade the developer that the

net value of his investment will rise if he supports the landmark designation; on the other hand, you don't want the small businesspeople who have their shops nearby to think that designation of a property on their block will result in automatic rent increases for *them*—otherwise they will very likely come into the hearing and speak in opposition to the landmark application. You need to study the market values and relationships between properties in your neighborhood before you make any assertions about valuation changes, up or down.

Property owners may also be of two minds about the effect of designation. This was demonstrated by the Scribner family, who owned the landmarked bookstore of the same name in New York. When designation of the exterior of the store was first proposed, the family opposed it, citing, among other reasons, the fear that the landmark's restrictions on development would lead to a *decrease* in the store's value. However, when they put the building up for sale, they asked for (and received) a *premium* price for it, based on the fact that it was a recognized historic landmark and so could attract a prestigious tenant. (The Benetton chain of Italy bought it, intending to gut the Beaux-Arts interior and turn it into one of their standard sweater-stores. After the New York City Landmarks Commission vetoed the plan, however, the company had little choice but to seek a bookstore tenant for the space. Brentano's, a subsidiary of Waldenbooks, Inc., has now restored the interior to its intended purpose of selling books—a move hailed by both preservationists and booklovers alike.

An Invaluable Aid to the Citizen-Preservationist

If you are considering working on getting a building in your neighborhood landmarked—or even if you aren't—there's a resource book available that can tell you everything you ever wanted to know about any conceivable aspect of any type of case. It's called *All About Old Buildings: The Whole Preservation Catalog,* and it's published by the Preservation Press of the National Trust for Historic Preservation (editor, Diane Maddex). Its 430 large-format pages are crammed full of listings of organizations to contact for support, places to go to get information on the law or historical facts or other research needs, and hundreds of recommendations of helpful books and magazines. I just can't say enough in praise of this book. It's saved me hours upon hours of legwork, and I know it can do the same for almost any neighborhood activist. It's an attractive-looking book, with many wonderful pictures, too. If you can't find it in your nearest well-stocked bookstore, you can write to The Preservation Press, c/o The National Trust for Historic Preservation, 1785 Massachusetts Avenue, N.W., Washington, D.C. 20036. A discount on the $24.95 price is available for National Trust members.

The use you make of any of the above factors will depend in part on the nature of the real estate market in your area at the moment, and how well the developer's proposal, and your counter-proposal, fit in with that market, as well as how skilled are the negotiators for each of the parties. Your developer probably is an old hand at deal-making, but he may be expecting the people from your side to be a bit naive. You'll want to show him that you've done a thorough and competent analysis of the site and that what your side is offering is not only practical from his point of view—it's attractive.

If anyone in your group has ever negotiated on a high level before (a banker, a lawyer, a broker, or a corporate executive), by all means make use of his or her skills. If you're all new at this, you may want to pick up any of the multitude of books available on honing your negotiating skills. (I think a short, snappy book like Harvey Mackay's paperback how-to, *Swim with the Sharks without Being Eaten Alive*, can provide a few simple tips to bolster your confidence and give you some good opening gambits.)

Archaeology

If you live in an area where the buildings are new, or lacking in architectural distinction, or if the property you're interested in preserving is land, not buildings, you may assume this chapter has nothing to offer you. But that may not be the case. In many states, land itself is covered under historic preservation laws, provided it is of archeological interest. It may have been the site of settlement by Indian tribes, or colonists from Europe, or immigrants from anywhere else in the world. Any artifacts they left behind should be carefully excavated, catalogued, and preserved.

Provided your state has such an archaeological section in the law, you should find out if any artifacts of possible significance have turned up during the digging of foundations of the building on the site. If so, work on the project may be halted, to give the experts time to evaluate the site and make recommendations for its proper archaeological examination.

How do you know if any archaeological potential exists? You will have to do some research into the history of the site. How far back was it inhabited, and by whom? You'll probably want expert help in finding this out, and you may get it from the members of the archaeology department of your nearest large university. If digging has already started, try to get permission for an archaeologist to visit the site and take a look at any items uncovered. Glass objects, bones, arrowheads, bricks, or stones that were once part of foundations to earlier houses are the sorts of things that indicate a need for further study. And that may be enough to bring the project at least to a temporary standstill.

Terrence McCarthy/The New York Times

This is just what has happened to a proposal to build an 80–million-dollar beachfront hotel on Maui in Hawaii. The discovery of an ancient Hawaiian burial ground has resulted in a moratorium on further construction. Opposition has surfaced, not just from neighbors, but from descendants of the Native Hawaiians, who wish to see the place of prehistoric importance recognized as sacrosanct to their religion. Their anti-development group is called Malama Na Kapuna, or "Caring for Our Ancestors," and their position is that the hotel, not their ancestor's bones, is what should be relocated because of the find.

In California, especially, strict interpretation of the California Environmental Quality Act has forced developers to consider the archeological impact of their plans on the land they intend to excavate. In December, 1988 in San Francisco an eighteen-story office project was halted while archaeologists sifted through the rubble of a recently demolished nine-story building for a treasure trove of artifacts from a Gold Rush settlement in Chinatown. The *New York Times* quoted Professor Allen Pastron as calling it, "The best site I've ever found in San Francisco and the first Gold Rush site ever in Chinatown." (See photo above.)

Of course, once the artifacts have all been collected and catalogued, the land will then be developable as planned. However, in some special cases where the archaeological find is of such significance and is so extensive that digging must go on for years, the developer will sometimes seek to sell or trade the unbuildable land for a parcel without the archaeological constraints. A developer with particular tax considerations and the right spirit of philanthropy may even be persuaded to donate the valuable land to a university or foundation for further research. Such an outcome may be a rare event, but there is nothing to be lost by suggesting that course of action to a developer once the archaeological find has been uncovered.

Walker's Row: A Case for All Seasons

Real life cases each illustrate a point or two about the historic preservation process, but no single case I've come across has all the major elements combined. So I have put together a composite story based on several different cases I've worked on to serve as an all-purpose guide.

The Challenge of Demolition

Posted on a pole installed in the middle of a city block this sign recently appeared: "COMING SOON! Luxurious Condominium Units. Parking. Close to Subway. All Amenities. For Preview, Call Ripperman Development Company." An artist's rendering showed an eight-story building, which was exactly as tall and as wide as the zoning on the block allowed. But the buildings now standing on the block are much smaller—they're modest brick rowhouses dating from the turn of the century, no more than three stories high. Curious about the change, one of the neighbors called the number on the sign, and soon received a glossy brochure in the mail. In it the architect of the new building (who was from a respected local firm) described the style of his creation as "contextural"—meaning it was designed to fit in gracefully with the forms of the surrounding buildings. It was certainly no bigger than many nearby apartment buildings (most of which were built in the '40s and '50s, before the eight-story limit took effect, and so reach heights of twelve to fourteen stories); and it was to be made of red brick, matching the color used most commonly in the neighborhood, and it would feature window ledges, pediments, quoins, and other bits of ornamentation, adapted (but not slavishly copied) from the surrounding buildings. Neighbors who saw it generally agreed it was a handsome piece of work.

Those same neighbors, even so, agreed without a second thought that it would be a shame to lose the three-story rowhouses that made up the old block. They, too, were handsome, and they were there first. Why tear them down to make room for something bigger but not necessarily better? Soon after hearing of the new plan, the neighbors met and discussed what, if anything, they could do to keep the old row intact.

No one had any experience in historic preservation, but of the eight people initially assembled, each knew enough to get the project started. John F., a lawyer, took as his task the reading of the state's law to find out what was involved in filing for a landmark, and what protection such a move would grant. Cindy D., a history major in college who now worked as a librarian, was to start researching the history of the building to see if it could possibly qualify for landmarking according to the criteria in the law. She was to be assisted by

Emily H., a retired dressmaker, who had lived all her life on the block and who remembered who some of the original residents were. Lisa K. and Frank G. were to get the word out to residents of nearby streets and apartment buildings that the demolition was planned, and solicit money, volunteers, and ideas on how to proceed. David B., a businessman, agreed to approach the developer on behalf of the group to see if he was set on demolition, or was willing to enter into negotiations for the block's preservation. Sam S., a union leader with a lot of friends in politics, said he'd call the city and state councilmembers he knew and sound them out as to their reactions to the proposal. Kathy M. would take notes at meetings and keep records for the newly formed organization on her home computer.

What each group member found out was encouraging from the start. The law did appear to be strong, and other buildings like the ones to be torn down had been landmarked in recent cases. The developer was willing to sit down and discuss the matter, and other neighbors were just as willing to contribute money and volunteer time, so that while the negotiations were going on, an architectural historian could be hired and a landmark application prepared, to be submitted should the negotiations break down.

Following a recommendation from the chairman of the city's historical society, a certified architectural historian, Nancy R., was hired to work on the case. Being immediately impressed with the quality of the buildings to be saved and shocked at the prospect of demolition, Nancy offered to take the case without a retainer, at one-third off her usual rate. She wanted to start working right away, without waiting to see what the group's fund-raising capabilities would be.

In less than two weeks she had compiled enough information to justify the filing of an application. The block qualified for landmark status, her report concluded, not just by virtue of its characteristically 1890s style, but also by virtue of who built it, who inhabited it, and how those people contributed to the cultural and economic life of the city.

She began by describing in detail the physical features of the houses themselves. There were nine of them, each with a slightly different pattern of brickwork, and different projections. Some had bay windows, some turrets, and some dormers. There was also a pleasant variation in the styles of the front stoops (some were straight, some curved, some with stone planters, some with wrought-iron railings, etc.) But for all these differences, the block formed a harmonious whole.

No architect had designed the houses; they were the product of the Walker Development Company, which had built blocks upon blocks of similar rowhouses in the city from the 1880s, when the company was founded, to 1931, when the Depression finally led to its bankruptcy. Many of these Walker blocks were in designated historic districts in other parts of the city. This block was the only one in this section of town, and was surrounded by larger apartment buildings constructed from the 1940s to 1950s. What made the rowhouse block even more unusual was that it was the first project undertaken by the company after its founder and first president, Eli Walker, had died, and had been replaced by his widow, Emma. She was the only female builder ever to leave her mark on the city, and being so new to the position, she paid special attention to the progress of the work. When she died, her notes on the project were found among her papers, which were then transferred to the city-history collection at the main public library. Those notes remain an invaluable aid to understanding much about life in her time: what sort of housing was wanted, how houses were marketed, how city approval was won, how labor and management battled over wages and working conditions, and a wide variety of other subjects, all minutely recorded by the exacting Mrs. Walker.

While Nancy, the professional historian, was focussing on the written record of the notes and the patterns of the buildings themselves as a guide to local history, the two amateur historians of the group, Cindy and Emily, were doing their own research on the people who had lived in the buildings, and planning an oral history presentation to supplement Nancy's scholarly nomination of the row as a landmark.

Emily wrote to her childhood friends, whose parents had been among the first owners of the houses, and who grew up on the street as she had done. Two responded with tape-recorded reminiscences of life in the twenties and even earlier, telling of the legend of the bootlegger who was supposed to have occupied one of the houses and made a fortune selling bathtub gin to shady characters who turned up periodically at the basement door. He disappeared without a trace just before the repeal of Prohibition, and the house sat vacant for many months afterward, as buyers all shied away on the fear that he (or his enemies) would someday return to claim the place. A few less colorful but more easily verifiable stories illuminated the lives of other early residents of the houses on the block.

Cindy's research concentrated on the period during World War II when the houses had become rather run down and unattractive for single-family use. A parachute factory had opened up on the next block (it was torn down after the war to make way for one of the larger apartment buildings) and the Walker row was acquired by the factory owners and converted into dormitory-style housing for the young farm girls who came into the city to serve as workers in the war effort. Newsreels of the day exist to show the new factory hands standing proudly beside their tightly-made beds, while a company dorm-su-pervisor, looking like a drill sergeant, checks to see how well each girl has done. Cindy has arranged to have this footage shown at the historic preservation hearing, so that commission members can see how the houses were refitted to be dorms at the time.

After the war the demand for housing for the returning GI's and their families was so great that the Walker houses were reconverted to private residences—though most were made into flats and small apartments, rather than restored to single-family use. Throughout the '60s, during the greatest years of urban flight, the row declined in popularity, and the stagnating rental market caused landlords to let maintenance slide, leaving the block in a shabby and unappealing condition by the mid–1970s. But late in that decade "urban homesteaders" had rediscovered the block, and buyers were vying to get the best deals on "shells" to gut and rehabilitate in the elaborately ornamented style that was back in fashion after so long an absence.

A decade later, in the late 1980s, those shells, once worth 15 or 20 thousand dollars, were going for 200 thousand dollars apiece, and the neighborhood was so "hot," the developer figured that he could sell new apartment units for $150,000 each. So instead of buying the whole block and selling the nine houses for a total of some 2 million dollars, it made economic sense to tear the block down, to be replaced by eighty units, to bring in some 12 million dollars. The tenants who still lived in the rental units in the houses were being offered $5000 each, to help them with moving expenses. After three elderly renters had expressed worry about finding a new place, they were promised units in the new building, at a considerable discount off the market price. This last piece of the block's history would not figure into the historic landmark application, but was useful for the group to know, to help it plan its approach to the developer in negotiating sessions.

Further Preparation for the Case

Members of the group (which became known around the city as the Committee to Save Historic Walker's Row) spent the last few weeks before the hearing in a mad scramble to line up witnesses and produce supporting letters and documents for their side. The National Trust for Historic Preservation sent a letter that lent its prestige to the effort; the Masonry Institute contributed a brochure on historic brick patterns showing a detail from one of the houses as an illustration; a Ph.D. candidate who was doing her thesis on the entry of women into the business world in post-World War I America was prepared to speak about the importance of Emma Walker as an early role model for female executives. And several of the World War II parachute factory girls were located; one had saved her letters from the time, recounting her experiences as a newcomer to the city and to war work, and these could be entered into the record as documentation of what life was like for residents of the building during that phase of its existence.

In addition, several neighborhood civic associations were planning to testify in support, as well as two members of the city council. Though some of this testimony might well be disregarded as irrelevant by the Landmarks Commission (whose strict charge is to consider only historic and architectural evidence), such information could still influence the outcome in subtle ways. John F., the lawyer, explained to the group what he was taught in law school: "If a judge tells a jury to disregard the reference they have just heard to a purple elephant, all they're going to be able to think about for the next few minutes is that purple elephant."

The developer, meanwhile, was prepared for his own side of the hearing. He has also planned to insert information about the economic necessity for the new building and remark on how badly the city could use extra housing units—though neither subject is properly discussed in a historic landmark hearing. He, too, knows the "purple elephant theory" for inserting useful, though not strictly relevant information.

The neighbors have learned that he has found a distinguished architectural historian, Professor P., to argue the buildings' lack of distinction. The townhouses are nothing special, the professor was expected to testify; they're just like thousands of others that can be found scattered in all parts of the city. There is no more reason to landmark these nine than to landmark any of the others.

Once the neighbors knew who the developer's expert was, however, they were able to prepare a good rebuttal. Though the professor was eminent in his specialty, Georgian Revival buildings, he had no expertise in economic history, worker housing, and urban demographics—all of which work to make the row unique and worthy of preservation. Its mere architectural configurations are not central to the neighborhood's case.

While some of the committee members dealt with the substance of the hearing, others worked to improve the political climate for the hearing. Their job was to see that the case got sympathetic press coverage; they arranged for hundreds of citizens to be present at the hearing; they held demonstrations and rallies where people chanted "Don't let it go!/Save Walker's Row!" and sold Walker's Row silk-screened T-shirts and tote-bags to help raise the money to pay for all the fancy color slides they hoped would impress the Landmarks Commissioners with the merit of their case.

After many heated budget discussions consensus was reached that the best use of the group's money was to pay for professional-quality graphics; they would use volunteer labor to present the findings of Nancy R.'s expertly researched report. If they had used her to do the presentation to the Commissioners, the cost would have been another $1000, and she had already been paid $1500 for her work in preparing the application for the landmark. By no means a rich group, the members decided to cut corners at this additional expense. So Cindy and Emily were ready to do the speaking before the Landmarks Commission on behalf of the group.

Last-Minute Serendipity

A few days before the hearing something wonderful occurred. The Landmarks Commission received a telephone inquiry from a seventy-year-old veteran from out of state. He heard about the case from his niece, who happened to read about it in the paper. The idea of landmarking the dormitory where the factory girls had worked was terrific, he told the Landmarks Commission secretary. If it wasn't too late to sign up, he'd like to testify at the hearing. He'd been a pilot during World War II, and his life had been saved by a parachute made at that factory. He'd been shot up at 10,000 feet over Italy, and, wounded and bleeding, had had to bail out of his plane. When he reached the ground safely, he tore up his parachute and used part of the silk as a tourniquet to bind up his arm. Then he'd hiked for two days until he made it back behind his own troops' lines. He still had the bloody scrap of parachute-silk, which he'd kept as a souvenir. Since he had heard that some of the former factory girls were going to be at the hearing, he wanted to come and give them a long belated thank-you for their work. Would the Commission allow him to speak?

The secretary said yes, the Commissioners would be glad to hear his story. So much of the testimony they are used to receiving is dry, academic discussion about brick and stone; it's not often they get a chance to hear history from those who made it happen. She put him down on the hearing agenda for fifteen minutes.

When the neighbors heard of the last-minute request, they were thrilled and confident that this added emotional boost to their case was all they'd need to win.

Apparently the developer thought so too, and the day before the hearing was to begin, he called up the president of the Walker's Row Committee, and for the first time, offered what looked to be a promising compromise. He would keep the facades of the rowhouses intact and build a new apartment building behind them. It would extend back further than the rear walls of the old houses, and all the insides would be brand new floor-layouts, with the old front doors sealed up and no longer leading anywhere. A new entranceway would be created in the center of the row, which would open to the building's new lobby. On top of the three-story-high roofs would be another five stories of

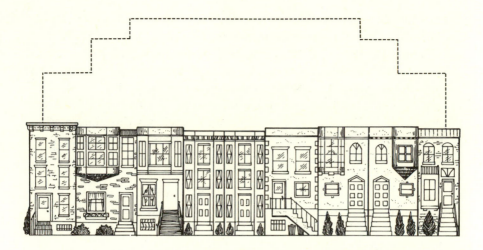

building, but these upper floors would be "stepped back" from the street so as to be barely visible when viewed from below. All the ornamentation taken off the backs and sides of the original buildings would be preserved and reattached in appropriate places to the facade of the part to be added on. The overall height and size of the combined new and old building would be close to what it was in the original plan: seven stories, and sixty-eight units (instead of eight stories and eighty units). But to people seeing it from street-level, it would appear that little has changed.

Compromise? Or Sell-Out?

The Walker's Row Committee was interested. Their case looked strong, but it was by no means a sure thing. A few said immediately, "This deal is the best we can do; we should take it while it's still offered." But several hard-core preservationists denounced the drawings as a "facadomy," saying that the old front, propped up by steel girders, without any of the old interior behind it, would be no more than a conjuring trick, a meaningless illusion of what once was, a kitsch version of its former self. One even said he'd rather see the block torn down than "saved" in this fraudulent way.

Another attacked the reuse of the old building's ornamentation, which would be added onto the facade of the new building: "Pastiche" was the term of disdain applied to this practice (it's French for "pasting" and can also be used to criticize the copying of historical elements on old buildings and attaching—or pasting—them onto new designs).

Despite the intensity of a few neighbors' dislike of the plan, the majority of the committee members were reluctant to turn it down out of hand. Slowly the idea emerged to return to the developer with a counter-offer, a compromise more to the whole group's liking. Restore the building, they would ask, and subdivide the original interiors into separate, new apartments as shown in the plan, but keep the existing doors in place, and make them separate, functional entryways into those nine ground floor units. The neighbors' version would still allow two more stories to be built on top, but these should be designed in the same rowhouse brick, so that the structure when finished would look much like the five-story rowhouses found on other blocks in the neighborhood. Under this scheme the developer could get about forty-five rentable units, or about two-thirds the amount of square footage he had proposed to build with his "facadomy" scheme.

The developer received the counter-offer the same morning as the hearing was set to begin, and so didn't have time to decide to take it or reject it. Instead, both sides agreed to a **continuance**, or postponement of the hearing, in order to try to work out a compromise in the interim.

Two weeks later the developer came back with his comments. His market advisers told him the neighbors' plan was unworkable; it was too expensive, and the new little upper-story apartment units wouldn't sell for enough money to make up for the cost of renovating the existing units on the first three floors. He restated his earlier eight-story plan.

The committee members, after some hours of internal wrangling, finally agreed among themselves that they would not accept a plan so strongly opposed by a substantial minority of their members. They returned to the developer and told him they would stick to their guns.

So the case was finally going to the hearing. All the witnesses from the previous month reassembled and were briefed on what points they should make. In this state hearings are run as a legislative process—meaning that there are no adversarial parties. The chairman of the commission calls the witnesses, and the members of the commission may ask questions, but no one else may cross-examine or raise objections to questions asked. The applicant (the organization seeking to have the landmark declared) has the burden of proving its case.

The panel had ten members, of whom half were experts in the various preservation specialties. Two were architects, two were historians (one a city historian, one an architectural historian), and one was an archaeologist. The other five were lay appointees of the Mayor, representing related professions and interests: One was a real estate agent, one an interior designer, one a writer of tourist guides to the city, and the remaining two were active members of the city's historical society. All served as volunteers for a stipend of $100 per meeting.

The chairman, who was the city historian, was known to be a temperamental egotist, who often started the meetings late and ended them early. The

Commission as a whole seemed most comfortable when rubber-stamping the recommendations made by their professional staff members; but in a big case like this, where powerful development interests were stacked up against powerful voting blocs, it was hard to predict what they might do.

John F., who was appointed the coordinator of the neighborhood's case, tried his best to fit his group's presentation into a form that would please the impatient Commission Chair. He warned all his witnesses to be as terse as possible, not to repeat each other's points, and to save for written submission any statements that would not fit into the time limits imposed. He also arranged for those witnesses who couldn't sit around all day waiting for a chance to speak (the elderly, the out-of-town experts who had planes to catch, and those experts who were being paid by the hour) to go on first, and let those with more flexible schedules do the waiting. He also explained to all the neighbors who wanted to stand up and say a few words that their best contribution was just to be present in the hall; the Commission Chairman was too short-tempered to sit still while citizen after citizen stood up to echo the same opinion.

The group's best hope was that the evidence alone would carry the case. What they brought with them was well above what was shown in many successful cases. The slides were beautiful, clear and complete, showing the buildings during the full span of their history, in all their phases of use. There were dozens of letters from supporting experts from universities around the U.S. There was the newsreel, and of course, at the end, there was the medal-bearing war veteran, who brought in his piece of bloody, battered parachute silk, and who tearfully thanked the "young heroines" who lived in the dormitory and who more than earned the landmark plaque on the wall to honor their efforts to their country in wartime.

After he was finished, the whole room burst into applause, including (with a rueful smile) the developer. Next it was his turn to put on his experts, with their slides. He had his expensive lawyer do the introductions of his witnesses. As expected they attacked the buildings in the row as mediocre and undistinguished. A statistician reported on his results of a survey of building types in the city. If these buildings are landmark quality, he concluded, then fully 53 percent of all the buildings in the city should be landmarked, too, because that is how many meet any of the criteria named in the Walker's Row landmark application.

The developer also tried to insert some testimony as to his dealings with the neighborhood, to show that he had been reasonable and offered them a fair compromise, but that hard-liners rejected his efforts. But the Commission Chairman cut him off, saying, "We're only here to decide the question of a landmark on this row, right now. We can't play arbiter in your private negotiations. Don't even bring it up."

The developer next tried to hint at the economics behind his development decision and to imply that landmark designation would send an anti-business signal to the city's real estate industry and hamper future growth—but he was cut off on that line of argument as well. "If we landmark your property, and you still want to change it, then we'll hear all about your finances," the Chairman interrupted. "But save that for the next hearing, please."

So, sounding a bit bruised and resentful, the developer quickly wrapped up his case. Following brief rebuttals by both sides, the Chairman declared the hearing adjourned, but gave each side an additional thirty days to submit any supplementary documentation for the record.

Three months later, without any fanfare, and with no advance notice from staff members that the subject was on the agenda, the Landmarks Commission took a vote on a motion to landmark the row. The motion carried, six to two (with one absent, not voting and one abstention on grounds of possible conflict of interest). The entire block, as requested, was included in the designation.

A great victory, the neighbors all thought when they heard the news—but it wasn't really...at least not yet. The battle was still only half-won. Under state law the developer could still move to have his plan approved, provided that he could persuade the Landmarks Commission that his plan qualified for one of several exemptions to the law. He could try to show that his alterations were compatible with the style of the landmarked building, or that his new project had "special merit," or that he would suffer "economic hardship" if barred from proceeding with his new construction as planned.

For a few months he studied his options. The only sure way to qualify for a project of special merit as the law defined it would be to make the new apartment into low-income units, or add in-home nursing facilities for the elderly, or stick in some other "do-good" sort of use—but then he wouldn't make as much money. Yet it would be hard to show economic hardship when it was clear that he could turn around and sell those nine townhouses for upwards of $200,000 apiece. So he figured his best chance was with the facadomy scheme—the plan the neighborhood had rejected. He would show the panelists the drawing of the townhouse with their facades restored, with five stories of new units added on top, and hope they would find the combination compatible, even though the neighbors did not.

In some states the hearing for alteration or demolition of a landmarked building goes to a different body than the commission that approved the designation. The new judges might be a state board as opposed to a local one, or they might just be a different group of appointees of the same executive who chose the original landmark hearing commissioners; but in this state the same panelists were to hear the developer's appeal. So he already had a fairly good idea of what approach they would take to the subject. Having found enough merit in the rowhouses to declare them historic, the commissioners were unlikely to view his planned addition as an actual improvement to the buildings, rather than a way to squeeze more dollar value from them.

Given this situation, the developer did not feel very confident going into this round of the fight. But the neighbors were not particularly happy, either, when they realized they were going to have to gear up for a hearing all over again. They would have to get back the same witnesses, and also do some economic studies to make the point that a complete interior renovation was a feasible alternative. But they were nearly out of money, and were terribly worried that the developer would hear of their financial squeeze and use it to his advantage.

Politically, too, the cohesiveness of the residents was beginning to fail. By then, the rowhouses had sat vacant and unused for more than a year. Vandals had broken the windows and sprayed graffiti on the brick walls, and rats had occasionally been spotted scuttling around the alley in the back. A few voices had been heard blaming the residents for not working out a settlement that would soon have the buildings back in productive use. The Walker's Row Chairman was getting tired of explaining to all who asked what the status of the case was, and why no progress was being made.

It looked at this point as if neither side could emerge the winner. But then someone new moved into the neighborhood and joined the Committee, bringing with him some fresh ideas. Where he lived before, the community and the developer in a similar situation were able to form a partnership, and develop a joint plan for a formerly disputed property. He said that might be worth trying here. He explained how it would work.

First the developer and the neighborhood organization would form a "CDC"—a community development corporation. Then that entity will apply for a "CDBG"—a "community development block grant," a government program designed to promote needed growth in decaying urban areas.* Rehabilitation of vacant housing units and preservation of a designated historic landmark would meet the requirement of the program that there be social utility in the spending of the funds.

A professional arbiter was brought in to settle some of the details of the partnership. A buy-in figure was fixed at a level the community could afford,

---

* Alternatively, application could be made to the Department of Housing and Urban Development for assistance under the "UDAG" program—that is, "Urban Development Action Grant"—to revitalize the block. Unfortunately, however, the HUD budget has been severely cut back in recent years, and such UDAG monies are now very difficult to come by.

and ownership percentages for each of the principals was hammered out. A new architect, chosen by agreement of the developer and the neighbors, was put to work designing a new plan that would suit the parameters of both developer and neighbors. She came up with a scheme to restore the rowhouses, subdivide their interiors into a greater number of smaller units, and build just two additional stories on top. This new upper part would be composed of luxury units with rents set so as to subsidize the older, restored part of the project. The new total number of units was fifty-five—about halfway between the forty-five the neighbors had proposed and the sixty-eight the developer had insisted he needed to make a profit. Because of the 20 percent tax credit available to rehabilitated landmarks, the "bottom line" of the deal looked good to all. The Save Historic Walker's Row Committee would get the high-quality renovation they desired, plus make a little money on the side; and the developer and his financial backers were going to make a lot more.

Everyone was now happy, right? Yes, but only because everyone was tired, frustrated, and looking for a way out of a hopeless bind. Nobody got exactly what they were after. The neighbors had to accept two extra stories on top of the row, and the developer had to settle for something less than the return he had originally dreamed of when he first bought Walker's Row. The "CDC" solution is neither for the community idealist nor the big-money speculator sort of developer. It's a rare and fragile thing, but when it works, it can be a wondrous thing to behold.

Eleven

KEEPING PUBLIC WORKS IN THE PUBLIC INTEREST

It's tough enough when the developer is a multi-million dollar corporation. Things get even tougher when the developer is the government, with the public treasury as its financial backer. When citizens organize in opposition to a government development plan, they know that their tax-dollars are going to pay the salaries of all the lawyers and staff people lined up against them. And others in government will act as judges, while still others write the regulations that guide the decisions to be made. The pertinent question here is the one that's been asked since the days of Ancient Rome: *Quis custodiet custodiens?* or: Who will regulate the regulators? Can the government evaluate its own development plans with the same detachment it shows to private property owners?

In all too many places, the answer must be a blunt "no," because the government has written itself outside the normal zoning rules. Government land is often left unzoned, or it may be assigned its own special zoning category, not subject to the normal review process. Special review boards typically start off with the assumption that what the government wants to build *must* be in the public interest. Such a system considerably handicaps citizen opponents, who (if they are involved in more than a one-shot effort) might be well advised to turn their energies to the reform of the government development process first.

But it's not always the case that the government gives itself favored treatment. Some localities do provide means for citizen participation, through use of a two-step process. First the case will go through the ordinary zoning process, but the outcome of the hearing will not be final (as would be the case for a private developer); the Zoning Board's ruling is simply advisory to a separate, special commission set up to review government building plans. In some jurisdictions the order might be reversed—that is, the special review board hears the case first, and its ruling will be advisory to the regular Zoning Board. There are also a number of other variants in the two-step formula: The Zoning Board's review may be followed by a final decision by the legislative arm of government, or by an agency of the administration, or by its chief executive. The existence of two steps might lead you to think that you have two shots to defeat the project, and in some states that might be true; but more likely than not, once the project is approved through the first stage, it has built the momentum needed to see it through the second stage, where it will merely be rubber-stamped. There is only the illusion that more time and attention is available for citizen input.

However, there are some cities and counties where the process of government development has been specially crafted to give greatest weight to the citizens who will be affected by it. Representatives of the neighborhood will be asked to serve on the study team that selects a specific site, design, or concept, or at the very least, will be consulted before any final plans are drawn. If the government where you live has devised such a system to address citizen concerns at the planning level, the only thing you will have to worry about is how sensitive and responsible are the neighbors who are chosen to speak on your behalf. It's up to you to find out who they are, let them know who you are, and brief them fully on any special problems you feel the development presents.

Here are some of the types of government plans that are most likely to arouse neighborhood opposition, and a sampling of reasons why neighbors try to have the development stopped or changed:

- **Highways, freeway ramps, interchanges, and other roadworks** may split the neighborhood in two, cause unacceptable levels of traffic congestion, noise, air pollution, and accidents. They are especially problematic if located too near to homes, schools, churches, or parks.

- **Bridges, tunnels, and subway lines** pose many of the same problems and several others as well. Bridges may cast shadows over the homes below, or intrude visually on the natural landscape; tunnel and subway excavations can damage foundations of nearby buildings; and any major engineering project can wreak environmental havoc on sensitive wetlands, shorelines, or waterways.

- **Large-scale buildings,** such as courthouses, records-centers, and administrative or legislative offices, pose all of the same problems caused by private office buildings, plus a few special drawbacks all their own: They are more likely to be picketed, to be the scene of a media crush, to be subject to bomb threats, and under some special circumstances (such as when high-level dignitaries visit) to require the roping off or barricading of surrounding neighborhood streets.

- **Municipal parking garages** are nearly always unsightly, and frequently become prime spots for muggers and other criminals. If parking is made cheap enough, mass transit use will be discouraged and commuter use of neighborhood streets may rise.
- **Hospitals, schools, libraries, and convention centers** are also large-scale government projects, but these are discussed in Chapter 14, on big institutions.

Strategies

After you've researched the ins and outs of how the government development process works in your area, and analyzed the specific problems posed by the plan facing your neighborhood, you must decide on a course of action: Fight? Negotiate? Try to fight on some points and negotiate on others? Concentrate on winning the hearing? Or save your resources for a challenge through the courts? Chapters 5, 6, and 7 give advice on forming an effective working group and deciding on your most productive approach.

In addition to the strategy suggestions contained in those chapters, here are some ideas that citizens have successfully used to curtail or modify ill-planned government development:

Strategy #1: Offer Alternatives

Government projects, you will be glad to hear, are almost always slow, tortuous affairs, that may take as long as five to ten years to be realized. In the time between the planning and the execution, conditions may have changed, and the necessity for the construction may no longer be so apparent. If you can demonstrate convincingly that what's about to be built is no longer needed in that form, you stand a good chance of sending the project back to the drawing boards—even if all approvals are finally in order.

For example: The government has approved a plan to add a freeway connection to the avenue that intersects your street. A few years have passed since the plan was first announced, and in that time, new subdivisions have sprung up all along a section of the avenue a few miles to the north. You get a traffic consultant (or better still, persuade the city traffic department to undertake the study itself), and his figures show clearly that the demand for the connection is now coming from the north. You propose that the access ramp be moved north, to better serve the new homeowners, who would otherwise be driving through your neighborhood to get to the freeway.

You might also devise an alternative to show that the same needs which led to the creation of the objectionable plan can be met by a different approach to the problem. Example: The county courthouse is no longer able to provide enough courtroom space for all the civil and criminal cases being litigated. The government wants to build a second courthouse very close to your apartment building, but you and your neighbors don't think it belongs on a residential street. You study the government's needs for space (and possibly have your own group's architect and site-planner analyze the problem) and you present a concept that will take care of the government's needs without impinging on your neighborhood. You show how the government can get two additional floors out of the old building by renovating its little-used basement space, and two more floors on the top from the construction of a rooftop addition. Your use-figures reveal that most courtrooms sit idle much of the time, and that more efficient scheduling could alleviate much of the need for space. Between the additions and the improvement in scheduling, there should be as much additional courtroom availability as contemplated in the new-building scheme.

Another approach to the courthouse problem would be to suggest an alternate site, one not so close to a residential area—perhaps in a somewhat neglected part of town, one where the shopkeepers would welcome the influx of new customers who work in the courthouse nearby. But caution: You must check with the area's civic or merchants' association before putting forward a site in someone else's neighborhood. Otherwise, you'll be accused of trying to foist your problems onto weaker, less organized citizens, and your group will come across as a bunch of bullies. With proper consultation, however, you can advance the alternative site as something favored by citizens from all sides of town, and make the alternative plan that much more attractive.

In pressing for alternatives, use the public pocketbook as another argument in your favor. If you can show that the cost of constructing a new courthouse from the ground up is far more than that of renovating and expanding the old building, you may win the government's own budget watchdogs over to your side, and they will make your case for you. But suppose you learn that the plan you're advocating will cost a few million dollars more? Then you need to draw up a balance sheet showing that other, nonmaterial gains are to be earned by doing it your way. Let's say you're talking about moving that highway interchange a few miles to the north. The length of the access ramp is going to be a little longer, and cost more—you won't deny that—but what the city is really paying for when it spends the extra money is not another mile or two of asphalt, but the future stability of one of its solid, tax-producing neighborhoods. With that freeway ramp threatening to bring in excess traffic, houses would lose value and those who could afford to move would do so. Increased safety (by not constructing the complicated intersection shown in the original plan) brings a long-term savings to society in the form of accidents prevented and lives not disrupted. An insurance actuary can help you arrive at such data. Planners, who often think of themselves as scientists, tend to want to have numerical backing for a decision that is really more a product of common sense (or good political judgment).

Now suppose you can't find a neighborhood where the people would welcome the freeway interchange, the courthouse, or whatever? Suppose the plan is for something so horrendous that nobody is likely to want it anywhere— yet the government keeps telling you, it's got to go *somewhere*. This is often the case with highways. The government tells you that the old commuter routes are crammed to capacity, yet still more subdivisions are going up, bringing in more people, who of course all own cars. So there has to be a new road to put them on, and your neighborhood just happens to be along the most logical route. What can you say to that?

Plenty. The first thing that springs to mind is: Isn't it time to stop giving permits for all those new houses? Why should your neighborhood have to pay the price for the county's failure to keep development within livable limits?

Second, you need to bring in evidence that road-building only spurs more growth, brings in more cars, and fills the new roads to capacity not very long after they're built. (It works something like a variant of the Peter Principle: Traffic expands to fill lanes available.) You can contact your state highway department or the Federal Highway Administration to find statistics on crowding of newly opened roads, or you can cite references from books written on highway planning (a few are listed in the Bibliography).

Third, and most important, you need to come up with some non-construction alternatives to building a new road. Perhaps the number of cars on existing roads could be reduced by a program to promote carpooling and discourage single-occupant vehicles? Perhaps the money to be spent on the new road could be given for construction of a light-rail line to run alongside the most gridlocked commuter route? Or an elevated tram-line might be built above the roadway. The government could also use the funds to buy new buses and subsidize the fares. Perhaps the buses might even be free (that would certainly get people out of their cars!). Or employers could be offered a tax break for running shuttle buses for their employees or otherwise using their own resources to reduce commuting by private car. Look into some of the creative solutions used by other cities, and even other countries, to find ideas you think might suit your situation. You need not present an expert-quality, thoroughly worked-out plan; all you really need to do is point to some ideas worth exploring, to show that more pavement isn't automatically the answer.

Remember, too, when you present your ideas, to hit hard on all the disadvantages of doing it the way the government had first planned. Measure the ozone levels on roadways comparable to the one the county wants to build. Is your government in compliance with the EPA's ozone guidelines? If it isn't (and very few big cities are), hint that there could be federal action taken if the level rises any further. Has drunk driving become a popular public crusade in your area (as it has across the country in recent years)? If there are bars anywhere along the intended route, use that fact as a point against construction. And of course if there are any schools, day-care centers, or playgrounds nearby, make an issue of the danger of children darting in front of cars. Perhaps some of your objections will be taken less seriously than others, but if you raise enough of them, and have enough people repeating them, you'll create a climate of doubt about the plan, and your offered alternatives will seem that much more workable for everyone.

If the planners seem skeptical as to the merit of any of your proposals, at the very least you should ask for a six-month study period for the government to consider what you have submitted. The tendency in all governments (except perhaps the most ruthless totalitarian dictatorships) is to study and re-study, rather than make a controversial move. In a democracy, controversy means that some voters will be unhappy over the outcome, and unhappy voters generally mean that some politician will be out of a job. But by studying a subject, government officials can show they are doing something about it, without actually disturbing anyone with action. Even if in the end the study goes against you, if you can delay the results long enough, you may kill the plan by attrition. (This may sound cynical, but I know of all too many cases where it's happened just that way.)

But suppose the highway plan survives all the study groups that have been appointed to deal with the problem. That tells you that powerful interests are undoubtedly pushing hard to get the road approved. Who are they, and just what benefit can they expect to get from the construction? If the answer to the question is that they are private developers, and that the value of the land they hold will double or triple because of the new accessibility of their properties—you should consider advancing one last alternative: a different method of financing the work. Let the private developers who want it, put up the money for the road. Why should you, the citizen, pay for something that's not in your interest?

This question has been the spur for legislation in California, Florida, and New York for "impact fees" to be charged to private developers when new roads, sewer lines, and other public works are necessary as a direct result of their development activities. In Orlando, Florida, these fees now range from $3700 to $4700 for each new house built. In vigorous real estate markets developers simply tack these additional costs onto the base price of the house, and so the development (both private and public components) goes on as planned. But in places and at times when the market gets "soft," the requirement for such fees can be enough to persuade the developer not to proceed— persuading the government, in turn, that the roadwork is no longer necessary.

The idea of "impact fees" is spreading rapidly now from state to state; so if there is not legislation in place in your jurisdiction now to assess such costs to developers, you might get a good reception from your politicians if you suggest it. Your local chapter of Common Cause (a lobbying organization for citizens' issues) could already be working for the proposal in your area. Why not look into it, and if there is a bill, help to get it passed. Unless, of course, you don't mind picking up the tab for the developers' goodies!

Strategy #2: Cut the Purse Strings

It's really very simple: Governments can't build what they can't fund. So if you can short-circuit the flow of money to a project somewhere along the line, you will be able to slow it down or stop it altogether. The key question in the matter will be timing. When does the project come up for review in the budget process? Your legislature will have a "budget season" when the executive branch submits its annual requests for X dollars for Y project, and the amounts and purposes are studied by the appropriate committees and by the legislature as a whole.

If the objectionable project is already funded by the time you hear of it, your task will be made much, much more difficult, if not impossible. So if you have any reason to believe that government planners are looking at usable land in your neighborhood for any type of development, and you want to have some input into the process, contact your elected representatives without delay. Ask detailed questions about the budgetary process, along with any questions you have about the nature of the plans being considered. Presuming you've caught it early enough, you will likely find that the project must go through a lengthy and tortuous route before it gets the money needed to make it a reality.

Here is a likely course for a single budget item. Let's say a city agency needs a new office building. Its administrators (or possibly outside consultants) present findings to the Mayor's budget office demonstrating the need for the building, estimating its cost, and perhaps recommending a site, or a few possible sites. If the Mayor agrees, the item may be added to that agency's budget for the next fiscal year. When the budget bill is submitted to the city council, it will first go to a committee, or very likely, several committees. The Budget and Revenue Committee will review the entire budget package, but requests for particular projects may also be examined by the committee with oversight in that area. For example, the Transportation Committee may look at requests for new roads; the Education Committee is interested in funding for a new school building; the Parks and Recreation Committee examines whether a new swimming pool is needed; and so on.

After the committees have finished tinkering with the bill (they may cut some items out and add others not requested by the Mayor; they may also change amounts or attach conditions to the spending of those amounts) it is sent on to the council as a whole. (For projects involving different levels of government, the name of the legislative body will change: For county cases, it may be your Board of Supervisors, in state cases, your state assembly, and in federal cases, the budget will be sent to the U.S. Congress.)

Once the budget bill is out of committee, anyone and everyone has a shot at everything in the budget bill—though in most places, committee recommendations tend to carry a lot of weight. Still, particular items may be cut, amendments for pet projects attached, amounts changed again, or parts could be sent back to the committee, or to a different committee, for further study. Administration officials play an active role in trying to see that what the Mayor wants ends up in the final version. So do various lobbyists for special interests groups (like developers) and so do individual citizens or civic associations.

Somehow, out of all this tinkering, dickering, and turf-protecting, once a year emerges a bill that most people can live with (though hardly ever is anyone truly happy with it), and that the Mayor is willing to sign.

But funding for your government project doesn't necessarily become a reality at this point. Many government funding decisions must be made at two or more levels. For roadwork, especially, your state may have voted the money to get it started, but the greater amount needed (often as much as 80 percent!) may come from the Federal Highway Administration. Your county may have voted to put in a new sewer line, but the project is still dependent on the state's decision to build that new sewage treatment plant nearby. Your town has allocated funding to build a parking garage next to the subway station, but the Regional Transit Authority (a multi-state agency) must first determine if the increased parking is in line with overall transit policy.

These multi-level cases increase your opportunity for input. If you fail to stop the project at the lower level, go straight to the next stage. Call your Congressman and try to get that federal funding held up (in these days of massive deficits and budget cutbacks, the task is a bit easier than it used to be). Conversely, if the higher level approval has already been granted, look to the lower level to get your objections in. To counter the argument that you are coming in too late to play a role, always point out that your neighborhood was not adequately consulted (or sometimes not notified at all) when the project was begun. Don't let your elected officials make you feel it's *your* fault for not being savvy about the complicated government development process. The failure was theirs in not keeping close ties with their constituents and asking you, *before* the plans got so far along, whether this project was something you wanted.

Though I've just said you should tell your politicians you're not savvy, of course, it certainly helps if you are. If there's someone in your group who is used to dealing with political causes, who knows when budget season is, who has testified at committee hearings before, who knows how to read the government register and can keep up with what the government is considering and when—then you have a great asset in your neighborhood. If you don't have someone with these skills, then you need to rely on the staff of your elected officials to guide you through the process. It's never too early (even if you're not sure yet that any plan is in the works) to have a delegation of neighbors pay a call on the office, introduce yourselves, and talk generally about what concerns you (now and in the future). Before you leave, ask that you be kept informed if anything touching on your expressed interests comes up in a piece of legislation.

As soon as you're notified that an item of importance to you is on the legislative agenda, your whole group should gear into action. Numbers count as much or more than content, so get those letters and petitions rolling. With testimony before government committees, you may well be held to a strict time limit (say as little as three minutes per witness), so you will need to plan for ways to get all your points across quickly. You might want to have five or six witnesses sign up to speak, and divide your most important points among them. But try to find people who can speak on behalf of separate organizations, if you can: for example, one from your neighborhood association, one from the PTA, one from a neighborhood church group, one from the local business association, and one from whatever others you can line up. They may all be members of your group, too, and make the points you've assigned them to explain, but when they appear wearing "different hats," it will seem to the legislature that a broad cross-section of the community has spoken, and more weight will attach to their words.

Just how you can tailor your testimony to have the most powerful impact is something full-time lobbyists and professional consultants are paid thousands to study and perfect. Obviously you're not going to be able to work your case like a seasoned pro—so use your average-citizen standing to your best advantage and ask the legislators' indulgence for any misunderstanding of the rules. You don't want to have your statement excluded from the record, for example, because you neglected to file your written statement fourteen days beforehand, as required. If you do want to put some polish on your presentation, you might want to go to your local library and do some reading about rhetorical techniques, persuasive speech-making, and the rules for government testimony.

Strategy #3: Take It to the Polls

Not all funding is through a legislatively adopted budget. Publicly backed bond sales are another common way of paying for government development. These may be issued by act of the legislature, but they may also appear as a ballot-item at election time. What you see may go something like this:

QUESTION 16: SHOULD BONDS BE ISSUED TO RAISE MONEY FOR THE INTERCOUNTY CONNECTOR HIGHWAY?

If a majority of the people vote for it, you've got a road; if they don't want to spend the money to pay the interest on the loan—no road. But someone's got to spend some money to explain the question to the voters and attempt to persuade them to vote one way or the other.

The government will certainly be banned from lobbying on its own behalf. The people most likely to do the spending are the ones who worked to get the measure on the ballot in the first place. If the idea for the road originated with development companies, they will undoubtedly pour thousands, even millions, into the campaign for its approval. The neighbors who are against the road will find themselves in a tough situation. Voting percentages keep dropping from year to year, and of those who do come to the polls, the number who vote on localized ballot questions (and nearly all bond issuances fall into that category) is shamefully low—frequently less than 30 or even 20 percent. So if one side does a fair amount of advertising while the other side can afford only a little—though out of the total number of county residents only a very small percentage may be on the developer's side—that small concentrated group of voters he's won to his view may be just enough to tip the scales in his favor.

This is exactly what happened in the fast-growing Maryland town of Silver Spring. The ballot item was a yes or no vote on a huge municipal parking garage to be built next door to a new in-town shopping mall, a private development. Without city-funded parking, the developers admitted, the project just would not work. At the beginning of the controversy it seemed that public opinion was running heavily against the construction. The area was in the midst of an explosive building boom, with a million square feet of office space already in the works, traffic woes spreading, and neighborhoods organizing and fighting for relief. The citizen-opponents of the garage saw the ballot-item as a sure vehicle for the people to express their discontent with the unmanageable rate of growth. The proposed shopping mall would be the largest of all the new buildings, and quite possibly the most profitable—especially if the parking structures on which it depended were to be paid for by the taxpayer.

Thinking their case was obvious, the citizens' groups paid little attention to fund-raising, advertising, and public outreach. Perhaps even if they had, the result would have been the same. The pro-development side raised and spent half a million dollars to get its message across—the most ever spent on a ballot question in county history! The citizens, in contrast, came up with a mere $10,000 for publicity of their views. So few outside the neighborhood got to hear the other side. When the votes were counted up, the citizens found to their dismay, that the developer had eked out a bare majority.

This is not to say that the initiative/referendum process will always be decided by who has the most money. But money is a big factor, no question about it. Still, money is only as useful as the time, expertise, and hard work it can buy. If you have enough volunteers to contribute these same necessities for free (or perhaps at cost, or at a discount), you could take on the richest opponent. So get those neighbors out walking door to door, tapping everyone they meet for their support. Maybe one of those contacted will be an ad executive, a public relations consultant, a graphic artist, or some other professional who will help you find the most appealing phrase to put your case across.

Remember, too, that your efforts must be targeted to the people who actually vote on minor ballot issues. It's no good slapping flyers down on car windshields if most of the cars have out-of-state plates or belong to teenagers or other non-voters. See if you can get a breakdown from your local elections board (or maybe from the political studies department of a local university) of what type of voter (young/old? middle/lower/upper income? etc.) is most likely to care enough to come out on election day and take a stand.

Members of organizations often follow the recommendations or endorsements given by their leaders. So make a special effort to win over the heads of local unions, religious groups, clubs, and professional associations, as well as the local political parties. With one or two large groups publicly on your side, you benefit, not just from their simple voting strength, but also from their prestige and influence over non-members. When issues are obscure, people often will look to see how some important person feels about the issue, and go along with that person's judgment. With one or two of these valuable endorsements, you could wrap up the numbers needed for a majority vote.

Strategy #4: Attack from Another Direction

You tried tackling the case head-on and couldn't get anywhere. You couldn't get the funding cut, and local election procedures won't allow you to have the question put to the voters directly. But you may be able to get at the project in a more roundabout fashion. Government developments are seldom straightforward affairs. They're almost always the product of circuitous deal-making, with hundreds of officials from many different agencies involved along the way. Not all of these people and organizations will be in agreement on the project, or even be aware that it's moving toward approval—or, as the old saw has it: "The right hand doesn't know what the left hand is doing." So it becomes your job, in a sense, to make sure that the right hand is coordinated enough to grab that left hand and stop it from following through.

Here is the sort of situation suited to this strategy:

The building permits department of the government has already approved a plan to construct an office building for one of its agencies, but the site chosen for the project includes a "paper street"—a piece of land shown on the city map as a named roadway, but which was never actually built. It's now up to the Department of Transportation to review and approve the closing (elimination) of that "street" from official records. Without this action, the plan cannot go forward, since it is illegal to build over what is technically a roadway—even if it's never been used for that purpose and likely never will be.

But you now have a whole new opportunity to press your case. If officials with decision-making power over the road-closing agree with your view, they could deny the closing and so put a stop to the project. You could be lucky to discover that one of the key officials of the Department lives in your neighborhood, or has a close friend who does, and so will see things your way. Maybe in the time it takes for the case to reach the top official's desk, some new evidence will have surfaced to make the plan seem unworkable, or politically risky, or maybe the city's budget crisis will have become so overwhelming that the funding will be cancelled. Your chances for winning may be remote at this stage, but at least the game is not yet over.

The involvement of a second agency may not, ultimately, put a stop to the plan, but it may provide you with some powerful bargaining leverage. Another transportation example shows how: Suppose the new office building will have a driveway that will release several hundred cars onto a major roadway during the a.m. and p.m. rush hours. That driveway will most likely need a traffic light. If you can get the Traffic Management Bureau to hold up on installation of that light for a specified period of time, you may be able to delay the opening of the underground garage, and possibly the whole building, while you press for other concessions. Say you'll remove your objections to the traffic light, provided that cars coming out of the building are allowed only to turn right (not go straight across the main road and onto smaller, residential streets). Say you want the government to operate a shuttle bus to bring its employees to the building from the main transportation nexus downtown, so that fewer cars will be coming up your street to get to the garage. These kinds of compromises are not only possible—they're expected whenever a large building, public or private, is at issue. Your Traffic Management Bureau will probably be used to acting as negotiator and helping to strike a deal in such cases. (Otherwise, you and your neighbors will be calling up constantly with complaints, and writing to your elected officials, asking for their intervention—and that's something all experienced bureaucrats will work hard to avoid.)

Other leverage-creating issues include:

- other traffic issues, such as street-widenings, creation of turning-lanes, curb cuts, sidewalk closings, installation (or removal) of parking meters, loading zones, specially reserved spaces, etc.
- placement of "street furniture," such as bus shelters, benches, utility poles, light fixtures, and other items dependent on the approval of other government agencies.
- planting of trees, grass, shrubs, flowers, or ground cover to be supplied by the city's Maintenance and Grounds Department, its Tree Department, or other agency.

This is by no means a comprehensive list.

I remember one case where the citizens were able to hold up a major project for two years because the permit for the closing of one alley was being withheld. In that case, the city council held the final say over the disposition of the alley, and the councilmembers were not willing to openly go against what the citizens' group wanted—even though another branch of the government had already issued all the building permits and the bulldozers were ready to roll. The citizens used the delay over the alley-closing to press for downsizing of the new building, and they succeeded. They also emerged with some significant traffic relief in the form of turn-prohibitions, dead-ends, and turnarounds. Once the compromise deal was signed between the citizens and the developer, the city council then went ahead and approved the alley-closing.

Strategy #5: Play One Agency Off Against Another

This is similar to Strategy #4, but this time you are not just trying to slow the bureaucracy down or gain some maneuvering room; you are looking to find one government agency that shares your neighborhood's interests and can act as the advocate for your position. This is not a frequent happenstance but one limited to special circumstances. It might occur in a situation like the following:

The Department of Interdepartmental Management (DIM) has expanded by 50 percent over the past several years, but the new employees are still crowded into the old building that has long served as headquarters. A plan has already been approved for an annex to be constructed on the grassy lot that is part of the present building's grounds, but which has long served the neighborhood as a playground.

Delegation after delegation of parents has called on the officials at DIM, asking them to find somewhere else to put the annex, so that the children can continue to play on the open space, but all appeals have been denied.

But then a mother gets the idea to bring the problem up to officials at the Department of Parks and Recreation, and there she finds a sympathetic ear. The Director of that agency is equally disturbed by the proposal, because the loss of play-space in that area will put pressure on her department to acquire some other land as a substitute for what was taken away. But any new capital expenditure this year will break her agency's budget. The Recreation Director brings the problem up directly to the Mayor, who's a close friend. He gives her his personal commitment to find some kind of solution to the problem.

Some weeks pass before the neighbors hear what kind of deal has been worked out. The Mayor has put together a **land-swap** within his government. The grassy lot will be added to the inventory of land under Parks Department jurisdiction; the DIM, in exchange, will receive an asphalt lot that was once the site of tennis courts (run by the Parks Department), but is now just surplus land. The surface is too cracked and broken to be restored to a playable condition for a reasonable cost, and the demand for tennis courts in the area is now served by the state college, which makes its athletic facilities available at certain times to residents of the surrounding community for a small fee.

The neighbors there are happy to see the unsightly, litter-strewn lot replaced by a building, and the DIM is happy to have a place where its personnel will feel welcome. And of course, the parents of the children who use the grassy lot are happiest of all, because now the lot will be officially declared a public playground and be protected for the long term from construction of new buildings.

Strategy #6: Make Use of Government
Land Preservation Programs

The land-swap described above exemplifies this strategy quite well. A variation on the same theme is use of **public easements**, which confer tax advantages on private developers who give up development rights for the public good. Let's say the grassy lot described in the case above is not owned by the government. A private developer has owned it for years, but never had any plans to sell it or develop it. Now the DIM approaches him with an offer, but it isn't very enticing. He knows if he takes the government's low bid for the land, he'll hear from all the citizens whose children now use it as a playground, and the press will treat him like the Grinch Who Stole Christmas. He cares about his public image—but he's not so philanthropic that he's willing to give the land away, without any sort of return.

The solution is for him to "rent" the land to the Parks Department for a nominal sum of one dollar per year, with a ninety-nine-year lease. Under the **public easement** program he can then take a tax deduction for the amount of commercial rent he has foregone, which will offset taxable profits from his other development ventures. The donor's tax attorney has advised him of how much he can claim each year. And of course he is now relieved of all property taxes and maintenance costs for the donated land. On top of these benefits, he will be feted in the press for his magnanimous show of public-spiritedness. That alone makes the idea sound better than taking the DIM's cash settlement. (Of course the DIM is still left looking for a place to build its annex...but that's not the neighborhood's problem.)

Easements, I should warn, work only in a limited number of circumstances. It's not often that a private owner will find more benefit in the tax break that comes with land donation than he would from sale. And, in some cases, even when an owner is willing to give an easement, the government is not willing to accept it. More and more, in these days of high government deficits, the Parks Department will not have the money to clean up, maintain, or improve the land as is necessary, and so will refuse to take control. Or government acceptance may hinge on the neighborhood's willingness to pay whatever upkeep or insurance costs may be entailed. If an easement seems a plausible solution to a land problem in your neighborhood, you might consider how much (if anything) you could contribute to the package financially, to make the deal acceptable to the government side.

Eminent domain is another useful legal concept when it is your neighborhood's goal to see private land acquired by your local, state, or the U.S. government for preservation as a park or wilderness area. The U.S. Constitution specifically confers upon the government the right to take land in the public interest, provided that the owner receive fair compensation for his property. The "Third Battle of Manassas" was perhaps the most celebrated recent demonstration of how eminent domain works. The Hazel/Peterson Development Company was planning to create an immense new shopping center/office/residential complex on land adjacent to the Manassas National Battlefield in Virginia. The U.S. Park Service had long hoped to acquire the acreage (the scene of some of the heaviest fighting of the Civil War), but Congress had never appropriated the money for an offer to the owners. Once the news of the private development became widely known, and the media broadcast the fact that boutiques and fast-food stands were going to be built where Stonewall Jackson's Army fell by the thousands, citizens all over America were appalled. Thousands of letters came pouring in to Congressional offices urging the government to acquire the land at any cost.

But while eminent domain was used in that instance to do what the majority of the people favored, eminent domain is not always so benign, from the average citizen's point of view. Governments sometimes use their powers to take property to make way for developments that neighborhoods oppose. For example, a group of houses might stand in the way of a planned highway, a nuclear missile silo, a dam, a military base, or any other large-scale project. As long as the owners receive fair market value (which is usually set by a judge, and based on an independently secured appraisal), it may be very difficult for citizens to challenge the transfer of the land for the unwanted use.

In such cases prevention will generally yield better results than any attempts at a remedy after the fact. Before there is any controversy on the horizon, establish a good line of communication between your elected officials and your neighborhood. Government planners typically consult the area's representatives before arranging any expensive (and possibly controversial) expansion into a neighborhood, and will defer to the politician's advice. If you've already made your group's presence known to your representative and briefed him about your feelings toward development, you can reasonably expect him to give your advice the same sort of deference, and advise the government agency accordingly on its development plans.

Of course, some kinds of development nobody wants nearby, and if your politician isn't very powerful, your district may get a project despite his best efforts. Toxic waste treatment plants, incinerators, landfills, and nuclear waste burial sites are just a few of the more obvious examples. But in such cases there is far more at stake than just the comfort and convenience of the immediate neighborhood. There are environmental, health, and safety issues of national consequence involved, and you and your neighbors will doubtless be linking up with national cause organizations to wage the battle together. Remember, it wasn't the residents of southeastern New Hampshire who led the fight against the construction of the Seabrook nuclear power plant—but they certainly were glad to have the outside help.

Strategy #7: Call Out the Press

When the government development agency is moving like a steamroller over all the obstacles your neighborhood is attempting to throw in its path, that may be because somewhere along the line someone has received a little extra incentive to keep the plans going forward. A politician may be using his influence over the process, to his own benefit, or to the benefit of his friends or supporters. Perhaps his campaign relied heavily on contributions from defense contractors, and now those contractors are anxious to avoid any delay in the construction of the tank-testing course they've been hired to build. It could even be that he's received some illegal payments for the assurance of support for the chosen site. (Things like that have happened more times in our history than most of us like to contemplate.)

But a politician need not be corrupt to push hard for a project some of his constituents will oppose. Oftentimes, the more construction and government contracting dollars a representative brings in, the more of a benefactor he is held to be by the voters in his district—all except, of course, that small fraction who happens to live under the shadow of the large new government development. If the proposed construction in a particular district seems to do less to serve the needs of the government agency than it does to serve the political boss's need to look like a good provider to his constituents, then the project may be easily condemned as an example of the **"pork-barrel"** at work. If, in addition, the project is susceptible to charges that it is poorly designed, unsuitable to its site, or duplicative of other government developments elsewhere, then the term you should use to describe the project is a **"boondoggle."**

Either way—boondoggle or pork-barrel—the press should be called to investigate the plan. Nothing excites a good investigative reporter so much as the chance to uncover a blatant example of government waste, favoritism, mismanagement, or fraud. You'll just need to give the press some kind of a lead to start working on. Just because you don't like a project, that doesn't make it a waste of the taxpayers' money. You should start looking for someone in the government who agrees with your assessment of the plan, and who is in a position to know—perhaps a disgruntled employee of the agency, or someone in the budget, accounting, or auditor's office, who has analyzed the costs. In an open society such as ours, officials just can't be stopped from leaking information, and when something big and controversial is involved, it's almost a certainty that someone will have reason to let out the dirty details (if indeed there are any to let out). Your own "Deep Throat" could just be waiting to see who, if anyone, is willing to act on the information he or she is ready to divulge.

Once you have some kind of solid tip to go on, don't be afraid to "call cold"—that is, phone a reporter you've never met and pass on what you've learned. Relay whatever facts you have at the time, without embellishment or hype, and suggest what you believe further investigation could reveal. To invest any time in the matter, the reporter needs to feel you are trustworthy and have reason to know what you're talking about. Offer to put the reporter in direct touch with the source, if possible; take him or her on a tour of the disputed site; and try to get him copies of any memos or other documents that support your contentions.

If you succeed in starting a media expose', the press may just do the rest of your work for you. Newspapers and TV stations love to show how they've saved the public millions by keeping a boondoggle or pork-barrel project from being built. They also like to make public heroes out of **whistleblowers** (which is what you would be if you brought a spending scandal to light).

Even if the press scrutiny ultimately fails to stop the construction, you will likely see greater attention paid to how it gets built and what impact it has on the neighborhood. You may be able to get some particularly obnoxious elements changed, or the size scaled back, or receive some concessions in the building's outward appearance or operations. So there is always something to be gained by calling press attention to a project, and little to be lost. The worst that will happen is that your leads won't pan out, and the story will just never get written.

Signs like this one let you know that Uncle Sam is a developer, too.

Federal Projects Involve Special Rules and Procedures

Whether your development problem stems from city, county, state, or federal action, any of the preceding strategies might be of help. But there are a few other techniques you can try that apply only in federally initiated cases. These are based on the fact that the federal government has established for itself a rather stringent set of rules governing how it selects sites, how much it may pay for leases or purchases, and how its buildings must be run after they are in use.

1. The General Service Administration (GSA) is the agency in charge of the maintenance and disposition of federal properties, and its chief duty is to see that the U.S. government gets the necessary space and services it needs at the cheapest possible price. If you can show that the deal being worked in your neighborhood is not the best the government can do—that the government is paying more than the fair market rate, or that more space is available for less elsewhere in the area—you stand a chance to see the unwanted facility relocated to a more acceptable spot.

2. Federal buildings have to conform to a host of standards and regulations that are more stringent than those applied to most privately held buildings. By law they must be handicapped-accessible. They must be free from asbestos, lead in the water, radon, and other hazards. It must be feasible to arrange for security of all exits and entrances, to reduce the danger of bombings, or theft of documents. If you suspect the new federal building in your neighborhood will not conform to any of these standards, put in an immediate challenge to its opening. You should be able to get a few months' delay, at the very least, to allow time to study the suspected problem. And even if the problem can be fixed, it could well turn out that the cost for bringing the building up to the federal standard is so high that the contemplated use is no longer acceptable to the GSA's vigilant cost-accountants.

3. Assuming you've followed the advice in the preceding section and contacted your district representative for his help in opposing the government's action, and assuming he has refused to help...start lobbying the rest of your state's delegation. You have two senators to influence, and other representatives as well. If you can get a number of the more important members, or better still, a majority of your state's delegation to support your neighborhood's position, then your own district Congressman may well change his mind.

4. Remember, also, that Congress works by committees and subcommittees. Find out who is chairing the committee with oversight in your area, and shift your lobbying from your individual Congressman (assuming, once again, that he has not been supportive of your position) to the committee-members. For example, if you've been trying to secure a promise from the federal government not to sell off a piece of national parkland to private developers, you would go to the House

Committee on the Interior and Insular Affairs, and its Subcommittee on National Parks and Public Lands. At the same time you should probably also bring your case to the attention of the Senate Committee on Energy and Natural Resources, through its Subcommittee on Public Lands, Parks, and National Forests. Finding the right committee may require some study of the committee structure and a lot of time on the telephone attempting to get direction from staff-members...but nobody promised you this was going to be easy. If you can afford it, you might do well to hire an experienced political consultant just to get you moving in the right direction through the Congressional maze.

5. In certain areas such as environmental policy, federal legislation generally is more protective than state or local ordinances are. In January, 1989, the Environmental Protection Agency (EPA) unveiled a far-reaching set of new conservation measures making it much tougher for developers, both public and private, to encroach on the nation's remaining wetlands. Several agencies besides the EPA will be involved in enforcing the new standards, including the Army Corps of Engineers, the Soil and Conservation Service, and the Fish and Wildlife Service. Any of these may be approached by citizens who believe that inappropriate development is about to take place on land that federal legislation seeks to conserve.

6. Special mention needs to be made of the Endangered Species Act. Many citizens mistakenly believe that if a development threatens to cause the extinction of any species of living creature, no matter how small, then the law decrees an end to the habitat-threatening project. Not so. Only federally funded projects are subject to the law. However, a substantial percentage of state and local projects are dependent on federal contributions or matching funds. Highways are typically joint state/federal ventures, and so the Act may be cited in these cases. This happened most recently in Delaware, over a 1.5 mile segment of roadway over land possibly inhabited by the rare bog-turtle (a species distinguishable from the common spotted turtle only by an orange patch behind its eyes). The 25–million-dollar project has been brought to a halt while scientists comb the area, looking for the four-inch-long turtles and checking the color of patches behind their eyes.

7. Special types of federal facilities have to go through specific federal review boards set up by Act of Congress. For example, the U.S. Commission of Fine Arts reviews all plans for federal monuments, memorials, and statues. The National Capital Planning Commission passes on the design and site-planning of federal buildings in the National Capital Region (Washington, D.C., and environs). The U.S.

The U.S. Army wants to tear down this miniature lighthouse, but first there must be at least four hearings.

Army holds its own hearings on planned construction or expansion of its facilities on U.S. soil. Provided citizens find out when the relevant review board is holding the hearing and file a written request to testify far enough in advance, they will be accorded time to air all their problems with the proposed construction in their neighborhood. Preparing for one of these special board hearings is the same as preparing for a local zoning hearing—supporting documentation from experts should be lined up, witnesses to cover each of the various points should be found, and photographs, maps, videos, and other graphic materials helpful to getting your views across should be presented.

8. In this era of limited federal funds, the government increasingly enters into private-public partnerships to get its buildings built. Let's say the government owns a fifty-acre tract of land, and wants to develop fifteen of those acres as offices and administrative headquarters for its personnel. It may find a private development company to build the needed buildings for it, in exchange for permission to develop other offices, residences, or stores on the remaining thirty-five acres for private profit. Because the land is still federally owned, it is exempt from local zoning controls—even though the greater part of development on the land will look, function, and create problems for the neighborhood just as if it were a wholly private endeavor. The U.S. military base at Ft. Belvoir, Virginia is now considering a major expansion to be carried out under just such a partnership arrangement. Each time such a plan comes up anywhere for review (and the Ft. Belvoir plan just cited will go through at least *five* stages of federal hearings), opponents should

do their best to show that the deal serves the private interest far better than it does the public-at-large.

You may want to argue that an unhappy surrounding citizenry makes a poor working environment for federal employees. When you speak up against such arrangements, you are in a sense defending one of the fundamental precepts of our democracy: that good government depends on the consent of the governed. The consideration that governments show to those of the governed who live closest to the buildings where the governing goes on is a reliable index of how sensitive the government is to the wishes of its people.

But you may have to work hard to see that your public officials are properly sensitized, before you are shown the consideration you know your neighborhood deserves.

SAVING THE SUBURBS

The New York Times

Dense residential development in Johnson County, Kansas, southwest of Kansas City.

When most people think about overdevelopment, they picture skyscraper-filled cities and densely congested urban streets. But "Manhattanization" of our cities isn't the only problem on the minds of anti-development activists these days. Some of the most heated battles going on now are between developers of new suburban subdivisions and the residents of the brand-new towns and villages they have built. Thinking they were getting away from the crowds, noise, and pollution of the big city, oftentimes the buyers of suburban homes are shocked to find, not long afterward, that the hustle, bustle, and development of city life has followed them on their path out of town. And they want to do something about it.

Here's a typical tale: A family visits a new subdivision, they see a model of a house they like and can afford, and though it's nearly an hour's commute from town, they decide to buy and move in as soon as their section of the development is complete. They like the tall stand of trees behind their lot and the fact that it's on a cul-de-sac. What they do not realize is that the developer has plans to cut down all those trees to make more building lots later on, and to turn the cul-de-sac into a through street to reach the new development section once it's complete.

Of course the buyers of the lot feel cheated and want to fight. But that may not be so easy, they find out to their dismay. All of the residents are as new to the area as they are, and so the neighborhood lacks the cohesion and leadership more often found in older, established urban places. Even if the people manage to organize themselves into an effective group, they may find they lack legal grounds to object to the changes. The sales-contract they have signed contains fine print clauses alluding to future development of houses and roads—though none of the buyers believed the new construction was to go up anywhere near them.

Still, the residents want to press their case. But when they tell their story to the local newspaper, they're surprised at how few people rally to their cause. The common attitude seems to go something like this: "That subdivision is already a sprawling mess of houses where there once was only green. Why should we object if a few more trees are being cut to build a few more tract houses?" No groups are charged up and ready to defend the character of the suburban village, the way they would be if one of the older, more familiar parts of the big city was threatened by the bulldozer. Once a place gets a few too many houses, shopping malls, or asphalt, it's as if people throw up their hands, say, "It's already ruined," and the hell with it!

These are just a few of the hazards you face if you're fighting for your suburban neighborhood—but they can be overcome, if you have strategies ready to deal with them as they occur. Other suburbanites around the country have shown it can be done in the cases they have won. As I often advise, if you know of any successful anti-development battles like yours that have resulted in citizen victories in your area (or know of any that are ongoing), it's always a good idea to call the people involved and get the benefit of their experience. People generally like to do what they can for neighbors in a similar situation. (I know I do when strangers call me for advice.)

Contracts and Covenants

In many suburban cases, the best advice you can get is to look into the future development picture very carefully *before* you sign anything, or even make an offer. When the real estate agent is first showing you around the area, ask all the questions you can possibly think of, and where the answers are important to you, try to get them down in writing. If the agent can't give you the answers you need, put the question to the development company directly, and look to get back a written reply on the company letterhead. If you're worried about possibly losing out to another purchaser while you're waiting for the reply, go ahead and put in an offer—but make your offer *contingent* on satisfactory answers to your questions.

While your questions must be tailored to the specifics of the house, lot, and subdivision that interest you, here are some typical issues to raise when looking over a house in a not-yet-completed development area: Is the wooded land behind the house going to stay that way? Who owns it? If it belongs to the development company, and they tell you it will stay wooded, what guarantees are they willing to give to that effect? What happens when the land is sold? Do the guarantees convey with the land?

What about county, state, or federal land nearby? What plans does the government have for its use or sale? What about power lines, power plants, sewer lines, garbage pickup, and other services and utilities for the subdivision? What's the plan for placement of utility poles, dumpsters, satellite receiving dishes, and other mechanical structures?

Who has authority over what homeowners can do on their private lots? Is there a homeowners' association? Does the development company have any seats (or even a majority?) on it? What special requirements, restrictions, or **covenants*** will you have to sign if you decide to buy? Are exceptions ever made, and under what circumstances?

What about other subdivisions or undeveloped private land nearby? What's it zoned for? What is known about the adjacent owners' plans for it? Is there a county master plan that sheds light on the type and density of development contemplated over a long term? If there are any documents available for you to see that will answer these questions for you, by all means obtain them.

Never rely exclusively on the promises made to you on the spot by agents or development company representatives. Their words of reassurance may be empty of reality. Your real estate agent tells you, "Oh, you don't have to worry about those willow trees coming down. The company would have to be crazy to let them go—they're such a selling point for the lots on this street." Yes,

---

* These are private agreements that bind all the owners of land in a particular area.

they'd be crazy to cut them *now*...but after all the lots on the street have sold, it wouldn't be so crazy to cut them down and make one more buildable lot on the land to sell.

If such assurances are not written down in a contract or a letter, they don't exist.

Unless you've had a lot of experience buying and selling houses, it's usually worth it to have a closing attorney go over the contract and any covenants or homeowners' association by-laws involved, before the deal is final. The cost is just a small fraction of the purchase price—which for most people is the biggest investment decision of their lives. Tell your settlement attorney about any oral assurances you may have received before you sign, so he or she will know what written guarantees to look for (or write in, if they're not there). Also mention any special plans or additions you may have in mind for the house in the next few years. The attorney may think it's perfectly fine for you to pledge to continue to use the same wood for repairs of any shingles, trim, and fences on your property—not knowing all the while that you're planning to replace the cedar-shingled roof with a more fireproof asphalt shingle. It's only after you've hired contractors and had half of the old shingles torn off that the homeowners' association brings the work to a halt, and you learn that the covenant you signed forbids you from changing roofing materials.

To avoid this sort of situation, have the attorney go over the contract and other documents with you, paragraph by paragraph, in plain English, like this: "This part says if you want to replace the roof or any of the trim, you've got to use cedar that matches the cedar used on all the other houses. This next part says if the Homeowners' Association Board votes by a majority to allow it, any of the common areas—including the park near your house—may be sub-divided for development as more townhouses."

If there are parts of the contract you don't like, see if you or your lawyer can negotiate changes before you buy. It may be done as simply as crossing out some of the printed clauses and having all parties initial the changes made. With more detailed changes, you may want to attach an addendum or exchange letters describing the revisions you have worked out.

If you can't get what you feel you need to live the sort of lifestyle you enjoy, then you had better not buy. The courts have generally been unsympathetic to competent adults who sign agreements to conform to certain rules, and then try to change the rules after they've moved in. The one great exception to this principle comes when the covenants or contracts violate the law, the Constitution, or public policy. So a covenant that forbids you to practice Hinduism (if that's your religion) cannot be enforced because it violates the First Amendment, which guarantees your religious freedom (this principle is discussed in more detail on pages 278–81.)

Problem: The Privatization of Suburban Towns

More and more of the functions that governments used to assume—the collection of trash, the maintenance of streets, provision for pedestrian safety, patrols to protect the neighborhood from crime, etc.—are being taken over by the developers and by homeowner's associations in suburban enclaves. When citizens get into conflicts with these private corporations or organizations, government officials are usually reluctant to intervene.

The phenomenon was well-described by *Washington Post* reporter Sam Hankins in an article in that newspaper on June 11, 1988:

"Local governments once took care of community facilities, but now they are reluctant to do so in the face of tight budgets. Roger Winston, a Silver Spring [Maryland] real estate attorney and chairman of the local community association's legislative committee, noted that 'Twenty years ago, playgrounds, basketball courts and pools would be found in public parks that a developer would dedicate to local governments. But now, more and more planners are saying, don't give us the land. Now they ask developers to put in pools and jogging trails and then form homeowner associations that will be required to maintain these amenities.'"* Where there once were publicly legislated laws and ordinances telling citizens what they could and could not do in their homes and on public property, each subdivision may now have its own peculiar set of rules and regulations, which new residents must attempt to understand. Because they frequently are not aware of what's allowed and what's banned at the time they moved in, homeowners are increasingly in conflict with their subdivision associations, and are looking to the courts for better definition of their rights and responsibilities. Hankins provides three examples that clarify the state of the law.

The first concerns restrictions on *use*. A homebuyer had established a day-care center in her house—a home occupation expressly permitted under the county's zoning code. Covenants governing the subdivision, however, prohibited all home businesses. The homeowner argued that caring for children whose parents were working during the day was a community service more than a business...but she lost. The unhappy ex-day-care provider told the *Washington Post*, "There's no way I would have bought the house had I known about the covenants."

A second case speaks to homeowner **obligations.** A buyer of a half-million-dollar house in a development of large estates and mansions learns that, under the rules of the homeowners' association, he is required to pay a hundred-dollar-a-month fee to have a professional lawn service maintain his grounds. He wanted to mow his own grass, and so he sued for the privilege. But after his

---

* "Covenants a Source of Conflict," p. E1.

lawyer told him what it would cost him to pursue the matter in court, and how little likelihood he had of winning, he decided to pay up and withdraw his case.

Both the millionaire homeowner and the hourly-wage-earning day-care worker learned the same lesson: WYSIWYG, or What You *Sign* Is What You Get. But covenants are enforceable only if they are applied equitably to all members of the community. Hankins gives an illustration of the point: If the homeowners' association requires all fences to be made of wood, but then takes no action when some of the homeowners put up chain-link, it can't suddenly go after the last one to substitute metal for wood. The homeowner can successfully argue that the rule has been **waived in practice** and so has become unenforceable.

Rules also must be **reasonable** to be upheld. A third case in Hankins' article involves the "reasonableness" test. A covenant prohibited homeowners from parking commercial vehicles on the street in front of their houses. A resident owned a truck, painted on the side with the logo of his employer's company, but he fashioned a removable magnetic panel to cover up the offending commercial lettering while the truck was in front of his house. The homeowners' association argued that the covenant had been broken, because the commercial logo was still there, even though no one could see it. But a judge ruled for the resident/owner of the truck, saying that he had done as much as any reasonable person could do to comply with the association's rules. He would not have to sell his truck (and possibly give up his job for the company whose logo it carried) in order to abide by the rules in the most literal sense.

Though these three cases taken together shed some light on the circumstances in which privately run associations can make rules for homeowners, there is an infinite variety of other situations and conflicts not yet settled in our courts of law. Exercising your greatest powers of foresight, you still cannot anticipate every potential conflict you could have if you move into a subdivision where many previously governmental responsibilities are now in private hands.

What should you, the citizen, do in this situation? Not buy into such a town? Some would say, if you wish to preserve your individual rights, that is your safest course. My own advice would be, run for the board of the homeowners' association, and encourage others who think like you to run for the other seats. Together you can change the rules and make your new subdivision town over into a more tolerant and easy-going kind of place.

Problem: The Sub-subdivision of the Subdivision

Let's assume you read the contract and all the covenants quite carefully before you signed on the dotted line. You are confident that no further building can go on next door to you, because the lots have already been developed, and the contract expressly forbids any further subdivision of developed land. What problem could there be?

You've forgotten that your homeowners' association has the power, by majority vote, to change the rules they have written for themselves. Now suppose there is a proposal to take a few of those extra-generous back yards to houses near yours and re-subdivide them to create space for extra "infill" houses. Only a few of the residents whose houses abut the newly created lots are objecting to the change. The rest live too far away to care one way or the other, or they look on the additional fees to be generated by the added density, and they're in favor. The development company has three permanent seats on the association board, and of course they're all for the plan (in fact, they proposed it). So you and your immediate neighbors find yourselves in a small minority. Do you have any recourse?

A case like this was recently decided by a judge in Prince Georges County, Maryland. He found that association rules could not be waived on a lot-by-lot basis; to do so violated the "uniformity principle" of zoning (discussed in Chapter 8). The rule applied even though the land-use regulating agency in this case was a privately run association rather than a county zoning board. All lots in the same general area, sharing the same general characteristics had to be subject to further subdivision, or none could be. It was unfair to the few association members whose houses bordered on the subdividable land to create more building lots near their property, but nowhere else in the subdivision.

(Of course, if the case had been tried in a different state, or before a different judge, a different opinion could have resulted. If you find yourself in a similar situation, you'll be well advised to look up the closest precedents in your state.)

Problem: Conflicts between Covenants and Other Rights

How binding are private agreements between parties on purely personal decisions, such as who you live with and what you do behind closed doors? This is a matter that land-use and civil liberties lawyers find themselves debating more and more. Weighty tomes have been written about the subject, but I will only look at two cases, one to show how covenants may *not* restrict your personal choices, and one to show how land-use regulations can legitimately be used to curtail specific activities.

Example #1: You buy a house in a subdivision and move in with your longtime companion, her adult stepson by a previous marriage, your eighty-year-old invalid grandmother, and her full-time attendant. The homeowners' association wastes no time in telling you that you've violated one of its most basic rules: that homes are for "single-family use only"—single-family being defined in their covenant as husband, wife, and children, period. But your state has its own human rights legislation, which forbids discrimination on the basis of age, infirmity, sexual preference, and many other conditions; and your lawyer tells you that you have a constitutional right to privacy and freedom of association. You're not about to give up your home without a fight. But can you win?

If you live in New York State, the answer is yes. A March 23, 1989 decision by the state's highest court overturned a local regulation because it restricted the number of unrelated persons who could live together, while imposing no such restriction on relatives. But in Florida and Arizona, where state law is less protective of individual rights, private developments have been permitted to make certain exclusions on the basis of age.

"Retirement villages" have been found to be within their rights to insist that children—even grandchildren on a two-week summer visit—be barred from living in a privately run complex. In many other states, cases are pending to determine the question. The law can be described as being in a state of flux—with the trend going in the direction of expansion of the definition of the term "family." Still, there's no sure predicting of the outcome of any one covenant-vs.-privacy case.

Example #2: You are a minister and you own a large home in a subdivision, with a swimming pool in the back. Every Sunday you have upwards of thirty children to your house for instruction in the tenets of your faith, and on occasion you use your swimming pool to conduct full-immersion baptismal rites on members of the congregation. The homeowners' association tells you that what you are doing violates the rights of your neighbors to enjoy a quiet Sunday in their own backyards. The congregants' cars take up all the parking spaces on the street, and the shouting of prayer responses at your sunrise service wakes people up at 6 a.m. You respond that you are bound by your conscience to proselytize for your faith everywhere you go, at home as well as abroad. You believe the First Amendment of the Constitution gives you the absolute right to continue with the religious classes and ceremonies.

Whose rights take precedence? This type of case has generally been easy for the courts. You do have the right to lead your congregation as you see fit, but you must find an appropriate place to do it. You need a church or some other building suitable for large crowds, located in a zone permitting institutional use. That building, like any other non-religious structure, must have sufficient fire exits and meet all the load standards necessary to ensure the safety of the number of congregants who use it. The courts have consistently found that there is a legitimate public interest in regulating what types of buildings can be used for different purposes, and that religion cannot be used to claim exemption from basic health and safety requirements.

Your home ministry will certainly be problematic from this point of view, as was the religious school a Virginia pastor attempted to open in two private houses he owned in a Fairfax County suburb. The court issued a restraining order barring the minister from setting up the school, which neighbors claimed would have overburdened their residential streets with school-bus traffic and faculty parking.

Both examples together, though they may seem contradictory on the surface, illustrate the same general principle, which may (somewhat loosely) be stated thus: What you do in your own home that affects only you is protected; when the effects of your home activities spill over into the neighborhood, some means of community regulation (whether by public law or private covenant) is in order.

Ownership Roulette

What if you've been unable to deal effectively with the development plans for your subdivision because the ownership keeps changing on you? This has become a problem in many of our explosively growing suburbs. Investors get the idea they can't lose in real estate, they form a partnership, buy some land, start to build some houses, and then sell out (or go bankrupt) partway through the project. It often goes like this: One partnership is formed to buy the lots, which are then sold to another group that develops plans, which in turn sells the plans to a builder...who then goes belly-up and has his assets taken over by creditors, who find a different developer to complete the project, which, after completion, is sold to some other corporation that will run it.... Well, that's seven owners so far, and the subdivision is hardly more than a few years old.

In situations such as this, the new ownership company will typically want to free itself from the contractual obligations of the prior developer. It may attempt to prove to the buyers of the houses that the original terms were unfair, too harsh, or can no longer be met by a company that hopes to stay in business (the proof is often the fact that the previous company went under). But the truth may be that the old company was poorly managed, founded by inexperienced investors who paid too much for the land, or built units too small and too shoddy to be sold at their astronomical asking prices. The trouble is that without greater access to the facts, residents often accept the first explanations they're given, and permit agreements to be changed to their disadvantage. My advice is: Hang tough, and make the new owners prove, not just to your satisfaction, but to the satisfaction of some mutually-agreed-upon outside auditor, that any concessions asked are absolutely necessary and cannot be avoided by cutbacks on the developer's side of the ledger.

Consider, too, that sometimes the "new owners" aren't really new. The way some developers slip around an unprofitable situation is to appear to have a new regime in place, when it's really just a name change, or a change in some of the cast of characters. In one case I worked on, a development company suffered a major setback when its rezoning application was disapproved; so the development corporation that had filed the application was dissolved, and a new owner/developer, with a new idea, materialized. It took some digging around in the deed and tax-records on the neighborhood's part to discover that the head of the "new" company was in fact the silent partner from the former development corporation. He'd just picked a new name for the letter-head and hired a different law firm to represent his plans to the community. The money was still the same; only the name had changed.

Sometimes the company doing the developing is a subsidiary of a bigger corporation, and when corporate restructuring goes on at the higher level, the developer you had assumed was in control disappears, to be replaced by new faces and new titles from different parts of the corporation—though no money and no papers have changed hands. You need to find out, in that case, whether a new development philosophy has come in along with the new faces. Don't be afraid to ask who's really in charge, if you're confused by the changes. If you don't get answers right away, you may have to wait until the dust settles, but be persistent. Your steadfastness during this period of internal shake-up could have a lot to do with whether the higher-ups decide to go through with the development as planned.

Occasionally the names and faces will change, and you will be *told* the philosophy has changed—your new contact will tell you, "This developer wants to be more sensitive to the needs of the community" than the old company was, and "He wants to work with you," and be "more open, do things the right way," etc., etc. —and that all sounds fine; but remember: "Watch what they do, not what they say." Conciliatory words are a nice start, but don't give up anything until they show you how nice they can be for real.

On the other hand, a change in development philosophy, along with a change in ownership, could easily be for the worse. The new developer may tell you he intends to do things quite a bit differently from the old owner, who was "too soft." It's No More Mr. Nice-Guy for you. Developers like this will try to put on a tough show. They'll tell you, "Look, you people were so damn demanding, so rigid, so intransigent, you caused Mr. Nice-Guy to take a bath. You imposed all those conditions and costs on him, and he just couldn't stay in business. But we're not going to make that mistake. We're not accepting any of his concessions. It's a whole new ball game, and we're starting again from zero."

This kind of talk may make some of your neighbors feel they are playing out of their league. They may want to take what they're offered or give up. But you'll try your best to keep everyone's resolve firm. Just keep reminding everyone, you're not there to guarantee anyone's profits. The developer bought the land, and he's got to deal with all the factors that came along with it—including a group that had already made its views known to the previous owner. He should have to deal with your presence as a given, just as he would do with silty soil conditions or other difficulties of the site. The costs of dealing with the real needs of the neighborhood are just as important (maybe more, in your eyes) than the cost of dealing with the soft footings on which his building will rest.

What do you do when there has not yet been an ownership change, but you're being threatened with the prospect if you do not give in on some important demands? The developer tells you, "Either accept the development as I've planned it, or I'll dump the whole project, and you don't know who you'll end up with." The next guy may be worse, or he may be better, but in the meantime the land will sit vacant (possibly with a giant hole dug in the middle of it) and it could become an empty, unsightly no-man's land.

This is indeed a good reason to try your best to reach a *reasonable* accommodation with the owner now—but that's not to say you should abandon your community-established priorities. You worked too hard to come to a consensus about what's important to your neighborhood, and you can't let yourself be scared away from that by the threat of ownership roulette. You'll feel somewhat more secure, whether the threat is good or it's a bluff, if you've taken certain precautionary steps:

- You've done your political homework and can count on your elected and appointed officials to stand by your community's position, and not switch sides merely because the ownership has changed hands.
- You know the relevant city/county codes and enforcement procedures and so know what to do if the owner ceases to maintain his property as he is required to do while he is looking for a buyer. You're willing to call the building inspectors out to cite him for every violation of fire safety, health hazards, etc., and people will call the police with tips if they see any drug dealing or other crime transpiring on the vacant lot.

- You've worked out among your own neighbors different scenarios and contingency plans so that if ownership changes and new plans suddenly arise, you can react to them swiftly and make counter-proposals as may be necessary.
- You may have also explored the possibility of raising capital from within the community so that you can make a competitive offer for the land, should it go on the market. You could also see if there is government interest in acquiring the land and dedicating it to public benefit, or entering into a partnership with a "Community Development Corporation" to build something that will both make money and serve some public purpose.

When a community knows what it wants, and what laws and codes protect it, and can act coherently in response to developers' moves, it will not be the loser in the game of ownership roulette. But even so, it's never any fun to have to sweat out what chance may bring you next.

Building Unity Amid Suburban Separateness

The isolation and insularity of suburban towns can be a powerful obstacle preventing residents of different parts of the county from joining together to fight overdevelopment. Sometimes the residents of one subdivision end up fighting the residents of another, rather than the developer whose dense building scheme is threatening both.

It can happen this way: A developer goes to the county planners seeking an upzoning of land so that he can build a dense apartment complex. It's county policy to encourage the production of affordable housing units, and so the planners encourage him to proceed with his application. Their question is not whether any land should be upzoned, but which parcel of vacant land in the county is the most suitable site. There's a north county site, but the residents of the nearest single-family subdivision will protest if the complex is put near them. They think it should go on a site farther south, but the residents of subdivisions down that way don't want it either.

Leaders of each residents' association are calling the other names. It's the Divide-and-Conquer Ploy—but this time it isn't the developer exploiting the division; it's occurred naturally, because of the patterns of residential separateness of suburban growth. Each little subdivision defends its own turf. Alone, each stands little chance of winning. But their efforts to control the number of new units and shape of the complex would be increased if all the heads of the homeowners' associations met and came to some agreement on what they would say about the plan, wherever it is sited. They may not be able to unite on all the minor planning details involved in the case, but they should at least be able to come together over a few broad principles, which could be applied to development, wherever it will occur. These might be that:

- No development permits should be issued for a project unless it has been demonstrated that road capacity for the increased traffic already exists. Promises to study traffic problems and plan for future road-building or other traffic-mitigating measures are not sufficient to remove opposition.
- Buffer zones of trees or open space should be maintained between existing developments and the new project.
- Parking lots or other large paved areas must be screened from view by trees, shrubs, fences, or other landscape elements.
- Access to public transportation must be arranged for residents of the new complex.
- Care must be exercised to protect environmentally sensitive features (such as streams, creeks, marshes, glens, or animal habitats) from development disturbance.

Once you have your basic points of agreement, write them up in a joint statement or position paper that you can quote to county planners, elected officials, and the developer. That way they will understand that it's not just you and a few neighbors who are grumbling about your own back yards. You will show organizing power and voting strength through your united effort. It would help if, in addition to defining the type of development you would oppose, you could list some qualities of development you would like to encourage in the area. This shows that you are not just a bunch of obstructionists, but have some positive ideas to contribute.

You should also seek support from as many different types of communities as can be found in your county or region. Seek common ties with leaders from other neighborhoods and incorporate their wishes into your document, if you can. Would they like to see more land acquired by the county for parks, playgrounds, libraries, or schools? If enough communities begin pressing for a specific use of the land in question, you may be able to persuade the county that its policy directives to private developers need to change. You might even start a grass-roots campaign to get the government to buy the land itself and dedicate it to the preferred public use.

The county could also figure into a private/public partnership deal, whereby some additional housing is built, and the rest of the land is given over to public use through the donation of an easement. Deals of this sort require goodwill on all parts—and some hard "number-crunching" to make them work, but when they do, it's a thrill for all involved. You get the feeling that you've saved not only your own neighborhood, but done something good and lasting for the residents of the whole county, and that's a very gratifying sensation.

The "Barn-Door" Argument

Another obstacle in your quest to check suburban sprawl is the common perception that you're trying to "close the barn door after the cows are out." The outskirts of all our major cities have already reached a high level of development; but now those same people who bought houses built over what once was verdant farmland are telling newcomers, "You shouldn't settle here—you're taking away what's left of the open space." The earlier suburbanites are like those cows that have escaped from the barn, and now they're trying to keep the pastureland all to themselves. What does it matter if a few more cows are allowed in to share the clover? The landscape is already trampled by so many hooves.

You must be prepared to counter this argument if you hope to generate any enthusiasm for the cause. You can do this in one of three basic ways.

1. You can show that your subdivision is in some way exceptional (because of the diversity of the people who live there, or because it was planned to provide some special features, or because it serves as a model solution to some particular problem) and is therefore worthy of the extra effort to protect its qualities. Or, if you can't show that, then:

2. You may argue that just because some of the land is already blighted by poor development, that's no reason to add to the area's problems. On the contrary, planners should have learned from the mistakes of the past, and now see to it that things will be handled differently this time around.

3. If your area is neither exceptionally well-planned nor particularly blighted, you can argue the passage of time: that when your subdivision was built, no one could have foreseen the problems inherent in the spread-out subdivision style of building. Back then things were different, gas was cheaper, and land seemed endlessly abundant. But the '80s and '90s are not the '50s and '60s, and so building patterns have to change. Growth must now be checked, while there are still some trees and natural beauty left.

As with any anti-development theme, you must be prepared to back up your arguments with evidence, hard facts: car counts, A.Q.I. readings, economic projections based on valid surveys, photographs, and expert witnesses' testimony. People will set aside their prejudices and confirmed views, if you are able to give them a clear, coherent picture of the situation, composed of the pieces of evidence you have assembled in a form they can easily understand.

The Last of the Wide Open Spaces

The suburbs have development problems not experienced in crowded, high-density cities, because they have one important attribute that cities lack: large stretches of undeveloped land. These appear as open invitations to certain types of development not possible in the city—shopping malls and airports, to name just two. Even the open space you may have thought was set aside in perpetuity for special purposes (a cemetery, for example, or a rail-spur), you may find to your shock has been bought up by a developer who plans to build more houses, offices, and shops on it...if you let him.

But different large-tract problems need to be addressed in different ways. The following are a few of the common problems facing suburbanites, with suggestions for citizen response.

Shopping Malls

Confession time: My uncle is a shopping center developer. He builds Leviathans of selling space—hundreds of shops encased in a shell of concrete, surrounded by a sea of asphalt. Once inside, you can't tell if you're in Tampa or Nome—it's all the same. And people all over seem to love them just the same; that's why he keeps building more and more of them. The only ones who don't seem to love them quite so much are their nearest neighbors (if there are any). The common strategy of shopping mall siting is to find a place out in the middle of nowhere to put the thing, so that as few citizens as possible will come in with objections to the idea.

But the middle of nowhere has a way of shifting over time, and often after the far-away shopping mall has proven a success, other development will follow. The land along the road leading to the mall is bought up and developed with office parks, dense housing complexes, and smaller malls. The area then takes on a certain glittery appeal for retail sales, until along comes a plan for a brand new mega-mall—only this time it's got plenty of neighbors—the owners of homes in the new subdivisions and apartment buildings around the old mall. And they all think enough is enough.

They can organize and fight the mall in the conventional ways, at any number of hearings that must be held. (Shopping malls, being complicated projects, will typically go through several stages of review, including: rezoning hearings, site plan reviews, highway plan amendments, and county master plan adjustments.) Although a large number of officials may have a say in the process, they often give shopping malls favored treatment. Counties may do their best to speed approvals, on the theory that to do so creates a "favorable climate for business"—key to a healthy economy. Upscale malls especially are supposed to give a county a positive image, bringing more jobs, taxes, and consumer options to an area—things we are all supposed to want.

When fighting a mall, you will need to counteract this overly rosy view. You could go about this in several ways:

- You could compile statistics and retail marketing demographics (which you will probably have to pay a high-priced research firm to obtain) to show that the area is "over-malled."
- You could use area unemployment data to show that the mall will not provide jobs to those who need them—that there is, in fact, a deficit of young entry-level workers to serve as store clerks, for example.
- You could show that traffic on the surrounding roads is at the saturation point—though this is just what the developer will expect you to do. He will have his own study to say the opposite, and the two studies will most likely cancel each other out. At zoning hearings, you might be better off to stress the negative economic and environmental impacts, and save the traffic issue for any corollary hearings that may be held separately by whatever body has oversight over changes to the road-system in the area. If the government is expected to foot the bill for the new roads, you could also go after the roads in the budget process.
- You could score some points off the general crassness of malls, especially if the land-area to be turned over to merchandising has some historic or environmental value. The premiere example of this technique was the successful fight to prevent shopping center construction on ground where the Battle of Manassas was fought. The public at large instantly grasped that it was vulgar to sell blue jeans and hamburgers in the place where thousands of young men had fought and died. But if you don't have the memories of the dead to preserve in your case (and Manassas was a rare example), you may well have the habitats of living creatures to protect. The public could be moved by the thought of harm to baby foxes, deer, rabbits, beaver, and even (as in one California case) swarms of butterflies.

- Hit hard on all the other environmental problems implicit in the plan: increase in ozone levels, surface heat generated by added acreage of blacktop and parked cars in the summer sun, freon leaks from the massive air conditioning units needed to cool a large indoor space (which would contribute to the "greenhouse effect")—anything and everything you can think of.
- Get parents or child psychologists to speak about adverse affects of the "shopping mall culture" on teenagers. Possible points to develop: The conversion of open space to selling space transmits a message to the young about a value system that places material desire about all else. The massive, anonymous nature of the shopping mall (unlike the corner store of small town life) voids personal relationships between seller and buyer and subtly encourages shoplifting. Other psychological and philosophical arguments against the shopping mall are advanced by social theorist William H. Whyte in his book *City: Rediscovering the Center* (pp. 208–210).

If the drive for the shopping center has already built up some momentum, it may be too late to argue underlying philosophies or proper siting. You may only be able to exercise damage control, and try to win certain concessions on the size, shape, hours of operation, traffic patterns, and retail mix of the tenants of the space. Opponents, even in small groups, can be a nuisance, and to keep things rolling smoothly, a developer will sometimes be willing to fulfill small requests, in exchange for your promise not to try to block the entire project. If you've sized up the situation and concluded that you have little chance of winning the whole war, concentrate on taking whatever little victories you can get. You and your neighbors may even receive a good offer to sell all your homes to the developer—which may well be preferable to living under the shadow of a retail megastructure. But if you decide to stay and press for concessions, here are some things you could reasonably request:

- Traffic diverters or barriers to keep the shoppers from driving or parking on your residential streets.
- Compatibly designed walls, fences, or a berm to screen the mall and its parking lots from view of private houses.
- Landscaping for you and your neighbors to increase the sense of separation between you and the shopping area.
- Restrictions on special events at the mall, such as fireworks, outdoor band performances, light/laser shows, circus shows, or carnivals in the parking lot, to certain hours, or total prohibition of such events.

- Agreements or covenants between you and the mall-operator
  forbidding expansion or applications for variances in the future.

With any and all such concessions you have gained, make sure you have
some mechanism for enforcement written into the agreement, and that you
know who to take your complaint to should any dispute arise over the
performance of the parties.

Farmland

So you've had it up to here with urban congestion. You hate suburban
sprawl even more, so you moved out to the country, to enjoy clean air and
sunshine and grow your own tomatoes that taste like something other than
sawdust. You love to take long evening walks along unpaved country lanes in
the evening, and are perfectly content...until one day you pass by your
neighbor's spread and see the sign he has tacked up to his elm tree:

**60 ACRES OF PRIME DEVELOPMENT PROPERTY
FOR SALE. CAN BE REZONED FOR 250 HOUSES.**

Then you realize that the suburbs are coming to *you*. You ask your neighbor
what's going on, and he takes a chaw on his tobacco plug, and gives you his
answer in his usual good-ole-boy drawl—except that now he's spewing figures
like a Wall Street banker. Crop prices are down 33 percent, and he needs new
equipment costing $110,000, and the dry spell last year ate up all his profits.
The interest on a loan is back up in the double digits; real estate taxes are
skyrocketing—and the developers now are paying $75,000 per acre—that's
four and a half million dollars—so he's decided to sell up and leave. He's sad to
see the old way of life disappear, and is mourning all the way to the bank.

You wouldn't mind so much if his was the only farm that's being turned
over. But this move is just the latest in a series of farm sales all around you. If
things keep going on this way, there will be no place within a half-day's drive
where anyone is growing any fresh food anymore. Everything will have to be
shipped in from far away, and your children will grow up believing that eggs
come out of styrofoam containers and that meat is a thing wrapped in plastic.

Even if one or two farmers really loved their lives and wanted to stay in
the area, once development reaches a "tipping point," they probably would
not be able to do so. Conflict between them and the residents of the new
subdivisions would be constant. The new people would complain about
crop-dusting, and the slowness of tractors moving along the highways, and the
noisiness of farm-life—the crowing of roosters, the mooing of cows, the
bleating of sheep—not to mention the smells.

Scenarios such as this are widespread across America, but the problem has not been very amenable to solution at the local neighborhood level. But some measures passed on the statewide level have worked to ease the crisis. Maine's 1988 legislation has been the most far-reaching. It prohibited construction of houses, restaurants, campgrounds, and wells within 150 feet of a working farm (defined as at least five acres in size, earning at least $300 per acre, and using pesticides); the 150–foot buffer must be on the land of the non-farm-operating neighbor. The law is the first of its kind in the nation, according to Nancy Bushwick, Director of the Farm Land Project of the Research Foundation of the National Association of State Departments of Agriculture.* It was passed in the hope of stemming the loss of farmland, which in the past thirty years has exceeded a million acres, or over 10,000 individual farms.

Though Maine farmers generally supported the move, in other states farm-retention bills have been eyed more skeptically by the farmers they seek to protect. In semi-rural but rapidly suburbanizing Howard County, Maryland, a measure was introduced to zone land for farm use only, by allowing just one house to be built per twenty acres; but the farmers who wanted to stay on their land argued against it. They said that their borrowing power would decline, if the development potential of their land was so diminished.

Farmers are more likely to look favorably on the tax-abatement approach, which has been tried with varying success in several different states. New Jersey's Farmland Assessment Act of 1964 is a case in point. To qualify for the lowest assessment rate, a farmer need only produce $500 worth of food products a year on the first five acres and $5 worth on each additional acre. However, the twenty-five-year old law desperately needs updating, as developers have proven. They have been buying up farmland, keeping a few acres under production to qualify for the tax-break, and developing the rest of the property at great profit to themselves. The suburbanization of New Jersey farmland is far from being checked.

On Long Island, in New York state, a far more active approach was taken when the government decided to pay farmers outright for the purchase of their development rights. The farmers received fair compensation for the potential sales profits they have forgone, and the public received the assurance that those few remaining farms would continue to produce fresh food for the county, rather than be converted into more houses or offices. But in these days of crunching budgets, few governments have the extra cash needed to duplicate the Long Island solution.

If you are fighting right now to prevent the farms around you from being covered over with buildings, you won't have the time to go lobbying for

---

* Quoted in Lyn Riddle's article in the *New York Times* of July, 17, 1988, "Zone Cushions Farms from Change."

legislation at your state capital. You will have to prepare your hearing against
the proposed upzoning or fight whatever permit applications your developer
has filed, and you can do that just as described in the more general sections of
this book. But added in with all the strategies and arguments described in
earlier chapters, you may want to raise a few other points specific to the goal
of preserving farmland:

- Use to your advantage the nostalgia that generally exists in rural
  areas for the farming way of life. Point out how alien to the local
  culture is the business world (if the development is to be an office
  building) or dense residential living (if the development will be in
  the form of townhouses or apartments).
- Research the history of the area, even if there is no historic
  preservation argument to be made for the farm-buildings themselves. You may find that the land has been continuously used for
  farming for a hundred years or more. In that case there may be more
  reluctance to permit a new use than there would be for land with
  no consistent historical purpose.
- Tie your case to the trend in other parts of the county and the state.
  If farmland is dwindling all over, each remaining piece has more
  significance for the future. Ask the zoning authorities to consider
  the future without any farms at all in the area. Appeal to their pride
  in local traditions and their desire to have their children inherit
  an environment as abundant and life-producing as what is now
  enjoyed.

Rail Spurs

As threatened as is the family farm in America is the old railroad line—
especially in suburbs that were once independent towns. Back in the early days
of settlement the only regular link to the big city was often provided by the
rail spur that fed into the main line at the major railroad hub. These spurs have
long been supplanted by highways, on which both freight-loaded trucks and
passenger cars are driven into the city. But the tracks and the underlying slivers
of land on either side may still belong to the railroad company, or if that
company is defunct (as is often the case), it may belong to a bank, or have
been taken over by the government, or bought up by private investors. What
happens to this unused land usually depends on how alert are the nearby
neighbors at the time any sales or deals are being struck.

If the rail spur has been sitting idle for many years and no plans are on the
boards, the neighbors may have a great opportunity to act before a developer
gets any ideas, before prices rise, before it occurs to anyone how easily a row

of townhouses could be built along the line. Rail spurs can contribute to the neighborhoods they once connected, if the development is tailored to suit the public interest. Here are just three ideas of what can be done:

1. **Bike and Hiking Trails**. Macadam can be put down over the tracks to create a lane just wide enough to allow bikes to pass, leaving a side-area of packed earth so that joggers can run alongside. This not only gives the community a major recreational asset, but can also encourage commuting by bicycle or on foot. If the spur contains enough land area to support the use, parcourse exercise equipment may be placed at appropriate intervals to allow for a full aerobic workout for users. Some cities, including my own, have been successful in finding corporate sponsors to help finance the creation of such a course, which then will host road races and other sporting events, generating good publicity for the corporation as well as fun for the participants. If the races become a popular annual event, the entrance fees could even help to pay for the maintenance of the course.

   Municipalities tend to balk at the cost of acquiring the land, and so conversion to recreational space will be much more likely if the holder of the abandoned rail spur can be induced (with tax incentives or through a land-swap arrangement) to give the land over to the Parks Department. Even so, a city may be unwilling to lose out on the tax revenue that would be generated if full development were to take place. A well-orchestrated public campaign is advisable if government appears to favor private over public development of rail-spur lands.

2. **Mass Transit Line**. Another development project citizens' groups may wish to pursue is conversion of the old tracks into a useful modern transit route for residents to reach their jobs. A commuter train, tram, or trolley—what is called "light rail" in today's transportation jargon—could run on the route, with modifications as are needed. However, neighbors need to be assured that the new trains will be quiet and that guard rails and other safety measures are in place for the protection of people living close to the tracks. Even with the greatest caution, opposition is to be expected from those whose property directly abuts the rail-spur land, but the whole community may be willing to alienate a few in order to bring about a decrease in traffic congestion for everyone else.

3. **Community Gardens**. "The wrong side of the tracks" is the stereotypical view of the houses built right along a rail line, but city planners are often receptive to ways to help change the negative image of the housing found in such a location. One way that has been shown to

work is through the creation of community gardens on otherwise undevelopable pieces of land. Community spirit and pride grow as the residents of an area learn to organize themselves and work together to make the garden bloom. In many cities around the country, from Berkeley, California to Washington, D.C., there are city-wide organizations that help neighborhoods acquire suitable land and get the project running. The Agricultural Extensions of universities have also been known to assist in such efforts.

In Boston the community gardens movement has been particularly successful in turning once-blighted areas in the Roxbury and Chinatown neighborhoods into oases of green. Boston Urban Gardeners, a foundation-funded non-profit corporation, has put together deals to prevent development on neglected parcels and to see that the land is saved for the community's benefit. It also has an outreach program to share its planning expertise with organizations from other cities and towns. Call 617/423–7497 if you are interested in turning your abandoned rail spur (or any other vacant and neglected tract of land in your neighborhood) into a set of productive, vegetable-growing plots.

It may be too late to put any of these options into effect, because building plans have already been announced. In addition to the normal zoning process, your community may be able to have input at another level, through your state or Interstate Commerce Commission. Before an existing rail line can be shut down and the tracks removed for development, it will be up to a particular government agency to declare the line officially closed. You may be able to object to this action, not on land-use planning principles, but on state and federal transportation policy grounds. Under the rule, the landowner may be obliged to show that he has made every effort to find a buyer who will agree to keep the tracks for transportation. Only after he has exhausted that option may a closure be approved. But check first by phone inquiry to either the state or federal agency to discover what rules and hearing procedures are applicable.

Now suppose the developer is already past that obstacle and has gone ahead and obtained permission to remove the tracks. What then? Rail-spur lands nearly always create long, narrow building lots, which can lead to some very odd building shapes and designs. You can criticize the resulting development plans on both aesthetic and practical grounds. The buildings are awkward and unworkable; too many variances are required; the result will not be up to community standards; etc. Though planners like to encourage creative solutions to parcel size problems, it must be acknowledged that on certain lots the potential for development is limited to nonexistent.

But suppose the building's design or site-planning is not vulnerable to your criticism. You may have one last chance, if you're lucky. Many rail spurs date back a hundred years or more. Dig deep into the archives and find out all you can about the original transfer of the land. Those old railroad companies were notorious in their day for swindling and cheating people to acquire any property along the preferred rail route. You may find evidence to show:

- that the rail company failed to secure clear title to one or more parcels of land where the tracks were built.
- that the land was acquired through a treaty with an Indian tribe under unfair terms. If that's the case, waste no time in contacting the modern leadership of the tribe. In many parts of the country Native Americans have been very aggressive in their attempts to right the wrongs done to them in the past, and in a few cases, they have prevailed in the courts.
- that at the time the land was given over for track-laying, a covenant was recorded stipulating that if trains ever ceased to run, the land would revert to its original owner. Such covenants are typically written for ninety-nine-year intervals, and may renew automatically, unless specific action is taken to reverse them. A title company may be of help in conducting such an investigation.

Challenges of this nature may not stop development, but simply cause a few months' delay, while the developers' lawyers sort through the confusion of old papers. Generally, whenever development is slowed down, you gain negotiating leverage, which may be all you need to obtain the buffer zones or traffic-access concessions you will need to transform the development into an acceptable neighbor.

Cemeteries

In older, more sentimental times, people from the cities used to take regular Sunday outings to the cemetery to pay their respects to their departed forebears. The trip took them out past small suburban villages, out to tranquil, verdant valleys, far from the workaday world. But economic reality has intruded into even this peaceful landscape, as suburban real estate prices have climbed toward urban levels, and landowners see more value in the development market than in the comfort of bereaved families. And so many graveyards have been put up for sale. That gets us into the scenario which has been the basis for all the *Poltergeist* movies: houses built over land that was meant to be consecrated in perpetuity as the resting place of the dead.

But it's not ghosts that are doing the wailing and screeching in protest. It's the cemetery's neighbors, joined most often by the families who own the plots. For the latter, the prospect of relocation of graves can be an emotionally wrenching experience, especially if the widow or widower had been reassured by the dying spouse that "everything was taken care of," and no decisions had to be made. Now they will feel betrayed and brutally damaged by the change, and often will fight it harder and longer than even the most militant of neighbors.

But families may need to be reminded—gently of course—that you can't win a case on emotion alone. You need legitimate legal grounds on which to protest the move; you need facts, and wellspoken witnesses to make a case at a public hearing.

You might be better off, tactically speaking, to let two separate groups go in opposing the zoning change: one composed of neighbors, who will make a reasoned, dispassionate case why the new development should not be allowed; and another composed of relatives and owners of the cemetery plots, who will simply protest the relocation. The latter organization will probably have little trouble finding people who are angry and upset enough to pound the pavement for petition-signatures, write letters to political figures, and pack the hearing room to make clear to the zoning officials the depth of community sentiment.

When seeking broad support you might also try contacting any local genealogical or historical societies. Cemeteries are recorders of our history as well as parcels of real estate. Tombstones and their inscriptions tell us many things about how people lived in other times and what they valued most from their lives. If the cemetery is filled largely by a particular ethnic group—say, black sharecroppers in the rural South—the cemetery may be the last real link with a vanished way of life. Those graves will speak to generations of oppression, lynchings, and struggle, which must not be allowed to be paved over into oblivion. Obtaining historic landmark status would be one way to preserve that record of the past.

That may be next to impossible, however, if the descendants of the dead no longer live in the area, or simply don't care that much about their ancestors' lives. In old western mining towns, the fortune-hunters who came to pan for gold were often single men, who, when they died (penniless, most of them), were buried in unmarked graves. Yet these paupers' graveyards are among the most historic in the country, and national preservation organizations should be contacted and brought into the fight to preserve them in their original settings.

You could also use the "crassness factor" (discussed earlier, under *Shopping Malls*) as a point in your favor. Why should we have yet another bunch of tract-houses or offices thrown up on land so imbued with meaning for so many families? Why must the feelings of the bereaved be sacrificed for the pocket-books of the money-men? Why can't they put their buildings on some lots where it will do good, not cause pain to so many people? Such questions help to build pressure on the developer to justify his choices. If he's sensitive about his public image, he may even be scared away from the deal he's contemplating. If he's not the sensitive type, however, you had better be working on the legal and economic side of your case, just as hard as you're working on the emotional and political side.

Country Clubs

The vast, green expanse of the golf course is, for many of us, the very epitome of the suburban image. Yet even the country club, bastion of wealth and power, can fall before the mighty developer's bulldozer. A country club can always relocate to cheaper land, further out, taking the millions in profits it reaps from the sale to build bigger, glitzier clubhouses for its members. And so a thousand or so houses will rise where golf balls once flew.

The first group the neighbors should seek out as their allies are those country club members who like the club where it is right now. Unless the club is planning to use its profits for a generous rebate on its membership fees, you will likely find a good number of the members on your side. You may even be able to foment a revolt from the inside that will block the sale. If not, you will at least have some persuasive witnesses who can testify that the club works well where it's always been, and that the move is unnecessary.

If the club has received a tax exemption (and nearly all country clubs do), you can point out that the tax-exemption policy exists expressly to encourage the retention of open space and greenery in the part of the county where it is most needed. If the club proposes to allow that land to be densely developed, and to create open space further away, where fewer citizens will have the benefit of it, then perhaps the club's tax exemption should be restudied, and possibly revoked. The club may not wish to enter into a deal that could result in a court challenge to its tax-exempt status.

One difficulty you may face is lack of public sympathy for your cause. Country clubs are widely seen as preserves of an over-privileged elite, and you may hear people express some desire to tear down the gates and let the people have their condos, stores, and offices, if that's where they want to put them. Spokespersons for the neighborhood should avoid using the term country club, but talk generally about "green space," "openness," "trees," and other qualities the whole public can appreciate. They should also try to look as "down-home" and un-clubby as possible, never appearing before the press in golfing slacks, for instance, or wearing a blazer and an Ivy League tie.

If possible, you will want to make common cause with the club's employees (many of whom may lose their jobs or not be able to afford the commute, should the club move further from town). Caddies, bartenders, waitresses, and groundspeople should be the ones to point out to county officials the economic value of the club.

In truth, it may be a lost cause to try to retain a large country club in a rapidly expanding real estate market. Your energies might be more productively spent in negotiations to control the density of what the new owner wants to build. You might also try to persuade him, in deference to the club's long history in the community, to dedicate a portion of the site to remain as open space, accessible not just to former members but to the neighborhood as a whole. That could well be the part with the swimming pool, or two of the tennis courts, which could then be operated by the county Parks Department.

If the clubhouse building itself has any architectural merit (and oftentimes they are gracious, older structures) you could also negotiate for its preservation. This could well be economically feasible, if the developer then rented the building out for functions, such as weddings and formal dances.

About Transfer Development Rights (TDRs). A complication may exist if the country club (or any other large tract of land) is not subject to simple sale, but is part of a package deal involving the transfer of development rights from one parcel to another. It might go something like this:

The country club's land is combined with some other parcel of land and the development rights of each are put together. (Under the law in some areas, the parcels need to be contiguous; in others, they need only be within the same jurisdiction.) Let's say the country club has fifty acres of land, now zoned to allow four units per acre. The other parcel of land, a vacant, one-acre tract at the edge of a suburban township, is also zoned for four units per acre, but it's owned by a developer. He offers the country club a nice sum of money, in exchange for which its Board of Trustees transfers to his parcel the club's right to develop its land. That is, the Club has now forever forfeited the right to build any housing units on Club property (something they never wanted to do anyway), and the developer now owns the right to build the 200 units the club's land could have accommodated. He adds that to the four units he can already build as-of-right, and now he can put a 204–unit apartment building on his one-acre lot!

To you, the anti-development neighbor, the deal looks like a bogus paper-sale. The country club has given up nothing it ever intended to use, and the developer has got something that lets him bust the zoning and radically change the look and quality of the neighborhood.

TDR deals may in fact be conducted according to the letter of the law, while they violate its spirit in ways evident to a ten-year-old child. You'll need to know how your local and appellate courts have viewed such deals. How many have been challenged? How many have been declared illegal?

If the TDR package requires zoning hearings for variances, look closely at the criteria for approval. The language of the statute may require the board to see to it that the outcome does not "circumvent the intent of the underlying zoning"—or words to that effect. If such a clause exists, you can make the case that the proposal represents an abuse of the process, and should not even be entertained.

The TDR was designed for and best used in situations where a developer has a piece of land of scenic value, which he would like to preserve. He is entitled to build a large number of units, which, for example, would block views of a mountain; but if he is allowed to transfer his right to build those units elsewhere, he can afford to leave the view unobstructed. The new units can be built on a parcel well suited to added density, perhaps in the middle of a city, far removed from the hills.

If you're fighting a case involving TDRs, you may find it helpful to cite a nearby example where the process was put to good use, for comparison's sake. That way the planners will know you are not trying to undermine the TDR concept (which nearly all city planners endorse) but are simply demonstrating, in this instance, that it has been inappropriately applied.

Airports

When they first built the airport, fifty-odd years ago, they put it in a cowfield. No planes ever flew at night, so the farmers didn't miss any sleep. The runways were short and the flights were not so frequent. Now there are suburbs sprawling in all directions, and takeoffs and landings occur every two minutes. Runways for jumbo jets stretch far into the distance, the engines are louder, and flight paths spread noise over thousands of homes.

If all that wasn't enough, now you've learned they want to expand the airport, to build Airport Annexes C, D, and E, plus two cargo and express-air delivery hangars and some small craft landing strips. But when you bought your house those many years ago, you were assured there would be no expansion, that new engines would be quieter, and that no flights would be allowed to land past 10:30 at night.

You go to the first few public meetings scheduled to discuss the problem, and are surprised to find most of the public is against you. They're all for having a newer, nicer, bigger airport, with more parking and greater choice of flight schedules. As for your complaints, they tell you, "Too bad! You knew there was an airport there when you bought the house," and "There's nothing to be done. The airport's going to have to expand to meet the increased demand,

and that means somebody's going to have to suffer. You're just going to have to learn to live with it."

It's not the purpose of this book to tell anyone to give up, but in situations like this, your best chance of obtaining peace and quiet came and went when you decided to buy property in that location. No matter what they told you beforehand—if it's near an airport, don't believe it! Airports *never* contract; just the opposite: The number of flights rises to meet runway space available. And that line about the ban on night flights—if you can get a letter from the heads of each of the airline companies that use the airport, guaranteeing now and in the future that there will be no late flights—well, just maybe you could trust that that will be the case. Otherwise, you'd better brace yourself for some noisy nights.

But let's say you're a very deep sleeper, so deep that you're not bothered by the occasional rumblings overhead. You love the house so much, and the price is so attractive that you want to buy it, regardless. Then at least arrange to see it at different times of the day, on weekends and on weekdays, and sit outside for a while on each visit, to get a sense of what it will be like to be there all the time. After that, if you think you can stand it, make your lowest plausible offer.

But what if you're already in the house, and you just want to keep the situation from getting worse? Expansions, though difficult to fight, can be attacked from several different angles:

- **The Environmental Angle.** There will doubtless be several organizations, some local, some regional or national, gearing up to fight the change. Bigger airports mean more concrete poured over grassland, trees, swamps, or other wildlife habitats. Some groups will protest anything likely to cause more noise pollution, or to spew more exhaust into the atmosphere. You'll need to work with scientists who can monitor decibel levels, air quality, and other adverse effects on the land. You might even find a psychologist who can speak about the effects of excess noise and rattling of windows on the elderly, small children, and people who have nervous dispositions.
- **The Traffic Angle.** Join forces with residents of all the communities spread out along the major road to the airport. It will be in their interest not to see traffic increase, affecting their commuting time or causing spillover onto neighborhood streets. Get calculations of the number of cars per hour to be added, and make projections of what will happen at various intersections at the peak hours of the day. Will light cycles get backed up? Will certain streets be taken as short-cuts? (Actually, these may work better as

reasons for the planning board to insist on improved mass transit access to the airport, but not to deny expansion.)

- **The Better Alternative Angle.** If the region has other airports, check to see if they are under-utilized. You can make a case that it's a better use of limited resources to get more value out of other existing airports than to spend money on an expansion so close to a residential neighborhood. This study needs to be professionally done to be persuasive to the authorities who will have the final word on the case.

- **The Demographics Angle.** The expansion may be based on projections that the region will grow by a certain percentage each year, increasing passenger demand. Look a little deeper into the demographics and see what they mean. Do the planners believe growth will continue, unchecked, at the same rate as in the past? Have they considered the impact of any new environmental legislation that might restrict growth, or considered any of the other dozen or so factors that might cause the trend to slow down or reverse? If you can cast serious doubt on the future need, you could make the desire for a bigger, newer airport seem to be nothing more than an expensive form of civic boosterism, the desire to have something grand and new to show up the other cities.

- **The Cost-Efficiency Angle.** Show that the airport can increase its passenger service and accomplish many of the other goals behind the expansion idea, without the great expense of new buildings, runways, and parking lots. Show that a renovation and reconfiguration of the existing terminal would be far cheaper and just as useful for the airlines as construction of additional space. Show that "mobile lounges" can work to take passengers to planes more efficiently than building a new annex at the other end of the runway. An elevated rail line or tramway from downtown could alleviate the need for additional parking lots. Again, you will need cost-accountants and other experts to develop the supporting data for your case.

How to Cope with Airport Expansion after the Fact. So they've done it. Now the airport is a lot bigger, and from your perspective, a lot harder to live with. What can you do to abate the consequences of the change?

- Demand that the airport pay for (or at least split the costs for) noiseproofing your house. You may not get it, but you have nothing to lose by asking. New insulating materials and draperies will work fairly well to screen out sound. (Of course your back yard and barbecue are still useless...but that's life.)

- Lobby for a "scatter plan." This was tried around National Airport, serving the Washington, D.C., region. Residents of all the neighborhoods along the flight path pulled together and lobbied hard for a change in the path airplanes must follow in their ascents and descents along the Potomac River. Their concerted efforts paid off, and the authorities agreed to a six-month trial period, during which pilots of different planes were given instructions to scatter—that is, fly different routes over different parts of the city on their way to and from the airport. During that period, the neighborhoods along the old flight path experienced a considerable relief in jet engine noise, from a landing or takeoff every two minutes, to one every five or ten minutes.

  However, neighborhoods that had never experienced any airplane noise before were now being disturbed on a regular basis—and they all began a counter-lobbying effort. Since there were many more citizens angered by the change than there were citizens who favored it, the political momentum was strong for reversal, and after the six-month period was up, the old flight patterns were reinstated. Though the experiment didn't last, I offer the idea as one worthy of consideration by airport neighbors in other cities. Perhaps you will be able to find alternative flights paths to scatter the airplanes which will excite less opposition from other neighborhoods. Perhaps the residents of the neighborhoods experiencing airplane noise for the first time will be more willing to share the burden, or less capable of fighting for reversal than were the citizens of Washington, D.C.

When all else fails, here's one last tactic:

Sell your house to a plane buff. Some people find it thrilling to look up into the giant underbelly of a jet aircraft on the ascent. They love everything connected with flight, including the noise and the rumble of crockery in the cupboards. Maybe you could even arrange for a house-swap with such a person.

Final thought: Buy yourself a set of those padded earphones the ground crewmen always wear, and pretend you're part of the airport team. You might eventually get into it and become a plane buff yourself!

Thirteen

SAVING THE CORNER STORE

Imagine a neighborhood without a single grocery store, with no real drugstore—just a premium-priced cosmetic boutique that sells a few odd sundries—no gas station, no dry cleaners, no lunch counter, no used bookstore, no deli.... What you'd find instead behind the storefronts of brass and glass are banks, travel agencies, opticians, reservation-only restaurants where everyone eats on an expense account, fast-food chain outlets where all the products come packaged in styrofoam, chain bookstores stocked only with best-sellers, and chain sweater stores selling clothes designed for teenagers.

You wouldn't call that a neighborhood, would you? It isn't, because none of the businesses depend for survival on the repeat patronage of the people who live in the area. The customers are all office-workers who leave the street deserted at night, tourists who go back to their hotels, corporate spenders who aren't looking for bargains, and impulse buyers who have just happened to wander past.

But this is an accurate portrait of the retail areas in many of our downtown neighborhoods today. Small businesses that cater to neighborhood residents—the "Mom and Pop" stores—have become an endangered species, threatened by the

Though the sign is still there, this hardware store has long since been replaced by trendy boutiques.

relentless territorial expansion of the big chains and the pricey little boutiques, and the drawing power of the big suburban malls.

What is the point of fighting to keep your neighborhood's housing down to human scale if all you can do is sleep there, and you have to get into your car and drive a couple of miles just to buy a loaf of bread? Yet it's generally far easier for citizens to grasp the importance of working together to preserve the character and charm of the houses and apartments in an area; it has always been harder to get them to focus on the need to protect the interests of the merchants who serve them. Businesspeople in America are traditionally supposed to look out for themselves—or go under. When they do, we rationalize that they just haven't been running their places right, and aren't meeting the demands of the marketplace.

But what really could be going wrong has nothing to do with the owner's management skills, or the desirability of his product or the quality of his service, or the loyalty of his customers—all the things that are, in theory, supposed to determine whether a particular merchant makes it or dies. Decisions made by real estate speculators, landlords, and tax-assessors may be the real forces for change on the block.

As cities around the country get older and more densely developed, land and floor space becomes scarcer and therefore more expensive. Rents and taxes rise, sometimes so much in one jump, that small-business owners can't make the price adjustments necessary to keep pace. Independently owned grocery stores, with their average 1 percent markups, are particularly vulnerable to sudden rent-hikes, and their steadily declining numbers in our cities are an index of the extent of the problem. But high-markup merchants, such as boutiques, or retail outlets with the financial backing of a national chain, are better equipped to cope with the vagaries of the real estate market.

Developers know this, and when they go seeking tenants for the ground floor space of new buildings, they go after the well-known names, the chains, and the marketers of upscale products, as their preferred tenants. That's one reason you see all the same stores in newly built space: the Benettons, Limiteds, Hallmark Cardshops, McDonald's, Waldenbooks, and Sharper Images— whether you live in Omaha or Orange County.

When the owners of older buildings discover how much rent per square foot the new development is bringing in, their response is frequently to jack up the rates to their own tenants, and the squeeze is on. The smaller, weaker service-places and shops just can't generate the income, and so they fold or move out to the far-flung, low-rent suburbs. And the neighbors are left having to do their weekly shopping at a gourmet shop that stocks more champagnes and caviars than it does milk and eggs.

But owners and neighbors don't always accept changes in the commercial part of their community with quiet resignation. Though examples of small-business/citizen cooperation are still rare, there have been a few cases that show how effective it can be. Here is one such story.

Santa Barbara, California is a pretty beachfront town whose very charm and neighborliness were the source of its popularity to real estate investors all through the '70s and '80s. The Earthling Bookstore, founded in 1974 by Terry and Penny Davies, did a good business selling books to residents interested in "New Age" phenomena, such as astronomy, psychic experiences, Eastern religions, and metaphysics. The Davieses knew Santa Barbara was expanding, but they also knew more people meant more customers, and so they paid the yearly rent-increases without complaint the first few years. They more than made up for the difference in increased clientele, and even were able to expand the store; but as rents continued to rise over the years, they decided to look for a better location, and so they moved over to the main shopping block of the town.

While business was doing better than ever in their new location, the Davieses heard a rumor that the city redevelopment agency had slated the area for demolition. A major department store had its eye on the block for its new site, and the city planners were all for a new and improved downtown. No one from the city ever directly notified the business-owners along the block of the change.

Totally unfamiliar with development politics, Penny Davies had the good luck to remember an article she'd read in a 1982 *Publisher's Weekly*, describing how the owner of a bookstore in Knoxville, Tennessee had successfully handled a similar challenge. He'd taken out full-page ads in the local newspaper asking readers how they would feel if their homes were to be taken from them and given over to developers. The Davies ran their own ads in the Santa Barbara press and posted signs in their own and other store windows around town, as well.

The publicity helped them to attract a good attorney to represent them in their fight against City Hall. He put them in touch with a group of local activists known as the Network, who were putting together a campaign against the redevelopment plan. They knocked on doors, raised money, and collected 15,000 signatures on a petition to put a question on the ballot in the 1982 election.

Though city councilmembers—who also constituted the redevelopment hearing board—campaigned hard for approval of their urban renewal plan, the Davieses found the people of Santa Barbara receptive to their pleas. When the ballots were counted, the demolition was defeated by a resounding 60 percent of the vote.

The Earthling Bookstore has ever since had a policy of making window space available to other citizen causes, as a means of repaying their neighbors for their support. The political fight also proved good for business: When it was all over, a poll showed that 75 percent of all Santa Barbarans knew where the bookstore was. Now the store is doing so well that the Davieses are negotiating to buy it from the owner. If they succeed they will never have to fear their rents suddenly doubling or tripling, or the launching of a new demolition drive.*

Strategies for Citizens and Business-Owners

The Earthling Bookstore case can't serve as a model for all purposes. Not all situations allow for direct voter participation, nor will the government be the initiator of most small business dislocations. The citizens of Washington, D.C., found out, to their dismay, the limits of popular vote on the disposition of private property. They had organized to save Rhodes Tavern, the oldest original building along the Pennsylvania Avenue inaugural parade route, by putting an initiative on the ballot, which the voters approved by a clear-cut majority. But then the courts ruled that demolition was the owner's right, not something over which the voters had any say. The demolition permit was issued, and the building came down, amid a crowd of angry, mourning protestors.

---

* This story was based on a report by Joan Barthes in the *Publisher's Weekly* issue of October 7, 1988, "Earthling Bookstore Stands Its Ground."

Moral Suasion. In other instances, even without legal power, well-organized citizens have been able to achieve great results. My own neighborhood's Save Our Supermarket organization won its results with moral suasion alone. We talked to the landowner who had put the grocery store space on the market—an elderly lady, a lifelong resident of the neighborhood, who, when she heard how upset people were at the prospect of losing their only grocery store in walking distance, agreed to seek out another grocery operator as a buyer, even if it meant turning down a higher offer from a developer! She actually had written into the sales contract that the buyer had to operate a grocery business in the space.

An independent food retailer, seeing the numbers of people who had signed the petition or done volunteer work for the SOS Committee's campaign, was impressed with the size and strength of the consumer market in the area, and so met the owner's asking price for the store. He has earned thousands of grateful, loyal customers by his decision.

But landlords like the grocery store owner are unfortunately rare. When moral suasion alone is not sufficient motivation, stronger measures will be called for. The following are some other techniques that may be effective, alone or in combination with each other.

Boosting Patronage. Neighbors may not realize that a beloved neighborhood shop is in financial trouble or in the process of being forced out, until it's gone. They may have heard the owner complaining from time to time about high rents and crunching competition from chain-stores, but they may not have considered what they could do to help. To hang on in a marginal situation, the business may just need a higher profile and a little added patronage to boost its income. Existing civic associations can help to get the word out. If the neighbors can be made to reflect for a few minutes on the value of the shop and what it would be like if it were gone, perhaps they would be willing to shop less often at the bigger, more convenient stores that they must drive to, and spend more of their dollars in their own neighborhood. Civic association members can also help to get the word out to their friends in other neighborhoods, and help the store to attract a wider following.

Neighborhood professionals in design fields or advertising might also consider lending their expertise to help the store improve its appearance or promote itself in ways that will draw in newer, younger residents of the area. Helpful advice could be something as simple as recommending that the store stock a certain item that is popular today. Some longtime store operators tend to get stuck in certain retailing patterns and don't keep up with what's attractive to new customers in the area. But many would appreciate a few suggestions as a welcome indication of your interest in their survival.

The store owner can contribute to building customer loyalty through his participation in neighborhood activities, perhaps by sponsoring a booth at the annual block party, or by donating items to the PTA fundraising auction. In some cases where an owner is being nosed out, the neighborhood just sits by and lets it happen because they don't feel any connection to the business, no matter how long it's been on the block. Owners need to dig their roots deep and spread them wide, if they expect to be able to stay firmly in place during rough times.

But then again, all of these little preventive measures may not add up to much. When rents double or quadruple, it will take more than neighborhood boosterism to keep a place in business.

Affirmative government intervention may be in order. By the time you get your government to recognize the problem, however, you may have already lost your basic services, and the neighborhood is in a state of decline. Then along come the planners and economic theorists with their packages of tax credits, reassessments, abatements, or low-interest loans. Whether such programs will help depends a great deal on how well they're written, and how time-consuming it will be for an owner to qualify for assistance.

Good legislation should specify what uses are to be encouraged (grocery stores, drugstores, hardware stores, etc.), and then define what constitutes an example of each type—for example: "A grocery store shall devote at least 60 percent of its shelf space to the sales of foods and non-alcoholic beverages" (so that convenience chain-stores or liquor stores will not be able to qualify for the benefits). The aid should be available only to those businesses located in "under-served" areas, defined by a geographic limitation fixed in feet or miles, so that the businessman who chooses to open his grocery store next door to a competing one will not qualify; but if he opens the same sort of store in a neighborhood where the nearest grocery store is two miles away, he is eligible for all the benefits of the program.

After the city council failed to pass a tax abatement bill, this urban supermarket fell to the bulldozer.

Though legislation of this type has been shown to have a good effect in areas as far apart as rural Crawford County, Missouri and suburbanized Connecticut, it's generally difficult to get local legislators to adopt such bills. They may be used to looking to the federal government to pay for aid programs, or be reluctant to try out new government programs in an age where self-reliance and volunteerism are values in vogue. That was the case in Washington, D.C., when, despite the united pleas of residents in neighborhoods without grocery stores all across the city, the council killed a bill to give tax incentives to businesspeople for opening new stores.

Government planners tend to be much more comfortable with the idea of enacting new land-use regulations than new tax deductions. So neighborhood activists may be better advised to try to correct the anti-small-business workings of the real estate market through changes in the zoning.

Methods of relief can take many different forms: One can redefine allowable uses, pushing the higher-rent-paying businesses into the denser-category zoning districts, leaving the lowest commercial category with only those uses the neighborhood wishes to encourage. Or one could create a whole new category of commercial use, called, for example, "Neighborhood Shopping Zone" and include in it the grocery stores, dry cleaners, drugstore, etc., but exclude from it fast-food outlets, movie theaters, or other high-volume users. Or one could set limits within the neighborhood shopping zone on the numbers of certain types of establishments (e.g., bars, restaurants, night clubs) that can occupy the same block. One could also write in some restrictions on layout, setbacks, signage, and parking, so that the traditional storefront streetscape of a town is maintained (keeping new competitors from overwhelming their neighbors with over-scaled signs, or breaking up the visual coherence of the block with drive-through lanes or front additions that project into the sidewalk, obscuring the other shops from view).

In my own neighborhood citizens worked with city planners to create a special zone tailored just for the conditions of our commercial strip. Called the "Cleveland Park Commercial Overlay Zone," the new zoning rules require:

- at least 50 percent of the ground floor space of commercial buildings to be reserved for retail use;
- a maximum of 25 percent of the linear street frontage to be taken up with bars and restaurants;
- a maximum height limit of forty feet, or twice the height of the lowest abutting building (whichever is the lower);
- a prohibition on curb cuts and drive-throughs;
- all retail uses must be consistent with the nature of the "Local Neighborhood Shopping Center" (a term defined in the city's Comprehensive Plan).

In San Francisco city planners and community leaders grappled for years with the problems of trying to keep small businesses from being driven out by large-scale development. Ultimately they devised a city-wide plan identifying and classifying every single commercial block in the city, and targeting those which served residential neighborhoods for stringent development limits. The plan has been in effect only a few years, and most of the business community is still complaining that the restrictions make normal business expansion too difficult; but most citizens I've spoken to think the plan has at last provided local neighborhoods with the protection they need.

Keeping the Neighborhood from Becoming "Over-barred." If your city planners can't or won't find zoning solutions to the problem, you may be able to deal with it, at least in part, through the alcohol licensing process. This technique is useful for the neighborhood bordering on the night-life center of town. Examine carefully all the liquor licensing regulations. How much discretion does the licensing board have to grant or deny an application? Is every adult, non-criminal business-owner entitled to a license if he submits all the proper forms? Is there a hearing that the public can attend? If so, how does a citizen receive notice of the hearing? Are citizens allowed to speak, and what kinds of evidence carry weight with the board members? Petitions? Histories of undesirable effects in other neighborhoods caused by establishments owned by the same applicant? Photographs of the neighborhood? Accident and drunk driving statistics for nearby intersections? Are board members bound to consider any special features of the neighborhood? Such as how many other bars are within X-number of feet of the applicant's place? Proximity to schools, churches, private homes? Is the owner required to make any guarantees about noise levels at night? About parking for his patrons? About crowd control? About transportation home for those too drunk to drive? What are the penalties if he's found to be serving minors? Or breaking any of the other rules the licensing agency has imposed? Will he lose his license, or will it be suspended for a period of time?

The answers to these questions may discourage you. In many areas, qualifying for a liquor license has become a routine matter. Seldom is a challenge mounted, and almost never is one successful. It's only in a few neighborhoods where the number of bars has proliferated uncontrollably that residents have begun to exercise their rights to appear and question the automatic granting of licenses. But when neighbors keep at it, and document all the problems caused by too many alcohol-serving establishments concentrated in a small area, they are bound to make an impact...eventually.

If no one has mounted a successful challenge before to a bar-license in your area, you should probably be prepared to lose the first few challenges you file. The board members may not know what to make of your objections. You may be treated as a prohibitionist, or a sanctimonious fuddy-duddy. You should make clear that you're not trying to impose your standards of morality on anyone; all you're doing is trying to do is protect the peace and quiet of your own home.

When enough citizens and voters come forward with the same complaints, the politicians (and the officials they appoint) eventually get the message. This has been the pattern in the Georgetown neighborhood, which includes several blocks that now form the night-life center of the nation's capital. Organized residents had been trying since 1979 (when there were 70 alcohol-serving establishments in the area) to have a moratorium declared on the issuance of further licenses. At their first attempt, their pleas were denied, and six years later, there were 108 licenses, and five years after that, 134. The number having nearly doubled, and the problems now being apparent to even the most obtuse bureaucrat (as each weekend night police arrest dozens of drunken youths and tow scores of illegally parked cars) the Alcoholic Beverage Control Board is at last ready to grant the residents' request. Though many Georgetowners believe the ban on more bars comes too late to do much good, the case history makes a good object lesson for other neighborhoods where the trend is just beginning.

Negotiating for Neighborhood Businesses. Tax abatement legislation and new zoning controls can take a long time to be put in place. What if a developer is putting up a new office building in your neighborhood right now, and you're anxious about the type of stores likely to occupy the ground floor retail space? You're sure, if you do nothing, that what you'll get are more cookie boutiques, designer chocolate stores, exclusive jewelry shops, and other stores of no use to the neighborhood—plus a new round of rent increases for the owners of the old shops on the same block as the new.

Express those fears to the developer. Call a meeting between the company representatives and a group of neighbors, and try to get them to consider the community in their marketing strategy. Point out that basic neighborhood-service shops —while they may be low on glamor—make for a more convenient and attractive workplace for the companies considering renting the office space on the floors above. Office workers need a nearby place to buy trash bags, cleansers, paper towels, and other mundane household products, just like everyone else. And of course the residents of the neighborhood will be better disposed to cooperate with the managers of the building on any future issues of concern, if the building provides some essential neighborhood-serving shops.

If the new building is displacing stores that have served the neighborhood for years, find out if any offer has been made to the owners of the old businesses to let them rent space in the new building. Your bakery owner, your sandwich shop proprietor, your tailor, or your hairdresser will most likely want to stay in the same location, for the convenience of longtime customers, but they could easily be stymied in their negotiations for a lease. A strong expression of support from organized neighbors could be the push needed for the developer to agree to let the traditional neighborhood store become part of his retail package, on favorable terms.

Popular pressure certainly helped to persuade developers in downtown Washington, D.C., to save a place on "expense account restaurant row" for Scholl's Cafeteria, a low-priced, longtime favorite of senior citizens, families, and tourists on a limited budget. On the other hand, despite all protests and complaints, developers have forced out several beloved family-run businesses: Whitlow's Tavern, Swing's Coffee Shop, and the Reeves Bakery. In the latter two cases, it appeared to the community that the developer was going to find space for the stores, but in the end the deals fell through.

When the stumbling block to successful relocation is the rent to be paid, you may be able to look to your city planning office to apply some pressure on your behalf. It's in line with the current ideology taught in most city planning departments of universities that planners should take an active role in preserving a "lively streetscape" with "an appropriate commercial mix." If you can get planners to do your negotiating for you, you'll likely find that their words carry more weight than yours. They may have special incentives to offer the developer to include the retail tenants you want; but even without any special programs or subsidies at their disposal, they will have the greater ability to win cooperation. The developer is always aware that he must deal with city officials again and again; it's in his long-term interest to rack up some merit points while he can, to be cashed in on a future project requiring special approvals.

Use of the Historic Landmark Process. Here is a technique of powerful but limited application. If the store or business you are working to retain is in an old building, you may be able to file a historic landmark application to save it. Now you may assume, since the landmark decision only covers the bricks and boards that physically comprise the building, that a designation as a historic structure will do nothing to control the use. And that is true enough— but it sure can do a lot to encourage it.

The technique works best with movie theaters. Let's say your neighborhood is about to turn into a hometown version of *The Last Picture Show*. The one remaining movie theater was built in 1932, in the heyday of the great Roxys, Odeons, Bijous, and Loewe's Palaces. It may not be on the grand scale of Radio City Music Hall, but it will still be worth your while for you to research who was the architect, what was said about it in the press when it held its first premiere, and what are the terms to describe any of its design motifs.

Seemingly little things, like a piece of zig-zag aluminum trim, may make it worthy of preservation. The Silver Theatre, in Silver Spring, Maryland, appeared to many residents to be a shabby little example of the Art Deco style, but after historic research was begun, they were pleased to find many eminent architectural historians enthusiastically supporting the case for its preservation.

If you do win a landmark for your theater, you will be able to save the marquee, the box-office window, the poster mounts on the street frontage, and the other outward elements that give it that distinctive movie theater appearance. That, in turn, will make it that much harder for the owner to convert it to a different use inside. In some localities, New York

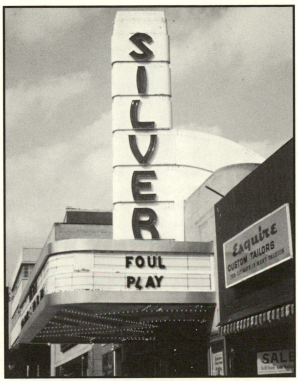

Its last marquee reads like a protest against the proposed demolition of this movie theater.

City among them, it is possible to apply for a landmark on the interior of a building. If granted, then the theater's auditorium, the curtain, the pillars, archways, footlights, etc., must all be catalogued and protected from removal or demolition. This almost guarantees the continuation of the building's original use. But in many states there is no provision for an interior landmark, and where there is, it is one of the hardest cases to win.

If you choose to pursue the landmark strategy, look for support from national or local organizations formed by enthusiasts of the style of the building you want to preserve. Your local historical society may be able to give you leads on contacts who may be of help. You might also check with the AIA (American Institute of Architects, 202/626–7300) to find a local member architect who specializes in renovation of the style of building that interests you.

Besides old movie theaters, many different types and styles of commercial buildings are likely candidates for preservation. Some of the more commonly occurring cases are: diners, federal-style banks, farmhouse-style farmer's market-buildings, fancifully shaped roadside stands (the coffee shop in the shape of a giant, steaming cup, for example), old ice-cream parlors/soda fountains, department stores, general stores, and taverns or saloons. This list is by no means exhaustive. Appreciation of the commercial styles from the past is growing, and there's no telling what may now be considered by experts qualified for landmark recognition. Years ago, the Art Deco style was considered passe'. Now it's been rediscovered and whole historic districts created to celebrate its qualities. The shop around the corner from you (however shabby it may appear right now) could well be in a style that will be tomorrow's trendy rediscovery. So look carefully behind the plastic signs that may obscure the original facade; tap those false-front panels and find out if there's stonework underneath; ask the owner what gargoyles or cornice-pieces he may have removed from the roof and still have stored in his basement. There are treasures hidden all around you, and if you keep an open mind and a sharp eye out, you just might find them.

Bringing Back America's Main Streets

In some towns it isn't a single commercial building that's at issue—it's a complete ensemble of buildings that form the commercial core of the town. Residents and merchants alike want to protect the viability of their business centers to keep consumer dollars from migrating to bigger, fancier shopping malls in outlying areas. Historic preservationists are also interested in retaining the historic character of these small-town shopping streets.

All three interests have come together in the "Main Street" program, under the sponsorship of the National Trust for Historic Preservation, which provides business and community leaders with practical advice and resources to help businesses in the old town's heart to survive and prosper.

If you think your town could benefit from the program's lectures, brochures, videos, and other materials, write to: The National Main Street Center, 1785 Massachusetts Avenue, N.W., Washington, D.C. 20036. You might also want to get a copy of *The Main Street Book*, by Peter Hawley (The Preservation Press, 1986), which covers everything from history to design to grantsmanship to preservation laws and all aspects of the Main Street Program.

Where there have been dedicated townspeople and merchants willing to work together for the good of all, the program has achieved some gratifying turnarounds and brought new and exciting life to some once-depressing small town streets.

Commercial Rent Control. As a final suggestion—though some may consider it too radical—you may want to explore some form of rent control for commercial buildings. As far as I know, this has been tried in only one city, Berkeley, California, and the results are not yet clear. The voters there believed it was as logical to try to protect small businesses from escalating rents as it was to protect residential tenants.

But as with residential rent control, the idea stirs heated debate. Opponents argue that it strangles the marketplace, causing tenants to remain in one place, regardless of how well the space suits their present needs, and it can become close to impossible for those looking to relocate to find anything in a moderate price-range. Supporters retort that, without it, landlords are free to keep raising prices, regardless of the condition of their buildings or the actual costs to maintain them. With a for-profit business as the beneficiary of rent control, landlords will say they are being unfairly discriminated against. Why should the government impose cost-containment on one sort of business expense (rent) but not on any other cost, such as labor, transportation, or supplies? Business tenants may reply that space is a far more limited resource, and there is greater public interest in seeing that it remains available for a wide variety of businesses, not just the most profitable few. Just as we use anti-trust laws on the national scale to protect the least powerful companies from the most powerful, so commercial rent control will work on the local scale to protect small businesses from big-time developers. The public benefits in two ways: in the continuation of basic services in the neighborhood, and in the increased opportunities for all classes of people to find suitable space to be able to start up their own businesses.

A carefully crafted bill could introduce commercial rent control on a one-year trial basis, with modifications and special exceptions drafted in response to the particular problems of the area to be covered. Adjustments and increases may be allowed under a specified set of contingencies, or as approved by a board, to provide for flexibility. If the experiment seems to help to stem the out-migration of neighborhood businesses, then permanent legislation could be considered. But if there is evidence that the concept is doing more to close off the commercial market to new entrepreneurs, then the area can revert to its prior unregulated state.

Should your town or city participate in such a trial program, I would be interested in hearing the results.

WHEN BIG INSTITUTIONS BECOME BIG DEVELOPERS

Here is a sampling of what I hear from people who live in the shadow of a big institution:

"The university treats the whole neighborhood as an extension of its campus."

"The hospital administration believes our neighborhood streets are simply different ambulance routes. Since their mission is to save lives, if we raise any objections, they practically accuse us of wanting to kill their patients."

"City officials keep telling us how good it is for the city to have big hotels that attract convention-goers' dollars. I wish they thought as much about the needs of the people who live here year-round as they do about the business travellers who come just for a few days."

"When they built the power plant out here, they made all these promises to the neighbors: The plant would be *safe*, it wouldn't make any noise, it would be clean and well-run—but now we're living with this smoke-belching, noisy monstrosity. The late-shift employees get off at 2 a.m. and are loud and frequently drunk. And we can't seem to get any action on our complaints."

"I just wish the Cathedral could be guided by this rule: 'Develop unto others as you would have others develop unto you.'"

If I listed all the complaints I've heard, they would fill volumes. In my ten years of dealing with development, I haven't yet heard from anyone who actually liked living next to a big institution or who considered it a good neighbor. The common image is of a Goliath next door—and you are David without a slingshot.

The situation is frequently made more frustrating as city officials support the worthy, prestigious institution in the dispute, over the complaining citizens. In some cases the institutions are built, or expanded, with government-backed bonds and are given special treatment in the approvals process. There are also institutions, such as public hospitals and state colleges, that are entirely government-run projects (if so, you can use the techniques discussed in Chapter 11). In other cases they may be private/public partnerships, which can receive all the privileges reserved for public projects, while generating profits for their investors as a private enterprise. Convention centers, such as have been built by several major cities in their downtown neighborhoods, are often the result of this type of arrangement.

The trouble is that each city and each county may have its own unique way of treating the development or expansion of its large institutions. In Washington, D.C., for example, most large-scale plans fall under the purview of the Zoning Commission, but campus plans, for unknown reasons, are in a category all their own. Hotel plans, on the other hand, will come up on the Board of Zoning Adjustment or the Zoning Commission agenda, depending on what sort of zoning district they're in (whether classified commercial or residential).

The burden is on you, the citizen, to learn everything you can about the way your jurisdiction treats the particular institution you're worried about. If you do find that it gets special treatment, it will probably be based on the assumption that whatever helps the institution to serve more people is automatically in the public interest. To counter this idea, you must keep bringing to the officials' attention that you, too, are the public, and that you have a right to a certain quality of life, which you expect your government to respect. Come up with a list of those restrictions and guarantees you feel are necessary to assure the continued livability of the area. Ask for these to be written into the zoning order as conditions for approval, and be sure to get enforcement clauses included, so that all parties know what will happen if the conditions are not met.

In order to know what conditions to ask for, you need to examine thoroughly the likely effects the big institution's presence will have on your neighborhood. Don't rely too heavily on whatever its administrators may tell you about its operations. You are much better off spending some time talking to the neighbors who live next to a similar institution, to find out in practice what the problems are and what restrictions they think would help to alleviate them.

As with any development, you will also need to know the basics about the plan: the square footage, height, setbacks, lot occupancy, number of parking spaces, number of employees and visitors, method of garbage collection, venting, landscaping, hours of operation, points of access by public transportation and private car, the design style of the building(s), and other information you would get for any sort of development.

But for a big institution you will also need to ask (and receive clear, non-evasive answers to) many questions specific to its function. The following is an incomplete list of questions and issues raised by the development of different types of institutions.

Hospitals

(Many of the same issues are also raised by nursing homes, convalescent homes, and hospices.)

How many beds will there be? What specialties will the hospital provide? If it will be a pediatric hospital, what accommodation will be made for the families of the children? If it's to be a psychiatric hospital, will it have locked wards and/or a prison-like appearance? Will there be fences or walls around the perimeter? If there is to be substantial outpatient treatment, will there be halfway houses affiliated with the hospital built nearby or on-site?

What will be the ratio of staff to patients? When do shifts change? When the night shift changes, will employees be instructed to move quietly? How will that rule be enforced?

How will community/hospital relations be handled? Will a joint panel be formed to work for certain shared goals and to deal with reported problems? Will the hospital have an ombudsman?

What about medical wastes? Will there be a guarantee that they will be properly disposed of—and prompt redress if they're not? How about dangerous drugs: How will security be handled?

Find out about the record of other hospitals run by the same operator. How do they rate in terms of patient care, physical plant, management, and community relations?

What about ambulance access? What streets will be used? Will the drivers be instructed that they may use the siren only in true emergencies (not when they're simply running behind schedule for a non-emergency transport)? Will there be any other type of emergency transport, such as by helicopter? If so, where will the helipad be? On the roof? Or at ground level?

What about access by private car and walk-ins? Will entrances for different types of care be clearly marked, so that patients won't have to circle around the neighborhood? What about parking? Will all staff and patient cars fit on the hospital's lots? Will patients be charged a fee (which will cause many to search for free parking on neighborhood streets)?

Does the neighborhood have adequate support services nearby? Doctors' offices, pharmacies, surgical supply rental stores, physical therapy centers, etc.? Will the hospital staff be concerned about where the patients go once they are released from care? (You wouldn't want this situation to occur: An Alzheimer's-affected patient has received in-hospital treatment, after which he is escorted to the front door, and just left there on his own to wander the streets of your neighborhood, looking for a friendly person to help him find his way home.)

After you have looked into all the specific questions you can think of, consider the overall picture. Does a need exist for a hospital of this type, in this location, now and into the future? Your state's Health Planning and Development Agency (usually abbreviated SHPDA, and pronounced "ship-da") may be required to hold a public hearing before a hospital can receive an operating license—though it may be difficult for you to discover when that hearing will be held and how you can participate. As soon as you first hear any suggestion that a hospital may be planned for a site, call your SHPDA office and ask whether any plans have been filed and if so, what are the next steps in the process. If you let them know early enough that you expect to be contacted about hearings, you probably will be.

Universities and Other Schools (Public and Private)

"Town and gown" antagonisms have been recorded as long ago as the Middle Ages at Oxford and Cambridge, and they are not about to go away. But you can help keep them to a minimum, if you watch out for areas of conflict when the new school (or school's expansion) is being planned. Here are some of the questions you'll need answered.

How many students? teachers? administrators? other employees? How many in each category are expected to arrive by car, and where will they park? How will school-bus routes, school crossings, and children's special safety needs affect the traffic patterns in your neighborhood?

You should be especially concerned about three special elements in the development of a school or college: 1) athletic facilities; 2) auditoriums; and 3) eating arrangements.

1. Will there be a gym? ball field(s)? pool (indoor/outdoor)? How often are games held? How many spectators? Where will they park? How noisy will the game be? Will there be loudspeakers? lights? banners? Consider this: Living near a school with a successful sports team can be like living near the football stadium where the Superbowl is to be

*University develop-
ment means more
than just class-
rooms to a neigh-
borhood. This
seven-story build-
ing is actually a
student parking
structure.*

played. On the day of the Big Game, the neighborhood may require traffic diverters and temporary one-way streets to keep residential streets from being overwhelmed. You should consider a worst-case scenario, draw up a plan to deal with it, and seek the school administration's promise to put the plan in effect on the days when large crowds are expected.

2. The University drama department may have a successful run of a play, which for you, the neighbor, will be just like living near a successful commercial theater. The music department may hold performances, recitals, operas, or competitions, just as Lincoln Center does. The film department may operate a movie theater, open to the public, just as any other movie house in town does. For each of these departments you need to find out how often events are held and how many ticketholders the auditorium can accommodate. If rock concerts are to be held, you should also ask about sound spillover beyond the walls of the building, crowd control, policing for underage drinking, and provision for waiting lines for those buying tickets (fans sometimes line up two or three days in advance of sales, trying to get the best seats).

3. Is there a cafeteria? Sandwich shop? Vending machines or vendors' carts? If the students are high school age or younger, will they be allowed off campus during the lunch hour? Will littering be a problem? What attitude will be taken toward student patrons by nearby restaurants and bars? Neighbors generally dislike seeing their local taverns and cafes turned into student hang-outs. Will any establishments be off-limits?

To what extent will the neighborhood be able to use the university as a resource and community center? Can non-student neighbors obtain library privileges, or buy a membership in the athletic facility? Will they be able to take classes of interest, not for credit? Will university students be involved in projects of interest to the neighborhood, such as oral histories of elderly residents, or special education of children with learning disorders? Will law students help work out neighborhood disputes?

What about fraternities and sororities? Are they allowed? If so, are they under control? How is hazing treated—as a prank to be expected of kids, or as a serious offense, calling for serious punishment? What about graffiti? Will the university clean it up? What about smoking? Is it restricted to certain areas of campus, or banned altogether (for high school students or younger)? Does the school assume any responsibility for student behavior off campus? Will students be liable for punishment by the administration for fighting, reckless driving, or other offenses committed on neighborhood streets?

Here are some less obvious issues to bring up: What kind of research does the university do? If laboratory animals are involved and are kept under poor conditions, the research building may draw crowds of protesters, or even be the scene of a break-in by animal activists. If scientists hold contracts for defense research, the same cautions are in order. You may also want to question how securely chemicals and radioactive materials are kept. If there were any accidents and hazardous conditions were created, would neighbors be informed? How? What about controversial public speakers? Who invites them, and what security arrangements would be made to protect those with known enemies (such as political leaders in exile, or those holding extremist views)? Would neighborhood traffic patterns need to be altered temporarily for security reasons?

What about commencement exercises? Are they a one-day trauma for the neighborhood, or does each department conduct its own ceremonies, imposing graduation-day traffic on the neighborhood several times over a two-to-three-week period? Will visiting parents have a place to stay? To park?

About university expansion: Forget what administration officials tell you about their limited funds or their contentment with their current size; they are *all* ambitious, *all* planning for that extra lab, that new pool, a new administration building, just as soon as that rich old alumnus dies and leaves the school all his money. You should try to get some ideas from the school's board of where they might be likely to put any additions, and just what the upper limits are on student-body size, number of departments, and special programs or course offerings. If a school has two campuses, watch out: From the administrator's point of view it will be highly desirable, at some point in the future, to be able to combine all the uses from the secondary campus onto the main one in your neighborhood.

I have saved the thorniest school issue for last: off-campus housing. In big cities it's nearly always a problem, since rents are too high for most students to afford, and not enough dorm space exists. What typically happens is that apartments in buildings close to campus are rented out to groups of students, sometimes as many as five or six sharing a two- or three-bedroom unit. Some student-tenants like to play their stereos at top volume all night, and throw huge parties at which the guests are likely to drink to excess and then throw up out the windows or pass out in the stairwells. People like that do not tend to make very good neighbors (to put it mildly). It's annoying enough when there are one or two such groups in your building, but it can become unbearable if the building becomes one-third or one-half populated by students.

In their quest to help keep housing affordable for their students, universities may make matters worse for neighbors. After a building has become home to a great many students (usually after it has become run-down, as well), the university may offer to buy it from its owner and convert it into a dormitory or into subsidized housing for graduate students. The longtime non-student residents will then be forced out. Fighting this sort of dislocation will be difficult, unless the tenants can raise the money to match the university's offer and buy the building themselves.

But tenants who are elderly or have little income should not give up entirely. They may be able to win with political power what they can't get by financial power. After all, tenants are permanent residents, who can vote, while students are often registered out of state (if they bother to register at all). The press, too, can be expected to give sympathetic treatment to the plight of the older residents who are being forced out to make way for the young college kids. With politicians and the press as allies, it should be possible either to reach a favorable negotiated settlement with the university (either for money to pay for relocation, or for a deal to reserve a certain number of units for older tenants), or to pressure the administration into finding another building to meet the students' housing needs.

A deeper, more intransigent problem exists when the university goes into the real estate business. This happens when the administration discovers it can raise a lot of its operating costs by buying up pieces of the surrounding neighborhood and leasing out the properties to developers of private offices or apartments. The pattern is most evident in big cities, as on the upper West Side of New York around Columbia University, or in the Foggy Bottom neighborhood near George Washington University in Washington, D.C. In the latter instance, the University bought up a long block of Pennsylvania

Avenue and developed it as a retail arcade backing onto a gigantic office building, destroying the look of some historic rowhouses in the process.

If you find yourself battling a university with a similar non-academic agenda, you should make a point of treating the school just as you would any other big developer. Don't be swayed by any of the university's usual rhetoric about its educational mission or the ultimate purpose of the profits being generated. When an institution takes on the role of big developer in its neighborhood, it should expect to be treated like one by the people who have to live with the results.

When you're gearing up to fight, you may find yourself with an ally from an unexpected place—within the university itself. There probably will be many students who don't want to see more of the area near campus turned into brick and concrete. They value the open spaces just as much as you, and those among them who have studied geology or engineering should be helpful in analyzing the environmental impact of tree-cutting, slope-grading, and bulldozing in the plan. Winning the students over to your side can greatly increase your odds of winning the whole case, as the administration may be reluctant to antagonize the population they are supposed to be serving.

Older officials may remember, too, what it was like back in the '60s when students and university administrations were commonly at odds. The University of California at Berkeley was the scene of perhaps the most famous (or infamous) student revolt, with demonstrations and sit-ins that actually shut the university down. You probably remember watching the protestors on TV news, but you may not recall what they were rallying against: a University development project. The administration wanted to build a new gym on a small plot of land the residents and students called "People's Park." Though students today seem quieter and less activist than a generation ago, they are still capable of causing considerable trouble if their emotions are touched in the right way. Most university officials would rather work with them and with their neighborhood allies to find a peaceful solution, than risk a return to the confrontational tactics of the past.

Churches, Cathedrals, Synagogues, Mosques, and Other Religious Institutions

Freedom of religion is something nearly all of us hold dear—and as a consequence, most of us are reluctant to raise objections when the developer is the representative of another faith. But the problems caused by development of religious institutions can be every bit as bad as those caused by any other big developer: buildings that are too massive for their neighborhoods (a steeple that's too high, or an auditorium that's too vast); traffic-drawing special events (weddings, christenings, bar mitzvahs, etc.), and designs that conflict with an area's architectural style (a stark, poured-concrete-walled temple amid blocks of Victorian bungalows). Then there are problems singular to religious institutions, like the ringing of bells or the Moslem muezzin's call to prayer from the top of the minaret tower, which can be loud enough to wake everyone in the neighborhood, not just adherents of that faith. Problems may also arise when the practices of religion go beyond the confines of the religious institution's property and into your neighborhood: Orthodox Jews want to place markers on the street to show how far one may walk to the synagogue on Saturday without violating the Sabbath rules; churches offer to pay for and build religious statues (usually surrounding a creche at Christmas time) in a public park or in front of a city-owned building in your neighborhood; or it may be that the pastor of a church stands on the sidewalk on Sunday mornings with a bullhorn, calling to all passers-by to come to church, and castigating as sinners those who choose to walk on.

Unless the institution is operating in flagrant disregard of local zoning and building codes (for example, one hundred congregants each week are coming to pray at a single-family house, or construction is underway for a new wing on an old church, without the necessary permits), the first thing to do is to try to work out a solution to the conflict with the religious leaders. Your approach to them should be respectful, showing sympathy for the special purpose of the institution. Above all, you should make clear that you are not trying to drive

Chester Higgins Jr./The New York Times

Brooklyn residents, seen here protesting the construction of a new headquarters building for the Jehovah's Witnesses, were careful to stress that their objection was to the proposed office building, not to the religious practices of its owner.

the institution from the neighborhood. (It would be helpful if you could find a member of the congregation who is also a neighbor to help arrange a meeting or serve as intermediary between the two groups.)

When you all first sit down together (preferably in an informal setting, such as your home—not the minister's office), you might want to start by saying how much the church and the neighborhood have to offer each other. Then see if you can get the church to accept suggestions from residents on ways to mitigate whatever problems you think exist. Let's say the church has an inadequate parking lot. Perhaps you can find a design-efficiency expert who can show you a way to re-stripe the parking lot so as to maximize the number of spaces. Or you might be able to put the church in touch with the owners of a nearby store (one that's closed on Sundays) with a lot that could be opened for parking by church members—the cost of the Sunday use to be taken as a tax-deductible contribution by the store-owners. It could be that the church only needs to hire a few traffic-handlers and car-parkers on certain crowded holidays. Maybe some teenagers from the neighborhood could handle the job for minimum wage, as needed. Whatever you offer need not be the perfect solution; it just has to be enough to show that you think the problem is a shared one, and that you're willing to help in the search for answers.

Now for a somewhat more difficult problem. Let's say the church wants to build a kitchen and a dining room extension off the back, so it can serve hot meals to the homeless. The church has already been serving cold sandwiches for months, in violation of city health and zoning codes. Rather than go in armed with ordinances and statutes, see if you can find a way to answer your neighborhood's concerns and let the church carry out its intended work at the same time. Your main objection might be that the food storage bins have been attracting rats. You might also be troubled by the lines of homeless men that stretch out from the church's back door all day (some of those waiting in line have been verbally abusive to the neighbors who pass by). Tell the church that if it can solve these two problems, you would be willing to withdraw your opposition to the plan. They can clean up the pantry to meet city standards; and they can open the church doors and let the homeless form their line inside, through the corridors. Perhaps under those conditions, the neighbors would not only be tolerant of the expanded use, but would actually be supportive. You might even find some who would be willing to do some volunteer work on the food-service line.

Why go out of your way to be so cooperative when the developer is a religious institution as opposed to a private businessman? Why not stand on your legal rights and insist that the zoning rules, the parking regulations, the food storage codes, etc. apply to the church, as they would to anyone else? Well, you could do that, and you might win your battle in the end. But you will certainly lose in the battle for press and public sympathy. Religious institutions have a tremendous public relations advantage. They can make you look as if you are fighting Charity, Mercy, and Compassion—if not God Himself. *Negotiate a solution if at all possible, even if you must concede far more than you would to any private developer.*

What if you try your best, you offer all the concessions that your conscience will allow, and you still get nowhere? Let's say the church has put a loudspeaker in its steeple and is broadcasting the pastor's sermons to the whole neighborhood. You tried to get him to lower the volume, but he is intransigent; he won't even agree to direct the sound transmission toward the main street rather than toward the residential side streets, nor will he limit his broadcasts to Sundays between 11 a.m. and 3 p.m. You don't want to give up. The problem exists and you have a right to have it redressed. So you will go to the city for enforcement—but when you do, be sure to maintain that same reasonable, unhostile tone you used in your negotiations with the pastor. Bring along whatever objective data you have: decibel measurements, sound recordings, counts of the number of houses where the broadcast can be heard. Hard evidence is important for proving your case, as the burden will be on you to show that you are not against the religion itself—just against some of its intrusions into your private life.

Even with indisputable proof, you will still be handing the authorities a difficult issue, one they will want to avoid. You may also find it necessary to seek political support for your position. But then again, it will be hard to find politicians who will stand up for you. Religious institutions frequently translate to blocs of voters at election time, and no politician wants to be seen opposing religion, if he can help it. When the media gets hold of a story, issues tend to get simplified, and all readers remember is that Councilman X got into a scrap with St. Y's Cathedral over something. That's a bad position to put your politician in. But you may be able to delete most references to the religious institution and focus more on the builder/contractor who is carrying out the development plan—that can help.

Take this case: The Diocese wants to build an archives building on the grounds of the cathedral, to hold all its records for the past 200 years. The building is to be a massive, warehouse-like structure, which will be placed some distance away from the beautiful church, with its blank wall facing some single-family homes. When discussing the situation with planning officials, introduce it this way: "The XYZ Construction Co. (not the Diocese) has begun to sink footings for the building within five feet of the nearest neighbor's property line, when the zoning regulations call for eight feet." You could add, "The architect has designed a windowless facade on the residential side." That way you have made clear that you are seeking help on technical and architectural issues, not anything having to do with the religious practices of the church.

However, there are cases in which religious freedom is unquestionably involved. Such cases are nearly always highly controversial, and the law may be interpreted differently, depending on what state you are in and what principles have already been established by precedent. On the question of religious statues on public land, the Supreme Court most recently ruled on the question in July of 1989 in two Pittsburgh, Pennsylvania cases. By a vote of 6–3, the Court found that a Jewish group was entitled to construct a giant menorah (a nine-branch candelabra used to celebrate Channukkah) on the grounds of a public office building, because it was part of a larger display that included symbols of other religions as well as some purely secular festive elements such as snowmen and lighted trees. However, by a narrow 5–4 vote the Court rejected a creche which stood alone in the entryway of a courthouse a block away. In this case, the majority found that the statuary, inscribed with the Latin motto "Glory to God in the Highest" conveyed the message of a particular faith and thus was an unconstitutional government endorsement of religion.

When the statue is entirely on private land the case-law becomes even murkier. The following is an example of a case with no clear outcome under the law today. Let's say there is a high hill overlooking your house, and the land at the top is owned by a Buddhist monastery. They have erected a forty-foot-high bronze statue of the Buddha, which is illuminated with bright lights all night long. During the day the shadow of the statue falls right across your window. You feel that, by its very size and positioning so close to your house, the statue represents an imposition of the monks' beliefs on you. But the monks are adamant about keeping the statue exactly where it is; to move it, they explain, would be impious.

A lawyer will give you an idea of your chances of prevailing in such a situation, but of course, different lawyers may see the case different ways. You may have to shop around to find one you think is well versed in the case-law, who also understands your point of view.

If your own right to practice your religion freely is in jeopardy, or if the state appears to be unduly favoring the religious institution over the neighborhood in a development dispute, you might want to contact the American Civil Liberties Union. There are ACLU affiliates all around the county; when a case arises involving separation of church and state or the protection of First Amendment rights, the ACLU represents its clients without charge. To find out if your case fits the organization's criteria, you would need to describe all the circumstances and put your request for representation in writing.

If you do go to court, remember, legal action will take months, if not years, to be resolved. Negotiations, especially when both sides are acting in the spirit of charity and good fellowship, according to the teachings of all the great world religions, can result in a faster, happier, and more just outcome for everyone.

Hotels

The neighborhood of Woodley Park to the south of my neighborhood has been locked in a fifteen-year battle with the largest single landowner within its boundaries: the Sheraton-Washington Hotel. Longtime neighbors have been worn out trying to deal with all the problems: the crowds of convention-goers, the traffic, the impenetrable taxi lines, the parking nightmare, the special exhibits that spill over beyond the hotel's inside space, and so on. The conflict reaches its peak each October as the hotel hosts an annual show of arms-merchants, and a parade of tanks and heavy artillery clanks down neighborhood streets at 6 a.m. on its way to the exhibition hall. And then, every four years, there are those Inaugural Balls—though most Woodley Parkers have learned to leave town at that time.

The neighborhood has raised and spent tens of thousands of dollars trying to make the hotel keep within all the rules and regulations governing its function within a residential zone. But the hotel managers have fought back. They have customers to please and a highly competitive business to run, and though they are always cordial in their talks with the neighbors and stress how much they would like to oblige, when it comes down to restricting their hotel's activities, they have been adamantly opposed to any concessions to the neighbors. The stand-off persists year after year because the needs of the two parties are basically incompatible. The hotel is already there and is not about to move. Neither are the homeowners who surround it on all sides.

Your best way to avoid this sort of situation is to try and keep it from developing in the first place. When a new hotel is proposed in or bordering on a residential zone, you should do your best to defeat it, or get it moved someplace else. For all their glamor—the sometimes stunning new design, the lush landscaping, the spectacular fountains, the celebrity visitors—a big hotel will always make a terrible next-door neighbor.*

But if you are not able to stop a hotel from being built, your next best course of action is to try to create a buffer zone between you and it, and get whatever other concessions you can wrest from the management to keep your area livable. Any restrictions or conditions the hotel agrees to accept should

---

* This section does not address small inns, bed and breakfasts, guest houses, and rooming houses, which (though they can bring problems) are typically much less burdensome to the adjacent residential neighborhood.

be spelled out in detail in a binding contract with a formal neighborhood organization.

What should you ask for? **More parking!** Think of all those rental cars and vacationers' cars with out-of-state plates (they can park anywhere they like and not worry about being ticketed); when the high season is upon you, they will park in front of your driveway, they'll park on the grass, on the sidewalk—anyplace they can find to squeeze in. So, push the hotel to take care of all vehicles on its own grounds, and in underground garages if possible. When calculating how many parking spaces are needed, think beyond the number of rooms and figure in the need for cars of those attending weddings, banquets, charity balls, political fundraisers, and any other large events the hotel will host.

If you can't get them to agree to enough parking to meet the peak demand, then you should push for the amount of large event space to be reduced, to match the limited parking amount.

Your second major headache will come from other forms of transportation: **taxis, limousines, and tour buses**. Taxi drivers will discover whatever short cuts they can find through your neighborhood streets to reach the hotel's front door the fastest. The limo-driver will think it's all right to idle outside your house for two hours while he's waiting for his passenger to emerge, or he may just circle endlessly around your block. Tour buses are the worst of the three. Very few of even our biggest hotels have the capacity for these behemoths to park, load and unload, or turn around. But no hotel that takes chartered tour groups should be allowed to go into operation unless they build adequate facilities for the bus traffic they generate. If a solution to these problem is not built right into the hotel's design, you will find, once the hotel is in use, that the management will avoid all responsibility, claiming that you must deal with the taxi, limo, or bus companies directly, if you want relief from neighborhood incursion.

Hotel health clubs are another feature of many of the newer, fancier establishments that have been problematic for their neighbors. Often featuring indoor or outdoor pools, Jacuzzis, jogging tracks, racquetball courts, weight rooms, and sauna, health clubs are expensive to build and maintain, and it is likely that the hotel will want to sell memberships to non-guests to cover some of the costs. And that means more traffic and more visitor parking for the neighborhood. On the other hand, if the hotel does not sell memberships, the neighbors will probably still experience some added noise from the pool or other outdoor facilities, without the compensating benefit of being able to sign up to use them, too. It's up to the neighborhood organization to decide whether to object to the inclusion of this sort of extra recreational space, or to try to encourage it as a compensating amenity for the community. The one thing to watch for, however, is the hotel without a plan for a pool or health club in its original design. Should the owners decide later that they need facilities of this type, the pool or club will have to be tacked on, frequently in a spot that poses some problem for those living next to it. If you see no plan for recreational facilities, ask about future needs, and if they tell you there will be no expansion to provide for such space in the future, *get that guarantee in writing*.

Back Alleys. Hotels are generally designed to grace major avenues, and so it is the back side that usually faces the smaller, residential streets. That is also where hotels tend to put their garbage dumpsters. The alley behind even the glitziest new hotel is likely to be a filthy, glass-strewn, oil-spattered stretch of concrete, lined with hulking metal containers that emit an awful smell. Employees may hang out there at night taking a smoking break, waiting around for friends to pick them up, or drinking and making noise. Back alleys behind hotels can also become places for prostitutes to pick up customers, for muggers to find victims, or for drug dealers to sell their wares. The neighbors should insist that the hotel do whatever is necessary to maintain security and keep the area clean. All trash should go in containers kept inside the hotel itself. Trash pick-up hours should be restricted to within the normal working day, and the same holds true for unloading by large, clanking delivery trucks.

Design Concerns. Though the front of the hotel may be gilded, sculpted, and ornamented like a wedding cake, often all there is at the back is an ugly brick wall. The neighborhood should insist that the part they see everyday be designed to fit in appropriately with the style of the surrounding neighborhood, no less so than the front facade.

Sometimes rather than look at the back of a hotel, however well-designed it may be, the neighbors would prefer to have the illusion that the hotel is not there at all (or at least is minimized). This can be accomplished by the use of various **screening devices:** the planting of trees, ivy, hedges, or other spreading plants, the building of walls, fences, or gates (which can be done in patterned brick or of fancy wrought-iron grillwork to make them more attractive) or the use of terracing and slopes. Commercial space

Neighbors who fail to note design details for the rear and sides of a hotel may end up with something like this.

in the rear could also help to create a comfortable transition between the hotel and the neighborhood. A coffee shop or cafe or a row of service establishments, such as a hairdressers, valet shop, or pharmacy could serve both the needs of the hotel patrons and those of residents who live nearby.

Where separation rather than smooth transition is preferred is in use of **roads.** You don't want the hotel's parking garage to be spilling a thousand cars out onto the street in front of your house after a big event. Even if the hotel's

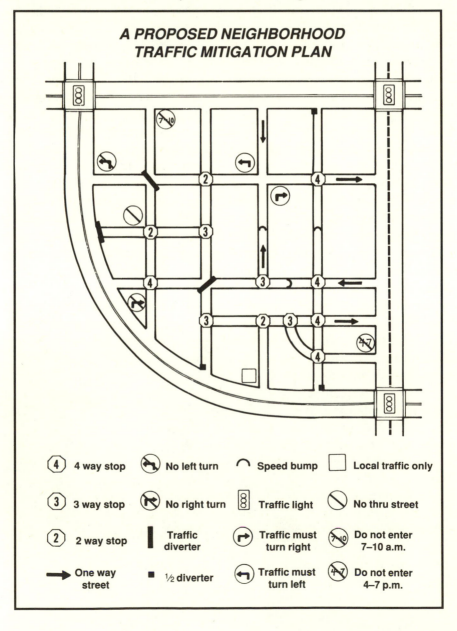

A PROPOSED NEIGHBORHOOD TRAFFIC MITIGATION PLAN

④ 4 way stop	⊘ No left turn	∩ Speed bump	☐ Local traffic only
③ 3 way stop	⊘ No right turn	🚦 Traffic light	⊘ No thru street
② 2 way stop	▮ Traffic diverter	➤ Traffic must turn right	Do not enter 7–10 a.m.
➡ One way street	▪ ½ diverter	➤ Traffic must turn left	Do not enter 4–7 p.m.

traffic circulation plan shows the hotel's driveways connecting directly to major arteries, you will still have the problem of drivers detouring onto your residential side streets to escape traffic jams.

Neighbors around the Sheraton in the Woodley Park area of Washington, D.C., dealt with hotel-caused traffic jams by creating a maze of one-way streets around the hotel, all of which steer hotel traffic back to the main road. In other parts of the country, residents have turned to even tougher tactics: They've put up barriers and diverters that prevent any cars from crossing over to residential streets. These may take any of several forms: concrete planter barrels that block the street entirely, or half-street "railroad crossing" arms that only stop traffic flow in one direction, or pop-up spikes set in the roadway that cause tire damage to drivers going the wrong direction.

The great drawback with the barrier idea is that it does nothing to cut down on the overall volume of traffic—it merely seeks to channel it somewhere else. That usually means some streets in someone else's neighborhood eventually get the overflow, and then they come in demanding barriers and diverters, too. These inter-neighborhood fights can quickly get ugly, with name-calling and screaming at officials for contradictory actions. So if you are considering a move to shut off certain streets from hotel traffic (or from any other big development), consider the impact further away. Then contact representatives of those affected neighborhoods and ask them to work with you to develop a plan you all can live with. When you have a set of recommendations that most of you think will help, you can present it to city officials as the work of the Coalition of Neighborhoods for the Mitigation of Hotel Traffic, or whatever name you choose to indicate that full consultation has been involved. Unity is always helpful in getting city response to your requests.

Another traffic measure you may want to consider is a ban on through-traffic by trucks and buses (except schoolbuses) for certain designated streets. The prohibition is easy to show on street signs and is particularly needed on streets that children frequently cross or play in. As an added advantage, your street will be freer from potholes if it is not traveled by such hard-wearing vehicles as tourbuses or trailer-hauling trucks.

With any traffic measures you get, you are going to need police enforcement. In order to be able to live in peace with their huge hotel neighbor, residents need to be able to count on the city to give them support for all the protective rules they've won for their neighborhood streets. Patrol cars should monitor trouble spots at random intervals, so that taxis will not drive around barriers or park in no-standing zones or otherwise block traffic. Special details should also be made available to handle the huge numbers of cars that come for special events. Officers are needed to direct traffic and write tickets for drivers who park or drive where they're not supposed to go. The hotel must also be held responsible for doing its share to see that drivers obey rules while on the hotel's driveways or internal streets.

If city officials, hotel managers, and neighbors all try conscientiously to anticipate problems and resolve them, the relationship among the three (while it will never be a particularly warm one, from the neighbors' side) should at least remain bearable.

Convention Centers

Take everything noted above about big hotels, multiply it by 100, and then you will understand the magnitude of impact a convention center will have on its surrounding neighborhood. Nobody who lives near the proposed site of one of these mega-monsters likes it—except perhaps for streetwalkers and souvenir vendors. Yet city officials *love* convention centers, and they're always eager for their city to have the biggest one around—almost as if they felt that manhood is measured in the gross square footage of exhibition space.

Though I never like to give defeatist advice, here goes: If your city has picked a lot in your neighborhood as the site for its convention center, *sell now*, and get out while the getting is good! Sometimes you *can* fight City Hall...and sometimes you can't. And when city officials become convinced that they need a huge convention center to boost the city's prestige, and that your neighborhood is the place to put it, the odds go heavily against you.

Residents of near-downtown neighborhoods in Seattle, San Francisco, and Boston all tried in vain to oppose the centers that now vie with each other for the biggest of the annual conventions. I wish I could point to a case where citizens have taken on city government over a convention center and won, but unfortunately, I haven't heard of one yet.

Libraries and Museums

Some of our most distinguished libraries and museums came about through donations of private estates containing collections of books or artworks. If that is the case in your neighborhood, you should be able to use the historic nature of the house and its contents as a factor in controlling development. You could file for landmark designation of the mansion, and so be assured of a public hearing at which you and your neighbors could express your concerns about alteration of the building or expansion of its institutional functions.

A number of libraries and museums are already designated landmarks, including the Nassau County Fine Arts Museum on Long Island (the former estate of industrial tycoon Henry Clay Frick), the Vizcaya Estate in the greater Miami area, and Hearst Castle at San Simeon, California. But a building doesn't have to be a hundred years old for its original design to be deemed worthy of protection. Some of our biggest and most popular museums are relatively new, designed by the finest architects of our time—Frank Lloyd Wright (the Guggenheim), Marcel Breuer (the Whitney), and I.M. Pei (the East Wing of the National Gallery of Art). Though these buildings are all less than fifty years old, they are designated landmarks, and must go through design review before they are allowed to expand. That process is underway as of this writing for the first two museums named, and neighbors and other supporters of the original architects' designs have been vocal in their disapproval of the size and configuration of the proposed additions. (In the case of the Guggenheim, a spiral, bowl-shaped building, the new addition was to rise like a tall block behind it, causing at least one architecture critic to scoff that it looked like the tank to a giant toilet bowl. A redesign has since been commissioned.)

When museums and libraries seek to expand beyond their traditional walls, one should also examine whether the increase is necessary to help it carry out its purpose. Institutions for the purpose of collecting things (which is what museums and libraries essentially are) have a tendency go on accumulating whatever it is they were built to show, whether further examples are significant or not. If money exists to maintain the collection, there will be little incentive to weed out the items which are better left in storage or sent someplace else. You will need the advice and testimony of the best experts in the field, however, to challenge the museum curator or librarian who asserts a need for institutional expansion.

In some situations there may be a definite need for exhibit space for a collection of one type of thing, but the museum or library that wants to build an addition to show that thing is not really the most fitting place for it. Example: Suppose your local library somehow acquired a collection of Einstein's childhood doodles. The directors announce plans to build a special wing to put the doodles on display. But all of the other important Einstein papers are in the library at Princeton University. Isn't that the most appropriate place for these newly discovered Einstein papers?

For this kind of critique to be effective you almost have to know as much about library science (or museum curating) as about land-use planning and neighborhood patterns. When you attempt to familiarize yourself with these new fields, however, you may find the library or museum directors maddeningly patronizing. They may imply, in genteel tones just barely laced with contempt, that you could not possibly understand the space requirements for hanging fossilized pterodactyl's wings. Only a few scholars alive could possibly be qualified to speak to the issue.

What you will need to make clear is that the needs of the museum to display the bones of an extinct flying reptile have to be balanced against the needs of the people here today to continue to enjoy open space in their own neighborhoods. And you all are the only fully qualified authorities on *that* subject.

You may be able to put the museum or library directors somewhat on the defensive if they have not always been as hospitable to the citizens of the community as a public institution ought to be. When was the last time they invited the neighborhood kids in for a special tour? When did they last host a reception, not for the big-money donors, but for the families who live nearby? What have they contributed to local clean-up efforts, to block parties, to school fundraising drives? If they have done any of these things recently, then they probably do want to be a good neighbor, and you should be able to sit down with them and work out a compromise on their plans. But if the institution has largely ignored or even been hostile to its neighbors, that's all the more reason why zoning officials should listen sympathetically to your side, and help you in your efforts to keep the institution in line with neighborhood scale and function.

The "LULU"

The acronym LULU, for "Locally Unwanted Land Use," covers a variety of disparate elements, from power plants (nuclear and conventional) to incinerators to sewage treatment plants to landfills to certain types of industrial plants (ones that have smokestacks or discharge wastes into rivers) to missile silos and weapons-testing ranges or other military uses. On the surface they all seem different—some involving large-scale building, some involving issues of air or water quality, some involving national security. Some are federally planned, some state, and some local, but they all have two things in common: All involve large-scale land use, and all generate immediate opposition.*

You may think a LULU is the same thing as a NIMBY ("Not In My Back Yard"), and in many ways they are similar. But there is a difference: NIMBYs are generally about social problems—housing for the poor, the ill, or the criminally convicted, or treatment facilities for the drug or alcohol abuser or troubled juveniles—that is, they are about *people*. LULUs are about *land*. And in general, LULUs are a great deal easier to fight.

First, you will have a lot of natural allies. If the LULU is a polluter, you will have the Sierra Club, the Wilderness Society, the Nature Conservancy, the National Wildlife Federation, the Audubon Society, and probably the Boy Scouts and the Campfire Girls as well. If it's a missile silo, you will have the whole of the peace movement behind you—SANE, Mothers For Peace, the American Friends Service Committee, et. al.—and you will probably be getting telegrams of support from Managua and Havana as well (a fact you will *not* want to mention on TV). Nobel prize-winning scientists will be volunteering to provide supporting data, validate studies and give testimony. Hollywood actors may show up for demonstrations, civil disobedience, and perhaps a symbolic arrest. In these kinds of situations, national support for your local cause is absolutely mandatory, to make clear that you're not just against the LULU because it happens to be near your house, but because it's a bad use of land, wherever it may be put.

---

* Certain types of maritime development have aroused the same response—e.g., offshore oil platforms, ocean dump-sites, garbage barges, and fisheries. Perhaps these activities should be referred to as "LUMUs," or "Locally Unwanted Maritime Uses."

You will not want to propose the alternative-site strategy, as you might do with a more benign sort of institution. That would only make it look as if you were willing to pollute someone else's neighborhood. What you will need to do is propose some alternative *form* of dealing with the problem. Example: Instead of saying, move that nuclear power plant to the next county, you could propose a series of mandatory energy conservation measures that would make a new electrical-generation plant unnecessary to meet future needs. Sometimes power companies will seek to build new plants, not to serve the energy needs of the citizens of the area, but to sell the energy off to a big city farther away—at a substantial profit. Showing where the real economic advantage lies can help to strengthen your local cause. If the need for the power is genuine and must be met soon, you could try to prove that a better type of plant could be designed than the one proposed. Find an area that has a working model of cleanliness, efficiency, safety, and capacity. It may use solar power, wind power, recycled garbage (which makes methane gas), or some combination of these energy sources; it may also be more expensive—but aren't clean air and water and community safety qualities worth paying for? What costs a little more up front may also be cheaper over the long haul.

In some cases you will want to push for reform legislation at the same time you are protesting the unwanted development project. Say the county wants to create a new land-fill in your area, to meet anticipated needs ten years from now when the current land-fill will be full. Get working right away on recycling and disposal legislation that will drastically reduce the need for the extra space. Get a ban on non-returnable bottles, ban disposable diapers (which now account for about 2 percent of all American land-fill space), and mandate recycling of newspapers, aluminum cans, and glass. Even if your efforts don't result in sweeping changes in the amount of trash your city generates, they will have this worthwhile side effect: Your city leaders will be alerted to the fact that your neighborhood is well-organized and politically savvy, and they will be less inclined to tangle with you in their quest to put the new landfill somewhere.

They will then probably pick some poorer, more isolated part of the county to stick their LULU landfill. If you and your fellow campaigners are really sincere about wanting to get at the roots of the problem (not just get the LULU shifted out of your neighborhood), you should then take it upon yourselves to help the residents of that more isolated town fight the LULU that government almost foisted on you. (You will feel much better for it.)

THE REALLY HARD CASES

How Not to Be a NIMBY

Some cases call as much for soul-searching as for sound development analysis. When you're sure a development will be harmful to your neighborhood's quality of life, yet you know in your heart it's being built for all the right reasons—to house the poor, to shelter the homeless, to rehabilitate the drug abuser, to ease the transition of the newly released convict into society, to provide a loving, home-like environment for the mentally retarded or the emotionally disturbed—what do you do?

First (and good advice for any situation)—think before you talk. Whatever your first emotional reaction is, it won't be as clearheaded, responsible, and useful as your second, third, and fourth thoughts on the subject. This goes for your neighbors, too. When you get together with them for the first time to talk about that homeless drop-in center, the drug treatment clinic, or the juvenile home, you will be fortunate to find among yourselves a clear-voiced and compassionate leader to chair the discussion.

In the private home setting for your get-together, it's good to air all the rumors you've heard, and get your worst fears out in the open, among friends, well before you speak to any city officials about the plan. (It may be that you won't be dealing directly with the city, because the contract to build the facility has been given to a private home operator. More and more, our city governments are turning to private contractors to provide the kind of care that city institutions used to handle.)

Start out by making lists about everything that is known about the planned facility. What type of service will it provide, and to whom? How many beds/patients/inmates will be there? Where do they come from? Are they referred/committed by the courts, or are they there voluntarily? What about the building: What's its square footage, height, number of parking spaces (and all the other data you would collect about any type of development)? How many staff-members will work there, and what are their qualifications? What type of oversight will there be? Random inspections? Check-lists to see that state and federal standards are met? To whom and how often does the staff have to report? What about visiting policies, locked doors, fences, walls, guards, and/or other security issues?

Before taking *any* steps, be sure you have the answers to these and other basic questions you may think of concerning the facility's operations. If you have trouble getting straight answers, and you feel you're getting a run-around, you should make clear to those proposing the development (whether they're city officials or private contractors) that you will do everything in your power to get hold of the facts, including filing a Freedom of Information Act (FOIA) case if necessary. As affected citizens, you have a right to be informed, so that you can have a proper say in what goes on in your own community. But make clear, too, that you are not seeking the information in order to start a fight against the project. You want to know because you would like to be able to make an informed, fair-minded judgment about the case. Whether you fight it or try to work with the project will depend upon what you find out.

Once you have all the relevant and necessary data for your evaluation, make a second list. This time have all those concerned neighbors give their reactions to what they've heard—what's wrong and what's right about the proposal. Too many residents for the number of staff? Too many people for the size of the house? The neighborhood already has more than its fair share of halfway houses? Does the private contractor have a history of poorly run group homes? Has there been violence, unsanitary conditions, or staff malfeasance at similar city-run facilities? Ask people to focus particularly on the things you will be able to document, whose effects you can quantify and possibly correct.

But also include in your list any of the things people are likely to be worried about, whether there is evidence for them yet, or not. Will the residents of the home attack neighborhood children? Will drug addicts be breaking into houses on their way to the clinic for treatment? Will there be winos sleeping in your garage, or pushers selling dope on the street corner, or any other scenario that scares you? Get it all out now.

Then go over the list and separate the legitimate neighborhood concerns from those that are far-fetched or paranoid, or that stem from misunderstanding or prejudice. See if you can work out an agreement with all the members of your group that each of you, when speaking publicly about the proposal, will stick only to those issues that are provable, relevant, and legitimately troublesome for the neighborhood. Agree not to say anything that might contribute to a sense of panic in the neighborhood. That will only hurt your chances for working out a satisfactory solution for all concerned.

Outside of your organization there are bound to be a few loud voices crying out some unsubstantiated fears about the development, but if your group is disciplined and sets the right tone for reasonable discussion, you can make them seem like a tiny minority, not representative of the neighborhood as a whole. Once you establish yourselves as a fair-minded, practical group, you should find the proponents of the plan willing to work with you to solve the outstanding problems.

The exception to this prediction occurs when plans for the facility are already far along before the citizens hear the news, and its establishment is presented as a *fait accompli*. Then citizens quite rightly feel they have been cut out of the process, their government having done all the planning behind their backs. Thinking themselves the victim of a sneak attack, they fall into a posture of defending themselves by planning a harsh counter-attack.

Though that's how nearly every citizens' group reacts, if you can persuade people not to, you will probably come out ahead in the end. It's fine for you to protest the lack of notice. But you shouldn't do it angrily; better to do it with a note of sadness. It's too bad that the city doesn't trust its own citizens to be open-minded and compassionate toward other citizens. The secrecy of the planning shows contempt for the community's judgment and is contrary to the principles of our open society.

Depending on what the laws provide for public access to government plans, you may have an issue you can use to get the process restarted from the beginning (either by filing an administrative appeal or a court case); but you should make clear that you are *not* taking this action as a means to be able to block the construction of the facility. You are doing it because you really mean what you say: The citizens should have a right to participate in development decisions that affect their lives. Once they have been fully informed about the plan, then they can decide whether or not to support it, seek certain changes or guarantees, or oppose it altogether.

Whether the proposal comes with advance notice or as a *fait accompli*, you will still need to move slowly and cautiously in your reactions to the project. After your group has identified the main concerns, you need to frame them in a form that will produce a useful dialog with city officials. That is, it's no good to start off by saying, "We're worried about people loitering outside the drug-treatment center waiting for it to open." That only invites an empty reassurance in response: "We will tell them they can't wait there," or "They will soon learn to come only during clinic hours." Better to put forward a positive suggestion for each of the problems you raise. Say, "The clinic should have a twenty-four-hour attendant, someone with the training to be able to refer people to the proper place—the emergency room or a homeless shelter—if they show up in need when the clinic is closed." Or, "Security guards should be stationed outside during the off-hours to prevent break-ins by people trying to steal drugs."

If the plan presents so many problems that the city can't afford to deal with them all, then and only then should you attack the whole plan as substandard and unsuitable for your neighborhood. Once you've reached this point, you will still need to be careful to emphasize, each time your neighborhood's opposition is brought up, that it is based on objective, enumerated deficiencies found in the plan, and not to the general idea of any sort of social service center in your neighborhood.

If the plan does have fixable elements, you should be very dogged and determined about getting the changes you feel you need. Don't let officials off the hook with vague promises. Be sure they put down in *writing* just what will be done to address the problems you have identified. With this public document in hand, you will know (and they will too) that you will have proof of their bad faith, should they fail to follow through.

But what if the basic problem has nothing to do with the design or functioning of the particular shelter or clinic, but with the multiplicity of such centers in your neighborhood? What if house after house, storefront after storefront, is being taken out of residential or retail service and being transformed into collecting-points for all the problem elements of urban society? This phenomenon is indeed a cause for alarm, and demands for reversal of the process. But you should base your opposition not only on the right of the residents to retain a healthy mix of private homes and stores, but also on your concern for the clients/patients of the new facilities to be added. A key reason for establishing social service centers in the community is to provide those being served with as normal a setting as possible. It's no good bunching them all together in one area; that just sends a signal to them that they are social outcasts, to be "dumped" wherever sufficient, cheap living quarters can be found. For their sake as well as your own, you may point out to city officials that your neighborhood is not a dumping ground for all the problems they can't solve.

If the city is set to go ahead with a plan to put one too many social service centers in your neighborhood, you might want to get in touch with residents of the facilities that already exist, and ask them to work with you on the problem. Discuss how you view the neighborhood mix, and let them know you value the presence of all types of neighbors, of all races, cultures, and conditions. Let them know you are concerned about the neighborhood losing its sense of community spirit. You may be surprised to hear that they value that spirit as much as you do, and prefer to live in a neighborhood composed mainly of families, rather than of facilities similar to theirs. They will almost certainly be pleased that you cared enough to seek out their opinions, and so be more disposed to cooperate with you in your effort to win community input over the siting of any new facility.

If you find you do share common concerns, invite some of the residents to be part of your delegation when you call on city officials. Or ask them to sign your petition or perhaps testify on your side at the public hearing (if there is one). That will do more than anything to prove that you care what happens to the people to be served by the facilities, and you're not just another group crying, "Not In My Back Yard."

One thing you should *not* do—no matter how much the subject is in your thoughts—is complain about what will happen to your property values once the new facility is built. Yes, your house represents your whole life's savings, years of hard work, your nest egg for your old age, and the greatest asset you will pass on to your children. And yes, when that fifteen-bed home for youthful offenders goes in across the street from you, it *is* going to hurt the value of your house. But bite your tongue, and see what you can do to get your neighbors to bite theirs, too. The property-value defense is the classic NIMBY stance, and once you use it, people will forget all the other arguments you've raised and just dismiss your complaints as the typical homeowner selfishness at work. "Enclave of privilege fighting to keep out the less fortunate" is how the story will play in the media. And your public officials will have a plausible-sounding reason not to respond to your requests for political support.

But just because you can't explicitly talk about your financial stake in your house, don't fear that the point will be lost. You can get the sense across, subtly, by talking about maintaining the neighborhood's charm or attractiveness, and the need to keep it "family-oriented." These amorphous qualities translate on the real estate market into higher resale values—still, it's far more acceptable for you to talk about them than about the money they can bring in.

But don't automatically assume that the social facility can't be made to fit in with the type of neighborhood you want. If a place is of an appropriate size and design for its site, and it's well-managed, it could coexist with its neighbors well enough. I know this for a fact. A block and a half from my house, the city has established a group home for eight severely retarded adults. The house is kept in good condition, the men appear well looked after, and the immediate neighbors have never had any complaints. But the staff of the home took the trouble to meet with the neighbors before the home was opened and answer all their questions and listen to their concerns. The neighbors came to understand that the house was not being turned into an institution; it was simply that another type of "family" was moving in. That is as it should be when all parties are willing to sit down and be realistic about each other's needs. And it can happen in more cases, provided the citizens are able to look beyond their back yards, and the city is willing to trust the citizens' abilities to respond fairly and participate responsibly in the development process.

This bungalow was skillfully and sympathetically adapted to become home to eight adults with severe mental retardation.

What You Should *Not* Accept

Some types of facilities are not appropriate for a neighborhood, no matter what the designers do to try to make them fit in. Any building where the residents will be locked in—a prison, a detention center, a reform school, or a hospital for the criminally insane—should be opposed absolutely by the neighbors. These facilities will require barbed or razor-wire fences, walls, watchtowers, electric gates, barred windows, and armed guards, and so will sit apart from the neighborhood like a fortress. Yet if facilities are built without these chilling features, the neighbors will probably live in fear of escapes by violent inmates—and that would be even worse.

The only place for such high-security institutions is in an isolated area, where the only neighbors will be prairie dogs and weeds. But as isolated land becomes scarcer and scarcer, as the crime rate keeps rising, and the public demands that dangerous people be locked up for longer periods of time, the need for more prison space becomes acute, and land sites are sometimes selected in haste with little regard for the effect on the neighbors.

Legislators say they are caught in a hopeless bind. No community wants a prison nearby, yet, as legislators frequently remind us, it's got to go some-where. If it's put in a location too remote from the cities (where most of the crime occurs), then the families of the inmates will find it difficult to make visits, which, criminologists tell us, is detrimental to prospects of rehabilitation. In some states, courts have ordered the closing down of substandard and oppressively harsh older prisons within a certain period of time, and so there is a deadline within which the new prison must be built, or else dangerous criminals will have to be set free.

These are serious problems, yes, but your neighborhood didn't cause them, and shouldn't be made to pay the price for the current crisis of need. Still, as citizens, you share the responsibility along with other thinking members of society of grappling with the moral, legal, and public safety questions posed by the prison population explosion. While you should stand firm in your opposition to any prison construction in your neighborhood, you should offer to work with others on finding an acceptable solution.

Perhaps you or other community leaders could serve on a search committee to look for a more appropriate tract of land for the prison. Perhaps it would be possible to refurbish and add onto the existing prison, to relieve overcrowding and bring conditions up to court-set standards. But you might also consider an altogether different approach from more cell construction: Explore the idea of alternative methods of punishment not requiring incarceration, such as victim restitution programs, house arrest, intensively supervised probation, and mandatory participation in drug or alcohol abuse treatment programs (since over 70 percent of all crimes in this country are committed by people with a drug or alcohol problem). Consider, too, that some 40 percent of all those in jail today have not been convicted of any crime, but are simply awaiting trial. Money spent for more judges, lawyers, clerks, and courtroom space would greatly relieve the overburdened judicial system and decrease the number of people now held in pre-trial detention centers. Since prison construction is tremendously expensive, almost any of these alternatives can be shown to be cost-effective.

Whether or not your ideas are accepted, you will have demonstrated that you are taking the problem seriously, and are not simply trying to shift the problem out of your own neighborhood and into someone else's.

Citizen Strategies

Suppose you have critiqued the facility proposed for your area and come up with a reasonable set of conditions you would like to see met, and suppose the city has looked over your demands, decided that it can't (or won't) fulfill them, and is determined to go ahead with the construction nonetheless. Now what do you do?

First (as always) you need to find out what type of approvals the new facility requires. Will there be a public hearing (either a variance hearing, a state health planning board, or other specific social agency hearing)? If so, you will have the opportunity to present your opposition, just as you would do against any other type of development. It will be up to you to persuade the hearing officers that the facility is inappropriate for the site, based on whatever evidence you can muster. Look for calm, objective types to be your witnesses, and discourage any offers of help from those who seem over-emotional about the issue, or whose opposition seems based more in prejudice or fear than on the plan's real flaws. Though in most instances when something new is proposed, the burden of proof is on the applicant to show that it is needed, in these types of cases, the real burden falls on the citizen-opponents, as public officials generally will assume (unless shown otherwise) that it's in the public interest to have more community-based treatment facilities.*

Chances are just as good, however, that your community will not get a public hearing for its position. In many states legislation has been enacted to remove the need for hearings and special approvals for such facilities, and to make them "matter-of-right." This is done exactly to keep the citizens from having any formal means to object to the proposed use. The law may declare that any eight (or ten, or twelve, or some other pre-set figure) unrelated persons living together shall be considered a family, and so shall be entitled to occupy a house within a single-family zone, without variances or special exceptions. Non-resident staff members most likely will not count against the occupancy limits, nor will their cars be figured into the parking requirement, since they would not be registered to the house address.

Remedies. If you find yourself in opposition to a matter-of-right facility, your options are somewhat limited. You could try to find some kind of *error in the application:* that the site dimensions are not adequate for the new addition that may be planned; that the building can't be adapted to meet all the applicable fire and health codes, or that some kind of special review process—to examine historic preservation or environmental issues—has been illegally skipped over. Or you could try to *challenge the state or local law* that permits the matter-of-right conversion of a single-family residence into a group home. It could be flawed in any number of ways: that its definitions are too vague; that it singles out some zone-districts for such facilities but not others; that there are other, higher laws that contradict it in some fundamental way.

Whichever strategy you choose, you will have to hire a lawyer and file for an injunction to stop the facility from opening. That will be expensive, time-consuming, and emotionally draining. However carefully you explain your stance in terms of the broad public welfare, you are sure to come across in the media as the classic NIMBY bigot. But if you are willing to endure a bad

---

* or CBTFs, as they are known in social-worker jargon.

public image, you might still come out with the result you desire, and prevent a badly-conceived or managed facility from going where it isn't wanted.

Another method that has been known to work, but which also brings with it bad press (because it really is a bit underhanded) is the **buy-out strategy.** It works like this: Say you've learned that the government, or a company holding a government contract, is negotiating to buy a house to be turned into living quarters for twelve parolees on a work-release program. You and your neighbors will do anything to prevent it, including taking a financial risk. So you find out what the asking price is and offer the seller more. Of course, you can only do this if you can raise the amount of the down payment and qualify for a loan. You can then sell the house to a family, presumably not for too much of a loss (and possibly for a profit, if values are increasing in your area). Be warned, however: Government treasuries have more money than even the richest neighbors can raise, and officials are aware that neighbors may attempt the buy-out trick. So they commonly purchase houses for half again or even double their true market value. You could end up provoking a bidding war you are not able to win. And even if you succeed in the current case, you may just leave officials frustrated and determined to place a facility somewhere else in your midst.

But only a few neighborhoods have the wherewithal for the buy-out or the legal grounds to file for an injunction. If that's the case in your situation, there may be nothing else for you to do except take your case to the media, try to see that your views are presented fairly, and hope that public sympathy will be with you, and will help to put public pressure on the city to reverse itself. But when controversial social issues are involved, media campaigns can have unpredictable effects. It's not at all like organizing against a big developer. You are not the underdog this time. And if things go wrong, you can very easily end up looking like the villain of the piece. So weigh your situation carefully before you start on this course. You need to consider:

- the composition of your neighborhood. Is it all of one race or income bracket? If so, you may come across as trying to preserve your exclusivity, and to shut your community off from the problems of society.
- the number and distribution of other social service centers in your city. If every neighborhood already has one but yours (and some have a concentration of facilities), you will be susceptible to charges that your community is avoiding its fair share of the burden.
- the professional and political credentials of your neighbors who will work with you in your campaign. You will want to find allies who have some expertise in dealing with the social problem the

proposed facility seeks to address: For example, if it's to be a home for the emotionally disturbed, can you get the support of those neighbors who are psychiatrists, psychiatric social workers, or clinical psychologists?

- the number of neighbors who are likely to say or do things in public that will hurt your case. Is an uncontrollable, anti-everything faction likely to emerge? Will there be people on your side who may be quoted spouting bigoted sentiments (lines like, "We just don't want those crazies in our neighborhood"; and "This is a decent neighborhood, not a place for riff-raff and street-trash"; and "People here are all well-educated—those retarded people just wouldn't fit in.") If you suspect that more than one or two would react this way, you should know right now, they will lose your case for you.

You've seen how it plays on the evening news. The crowded public meeting hall, the camera lights, the angry voices. The mothers holding up their babies, using them as stage props for their fears. "Those delinquents will be molesting our children!" they scream. The beleaguered city officials trying to stay calm. You can't help but feel sorry for them. And you get angry that no one is willing to give them a fair hearing. Instead, mindless fear seems to rule the hall. You wonder how these people can be so lacking in compassion. It seems a modern-day example of "no room at the inn." So you root for the neighborhood to lose.

That's the view the news-bite gives you. But here's the part you never heard: The group home for adolescent boys will be overcrowded from the day it opens. Several of the 14–20-year-olds have been convicted of serious crimes which carry penalties for adult offenders of ten to twenty years or more. The site chosen is not near any public transportation lines, and no thought has been given as to how families will come to visit or how the staff will get to work. There is only a very small front yard for the boys to use as recreation space. One of the neighbors may have told the reporters all this quietly, but that undramatic piece of videotape got left on the cutting room floor.

What's needed is a way to draw press attention away from the clash between the residents and the clients/inmates of the facility. That something should be interesting, positive, and creative, an innovative approach to a seemingly insolvable problem. You will need bright, flexible, energetic people to devise such a plan—and they may be hard to come by if yours is a neighborhood where everyone's working overtime just to get by. But where neighbors are free to put in the volunteer time and the mental effort, you might be able to follow this course:

Before you call your first public meeting, before you look to get any backing from anyone to oppose anything, first seek to define something you all can be for. Let's say the problem is a proposal for a shelter for homeless families. Your committee should not say one word against the creation of the 200–bed facility until you have worked up a fairly complete and worthwhile-sounding alternative. Then announce that the neighbors have come out in favor of a plan to build, not a temporary shelter that is likely to be expensive to set up and nearly impossible to maintain in good condition, but a small apartment building to provide for the families' long-term housing needs.

Don't worry about "making the numbers work," as you would do when negotiating with a private developer. The point of the exercise is not to prove yourselves better planners than city agencies, but to demonstrate your willingness to be part of a real solution to a pressing societal problem. The onus will then shift to the city to show why it's better to spend money on a scheme opposed by its citizens than to achieve the same good (or better) social result with something the citizens support.

Your alternate plan should have enough substance to it to warrant further exploration and development. Perhaps you could get an architect to come up with a sketch of a residential building of a size and design suitable to the site. You may not want to pay for drawings but simply write up the basic concept— the number of families to be served, the ratio of subsidized units to market rate units, sizes of units, placement of parking spaces, etc.—or you may want to put forward two or three variations on the theme.

Your proposal should be detailed enough to allow you to answer basic questions about it that may be raised by the press or city officials. You will then have succeeded in reframing the question in these terms: not whether to help the homeless or attempt to push them aside, but *how* to help them—offer them a spartan, temporary shelter (according to the city plan) or build something permanent, attractive, and suited for a family-oriented neighborhood (the citizens' plan). That will be the question that the news report will air.

You can expect city officials to react negatively to your plan, but then *they* will be the ones who sound callous. They will tell you that it won't work because the money isn't there. Federal funds would have paid for most of the costs of the temporary shelter, but they can't get funding to build a low-income apartment building. They could also say that the alternative you have offered doesn't suit the need—that right now there are homeless families who must have beds immediately. Your permanent housing plan will take too long to be of use to those who need it. Or they may tell you that your plan won't help the same number of people their plan was designed to reach, or that there is some other technical or logical flaw in your idea.

Much of what you hear will be excuses, but a few of the reasons will be valid. You must respond to them seriously, unless you are willing to have your campaign dismissed as a meaningless ploy by a group of obstructionist neighbors. To the funding problem you could offer this counter-question: Does the city have a real commitment to help the homeless, or is it only willing to do as much as someone else will pay for? If it can't come up with its own money to get the plan started, a better use of officials' time would be to lobby the federal government for a more flexible funding program to help pay for a plan that the citizens will accept, not one that will cause a deterioration in the quality of life in the neighborhood.

To the argument that the need for emergency shelter is more pressing, you can say that other emergency solutions would be faster and cheaper to put in place—for example, each evening after working hours beds could be moved into empty city offices, or, if there is a sizable percentage of unleased new office space in the area, suggest that any commercial space unleased for more than a year be taken over by eminent domain to be turned into temporary shelter space. Or you could ask that the state's National Guard barracks be converted to meet the need. It makes sense for other segments of society to take on the emergency problem; neighborhoods are more suited to contribute sites for permanent family residences.

To the argument that the plan is only offered as a ploy, and that it just is not logically or technically feasible, the only good rebuttal is your neighborhood's continued willingness to sit down and hammer out problems, lobby for funding, and do whatever else is necessary to make the plan a reality. But the very sincerity and compassionate volunteerism you have demonstrated can have a paradoxical effect: Rather than convince the city that it needs to work with you to get your plan built, it may just show them that they are dealing with people who are well-organized, politically savvy, and incapable of being manipulated into a losing position. That could be enough to get officials to back off from the idea of forcing a temporary shelter into a site near you. Though you did not put forward your alternative idea as a ploy, it could end up working like one, to get the shelter plan defeated, without bringing any alternative in its place.

But if, against all the odds, you can get a commitment to develop your community-based plan, you will truly have achieved a stunning resolution to a difficult problem. You will have found a way to turn your case from a NIMBY—Not In My Back Yard—to a SIMBY—Solved In My Back Yard. And that would be an accomplishment that would not only be of great value to your neighborhood, but could serve as a model for thousands of neighborhoods across the country.

The Cases You *Should* Lose

Not every problem can be worked out the way the neighbors would like. Sometimes the neighbors simply don't want different types of people to live in their community. It won't matter how well the facility is designed or managed, or how well it suits the site, because the objection isn't to the building, but to the people in it, and not because of any harm they might do, but because of what they are. They might be physically handicapped, retarded, or mentally ill, or they could be from a different racial or cultural background, or they simply could be poor.

These are the cases you *should* lose. Winning in this instance has nothing to do with saving the neighborhood, because illness, retardation, poverty, or ethnic diversity are not things it needs saving from. These are aspects of our society that affect us all, and we can't (or shouldn't) be allowed to zone them out of existence, or to try to make our neighborhoods into islands reserved for the healthy, the wealthy, or the representatives of a single cultural type. To me, that would not be a neighborhood, anyway—it would be a fortress, a place for an embattled, frightened few, and not a pleasant place to live.

It's not my intention for this book to be used to further exclusivist purposes, though I recognize that it could be. But fortunately, there are laws and court decisions that make it more and more difficult for citizens' groups to manipulate the development process for discriminatory purposes. Federal and state legislatures have mandated handicapped accessibility. Equal housing opportunity laws have given minorities the right to sue any real estate agent who engages in "steering" (that is, showing only those houses or apartments in minority neighborhoods). And banks can now be penalized for "red-lining" (designating a whole neighborhood as a high-risk area and refusing to write loans to home-buyers or businesspeople). But detection of these practices remains a problem.

Just how far the courts can go to try to equalize housing opportunity in the face of citizen opposition is tested in cases brought by civil rights and civil liberties groups. In 1988 two important new decisions struck down zoning approaches in two New York communities that were found to be discriminatory in effect, if not intent. In the town of Huntington, on Long Island, a federal appeals court ruled that the town had used zoning illegally to prevent the construction of apartment buildings in predominantly white, single-family-house neighborhoods. Since most Huntington blacks were looking to rent apartments, not buy detached houses, the practical effect of the zoning was, in the court's view, "perpetuated segregation." And in the city of Yonkers, in Westchester County, a judge took an even more activist role toward racial imbalance. Not only did he find that the town had discriminated by building its low-income housing projects in predominantly black areas, but he ordered the city council to enact a law providing for the construction of new projects in the predominantly white, single-family-house neighborhoods in town. The councilmembers appealed, but the U.S. Supreme Court on January 10, 1990 upheld the desegregation order, while overturning the lower court's assessment of fines to be paid out of the individual councilmembers' pockets.

Lower court decisions in other states have generally restricted the rights of towns to say what kind of people can be defined as a family under zoning laws; they have also rebuffed attempts to place a rigid population cap on a particular area. Where zoning has come in conflict with freedom of association, privacy, or equality under the law, more and more often zoning laws have had to give way. Anti-development activists are learning to take care not to encroach on anyone else's basic freedoms in the process of protecting their neighborhoods from developers. They are beginning to unite with housing activists and other advocacy groups to make a better community for everyone—because only an open, lively, welcoming sort of neighborhood is the kind worth saving.

PART IV

AFTER THE HEARING IS OVER

LOSING ROUND ONE

Grounds for Appeal

There are no guarantees that if you follow all the prescriptions in this book, you will win your administrative hearing. I have lost arguments before the Zoning Commission, the Board of Zoning Adjustments, and the Historic Preservation Review Board—as has any citizen-advocate. Sometimes you just can't pull together all the evidence in time; sometimes one crucial bit of proof eludes you; sometimes the hearing officials have made up their minds in advance, or the opposition was too clever at countering your case...or you were just unlucky. You may not even know why you lost. You only know the fight is too important to give up now. You're just waiting for the start of the next inning, keeping in mind the words of the immortal Yogi Berra: "It ain't over till it's over."

You can appeal.

In some areas there may be an intervening administrative step that must come before review by a court. You may have to file first with the Board of Zoning Appeals, or some other similarly named administrative appeals agency. Ask the director of the planning office (not any of the lower level staff members) about the procedure for appealing a land-use case decision. Any errors in the filing will waste valuable time, damage your credibility, and keep you from getting the second chance you need in your case.

Also before you go to court: If, in the first round, you relied on volunteer advocates, now is the time to hire an attorney. To save money you may want to use him or her only as a consultant to your volunteer counsel, or you could let the attorney handle all the work; but in either event you will want someone experienced enough to know what issues are appealable and what has worked in the past.

Decisions are seldom overturned because the appeals board or the court finds the facts at variance with the judgment rendered. They are far more often struck down on procedural or technical grounds: The hearing did not go according to all the rules laid down; the hearing officers may have prevented a certain witness from speaking, or admitted evidence that was, strictly speaking, irrelevant; the developer may have been permitted to submit a report for the record after the date of acceptance had passed; or notice was not properly given; or one of the hearing officers had a conflict of interest and should have abstained from voting, but didn't. These are flaws you can identify concretely with facts, dates, and names—but that's not enough; you also need to show that the flaw had crucial bearing on the outcome of the case.

If you are successful in showing that the hearing was flawed in this way, you're only halfway there. In all likelihood you will have gained a new administrative hearing at which you will have to argue your whole case over again, with all the same costs and effort involved for your side. The building you didn't want may have been built in the interim, and though the appeals court judge may direct the Zoning Board to consider the case **tabula rasa,*** you know in your gut there will be a strong presumption for the Zoning Board to come to the same conclusion that they reached the first time around. While it has happened a few times that owners have been ordered to tear down buildings they have completed under earlier approvals, such cases are extraordinary, and make front-page headlines whenever they occur.

Appeals courts don't always turn cases back for rehearing. Though judges tend to be reluctant to question local commissioners' decisions in questions of land-use policy, they have the right to do so, and when they find that the zoning panel has not properly interpreted the law, they may simply declare the decision reversed. For example, if an area is designated in your county's Master Plan to allow "moderate density retail development," but your Zoning Board has voted to permit a shopping mall—a high-density use—the court might side with you on the substantive issue of the meaning of the Master Plan. A court would also decide whether the applicant (usually the developer) has met his burden of proof; whether testimony of certain witnesses (such as certified experts, or government officials) has been given proper weight; or whether other rights (such as freedom of association or religion) have been illegally curtailed by the action of the Zoning Board.

Courts also hear challenges to the system itself. Even if your case was conducted according to all the rules and procedures, and the Zoning Board's decision was based on a fair reading of the evidence, you could still attempt to show that the way the Zoning Board handles *all* cases is in conflict with state

* Latin for "with a clean slate," meaning, in this instance, as if the new building had not been built.

or constitutional law. A notable recent case where this worked: In New York City all major land-use cases were heard by a special panel called the Board of Estimate. It was composed of one representative from each of the five boroughs, plus some other officials elected at large. Because the borough of Brooklyn has many times the population of Staten Island, and yet had no greater voting strength on the Board, the U.S. Supreme Court found that the city's land-use decision-making system violated the fundamental democratic principle of "one man, one vote." Literally hundreds of development cases are on hold while a new decision-making process is being crafted.

What makes a case appealable in one state may not work in another. Some states have laws to forbid discrimination against families with children, or the elderly, which may serve as your basis to appeal a decision that, for example, allowed construction of a building designed only for young single adults. Other states provide special protection for tenants against eviction or excessive rent increases, and provide the "right of first refusal," so that residents may bid on their units before anyone else is allowed to make an offer for redevelopment. If you don't know your own state laws well, have an attorney go over the transcript of the hearing looking for these and any other possible violations.

Just remember while you're doing this—developers can appeal, too. They have their own issues to watch for: "takings" of private property, "denial of fair use," plus any technical or interpretative flaws they can find. When a developer is the one filing for appeal, he is no longer challenging your neighborhood, legally speaking; he's going up against the government body that rendered the decision he doesn't like. It's up to the government, then, to defend what it's done. But that doesn't mean you can relax and let the government lawyers do the work. In all the developer-initiated appeals I've seen, the government has assigned young, inexperienced lawyers to handle its side. These poorly paid civil servants tend to get reassigned frequently, and seldom get to see a case from start to conclusion. So you and your neighborhood lawyers may well be the only ones who truly understand the case or care deeply about its outcome. If that's so, you won't want to see the government handle the appeal alone. You'll want to file an **amicus** to bolster the government's case. You might also find the government very willing to take all the help you can give it. Set up a meeting to brief the attorney(s) assigned to the case and make sure they know all the case-law and arguments for your side. If you find out they're well able to handle the appeal for you, you'll be pleasantly surprised, and can relax, knowing your neighborhood's future is in good hands. And if they're not...well, you know you've got some fundraising to do, to pay for a lawyer to file the best amicus you can compose.

Reopening Negotiations

The fact is, court appeals are *long,* and if the calendar is backlogged, may take years to be heard. They're expensive to prepare and nerve-wracking to go through, and unless the illegality of the decision is glaring, whether you win or lose could end up a crap-shoot. Despite all this, there is an advantage in filing an appeal, even if you suspect the pro-development decision will be upheld in the end; and that's chiefly because of the expense, aggravation, and continuing negative publicity your appeal will generate for the developer. That could be the spur needed to reopen negotiations that had broken down or were refused before the Zoning Board held its hearing on the case. The developer has the stronger hand in any post-decision negotiations—no question about it—and your side will have to offer far more than it did when the first rounds of talks were held. But it may be better for you to reach agreement over a few items you desire than to push your appeal as far as it can go and lose everything in the end. The developer's incentive to give you some of what you want is simply to get you out of his hair at last. Your appeal could cast a cloud over his financing, or complicate his plans to sell his development out to another company, and getting you to withdraw your appeal could well be worth the money to him. Keep in mind that *his* lawyer is not **pro bono** but will be working with a meter ticking at $200 to $300 an hour.

If your appeal does lead to renewed negotiations, then you are faced with all the same questions you had to consider the first time around. How much is enough to get you to give up the suit? How can you get your members to agree on a bargaining position? What do you do when some of you are ready to sign and drop the suit, but others are vowing to fight until the end? In order for you to bargain in good faith, you'll need to settle among yourselves in advance just what your goals are and what strategy you'll follow to achieve them.

However, there are reasons to appeal beyond hoping to reopen negotiations or win the case at a higher level. There are times you will want to appeal simply to restate the principle your organization stands for. I was involved in one such case. A garden supply shop and tree nursery applied to the Zoning Board to increase the capacity of its parking lot. My neighborhood organization objected, but the Board of Zoning Adjustments (BZA) ruled against us. We were not so troubled by the decision itself—the parking lot would only become larger by a few spaces—as by the way it was made. The BZA had invalidated the testimony of one of the neighborhood's elected officials on narrow, technical grounds. If in future we wanted his testimony to be accepted in similar cases, we needed to establish that the BZA should have given the official's testimony proper weight. So we appealed the decision to the court, and won. After the victory on that point, we did not ask the garden supply shop owner to reduce the size of the lot. We had won the legal argument, which would affect far more important cases in future than that dispute over a few square feet of asphalt, and that was what counted.

Still another reason to appeal is to establish the neighborhood **bona fides** as a tough, committed group. You may lose the case in the end, but you want all other developers to see that you went down fighting all the way. That may give the next developer pause before tangling with you. With few exceptions, developers prefer the easy course to the hard; weak opponents over strong; and compromisers to all-or-nothing risk-takers. A long-term fight (even a losing one) gains you experience, a high profile, and often, powerful, new allies the next time around. Your one defeat may be strategically acceptable, if it enables you to go on to other, more important victories.

Stacked against these reasons to proceed is the hard fact that appeals of administrative decisions are seldom successful. And when a higher authority upholds the ruling of a lower body, it reinforces the decision and gives developers legal blessing to do more of the same. So weigh all the factors carefully before filing your appeal. Consider all the risks, take stock of the costs and how much more money you can raise, how well your group's spirit and consensus will hold together, and whether you'll be able to keep those press releases flying. Only you can determine if the appeals course will work for you.

The Ballot Box as an Appeals Court

"Participatory democracy," that catch phrase of the '60s, has proven a useful tool for activists in the '80s who are challenging developers. From Irvine, California, to Putney, Vermont, with notable stops along the way in Ann Arbor, Michigan, Palm Beach, Florida, and Westchester County, New York, citizens have been vetoing by the ballot what zoning boards, county councils, and other authorities have already approved. Such a course is extremely labor-intensive, requiring dozens, if not hundreds of canvassers to cover the electoral area to gather the percentage of registered voters' signatures needed to put a question to a direct vote. But if you have the people-power and the commitment (and there is no easier course open to you), by all means pursue the public initiative/referendum approach.

One thing you will need to examine carefully: how your ballot question is phrased. Not all initiatives have the force of law. In Massachusetts, for example, voters approved a measure calling for a ban on further construction in the coastal area of Cape Cod, but its effect was merely advisory. (Fortunately, the state legislators got the message and passed a bill giving legal weight to the vote.) In the mid–'70s in Petaluma, California, voters approved absolute limits on new development and population growth, but the courts said the measure went too far, tampering with established private property rights and the freedom to choose where to live.

For a ballot initiative to pass legal muster, it needs to be written by someone who knows the language of the law, who can also write plainly and tersely, so that the idea can be quickly grasped by the voters.

After you have found the right phrasing, and brought in your quota of signatures, your work has just begun. The developers will gear up their enormous, professionally run campaign machine and try to defeat your initiative. You will have to mount a comprehensive, grass-roots campaign to answer their charges and keep the people on your side. You may expect to be outspent by 5 to 1, or 10 to 1, or even 50 to 1, but that doesn't mean you will lose. If you can get your people out, in good weather and bad, handing out your hand-lettered flyers and talking to their neighbors, you could win more votes that way than the developer with the slickest, most expensive TV advertising blitz.

Multi-Level Appeals

You need not restrict yourself to one level of appeal. This was demonstrated by the citizens of the Tenleytown neighborhood of Washington, D.C., who refused to accept the Board of Zoning Adjustment's ruling that a developer could build an access drive to an office building across a piece of public parkland. They initiated *five* levels of appeal, simultaneously. First, they followed the standard first course of action by filing an appeal with the proper administrative agency, the Board of Zoning Appeals. Second, they started a lawsuit to challenge the city's right to give away public land. At the same time they found city councilmembers to introduce a local bill that would take back the parkland by eminent domain; they also found Congressmen willing to start the eminent domain process in the House and Senate (based on the fact that the park had previously been under the control of the National Park Service). Fifth, they waged a media campaign against the Mayor, designed to force him to reverse his decision to give away the land, or else continually have to justify to the voters (during his re-election campaign) why he had taken the action that he did.

Three of these efforts were still steaming along when the developer, finally tired of all the fighting, agreed to a settlement that removed the road that had been built and turned back the parkland to the public. If he had not negotiated a settlement, in all probability, one of the bills introduced to restore the park would have passed, and the same outcome would have resulted—though it would have taken longer and been more expensive for everyone.

Knowing that one of the five avenues of redress had a good chance of succeeding strongly influenced the developer's decision to compromise. But even if the chance for each was slight, it still would have been worth the neighbors' while to start all five efforts. As long as each one still held out some kind of chance for success, there was incentive for the developer to negotiate, and generally, where there is talk between reasonable people, there is hope.

Money Talks

Non-court methods of appeal may be cheaper, faster, and more effective overall. What the Zoning Board thinks is all right, the developer's bank may bring to a halt. If you're thinking along these lines, then you need to do just as Deep Throat advised Bob Woodward: "Follow the money."

If the development is a publicly funded project, then the "bank" is the government treasury, in which case, you can attempt to intervene in the budget process, as described in Chapter 11. But with privately funded projects, you will need to be cautious. You just can't go to the lending institution and question the developer's plans to spend money on a building in your neighborhood. Such interference would leave you open to a multi-million dollar damage suit, if you did indeed cause the financing to fall through. But it is possible for the bank to reach the same conclusion you want it to reach, without any direct contact between you. If you can manage to make the development the object of continuing, unrelenting controversy, you could make the bank nervous about the developer's prospects for success. If nearly all the neighbors truly hate the development, they could well make potential tenants wary of moving in; they could also keep the new building from getting needed traffic measures (signal lights, parking meters, loading zone spaces, and other publicly approved details), and so make life considerably more inconvenient for the people who come to the building. Such things could turn a solid proposition into a losing one. For lesser reasons than these, investors have pulled out of projects before.

Citizens can also apply financial pressure more directly on a developer, in the form of a **boycott** of the stores and business that move in. Though the restaurateur, dry cleaner, or hairdresser may not be directly responsible for the creation of the building you hate, he or she did choose to move into the unwanted development, knowing in advance of neighborhood opposition, and so must share some of the opprobrium you feel for the developer. Retail tenants can also bring pressure on the developer to correct certain design problems.

For example, in an over-scaled mixed-use project not too far from my house, a large Chinese restaurant was set to open, when the citizens circulated a petition against yet another car-attracting business opening in a building with insufficient parking for the shoppers and office-workers who drove there every day. As a result the owners of the restaurant made arrangements with the developer for fifty spaces to be reserved each evening for patrons of the restaurant.

An even more dramatic change came about in an enclosed shopping mall in Washington, D.C., as a result of consumer pressure. In its first few years of business, the upscale Mazza Gallerie was failing to attract the number of consumers it needed to be a success. A survey revealed that most residents of the area considered the blank, beige facade of the development cold, stark, and uninviting. From the beginning neighborhood activists had complained about the fortress-like appearance of the shopping mall on the plan, but it took consumer displeasure to get the mall managers to act. Store windows were cut through the concrete walls of the building, and glossy black-and-white patterned tiles were added to give some life to an otherwise unrelievedly dull facade. Sales have since improved, and the residents are slightly more pleased with the appearance of their (still-too-big) neighbor.

The Uses of Shame

Though a developer may have won in the zoning process, in the courts, and in the business world, his victory could turn out to be something of a hollow one, if along the way he has lost the good image he enjoyed. You may not be able to make him to do the right thing by the community by the force of law, but you might still be able to get him to do it on his own, if you can shame him into it. Though it's rare, admittedly (since most developers care far more about making money than about making friends)—I do know of a case or two where it's worked.

In Arlington, Virginia, a big development corporation was set to renovate a low-income building, to turn it into luxury units for the upper-middle-class. Though the zoning was all on the corporation's side, and it had the money it needed to go ahead, once the tenants began to organize and protest—even though they had no basis in the law for what they were asking—the corporation delayed on the scheduled evictions and began to negotiate with the tenants to allow them to remain. Why? The press was portraying the corporation as a heartless monster, turning poor families out into the street. The corporate executives cared about their reputations too much to let the plan proceed.

They also had their eyes on the future. The "defenseless" poor were lining up many important politicians on their side, who were quoted on camera telling reporters how appalled they were at corporate insensitivity and greed. The next time the corporation wanted favors from the county—as its executives well knew—these same politicians would be able to express their displeasure in concrete ways. So the executives sat down with the tenant organizers and their **pro bono** lawyers (because of the publicity, the tenants had no trouble attracting free, first-class legal aid) and worked out a deal to provide renovated units at low-cost to some tenants, and relocation assistance to others.

Though not the perfect solution for all renters in the building, considering that the talks worked on shame-value alone, it was a remarkably successful settlement for all concerned.

Downzoning: A Systemic Approach

If you played by all the rules—administrative, legal, political, and economic—and you still lost your case, it could be that the rules as they're written give the developer the edge. If the zoning in place permits oversized buildings, if the law upholds the decision that allows that type of development, if the politicians tell you they don't have any role to play in the process, and you don't have the financial wherewithal to make deals with the developer, you could be out of luck in that case.

What you need to do is to change the parameters of development in your area. That means changing the zoning to limit size and density—i.e., **downzoning**. How to go about filing for this, and some ideas about bringing your application to a successful conclusion, are discussed on pages 209–11.

But how will it help to change the zoning if the new development has already won all the approvals it needs under the old, denser zoning? As soon as the zoning is adjusted downwards, the new building will be immediately **grandfathered** into its zone, meaning it's only permitted because it arrived before the rules changed. Grandfathered buildings are subject to certain restrictions: They can't expand without a variance, and if there is turnover in the retail space, certain high-density uses will be prohibited or limited in size. The owners of the building will have to come to the neighbors seeking support (and offering concessions) if they want to get around the restrictions of the new zone. So downzoning (if you can accomplish it) puts you in a favorable position vis-a-vis the developers who have already built. And of course, those developers who have not yet put up their buildings will have to conform to the newer, lower-density standards you just had imposed.

Block That Bulldozer!

Let's say *everything* you've tried has failed. Your administrative appeal, your court case, your attempts at economic pressure, political pressure, your application to rezone the block...all have come to nothing. You've even tried to sell out and move away, but with that ghastly development pending, no one will buy your house. What now? Give up?

For some people, not just yet. There's one more thing you may want to try, and while I won't promise it will do the trick, it did work for Gandhi in India, and many others after him. Forget the law and act on your conscience. Physically interpose yourself between the construction vehicles and the land. Chain yourself to a tree or a fence, or lie down in front of the bulldozer. Get all the protesters you can together and stand, immobile, on the steps of that historic house. Don't let that wrecking ball swing!

I did it, along with six others, rather than see a piece of parkland paved over into a road. Of course I knew, as you will too, that construction would eventually occur. All the developer has to do is call the police and they will come and take the protesters away. They will warn you firmly, two or three times, and then they handcuff you and put you in a paddy wagon and drive you to jail, where (if the system works fairly efficiently) you will sit for three or four hours, until you are brought before a judge who will release you on your own recognizance.

It is not pleasant (I can't emphasize that strongly enough). So consider all the negatives very carefully before you take on the law. Can you afford to spend a day in jail? Will you end up spending more time and money than you can afford on your defense? Will you be alone, or do many others feel as strongly as you? If convicted (as you almost certainly will be), will a misdemeanor on your record hamper your career, your security rating, your social or familial relations? Are you healthy enough? If you need any daily medications, even if you bring them along with an accompanying note from your doctor, you should expect the jail officers to take them away from you. They are creatures of bureaucracy, generally speaking, and are unlikely to see your case as an exception to their rigid rules.

But if you think you can take it, physically, emotionally, and professionally, and you know that others stand equally prepared to do the same, then get together and work out your strategy. Much has been written about *civil disobedience*, and if you haven't read any of the classics (Thoreau, Gandhi, Martin Luther King, Saul Alinsky, to name a few), that's a good start. Perhaps just as useful is talking to others who have done it. Nuclear protesters may give you some tips...or they could even talk you out of it. It's not for everyone, and there's no need to feel ashamed, should you decide against it. In the same vein, don't press others to join you if they seem to have misgivings. This action needs wholehearted commitment. Others can show their support by forming a crowd of witnesses to the arrests.

Your strategy group will need to consider how many arrests are needed to make the maximum impact.* Will TV and the daily papers cover only one? Call the reporters and ask! If only a few are ready for the challenge, consider using them sequentially, to draw the process out. You might want to have one arrest every hour, or one each day, depending on the number of volunteers.

Age and sex of the protesters should also be taken into account. If only two or three are to be arrested at a time, they'll most likely feel more at ease if they're all of the same sex. Men and women will be put in separate cell-blocks while awaiting arraignment, and it's always good to have a friend with you as

* A note of caution: You need to be careful about the framework for your planning. Make clear to all who participate that your discussion is theoretical only, not instruction for action. It will still be up to each individual, in the privacy of his or her own thoughts, to decide how, when, and whether to commit the act of civil disobedience. That way, when the volunteers actually come forward to be arrested, each can honestly say he or she acted on his or her own initiative, not at anyone else's instigation. This is necessary to protect the group's leaders from charges of conspiracy. While committing the act of civil disobedience may be a misdemeanor in your state, it's possible that those who conspire to cause others to commit a misdemeanor could be charged with a felony. And you don't want to leave any members of your group vulnerable to such a charge.

you go through this experience. Those under eighteen should probably be dissuaded from volunteering, as they are likely to be sent to a separate holding facility for juveniles.

When is the best time of day for acts of civil disobedience? The morning rush hour has many advantages. It will be easy to draw a crowd of spectators. You can call for cars to honk their support as they drive by. Print journalists will have time to go into the office and write up the story before the deadline for the next day's early edition. Camera crews will be able to have the film in to the editing room, ready to show on the 6 o'clock news, with maybe a smaller snippet repeated at the 11 o'clock as well.

What day of the week? Find out if there is any day that your daily paper likes to focus in on different sections of the metropolitan area—for example, on Thursdays the *Washington Post* runs a special section with various neighborhood reports. When calling for coverage, I spoke to reporters who work specifically for that section, and worked out the timing of the civil disobedience around their assignment schedules.

Does that sound too calculating? It's really only prudent. Though you're acting out of conscience, from the purest of motives, it won't count for anything unless people get to hear of it. The effort to block the construction is a physical reality, but its meaning is purely symbolic. You will be removed, and the construction will go on...at least for a little while. So you must base your actions on what makes the most potent, memorable symbolism that can become a rallying point for the whole community.

How you arrange yourselves at the site is also key to your impact. Some say you should face the bulldozer, to show that you're meeting the threat head on. But I follow contrary advice: Turn your back on it, as if to say you don't care where it goes, so long as it does not advance over the ground you are protecting. That implies that you feel within your rights to be where you are, and treat the bulldozer as the intruder, the trespasser. It also has the public relations advantage of allowing you to face the camera, while the bulldozer seems to be sneaking up on you from behind.

When I stood in the disputed piece of parkland, my back to the bulldozer, I was already thinking out my defense in my head. "There I was, your honor, standing in the park, enjoying the scenery, minding my own business, when all of a sudden this huge bulldozer showed up. I can't think what it was doing there!"

Whether people stand, sit, walk, or lie down, whether they carry signs, sing, chant, pray, or stay silent will depend on a variety of factors, including: the visibility of witnesses outside the fenced-off construction area, whether the land is sloped or flat, the size of the area to be bulldozed, the number and width of trees, and the number and personal disposition of people undertaking civil disobedience.

Whether few or many, the people need to be well-briefed and to come prepared. They should wear comfortable shoes (preferably ones without laces, which in some jails are confiscated during detention) and clothing that they don't mind getting dirty (bulldozers can kick up a lot of dust). What not to wear: jewelry and belts (since these will almost certainly be taken away before you are put in a cell). In case bail is required, bring about $100 in cash, and have the phone number of a lawyer to call in case there is some complication about your release before trial. It's a good idea to eat a big breakfast. You might not arrive at the lock-up in time for lunch, or if you do, you might take one look at it and decide not to touch it. And clear your calendar for the whole day; even if you're arrested at 8 a.m., you still might not be out until late in the afternoon.

With all your efforts to anticipate what will happen and to plan for maximum impact, you still won't be able to control the event itself. What happens will depend largely on what the developer does, and how the police react. The first day my group decided to commit civil disobedience, we all stood along the edge of the construction site, where posts had been dug to hold sections of chain-link fencing, our intention being to block the fencing off of the park. As the workmen unrolled the chain-link sheets, we chanted, "Roll it up, roll it up!" while TV cameras captured the scene on videotape. After a few minutes, the workmen stopped. The foreman, who had been conferring with the

Sharon Farmer

The author and a police officer having a disagreement about development. The policeman won in the short term, but 18 months later, the government sided with the protesters, and the park was ordered restored.

developer by portable telephone, suddenly called a halt to the work. Apparently, the developer was not ready to have a confrontation with the citizens shown on the three major stations, and so he cancelled the construction for the day. The workmen rolled the chain-link sections back up, loaded them in a truck, and drove away.

But the next day the developer had clearly made up his mind he was going to proceed, demonstrators or no demonstrators. At 8 a.m. bulldozers and dump trucks were lined up along the street, ready to roll over the grassy meadow of the park. The first three demonstrators willing to try to block them stepped in the middle of the vehicles' path, and stood, back to the bulldozers, waiting to see what would happen. Of course the bulldozer driver halted his machine. (None of us thought for a moment there was any chance of being run over; we knew the developer would not risk injury to us, for which his company could be sued.) The machine and the protesters remained in a stand-off for several minutes, while the developer called the police. About twenty minutes later, three squad cars appeared. After asking each demonstrator three different times to move out of the way of the bulldozer, and after receiving three polite but negative responses, the officers made the arrests and escorted the demonstrators away in handcuffs.

Some say one should not cooperate with an arrest over a matter of conscience, but I've never seen the point of that. There is less dignity, in my view, in being dragged off, bodily, than in walking off proudly, with head held high. There is a natural tendency, when your hands are held behind your back, to lower your head as you walk, but you should make a conscious effort to avoid this posture. It's why arrested people on TV so often look furtive and guilty. I tried to keep my eyes level with the camera, and look self-assured, even though I really felt nervous and scared.

Once we were charged and a trial date was set, our anti-development position had a new forum, a new focus. Though there would be no more zoning hearings at which we could argue our points, there would be a criminal trial, at which we could press our view that the land we'd hoped to preserve was a public park, not a private development site. As long as the developer was pressing criminal charges against us, he was the heavy in the press, and we were his victims. The four of us (since charges were dropped in three other cases) became symbols of the citizens' resistance to the depredations of developers, not just on that site, but all over the city. Donations, which had almost dried up after we lost our administrative appeal, started flowing freely again, and major publications invited us to write articles describing our cause. City officials who had dismissed us as having lost now had to recognize that the fight wasn't over, we were still there, and we weren't going to go away until the parkland was restored.

One tangential point: After having spent a full day in the cells of the D.C. "holding tank," all of us became outraged at the filthy and miserable conditions experienced by detainees. In civil disobedience cases it's tempting to get sidetracked on the issue of jail conditions, but if you complain of them publicly before you have your trial, you could well distract attention from your cause. The attitude is widespread in society that if you court arrest for any reason, you had better be prepared to be treated the same as those arrested for all other crimes. You mustn't expect jail to be decent. Though you may well feel (as I do) that those who have not yet been convicted of anything ought to be treated in a civilized manner while awaiting arraignment, you should also be prepared to set aside those feelings, to let the focus of your arrest remain on the development issue, and not on the treatment you receive while locked up.

To that end, although you may have chosen to contravene the law, you should always plead not guilty in your case. That way you will be assured of a chance to defend your actions, and in the process, condemn the developer for necessitating your stand of conscience. But if you get a chance to delay the trial at all, you should take it. Trials put issues behind them. Part of the point of civil disobedience is to keep the case in the public eye, to generate outrage, and keep up the pressure on the developer and city officials. Will the developer press the charges? Will he try to reach a settlement with you? Will the city prosecute or drop? Will the Mayor intervene and try to hammer out some kind of compromise between the protesters and the developer? The maneuvering period over these issues can go on a long time, if each side uses all its available reasons for delay.

The city may go slowly simply because its courts are clogged with more important cases. The developer, technically, isn't a party to the arrests and so won't have a say in the timing. You can ask for and get continuances based on illness, necessities of work, family duties, and long-made travel plans (up to a point, which varies depending on the patience of the judge and the practices of the area).

The city may not want to prosecute, especially if it appears that you will use your trial to reopen the development issue (although, when you actually get to court, the judge could well rule that the conflict over the development is really irrelevant to the case, and that you must restrict yourself only to the incidents immediately leading up to your arrest). Before trial, in the forum of public opinion, you can talk about what you see as the real issues in your case. Suggest that the Mayor and the Director of City Planning should be on trial, or might be subpoenaed to testify at your trial. Say that you intend to show that it is the development (not your own act) that is unconscionable, and a violation of the spirit, if not the letter of the law. Certainly ask for a jury trial, if you can get it (your chances of acquittal will rise dramatically). You may also want to consider what defense strategies have worked in other recent cases of civil disobedience. Your lawyer may be familiar with the successful "necessity defense" used in the trial of Amy Carter, Abbie Hoffman, and other co-defendants in Amherst, Massachusetts. A jury accepted their contention that in order to protest a great crime (in their case, apartheid; in your case, a development that will ruin your neighborhood), it was necessary to commit the minor crime of trespassing.

Whatever defense you use, don't be too surprised if you are convicted. As was the case in Alabama and Mississippi in the days of sit-ins and freedom rides, protesters tend to be judged guilty by the system that arrested them. You may treat your "record" as a badge of honor. About the penalty: In nearly all localities you need not fear a jail-term. The cells are overcrowded with dangerous criminals, and have no room for first-time offenders of non-violent crimes. You can expect a suspended sentence, probation (usually unsupervised), a fine (unlikely to be more than a few hundred dollars, which your organization, of course, should pay on your behalf), or community service. With the latter sentence, it may even be possible to receive credit for working for the same neighborhood association that organized the protest!

If the sentence is more than a slap on the wrist, you have another issue to keep the media's attention. Why is the city coming down so hard on protesters against overdevelopment? Why is it siding with developers against its own citizens? Without saying it in so many words you can get across the idea that the punishment was "wired"—that is, set up in advance to please big development interests. This is what we did after one of our number (in fact, the leader of the protest) was given an overly harsh sentence in the park protest case. Public disapproval of the sentence ran so high that the judge actually revised her original sentence (from one hundred hours of street and alley cleaning to twenty hours)—which our leader carried out, with help from his friends, while reporters took notes and photographers snapped his photo.

Afterwards, neighborhood residents and citizens from all across the city were made aware of what had transpired from the stories in the papers and on TV. Everywhere he went the Mayor had to explain his decision over the development and over the prosecution of the protesters. His political advisers could see that his image was suffering. The sentenced activist, on the other hand, had become something of a folk hero in the city, with his picture on the cover of a local newsweekly. And the controversy was far from dying down.

Some months later, the Mayor decided to try to win back the friends (and voters) he'd lost. He called up the organization's head and set up negotiations over the restoration of the parkland and the removal of the objectionable road.

More months passed before an acceptable settlement was reached. To announce it the Mayor called a press conference, at which the head of the organization handed over to him an engraved hatchet, to be symbolically "buried." The road is to be torn up and parkland to be returned to the neighborhood. We won everything we were asking for, when only months before, the conventional wisdom was that our cause was lost.

I have not a doubt in my mind that the arrests were what galvanized the community and turned the situation around. But even if the protests had come to nothing, I still would not have regretted my decision to stand my ground when the bulldozer was on the way. Sometimes you feel it's better to protest something for its own sake, than to accept passively what you know to be wrong. As my fellow arrestee, Phil Mendelson, so eloquently described his feelings in his *Washington Post* op-ed piece a few weeks after his arrest:

"I started my summer in jail. My crime was "unlawful entry" into a public park. It was only 8:30 Monday morning, but a developer was preparing to build a road to his new building and I was in the way. My arrest was by choice....

"For 18 months the genteel residents of Ward 3 have tried to prevail through normal governmental processes. We enlisted the support of D.C. Council members, filed comments with executive agencies and even went to court.

"But last Monday, all we had left were our bodies. I took mine to the park and wouldn't leave....

"Two weeks ago we tried to meet with the Mayor. He went out of town. His aides promised, though, that the city would not argue against our request to preserve the park while the judicial process is pending. We were double-crossed. On Monday the bulldozers came.

"We can accept this or protest it. I have come to believe that there is much more to be lost by acquiescence than by protest.

"As I took my first ride in a paddy wagon, my fellow protesters and I recalled the famous exchange between Henry David Thoreau and Ralph Waldo Emerson. Thoreau had been jailed for civil disobedience and his friend had asked, 'What are you doing in there?'

"Thoreau replied, 'What are you doing out there?'"*

If Thoreau's question has resonance for you, then civil disobedience may be the right course, whatever your chances of success. If you don't have that feeling of moral compulsion, that deeply personal sense of outrage that leads you to put your own body on the line, then you must look for other ways to carry on your fight, or be quietly resigned to an unhappy outcome.

---

* June 28, 1987. By permission of the author.

Other Last-Ditch Means

You don't have to get yourself arrested to keep your case on the front burner. There are other techniques you can try, short of civil disobedience, to show that you haven't given up the fight. You can dog the developer and picket his office as well as the development site. Dog city officials, taking the issue to social functions, banquets, awards dinners, anyplace you find them. Picket outside, and try to get your people inside, to ask tough questions and confront the officials with your displeasure. Don't worry about sounding obnoxious or embarrassing the official. At this stage of the game, you have to be willing to be aggressive, and less than gentlemanly or ladylike—or else give up.

Look also for creative ways to keep your cause alive. How about a little street-theater? Have your members don costumes and masks to play the roles of the developer and city officials and pantomime the deal that put that ugly new skyscraper in your neighborhood. You could even have someone come in wearing a cardboard costume in the shape of the big new building; have others dressed in cardboard reproductions of smaller, single-family houses, and have the big building act out the squashing of all the little ones. If your little play has dialogue, just be careful not to defame any living people—especially any private citizens who may have supported the development, who are not public figures.

Another attention-grabbing idea, well suited to groups protesting excessive traffic-producing plans, is the "drive-slow." Get all your members out in their cars at a pre-set date and time (the Friday evening rush hour would be a good choice), and drive in a line along the road you believe is now over-burdened with development-generated traffic. If the road has two or more lanes going in one direction, have your drivers cruise in all the lanes abreast. Go at exactly the legal speed limit, and not a fraction more. Stop for all yellow lights and pedestrians at crosswalks. Within a few minutes, your "drive-slow" should cause a massive back-up of commuters' cars, no longer able to use that street as a speedway because of your action. You will have demonstrated conclusively to your Traffic Management bureaucrats that the street is over-used by commuters, and only functions as a thoroughfare when the speed limit is routinely broken.

If they're not convinced by a one-time demonstration, repeat the drive-slow as many times as it takes to make them see the necessity for action on your behalf. The residents along the Reno Road corridor in Washington, D.C., tried this, and as a result, won left-turn prohibitions and lane-reductions that now severely discourage use of the street by commuters in the morning rush hour (residents are still pushing for measures to discourage commuting in the p.m. rush).

Banners and billboard-like signs could also express the continuing outrage of the community about a development decision. The residents of Adams-Morgan, a largely Hispanic neighborhood in Washington, D.C., used this tactic to good results many years ago. A gas-station chain had bought a large lot right at the crossroads of the neighborhood, the site of the traditional weekend community farmers' market. Though the big oil company (British Petroleum) that owned the gas station had every legal right to proceed with the development of the lot, it held off breaking ground, deterred only by the huge, anonymous sign that appeared on an adjoining wall, which read:

"¡BP, FUERA! ¡NO LE QUIEREMOS EN NUESTRO BARRIO! [Translation: BP, leave! We don't want you in our neighborhood!]

Eventually BP sold the lot to a local bank, which, before building a branch on that site, met with community leaders and promised to devote a certain percentage of its loans to support renovation and new enterprises in the community.

You can come up with many other ideas to keep your movement going, even after you've lost before the zoning board or in court. It just depends on how determined you are, and how far you're willing to go. You'll probably find that the more dire your situation looks and the more desperate you feel, the more vigorously you'll fight at the end. That's true in nature of any cornered animal. Chances are you'll either wriggle free, or your last-ditch struggle will attract others to intervene on your behalf, or the developer will tire of trying to beat you and will walk away or call for a truce. You may come out of it all a bit mauled, it's true—but then others will think twice before picking on you next time around.

WINNING AND WHAT COMES AFTER

A Show of Gratitude

So you've won your administrative hearing. Congratulations! Now you're wondering what to do next. For starters, throw a party! It's the best, most fun way to thank all the people who pitched in. Sending out a mailing with the date and time of the party also gives you the opportunity to get out news of your victory to those who may have missed it (especially if your local paper buried the story at the back of its local news section).

Victory parties serve another important function, too: They allow you to be gracious to those neighbors who were on the other side, or who sat on the fence. Invite all, regardless of what they may have said, or failed to say, in the heat of the conflict. By all means invite the zoning authorities, the landmarks commissioners, the planning office staff—whoever played a role in advising or determining the outcome of your case. Invite your elected officials, too, even if they were less than supportive of your efforts. You'll need the goodwill of all these people in the future, and now that you've proven your effectiveness as an organization by winning a big case, they'll see that they need yours in return. By attending your party, they have the opportunity to strengthen ties and pledge to work with you when the next case comes around.

Letters. Not everyone will be able to attend the celebration. To make sure that everyone receives some form of thank-you for their help (whether it's a one-dollar contribution or three-weeks' worth of volunteer labor), you need to send out thank-you letters. Use the lists compiled by your membership and fundraising committees to get names and addresses of recipients. If you have mail-merge software, you can make sure each contributor's name appears in the salutation. We all like to get a little personal recognition for our part in a hard fight (even if we realize that a computer has aided the letter-writer in recalling our names). We're also much more willing to lend a hand next time around if we know our help this time was acknowledged and appreciated.

And there *will* be a next time—you can count on that, as long as the real estate market in your area is growing. Winning an administrative hearing won't be the end of the case. If your developer was told he can't build the plan he wanted, he's probably busily at work, coming up with a new plan for the same parcel of land. Or he may put the property up for sale, bringing in a new owner, with new, and possibly worse ideas for its development—and there you go all over again. There's no rest for the weary.

You can sit and wait for this to happen, and you may have no choice but to do so; you're too exhausted and burned-out to do any more pavement-pounding and knocking on doors. And your friends and neighbors are all *maxed-out* (meaning they've given the maximum cash contributions they can afford). And you feel like screaming if you hear the word "development" one more time. In that case, take a break for a while. Don't worry about anything happening right away; there is almost always a "dormancy period" between plans. The developer's tired, too, and it should take him some time to figure out what he wants to do next.

Ready for Some Action?

If you're *not* worn out, but are hot to follow up on your success with more action—now's the perfect time for it, when the developer's already weakened and confused. He won't be expecting anything from you for a while, so you'll have the advantage of surprise. The following is a list of options to consider:

- File for **downzoning** (discussed in Chapter 9, and briefly again in Chapter 16).
- Attempt a **community buy-out.** You and your neighbors raise the money privately, make the developer an offer, and develop the land according to your own ideas of appropriateness. (This strategy is discussed in Chapter 15.)
- Press the government to acquire the land for the public benefit. This could be done through **eminent domain,** donation of a **scenic easement,** a **land swap,** use of **transfer development rights,** or outright government **purchase.** (These strategies are discussed in Chapters 11 and 12.)
- With the aid of local, state, or federal programs, form a **Community Development Corporation** (a CDC), buy the land, and develop it

according to the program's guidelines for public/private partnerships (discussed in Chapter 10).
- If your case involved historic preservation, you might also be able to pursue the option of the **historic district** (discussed in more detail, below).

Historic Districting

You've just won a landmark on that building you were trying to save, and you're thrilled at your accomplishment. But what about the buildings all around it? Wouldn't you also like to see them protected from incompatible development by historic landmark laws? A historic district could bring about this end.

Were most of the buildings in the neighborhood built at about the same time as the landmark? Is there any distinctive style to the neighborhood? Or perhaps it has an eclectic mix of styles, reflecting different stages of architectural fashion? Is the area culturally cohesive, having maintained a special ethnic flavor in its restaurants, stores, religious institutions, street signs, and decorations? Anything that gives a neighborhood a defining character could make it worthy of preservation. Did the whole area play a role in the history of the city or the region? Was it once a colonial settlement? a whaling seaport? a factory town—perhaps a hotbed of union organizing in its day? Ask yourself these and other questions, much as you did when undertaking the application for landmark status of an individual building. As you did then, consult with knowledgeable architectural historians and staff members of your state or local historic preservation office, and/or call the relevant architectural appreciation organization—the Victorian Heritage Society, the Art Deco Society, the Early America Society (for colonial architecture)—whoever specializes in the type of building found in your neighborhood. (*All About Old Buildings: The Whole Preservation Catalog* contains a comprehensive list of all the national, and many regional groups.)

You will also need to find out how historic districts work in your area. In some states the term "historic district" is more of an identifying label than a set of legal constraints on development. In other places historic districts impose strict regulations that must be followed for all new construction and alteration. Some districts won't even let you change the paint color of your house without design approval. You may not want to bother with the application process if the law is too weak, and you may not want to impose burdensome rules on homeowners if the law is too strong. So check into the historic district's scope, and consult closely with as much of the neighborhood as you can, before proceeding. Set up town meetings to explain the advantages and disadvantages to all. Weigh carefully how much control you will gain over commercial development (will the law help you to control size and density, as well as aesthetic features of the buildings?) as against the control that will be exercised over your own ability to remodel and add onto your own home. Will you face a nightmare of petty bureaucratic hassles every time you need to patch your roof? Or is the system designed to focus on the big issues, and help the small property owner get permits quickly and efficiently?

My neighborhood debated these questions in open meetings held over a period of eighteen months. We put on workshops run by experts who could answer homeowners' questions, and each resident received a hand-delivered invitation to one of sixteen coffees held in nearby private homes to discuss the pros and cons. We emphasized that there would be some restraints imposed on what owners could do to the facades of their Victorian, Queen Anne, or Arts-and-Crafts style houses, but as a trade-off, the community as a whole would have far more input into what developers could do to the small Art Deco commercial buildings along our shopping strip. Without a historic district, there was a very real possibility that all would be torn down, to make way for a concrete canyon of high-rise offices.

At the end of the study period it was clear that the vast majority of the citizens were in favor, so we sent in our application to the city's Historic Preservation Review Board, along with petitions and several hundred letters of support. In November, 1986, our Cleveland Park Historic District was created, and by April of the next year, it was listed on the National Register of Historic Places. Now any time a developer wishes to demolish or alter one of our neighborhood shops, there must be a public hearing, at which experts and residents can state their opinions about the change. The citizens finally feel they have some control about the future of their town (even as they have had to give up to others some say over what they can do to their own houses).

There are some widely believed myths about historic districts that you may have to dispel, if you want your neighborhood to come under the protection of your state's historic district laws. Four of the most common are that:

1. Property taxes are higher in historic districts.
2. "Gentrification"—the displacement of low- to moderate-income residents by middle- and upper-class buyers—always occurs when an area is declared historic.
3. Historic districts create neighborhoods frozen in time. No one will be able to adapt an old, inconvenient house plan for modern living; and striking, innovative design ideas will be forbidden.

4. The "design police" will dictate what you must do with your house. You will be required to pay for expensive restorations, according to someone else's aesthetic ideas.

To answer them one by one:

1. Assessments for property taxes are nearly always based on the real market value of buildings and land. If people keep paying more for houses in your area, then taxes will rise. If prices remain stable, so should taxes. Because historic status confers prestige on a neighborhood, it may make it more desirable, and that in turn could boost prices and taxes—though it's by no means inevitable. In Washington, D.C., real estate taxes have been rising steadily over the past ten years, but no more so in any of the twenty different historic districts than in undesignated neighborhoods. In commercially zoned areas, developers may be able to press for *lower* assessments, since their ability to develop their properties to the full extent allowed by zoning has been significantly diminished under historic district rules.

2. Gentrification is prone to occur whenever beautiful old houses are available at a reasonable price for those who can afford to restore them. This happens as often in undesignated areas as in recognized historic districts. Some of Washington's most historic areas are in relatively low-income parts of the city (Anacostia, Shaw, LeDroit Park), where little or no displacement has occurred. But in historic districts in other cities, community and government leaders have given much thought to ways to help long-time residents remain in their wonderful old houses, and resist the temptation to sell out to young professionals with the money to pay for restoration. Barbara Brandes Gratz devotes two chapters of her 1989 book, *The Living City*,* to strategies that worked in historic districts from Savannah, Georgia, to Pittsburgh, Pennsylvania, to make sure that residents can continue to live in neighborhoods now recognized for their architectural distinction.

3. All historic districts allow for compatible change. What differs from district to district is how stringently or liberally the guidelines are written for new design, and how those guidelines are interpreted by the historic review staff-members and panelists. In my own historic district we made a point to write guidelines encouraging creative design ideas for the expansion or renovation of the turn-of-the-century houses. We specifically discouraged exact copying of historical forms and style, preferring to be able to distinguish between what was original and what was added later. This is also what is prescribed in the *Secretary of the*

---

* New York: Simon & Schuster, 414 pp.

Interior's Standards for Rehabilitation, a booklet put out by the federal government advising owners and architects on the restoration of historic properties.

4. No historic district in the country requires owners to change what's already been built to conform to architectural standards, or to rehabilitate a building that's in disrepair. Only when owners initiate the change, either for demolition or alteration, will they be subject to design review; then they may be required to modify their plans to suit the landmarks commission's ideas of compatibility of style. If the district is working as it should, the owner should be well aware of what sort of changes are allowed in the district, and what sort are discouraged. A pamphlet or written set of standards should be available to the owners and their architects/builders, so that the decisions of the design review panel will not seem arbitrary, but will reflect certain reasonable and widely accepted architectural principles. The system should also be flexible enough so that it can accommodate trends and changes in lifestyles that people want and need. For example, if today's smaller families no longer need all the space in their four-story townhouses, they could be allowed to build new entrances to the basement level and create a separate apartment downstairs. Because residents have the opportunity to participate in hearings and argue for the changes they want (and against those they think will harm the neighborhood) the process should remain essentially democratic, and not turn into the design dictatorship of a few.

Redefining Terms

Downzoning, the buy-out, land-swap, CDC planning, and/or historic districting might not work for you, either because the approach to your problem is too sweeping (you don't need a whole historic district to deal with an issue that's confined to one block) or because the approach is too limited to help (the problem goes beyond the single parcel that's up for sale). What you might need instead is some adjustment to the language of the zoning code—some redefinition of terms.

Here are four situations in which this approach could help.

1. **The use-categories are too inclusive.** Here's a typical example of how this problem might affect your neighborhood: Your local shopping area seems to be turning into a strip of burger joints, fried chicken places, and taco stands. Gone are restaurants with variety in their menus, gone is waitress service, and threatened are other types of retail stores. Downzoning won't get at the problem, because restaurants are allowed

in every zone. What you really need is some way to distinguish between fast-food restaurants (which bring parking problems, litter, noise, fumes, and congestion to the neighborhood) from other types of restaurants that serve seated patrons a meal on real plates. You need an **amendment to the text of the zoning regulations** to create a new class of retail establishment—the "fast-food store"—written with precision, so that everything you recognize as a fast-food use will fall, indisputably, into that class. Then make sure that the fast-food class is listed as a non-permitted use in your local neighborhood shopping zone.

Washington, D.C.'s, city council did this, in response to citizen pressure, and the resultant change has considerably alleviated the litter problem in many neighborhoods, including my own. Now new fast-food businesses are restricted to high-density commercial areas that are more than 600 feet from residential zones.

Other changes in the definitions of zoning categories and terms might be tailored to suit the particular needs of your specific area. For instance, you might seek to redefine "grocery store" to exclude convenience stores, or propose new rules to prohibit certain combinations of uses (a gas station with a liquor store, for example, to discourage drinking and driving). Or you could ask that certain distance-limits be written into the code to provide for separation of certain uses (keeping a minimum of 300 feet, perhaps, between bars and schools, or between night-clubs/discos and private homes).

2. **Too many exceptions too easily granted.** If, every time a developer applies for a special exception or variance to expand a shopping center, a hotel, an office building, or other large-scale development, he seems to get it, then the standards used to determine need for the exception may be too vague, and should be tightened. The zoning code should spell out the types of circumstances that may be used to prove economic hardship, practical difficulty, or any other rationale for change, and should instruct the Zoning Board to deny permission when the difficulty is self-imposed (as when a developer buys a piece of land at a high price, knowing it is zoned to allow forty units, but he needs to build sixty units in order to turn a profit).

3. **The zoning bonus or incentive system is being abused.** Most cities could benefit from an updating of the regulations governing the granting of PUDs (or PDAs, MUDs, or whatever alphabet-combination is used to describe planned mixed-use developments in your area). Look at it this way: Most of these programs were written to give developers incentive to include substantial amenities and public benefits in the

buildings they put up—but most of our residential neighborhoods already enjoy a significant amenity in the low-scale, spacious layout of houses and stores. Why give the developer extra height and density in exchange for a bit of artwork or a fountain that the residents never asked for, while letting him take away the one thing they most prize—the peace and tranquility of the neighborhood? Why should neighbors have to organize themselves again and again, raise money, come to hearings, do lengthy analyses of plans, and argue against the ones they feel hurt their interests? Why not simply write rules that state clearly how much building is allowed, and in what form, and leave it at that? In other words, *ban the PUD* in residential areas, and do away with the uncertainty and subjective nature of the process, which citizens find frustrating and confusing.

Of course it will be hard to bring about this change in the regulations. Planners who were schooled in the '60s and early '70s are trained to regard the PUD as a wonderful tool, a way to bring in more and better development. They're usually puzzled at first by citizen hostility to the concept. But with patience and a few good object lessons, you should be able to help them to see the problem from your perspective. It took the citizens of my neighborhood some time to get their points across, but ultimately we did, and the PUD rules are now so restricted in my neighborhood that they are virtually inapplicable. (The new rules have left developers some flexibility in the footprint and setback of new buildings, but have taken away the bonus for height and density.) Because of these important changes, we really have very little left to fear from big developers who own property along the neighborhood shopping strip. As there is no more incentive under the rules for demolition and redevelopment, we can at last have confidence that the stores and houses we love will still be standing many years from now.

4. **There is no way under the code to challenge matter-of-right applications.** This problem commonly stems from vague language in the preamble to the zoning code, which gives the general purposes for the regulations. The opening paragraphs usually express the government's interest in regulating land in nice-sounding but overly general phrases such as "to promote public safety," "ensure adequacy of public facilities and services," and "provide for the common good." Environmental protection, maintenance of the infrastructure, and equitable treatment of citizens may also be among the themes used to justify the enactment of zoning in your jurisdiction. But these seldom will be followed by

specific **enforcement standards** against which zoning applications are to be judged.

What that means is this: Even if the roads in your area can no longer accommodate any more commuter cars, and the sewer system is operating near break-down, and the A.Q.I. exceeds all government standards, a developer still could come in with an application for a 600–unit apartment complex, in a zone that allows for just that number of units, and get it. You may *think* you can challenge the application based on the general language of the preamble—since the project certainly conflicts with the "public welfare" and the "adequacy of services," but in all likelihood the administrative agency (and the courts, if you sue) will rule against you. Unless the zoning code spells out some set criteria by which matter-of-right applications can be judged (and denied, if certain standards are not met), a developer will always be able to build as much as the zoning allows.

Writing specific enforcement standards for zoning categories, however, will be a tricky feat. You could, for example, press for a ban on the construction of new, traffic-drawing retail or office space in places where the A.Q.I. has been found to exceed 100 for more than thirty days of the year; but developers would be sure to challenge such a measure in court as unfair to owners of not-yet-developed land (since those whose buildings already draw heavy traffic suffer no curtailment of their economic activities). Such a measure would likely be struck down. An experienced land-use planner and lawyer are essential in the drafting of regulations that will stand up to scrutiny by the most conservative of courts.

The Moratorium

When development is happening faster than you can cope with it, you won't have time to propose new regulations and see them through the complicated legislative process. You need relief right away. A *moratorium* may be the answer. This will be a specified period of time—a few months, or perhaps as long as a year—in which no permits for new buildings over a certain size will be issued by the government. During that time the citizens and their elected officials presumably will be studying the overall development picture in the area, identifying problems, and tightening the zoning standards to protect threatened areas from overdevelopment.

A moratorium can be enacted by any of several methods. In New Jersey, the governor, by executive fiat, put a temporary halt to all construction along coastal areas and waterways, based on his emergency powers to protect the public from "imminent peril" to its health from pollution of the environment. The measure remained in effect until a legislatively created Coastal Commission was able to take action to protect the state's sensitive shoreline. In San Gabriel, California the voters approved a one-year ban on both commercial and residential construction, during which the city council, strongly influenced by a group called Citizens for Responsible Development, reassessed its policies on growth. In Seattle, a moratorium on new office construction came about by action of the city council, but its effects were limited to downtown and its duration was only for five months. That gave the citizens enough time to put a referendum on the ballot, and after its passage on May 16, 1989, more stringent, permanent development limits took hold.

Changing the Way the Game Is Played

Fair Play for All

You can rewrite regulations to level the playing field (that is, change the way land is treated for development), and that will be helpful, but it might not be enough if certain players (the developers) are still given favored treatment by the referees in the game (the officials who oversee the hearing process). In that case you'll want more rules governing who may judge a zoning case, how those judges are picked, who may speak at hearings, where they're held, and how different types of testimony should be regarded.

Some of the obvious reforms you should work for (if you don't already have them) are:

- **Conflict of interest** laws, prohibiting officials from participating in cases in which they (or their partners, or immediate family members) have a financial stake. In our post-Watergate era, you may have assumed that all governments have such basic ethics-in-government rules, but they are really far less widespread than you may have thought.
- **"Revolving door"** legislation, prohibiting former government officials from lobbying the government for a specified period (usually one or two years) after they have left their official positions for private employment. The law should also work in reverse, so that a zoning official who formerly worked for a private development company should be banned from judging any case he or she once worked on while at that company. (Persons who remove themselves from cases to prevent conflict with ethics rules are said to have *recused* themselves.)

- **Campaign finance laws.** If the zoning authority in your area rests directly with elected officials, you will want to be sure that your campaign laws require candidates to disclose which individuals and corporations are contributing to their campaigns, and how much. Office-holders should be prohibited from voting in cases brought by developers who have contributed more than a nominal sum to their election bid.

If you don't know where to start in pushing for such laws, contact your local branch of Common Cause. Ethics in government is a special concern of that organization.

A Rational Structure for Planning

The zoning judges may be operating according to the best ethical standards, but they're still heavily dependent on the advice and opinions of their professional planning staff. So the citizen-activist will be interested in:

- the quality of personnel in that office;
- the adequacy of its budget; and
- the relationship of that department to other government agencies.

To take them in order:

Personnel. By the end of a long, complicated development case, you've gotten to know the planning office staff quite well. How did they rate? Did they seem to know their jobs? Was the person assigned to handle your case familiar with your neighborhood, or at least willing to learn? Did they initiate contact with leaders in your community, or did they wait for you to bring your complaints to them? Did they listen when you spoke, and did they respect your views? Most important—did they see their job as helping you, the citizen, or did they view their role as fostering more growth, and helping the developer cut through red tape? Or did they cast themselves in a neutral role, and leave it up to you to try to figure out how best to persuade the zoning authorities of the merits of your position? Did they at least try to work toward a negotiated solution? Did they help you to understand the process, to know what papers had to be filed, and when?

If they failed to do any of these things, you should be talking to their bosses (not the appointed director of the department, but to the mayor or county council chairperson, who's the ultimate boss). You probably don't want to complain about any one person by name (unless that person's conduct was particularly egregious) but press for changes in the orientation and general attitude of the staff. They were most likely handling cases just as they were directed to do from above. When politicians understand that the voters are displeased with the way a department treats the citizens, they will give members of that department new marching orders, and changes will result.

At least this was what I observed in my own city. In the early 1980s the planning office staff nearly always sided with developers in disputes with the citizens. In the last few years there has been a citizens' revolt, and the voters have made it clear to the Mayor that they expect more support from their government. The Mayor has turned development policy around, and the planning office staff members have received the message. Now, whenever new plans come in for a development in any neighborhood, the planners call community leaders, first thing, and ask their opinions. And more often than not, these days, they do what the citizens ask. It certainly has been a welcome change!

The Planning Office Budget. The staff can only carry out as much as it has funding to do. If you want a better planning office, then lobby your council for a better budget for it in the coming fiscal year. Good staff members won't be hired away by developers if they are paid adequately by the city for their work. Nor will they be so prone to rely on developer-provided reports for their conclusions in zoning cases, if they have the resources to do the data-gathering and analysis on their own.

If you can get the funding for one more position, you might also suggest that the department employ a public education officer. This staff member would act as a guide to all citizens who come into the office with development problems, to help them understand the process, the zoning terms used, and what role each of the parties is supposed to play. He or she would help the citizens' group to get organized, file the necessary papers on time, and identify which issues are the proper province of the zoning hearing and which can't be heard in a land-use forum. The availability of paid, expert advice would do much to even the odds for the inexperienced citizens who are up against a big corporation with a team of professionals working for it full-time. The government already provides such a service, free of charge, to poor people accused of crimes; why not extend the same right to counsel to citizens who have done no wrong but to live in a neighborhood eyed by big developers?

The Relationship of Planning to Other Departments. If you go in to see the planning staff, and you find a plaque on the door identifying the agency as "The Office of Planning and Economic Growth" or "The Zoning and Development Department"—watch out! The name already tells you what attitude applies, and you'll want to work to change it. The planning staff should be concerned with how much new development can fit in and where it can go; the economic development office has as its mission the promotion of a healthy business climate. These are separate functions, and should be carried out by separate agencies. The two should consult with each other, of course, and both should be guided by an overall policy set by the chief executive and the legislature, but there should be a natural tension between them—the economists trying to bring more of every profit-producing activity to the area; the planners trying to see that the quality of life for residents is not sacrificed for others' monetary gain.

Another common problem in the structure of governments is that the planning function is split among several different agencies. The Parks and Recreation Department will have say over the disposition of open space, the Housing Office will rule over residential development, and the Economic Development Agency will control commercial and industrial growth. The problem is compounded if there are also special boards set up to deal with development in certain geographic areas (a Waterfront Commission, for example, or a South-side Urban Renewal Board). This means that decision-making is fragmented, and thus more susceptible to influence by special-interest groups.

As I see it, citizens are better off when there is just one agency that has set standards and practices that everyone can recognize and work with. It should either be an independent agency, answerable to the legislature, or part of the executive branch, for which the mayor or chief executive can be held accountable. In either case, clear policy directives need to be traceable to one source, and that source needs to be removable by the voters, if the job is not being done right.

Reform in the Small Details

Getting the right people in positions of authority, making sure they are responsive to citizen input, and that they are conducting themselves within a rational and ethical framework is all crucial, if the system is to function fairly. But now you need to make it convenient, too. What good is it to have sensitive zoning commissioners, who want to hear what you have to say, if you can't get to the hearing because it's held too far away or during your working hours—or you can't find the tiny public hearing notices that run in the classified ads section of your paper?

In that case you should work to get public hearings scheduled during the evenings, from 6 o'clock on, so that working parents can attend. You'll want them held in a public meeting place in the community near where the development is to occur, or to be at least easily accessible by public transportation to members of the community who don't have cars. All who live in the area affected by the development proposal (not just members of your organization) should receive word about the time, date, and place of the hearing, directly—either through the mail (sent to all *residents*, not just property-owners!) or through placement of large (at least quarter-page), plainly-written notices (preferably including a sketch of the proposed development) displayed in the general news section of a mass-circulation newspaper.

Citizens interested in attending should be able to call up the zoning office and easily find out who will be speaking, and in what order participants will be heard. Those who wish to testify should be given an approximate time to expect to be called (you can't expect a nursing mother or an eighty-year-old grandfather to sit on a hard bench for four or five hours at a stretch, waiting to speak for two minutes).

The means to be recognized as a participant need to be simple and clear. If your current regulations require that requests to testify must be made in writing, seven or fourteen days in advance of the hearing, and be marked with the case number in the upper lefthand corner—get those rules changed. A phone call the day before the hearing should be all it takes to be allowed to have a say.

Rules for acceptance of materials from organized citizens' groups likewise should be kept simple. Some localities require that all exhibits—whether written reports, photographic evidence, or graphs—be submitted in multiple copies, one for each zoning panelist, one for each of the parties to the case, and two for the case files. But photocopying fifteen or twenty sets of materials and reproducing pictures can be very expensive—enough to become a financial drain on a small citizens' group. The zoning authority's office should be the one to pay for the copying and arrange distribution of materials filed in the case. The same allowances that should be made for citizens during the preparation for the hearing should be continued during the hearing itself. Zoning commissioners need to be patient and courteous with citizen-participants, especially those who have never attended a public hearing before. They should not cut off a speaker if he or she exceeds the pre-set time limit by a minute or two. Hearing a time-bell ringing in the middle of your speech can be very disorienting. If the zoning commission chair rules certain evidence or testimony out of order, he should take a moment to explain what he is doing to members of the audience. He should also be sure that citizens understand when they will get a chance to rebut arguments that the developer is making, and when the developer will get the same chance. If there are additional days of testimony to be scheduled, or if there is a deadline for final submissions, or a date set for a vote, the citizens should be told exactly when and where, so that they won't have to send a representative to every scheduled zoning meeting, waiting to see if anything is happening with their case.

These reforms may sound like common sense, yet they are in place in very few localities. The chief obstacle to their implementation is the lack of a constituency to lobby for them. Citizens tend to get involved on a case-by-case basis. Only the developers' representatives follow the workings of the system on a regular basis; only they have the time and energy to lobby for rule-changes—and the more complicated and burdensome the process is, the more it favors them and handicaps the citizens.

Planning professionals, of course, should be the ones to undertake the redrafting of rules, but they will only make time to do so as directed by politicians. So in the end, it all will come back to who holds office and how much that person cares about citizens' rights in the development process. It's up to you to make the issue matter.

Master Planning: A Unique Opportunity

America, I noted in the Introduction to this book, lacks a long history of planning in its cities, and this is probably true for the city where you live, too. There will likely be no overall plan in effect to chart development policy over the next ten or twenty years, but decisions will be made piecemeal, in response to the pressures of the moment. To find out if that is the case, call your local planning office and ask: Is there a master plan? (It might be known by another term, such as comprehensive plan, or it might have a specific name, like the So-and-so County Development Plan, or it may be a subsection of a larger, regional plan, like the Tri-state Peninsula Plan.)

If the answer to your question is no—and you really want to protect your neighborhood now and in the future—you have a unique opportunity.* You can lobby your legislature to get the process started. A strong, enforceable master plan written to incorporate citizen goals is your most valuable weapon against the threat of overdevelopment. It will map out areas to be protected, identify other areas that are underdeveloped, where higher densities are to be encouraged, and help to ensure that spurts of growth in any one area do not outstrip the government's ability to provide the necessary roads, schools, and other essential services. It's a bit like zoning, but on a higher plane: Most master plans require the government administration to change the zoning to conform to the policy directives of the master plan. When you get an effective master plan that serves your interests, you no longer need to fight each new development plan that comes along, or try to persuade pro-growth officials that downzoning is justified; they will be bound by the dictates of the master plan to restrain growth in the manner outlined by law. And if they don't, you can sue and win.

How do you go about getting this marvel of citizen protection? You could approach it much as you would go about getting a downzoning action started—

---

* If the answer is yes, you may want to skip to the next section of this chapter.

but on a city-wide scale. Form a committee from among your neighbors, then link up with other civic, planning, and preservation groups in other neighborhoods in the area, form a coalition, and work together toward the goal. Use whatever expertise you have among your volunteers to tackle the various subtopics (transportation planning, housing distribution, commercial growth, mixed-use developments, historic preservation, parks and open spaces, shopping malls, and many other issues); but you will also need the skills of lawyers, architects, economists, and other experts (some of whom you may have to hire, at least on a limited consulting basis).

When you have arrived at the basic concepts you want to see incorporated in the plan, arrange a meeting with your local elected representatives, and with any other legislators you know to be interested in development questions and open to the idea of sponsoring legislation. You might also want to invite representatives of the county or city administration, including the chief of the planning office.

Lay out your ideas for the type of master plan you envision. The preliminary work your study group has done should be sufficient to show that your planning ideas are practical, balanced, and beneficial for all the citizens of the area. You should then be able to get the government working with you toward the drafting of a formal planning document that can eventually become the master plan law.

One thing to watch: If officials seem interested in pursuing the master plan idea, make sure they know you expect to be full partners in the process. You don't want them to start moving forward with the planning on their own. In that case, what will likely happen is the drafting of a plan that suits the theoretical notions of the planners, not the neighborhood reality you know. They will bring their plan back to you for your comments, and you won't recognize it. You may try to change what they've done, to put your own ideas back into it, but you'll find, once the momentum is going, that it will be difficult. So, rather than have to work after the fact to get the plan changed, insist at the outset that the citizens continue to be the initiators of ideas, not simply reactors to what the planning professionals have conceived. This requires far more work on your part, but I can tell you (from my own experience with the Comprehensive Plan in Washington, D.C.), the result will make the extra effort worthwhile.

For your citizen-initiated plan to work, it should:

- have a set time-table—10, 15, or 20 years are standard—after which the plan will expire, to be replaced by a more up-to-date version.
- identify specific neighborhoods and set general development patterns for each. It should *not* set limits on a lot-by-lot basis (it is *not*

a zoning map), but should contain enough information about each area, and the goals to be met within each, so that the zoning authorities will understand what approach to take when applications are filed for lots within any specified area under the plan.

- set clear categories, with well-defined limits of density and use. For example, the plan could categorize the residential areas of a city in five parts: 1) Low-rise/low-density; 2) mid-rise/moderate density; 3) mid- to high-rise/medium density; 4) high-rise/high-density; and 5) mixed-use/residential within commercial or light-industrial development areas. Though the plan may distinguish between categories based on FAR, height, and number of units per acre, there will be far fewer categories than on the site-specific zoning map, and the categories will not be described in the same precise detail as zoning terms are normally defined.
- set the boundaries of the Central Business District (downtown) and other high-density areas of the city, and describe what measures will be employed to ease transition between these high-traffic areas and adjoining neighborhoods.
- identify all major institutions, whether public or private, and set parameters for the future expansion of each.
- identify parks, open space, recreational areas, bodies of water, and other environmentally sensitive areas, and set policy to protect their borders from encroachment by developers. If a larger number of parks is desired, the plan should identify other areas suitable to be set aside as new parks or protected open space, and describe how and when such changes of use are to be carried out.
- identify buildings and districts of historic or architectural significance, whether already carried on the local or national register of historic places, or to be researched for possible application for landmark status. A timetable should also be set for completing studies of potential landmarks.

(The next three elements are crucial to the plan's success.)

- contain an **implementation section** telling how the plan is to be carried out. This is every bit as important as what the plan says about development. It's no use having clear ideas about the type of development to be permitted or restricted in different places if you have no plan for how the change is to occur. The plan should contain language along these lines: "The zoning commission shall act within one year to bring about conformity between the city's zoning map and this plan." Such a directive will require the zoning authorities to analyze the plan, compare it block by block with what the current zoning map prescribes for the city, and make the necessary zoning map amendments to bring about agreement between the two. Without such language, the master plan will simply be a citizen wish-list and nothing more.

• include a good wall-sized *map*, showing all existing streets (whether public or private, open or closed) and overlaying the categories described in the text onto the street-grid by means of colors or patterns. The map should be easily readable, with a simple legend explaining the meaning of each of the patterns or colors.

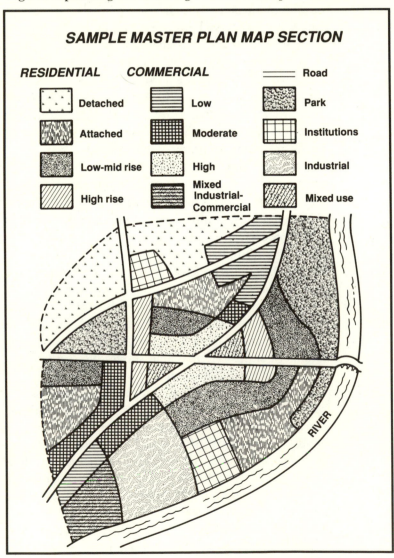

SAMPLE MASTER PLAN MAP SECTION

RESIDENTIAL	COMMERCIAL	Road
Detached	Low	Park
Attached	Moderate	Institutions
Low-mid rise	High	Industrial
High rise	Mixed Industrial-Commercial	Mixed use

- put forward rules for **vesting*** of development rights during the period after the plan has become law but before the city zoning map has been changed to conform to the plan's specifications. A developer should be able to establish a vested right to build only as much as is permitted under the density limits of the master plan—*not* what may still be listed on the zoning map (should there be a conflict between the two). This is essential, otherwise the same day the plan is approved, every developer will seek permission to build at the higher limits allowed by zoning, before the zoning commission has a chance to enact the restrictions of the plan.

In addition to these ideas, you will certainly benefit from studying the master plans now in use in cities similar to your own. If you live in a large city, I strongly recommend taking a look at San Francisco's city plan: It is highly neighborhood-oriented, identifying and extending a wide range of protections to 210 distinct neighborhood shopping areas. Since its implementation in 1986, high-density office construction—once exploding out of control—has been severely curtailed, and now every new development must be reviewed for suitability of location, needs of businesses already in the area, and quality of the building's design. Developers are also required to contribute to a city-administered fund to provide housing, transportation, child care, and open space to help fill the needs created by additional large-scale buildings. San Francisco also puts a cap on the total amount of office square footage that may be constructed each year—the only major city in the U.S. to do so. This feature of the plan was initiated, not by the city planning office or the Board of Supervisors, but by a citizens' group called San Franciscans for Reasonable Growth, which collected the signatures necessary to put the measure on the ballot. Despite concerted developer opposition, Proposition M, as it was known, was a clear winner with the voters of the city.

If your primary goal is not to restrain an overheated building boom, but to encourage the right kind of development in the right parts of town, you may find Philadelphia's Center City Plan a better model for your purposes. The *New York Times'* architectural critic, Paul Goldberger, in his column of June 12, 1988, found much to like about the plan, especially in its careful attempt to "balance growth and preservation." As he quotes Barbara Kaplan, the executive director of the city planning commission: "'We very much want to stimulate growth, and we believe we still have room for it, but we really do feel it is absolutely essential that we preserve what is valuable about downtown.'"

---

* This term is defined and its implications discussed on pp. 193–94.

The plan makes specific recommendations about where future large-scale growth should occur, and it also sets out priorities and desired features for development within the city's core, but, to my way of thinking (and that of most neighborhood activists), it has one fatal flaw: It is merely advisory, and does not have the force of law. That practically assures that some determined developer will come along in the future and construct a building that contravenes all the important guidelines of the plan.

If you live in a smaller town you will find the Philadelphia and San Francisco plans too focused on skyscraper development to be applicable in your case. Of more relevance might be the planning study done for the counties of Middlesex, Somerset, and Mercer in New Jersey. Citizens and government officials in those areas, long concerned about excessive growth, were able to band together in a tri-county forum, which produced a handbook called *An Action Agenda for Managing Regional Growth*. In reviewing the plan, *Washington Post* architecture columnist Roger Lewis called it a "cogent, strongly principled report" which "calls for sometimes radical measures."*

Lewis, a University of Maryland professor as well as a practicing architect, also considered a model plan drafted at an urban design seminar in Key West, Florida, that could be applied to neighborhoods around the country. Called the "TND Overlay" (for "Traditional Neighborhood Development"), it's a new zoning concept created by an interdisciplinary project team composed of architects, landscape planners, public officials, lawyers, engineers, and real estate developers, which draws upon the house styles and street patterns of the traditional American small town as an alternative to conventional suburban patterns in use today.

Many of the ideas incorporated in the TND Overlay, and discussion of other useful zoning and urban design concepts are discussed in detail in the lively and thought-provoking book *Shaping the City*, based on Professor Lewis's newspaper column of the same name.

When there is finally a city plan that works for your neighborhood and the wider area around it—a plan that allows growth to proceed in an orderly fashion, that protects the environment reduces traffic congestion, that city officials are willing and able to enforce—that's when you and your neighbors can sit back, relax, and breathe a sigh of relief. You don't need this book anymore, so give it to someone who does, and be willing to answer their questions and give them the benefit of your experience—to help others to do for their neighborhoods just what you have done for yours.

---

* Quoted in his regular *Washington Post* column, "Shaping the City," June 23, 1988.

When Your City Already Has a Master Plan

Get a copy and read through it carefully, paying special attention to what it foretells for your neighborhood over the coming years. If you don't like the scenario it lays out, get right to work and try to change it. Plans can be modified (by legislative amendment or by promulgation of new executive orders, depending on how it was originally enacted), and it's a far easier undertaking than starting a plan from scratch. Consult with your neighbors, civic association heads and other community leaders, urban studies faculty at local universities, public officials, and any other experts you can think of who might want to help.

You may not find any fault with the substance of the plan; the part you might want to change is the implementation section. If the plan is full of protective clauses and recommendations you would like to see imposed, but its language is merely advisory, then you will need to have it amended so that its directives become mandatory prescriptions to be carried out within a set period of time.

Call on your legislators and ask them to work with you to bring about any changes you seek. As with any particular land-use case, success depends largely on the amount of voter interest you can generate. Plans can and do become hot election issues—especially if you have concrete examples to point out, to show people how bad planning (or lack of planning) can affect their daily lives.

For books, pamphlets, or other resource materials with ideas to improve the planning for your neighborhood or to help you organize to bring about the changes you want, you should contact:

The American Planning Association
1776 Massachusetts Ave., N.W.
Washington, D.C. 20036
or
Regional/Urban Design Assistance Teams
The American Institute of Architects
1735 New York Avenue, N.W.
Washington, D.C. 20006
or
Partners for Livable Places
1429 21st Street, N.W.
Washington, D.C. 20036

Beyond Master Planning

When you have a city plan that puts forth a vision of your neighborhood for years to come, is that the end? For most citizens the answer is "yes." But in some cases the development problem you've been battling is only a symptom of a broader public policy issue, one that reaches far beyond the plot of land you've been working to save. If your beaches are eroding, stopping one shoreline condo complex won't make that much difference in the long run; if your air is overloaded with ozone and carbon monoxide, beating back one highway plan won't make it clean; if it's a forest you've managed to save from the logging company's chain-saws, might it still not die from acid rain?

For these and similar long-range problems, no new zoning rules or city plans will help. You need long-range answers, that apply beyond the boundaries of any particular county or town. Leaders in many local communities are coming to recognize the need for statewide and even multi-state planning. In drawing up measures to control development along the New England coastline, or in the northern rain forest areas of Washington and Oregon, or in Native American and other ethnic heritage enclaves that are threatened with encroachment of ski resorts, vacation home construction, and other tourist-driven development, planners must design measures that will have impact on investors, corporations, and developers based in urban centers outside of the areas to be developed. And more and more often these days, the purchasers to be affected by the land-planners' decisions are in foreign countries—in Japan, Saudi Arabia, Germany, or Kuwait.

In states such as Vermont and New Jersey, this type of broad area planning is already underway. And in Maryland, Delaware, and Virginia, officials, residents, and environmentalists have been working together to bring into being a regional plan to protect the fragile Chesapeake Bay area from the harmful effects of overdevelopment.

These movements, once dismissed as radical, or unmanageably bureaucratic, or as an assault on economic freedom, are gradually being accepted as necessary, if we are to continue to live in harmony on this planet of limited resources. Many creative planning measures will continue to be tried out, and if found to be too cumbersome to administer, reworked; if found too weak to have impact, beefed up—whatever is needed until practical solutions to development problems are in place.

Beyond state and regional planning, there is a trend toward national and international controls on development as well. In an age of alarms about global warming trends, holes in the ozone layer, disastrous oil spills, and radiation clouds from defective nuclear power plants, it's no longer hard to see how the development rules drawn up in the Amazon basin, or in Chernobyl, U.S.S.R., or in Valdez, Alaska, can affect us here in our own cities and towns. As former Speaker of the House Tip O'Neill has been known to say, "All politics is local."

This message was brought home once again when, in January 1989, *Time Magazine* named the Earth as "Planet of the Year." In a list of five recommendations that nations should implement to cope with the crisis, *Time's* number two was *"Establish comprehensive national zoning plans"* for preservation of the environment.*

You may not be able to concentrate right now on anything that is happening beyond the bounds of your own community, but you can feel assured, when you help to save the neighborhood around you, that you are also helping to save part of the one global neighborhood that is home to us all.

---

* *Time*, January 2, 1989, p. 32.

A Select Bibliography

Architecture

The American Institute of Architects Membership Directory. (Washington, D.C.: AIA Press, 1735 New York Avenue, N.W., 20006. 1553 pp. 1–800–242–4140) Need an expert to advise you on a particular building problem? This lists over 53,000 member architects and 10,000 firms, with brief descriptions of specialties practiced.

Goldberger, Paul. On the Rise: Architecture and Design in a Post-Modern Age. (New York: Viking Penguin, 1983. 340 pp.) A collection of columns from the New York Times's respected architecture critic, covering significant architectural events, not just in New York, but in cities all across America.

Harris, Cyrill M. Dictionary of Architecture and Construction. (New York: McGraw-Hill, 1975. 553 pp.) Over 1700 illustrations make nearly every term in architecture, planning, engineering, and the building trades comprehensible to the layman.

Hellman, Louis. Architecture for Beginners. (New York: Writers and Readers Publishing, 1988. 210 pp.) Concise, well-illustrated guide to all major architectural styles, with mini-histories of their origins, profiles of their greatest practitioners, and brief discussion of their problems.

Liebs, Chester H. Main Street to Miracle Mile: American Roadside Architecture. (Boston: Little, Brown—A New York Graphic Society Book, 1985. 259 pp.) The book that legitimized serious architectural study and preservation of automobile-related designs, such as gas stations, supermarkets, drive-in theaters, miniature golf courses, motels, diners and restaurants.

Longstreth, Richard. The Buildings of Main Street: A Guide to American Commercial Architecture. (Washington, D.C.: The Preservation Press, 1987. 149 pp.) Compact yet comprehensive guide identifying every style of commercial building you are likely to encounter. Many wonderful photos.

Wolfe, Tom. From Bauhaus to Our House. (New York: Washington Square Press, 1981. 128 pp.) Before skewering the worlds of high finance and high society in his novel, The Bonfire of the Vanities, the journalist/social-critic turned his acid pen on the world of modern architecture—and the result is as provocative, witty, stylistically original as one would expect from the inventor of "the new journalism."

City Planning and Public Policy

Architecture/Research/Construction, Inc. Community Group Homes. (New York: Van Nostrand Reinhold, 177 pp.) A design firm details the kind of planning necessary to provide social service clients with a truly home-like environment, not a mini-institution. A good sourcebook to help community leaders determine if a planned group home is well-designed, in keeping with architectural and safety standards of the neighborhood, and protective of the privacy and comfort of its residents.

Barnett, Jonathan. *The Elusive City: Five Centuries of Design, Ambition and Miscalculation*. (New York: Harper & Row, 1986. 210 pp.) An excellent brief history of city development and planning ideas, from Pompeii to LeCorbusier.

Cooper-Hewitt Museum (Lisa Taylor, Director). *Urban Open Spaces*. (New York: Rizzoli, 1981. 128 pp.) Large-format, illustrated guide on treatment of open space. Chapters on playgrounds, parks, waterfronts, pedestrian malls, public art, "street furniture," sidewalks, signs, community gardens, Neighborhood Land Trusts, model legislation, psychological effects of open space, and a host of other issues.

Gratz, Barbara Brandes. *The Living City*. (New York: Simon & Schuster, 1989. 414 pp.) Full of instructive anecdotes and fresh ideas of how community activists from Savannah, Georgia to Ithaca, New York are protecting their neighborhoods from overdevelopment.

Hayden, Dolores. *Redesigning the American Dream: The Future of Housing, Work, and Family Life*. (New York: W.W. Norton & Co., 1984. 270 pp.) How the use of space affects our private lives as well as our public interaction, written from a feminist point of view.

Jacobs, Jane. *The Death and Life of Great American Cities*. (New York: Vintage Books, 1961. 458 pp.) The classic that has so influenced the current generation of city planning directors—a brilliant, but highly-opinionated work, often misquoted by developers to justify high density plans. Must reading if you want to understand the history of planning in America.

Lai, Richard Tseng-Yu. *Law in Urban Design and Planning*. (New York: Van Nostrand Reinhold, 115 5th Avenue, 10003, 1988. 320 pp.) Untangles the maze of zoning and design laws today, written in scholarly but readable English.

Leavitt, Helen. *Superhighway—Superhoax*. (New York: Ballantine Books, 1970. 311 pp.) Incisive, thoroughgoing analysis of how highway planning is done in this country and why it so often destroys neighborhoods.

Lewis, Roger K. *Shaping the City*. (Washington, D.C.: The AIA Press, 1987. 315 pp.) A collection of *Washington Post* columns on city planning by a University of Maryland professor of architecture. Written in clear, jargon-free English, with wonderfully instructive illustrations; a good introduction to city planning for those encountering development language for the first time.

Middleton, Michael. *Man Made the Town*. (New York: St. Martin's Press, 1987. 240 pp.) Insightful essays on: the over-scaled nature of modern development, the disastrous effects of the automobile on the urban scene, the abdication of city planning powers to development companies, and other critical reflections. Surprising, perhaps, that this is the product of a grant from the Shell Oil Company.

Mumford, Lewis. *The Lewis Mumford Reader*. Edited by Donald L. Miller. (New York: Pantheon Books, 1986. 391 pp.) A collection of pieces covering cities, architecture, technology, and American culture, distilled from many books of the prolific and innovative writer/critic, whom Malcolm Cowley called "the last of the great humanists."

Spirn, Anne Whiston. *The Granite Garden: Urban Nature and Human Design*. (New York: Basic Books, 1984. 334 pp.) Much useful information on the relationship of cities to the environment. Sections on types of plants, animals, soil, and water conditions typically found in cities, plus discussion of problems of pollution, flooding and erosion, toxic wastes, and excessive heat generated by overdevelopment.

Unterman, Richard K. *Accommodating the Pedestrian: Adapting Towns and Neighborhoods for Walking and Bicycling*. (New York: Van Nostrand Reinhold, 1984. 232 pp.) Complete, illustrated guide to practical planning for streets, sidewalks, and pathways. Before-and-after studies of real places, information on uses of traffic data, discussion of available traffic management techniques, and rating of design solutions from safety, aesthetic, and other perspectives.

Whyte, William H. *City: Rediscovering the Center*. (New York: Doubleday, 1988. 386 pp.) One of the most innovative social theorists and planners of our age sums up decades of observation of street life and urban living patterns in this highly readable yet scientific study. Highly quotable for the neighborhood activist looking for a distinguished name critical of much of today's large-scale development thinking.

Community Organizing

Alinsky, Saul. *Rules for Radicals: A Pragmatic Primer for Realistic Radicals*. (New York: Vintage, 1971. 196 pp.) You don't have to be a radical to find Alinsky's advice on organizing, strategy-setting, and communications helpful.

A Blueprint for Lobbying: A Citizen's Guide to the Politics of Preservation. (Washington, D.C.: Preservation Action, 1700 Connecticut Avenue, N.W., Suite 401, 20009. 1984. 40 pp.) Though this booklet is written for the neighborhood preservationist, its advice on lobbying is transferable to other types of development cases.

Brigham, Nancy, with Ann Raszmann and Dick Cluster. *How to Do Leaflets, Newsletters and Newspapers*. (New York: Hastings House Publishers, 1982. Order c/o PEP Publishers, P.O. Box 289, Essex Station, Boston, MA 02112. 110 pp.) Planning, editing, layout, financing, distribution, libel law, and anything else you would want to know about publishing any type of material for your neighborhood organization.

Cooke, Holland. *How to Keep Your Press Release Out of the Wastebasket*. (Washington, D.C.: Holland Cooke Seminars, 1988. Order c/o Holland Cooke, 3220 N St., N.W., Washington, D.C. 20007. 130 pp.) A radio news director tells what makes him sit up and take notice of a press release, and what is a sure snore-inducer.

The Foundation Directory. (New York: The Foundation Center, 79 Fifth Avenue, 10003. 672 pp. Regular supplements available.) At $75 for the Directory and $30 for the supplement, a good buy if you are looking to foundations to provide a significant portion of your organization's income.

Kahn, Si. *Organizing: A Guide for Grassroots Leaders*. (New York: McGraw Hill, 1982. 387 pp.) Down-to-earth advice by a veteran community activist about leadership, meetings, research, tactics, publicity, fundraising, lobbying, coalition-building, and other topics of interest.

Mackay, Harvey. *Swim With the Sharks Without Being Eaten Alive.* (New York: Ivy Books, 1988.
    313 pp.) Quick, easy-to-follow tips about the business world—helpful if you're going to be
    entering into negotiations with a developer, fundraising, trying to "sell" your neighbors on
    your organization, or just want to build up your self-confidence to keep your battle going.

Organizing for Local Fundraising: Self-sufficiency for the '80s. (Boulder, Colorado: Volunteer
    Readership, P.O. Box 1807, 80306. 1984. $7.95) Written for the small community group,
    with practical examples of how others have run successful campaigns.

The Sierra Club Political Handbook. (San Francisco: Sierra Club, 530 Bush Street, 94108. 1979.
    76 pp.) Concise advice from an organization that went from being a small, committed band
    of wilderness-lovers to a nationwide, mainstream movement.

Trump, Donald. *The Art of the Deal.* New York: Warner Books, 1987. 372 pp.) You'll need to
    know how a developer thinks, and what better guide than the autobiography of America's
    number one overbuilder? Written in breathless, page-turning style, full of outrageous
    anecdotes that should get any neighborhood activist's stomach churning. Plenty of good
    object lessons—but not for the faint-hearted or easily discouraged.

Historic Preservation

Brolin, Brent C. *The Battle of Saint Bart's.* (New York: William Morrow & Co., 1988.) If freedom
    of religion vs. the public right to light and air is of interest to you, read this book; it tells
    the gripping and sometimes comic story of the quest of Saint Bartholomew's Church in
    New York to sell their air rights for the construction of an office tower, and the coalition
    of citizens' groups and preservationists that fought to stop the sale.

Coughlin, Thomas. *Easements and Other Legal Techniques to Protect Historic Houses in Private
    Ownership.* (Washington, D.C.: Historic House Association of America, 1600 H Street,
    N.W. 20006. 1981. 28 pp. Available as part of the "Old House Starter Kit" package of
    information pamphlets. To order call 202/673–4025) Explains easements, state and local
    tax implications, federal tax requirements; provides sample deeds of easement.

Hawley, Peter. *The Main Street Book: A Guide to Downtown Revitalization.* (Washington, D.C.:
    Preservation Press, 1986. 324 pp.) Everything you need to know about the commercial
    centers of cities and small towns and the National Trust's Main Street Program to help
    bring them back to life.

The Landmark Yellow Pages: Where to Find All the Names, Addresses, Facts and Figures You Need.
    (Washington, D.C.: Preservation Press, 1990. 320 pp.

Maddex, Diane, ed. *All about Old Buildings: The Whole Preservation Catalog.* (Washington, D.C.:
    The Preservation Press. 433 pp.) The single resource guide I would recommend to anyone
    concerned in any way with historic preservation. Also full of useful information, including
    organizations to contact and books to read, on related topics, such as grantsmanship,
    neighborhood organizing, zoning law, and city planning. If you can't find it in your
    bookstore, write to the National Trust for Historic Preservation, 1785 Massachusetts
    Avenue, N.W., Washington, D.C. 20036, or call 202/673–4200.

National Park Service. *Respectful Rehabilitation: Answers to Your Questions about Old Buildings*. (Washington, D.C.: The Preservation Press, 1982. 198 pp.) Easy-to-understand guide to the rules governing restoration of landmarked buildings in order to qualify for federal tax credits.

Naylor, David. *Great American Movie Theatres*. (Washington, D.C.: The Preservation Press, 1987. 272 pp.) If your local movie palace is in this book, and it isn't landmarked, file to save it now!

Urban Land Institute. *Adaptive Use*. (1090 Vermont Avenue, N.W. Washington, D.C. 20005, 1978. 246 pp.) What distinguishes this book from others about saving old buildings is the economic data; for the case studies, costs are figured from the start of the project through its completion and operation. No theories here, just practical models for solutions of problems.

Miscellaneous

Abbey, Edward. *The Monkey Wrench Gang*. (New York: Avon Books, 1975. 387 pp.) Ideas in fiction can be a lot more inspiring than a scientific study of a subject, and this novel contains some wild ones, as well as being an entertaining read.

Bennet, Jennifer. *The Harrowsmith Landscaping Handbook*. (Camden East, Ontario, Canada: Camden House, 1985. 176 pp.) Part of the comprehensive Harrowsmith Series on design issues. Tells how to read a landscape plan—particularly helpful if you need to analyze the landscaping of a development project. A complete guide to landscape design, with many illustrations of plants, what spaces are appropriate for which types, and how they should be maintained once planted.

Nichols, John T. *The Milagro Beanfield War*. (New York: Ballantine, 652 pp.) If you enjoyed Robert Redford's movie version, you'll like the novel, too. A bulldozer-run-amok is as much the villain of the story as any of the human characters. Shows what a small, impoverished community can do, even if it's up against a big, powerful corporation.

Glossary

A-O-R. See **As-of-right**.

A.Q.I. See **Air quality index**.

Accessory use. In multi-family buildings in residential zones, the inclusion of small shops (usually dry-cleaners, hairdressers, and convenience stores) or offices (usually medical). In single-family zones, basement apartment units and **granny flats** may be allowed as accessory uses.

Adaptive reuse. Preservation of a building of historic or architectural distinction through modifications to allow it to serve a modern purpose. Through adaptive reuse, old industrial lofts have become apartments, fire stations have become theaters, theaters have become office buildings, blacksmith shops have become restaurants, and so forth—although on occasion the modifications made in the adaptation process have been so extensive or ill-conceived that the original historic purpose of the building is obscured.

Air quality index. A federally set standard for measuring the amount of pollutants (generally carbon monoxide and ozone) in the atmosphere. Levels under 50 are considered good; above 100 is classified as unhealthful.

Air rights. The unbuilt space above a building, roadway, or land area. If an owner has a three-story building in a zone that allows ten stories, he has air rights to seven additional stories, which, in some localities, he may sell or trade to other property owners. Once he has sold his air-rights, he has forever given up the option of putting a ten-story building on that property.

Amenities. A term often used in zoning bonus cases to describe desirable features offered by the developer as a trade-off for extra height and density, above what the zoning allows. Common amenities are: fountains, plazas, atriums, artwork, benches, special landscape features, underground parking, public transportation links, art galleries, theaters, day-care centers, senior service centers, public meeting rooms, and housing.

Amicus curiae. Latin for "friend of the court." A brief submitted in a lawsuit by someone not a party to the suit; for example, when a developer sues the city over denial of building permits to which he feels entitled, a neighborhood organization would file an *amicus curiae* (generally shortened to *amicus*), supporting the city's position.

Area. The measurement of a flat surface, such as a building lot, arrived at (if you remember your basic math) by multiplying the length times the width. The result is expressed in **square footage**.

Art Deco style. An architectural style popularized by the 1925 Paris Exposition des Arts Decoratifs et Industrielles Modernes, and widely used through the mid–1950s, after which it fell out of fashion for some twenty years. It has now made a strong comeback, evidenced by the number of Art Deco historic landmarks that have been added to the National Register of Historic Places in the past several years. Art Deco characteristics include: use of glass block, aluminum trim, zig-zag or angular ornamentation, and streamlined curves.

As-of-right. Development permitted under the zoning of a site, without variances or special exceptions. A synonym for **Matter-of-right**.

Assemblage. Purchase by one owner, or cooperating group of owners, of all properties within a specified area contemplated for large-scale development. If the properties are improved (that is, have buildings on them), demolition applications may be filed simultaneously with the transfer of deeds.

Berm. An artificial hill, often built to separate incompatible elements of a development plan.

Boondoggle. A government development project that is unnecessary, poorly planned, or otherwise wasteful of the taxpayers' money. Compare **Pork-barrel.**

Bonus zoning. A system set up to encourage development in specified areas (often low-income areas bypassed by investors) through the incentive of permission to build more height and density than allowed under the zoning code. Bonus programs may require the developer to include certain amenities in the project to qualify for the extra space (see **PUD**), or make a contribution to a city-administered fund to pay for low-income housing or other public benefits (see **linkage**).

Building restriction line. The demarcation of an area within a lot on which no construction can occur. Typically, a building restriction line will be established X-many feet from the street, to ensure that a uniform set-back is maintained or that power and sewer lines are not built over but remain accessible to work crews.

CBD. See **Central Business District.**

CBTF. See **Community-based Treatment Facility.**

CDBG. See **Community Development Block Grant.**

CDC. See **Community Development Corporation.**

Central Business District. The highest-density zone in most city zoning plans—what is generally known as "downtown."

Community-based Treatment Facility. May be either for out-patient treatment or residential care. Typical CBTFs include: group homes for the mentally impaired, halfway houses for juveniles or adults under the jurisdiction of the courts (through parole, work-release, or probation programs), supervised living arrangements for the emotionally disturbed, and clinics for drug or alcohol abusers.

Community Development Block Grant. A program administered by the U.S. Department of Housing and Urban Development through which grants and guaranteed loans may be made available to neighborhood organizations, local governments, or private/public partnerships for ventures judged to help revitalize a deteriorating neighborhood. Some states and cities also have their own versions of the CDBG.

Community Development Corporation. A development company created through the partnership of a neighborhood organization, or individual neighborhood investors, with a private development company. The CDC may be established through government action, or come about entirely by agreement among the private participants; it may use government loans or grants and work according to government-set rules, or it may be an entirely independent corporation—though the former is far more frequent than the latter.

Comprehensive Plan. See **Master plan.**

Conflict of interest. An ethical problem arising when a person has power or influence over a matter in which he or she has a direct or indirect financial stake. Conflict of interest most commonly occurs in zoning cases when politicians are allowed to take action on applications from developers who have contributed to their election campaigns; but the same term also applies when a lawyer is asked to represent a neighborhood group against a developer whom he or she (or any other members of the same law-firm) has previously represented. By the American Bar Association's ethical standards, that lawyer should be bound to decline the case.

Contexturalism. Architects' jargon for taking into account a building's surroundings during its design. (See photo.)

Continuance. A postponement of a hearing or court case.

Covenant. A private agreement, generally between a home-buyer and the development company or homeowners' association in control of a subdivision. Covenants may restrict your ability to add onto or change the architectural style of your house, sell off any of your yard, or otherwise impose restrictions not found in the city's zoning code. A properly written covenant will, in most cases, be upheld and enforced in a court of law.

Curb cut. A break in the sidewalk for a driveway, roadway, or ramp for wheelchairs, strollers, or other small vehicles.

Deconstructivism. A recent style of architecture that makes use of dissonant, asymmetrical, paradoxical, and chaotic forms to express the disorienting, random, contradictory spirit of our times. Its foremost practitioners are Frank Gehry, Peter Eisenman, and Bernard Tschumi, whose work in architecture today has been compared to the work of John Cage and Phillip Glass in music.

Demolition by neglect. Describes a tactic, illegal under many state historic preservation statutes, of allowing a landmarked building to deteriorate beyond the point at which it is still feasible (architecturally or economically speaking) to restore it. The owner may then use either "practical difficulty" or "economic hardship" as a reason to seek a demolition permit.

Density. The bulk, mass, or volume of a building or buildings, generally measured in **FAR.**

Downzoning. Changing the zoning on a parcel of land from a less restrictive to a more restrictive category. Compare **Upzoning.**

EIS. See **Environmental Impact Statement.**

Easement. An arrangement whereby an owner gives up the right to alter or add to part of his property, in exchange for some consideration—typically tax benefits, occasionally, rental payments. Two of the more commonly seen types of easements are the **facade easement,** whereby the owner assigns design control over the front of his building, usually to a non-profit historic preservation organization such as the National Trust for Historic Preservation, for which he takes a one-time tax deduction; and the **scenic easement,** whereby the owner gives to the government control over his undeveloped land (usually located next to parkland, or along a coastline or in other environmentally sensitive area), and likewise receives a tax deduction for the value of the development profit he has forgone.

Elevation. An architectural drawing showing a view of a building from top to bottom, on one side only. (See illustration.)

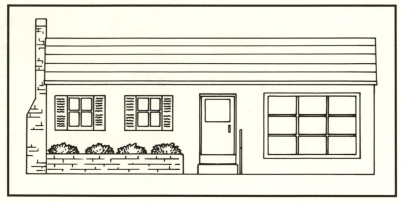

Eminent domain. The right of the government to take private property for public use, with fair compensation paid to the owner. The price may be based on an appraisal of the property's current market value, as approved by a judge, or panel of judges.

Envelope. The maximum amount of space that may be developed on a lot. The envelope is determined by zoning limits on height, **FAR, setback,** and percent of **lot occupancy.**

Environmental Impact Statement. A report prepared usually by the government agency in charge of environmental protection (whether federal or state) on the effect a building will have on the land, air, and water around it, and the animals and humans who inhabit the area. Some localities require a satisfactory EIS before granting development permits; in other places the recommendations in the EIS will be advisory only, but may still have a significant effect on the outcome of a case.

Ex parte communication. Latin for "one-sided" communication, used to describe any conversation that occurs between one of the parties to a case and any official with decision-making authority over it. Because the other parties will not have an opportunity to hear what is being said and to respond to it, such discussion is inherently unfair and is not allowed under law.

FAR. Stands for **Floor-to-Area ratio,** but is normally spoken as a single word, or pronounced by its abbreviation. FAR is the standard measure of **density,** and is arrived at by adding up the **square footage** of all the floors of a building and dividing by the **area** of a lot.

FOIA. See **Freedom of Information Act.**

Facadomy. A term of abuse among historic preservationists. Describes the practice of saving only a small fraction, usually the front wall, of a historic building and constructing a new building around it, often considerably larger and in a pseudo-historic style. (See photo.)

Fenestration. A fancy term for windows.

Footprint. The outline of the base of a building on its lot. (see sketch, p. xvi.)

Freedom of Information Act. A piece of federal legislation requiring the federal government to make available to citizens its records on any of its public activities, exclusive of what may be withheld for reasons of national security or protection of an individual's right to privacy. Helpful to the citizen interested in discovering how the government arranged for bids on contracts for public works or how other development policy decisions were made. The citizen filing the FOIA request will be charged all the costs of fulfilling it. Some states, counties, and cities have their own versions of the federal FOIA process.

Gentrification. The shift in housing patterns in urban neighborhoods that occurs when middle- to upper-income buyers (usually white professionals, either couples or singles) renovate old rowhouses or apartment units in mostly lower-income, inner-city, black or Hispanic neighborhoods, and move in themselves, or rent or sell to other higher-income earners. Gentrification is generally held to be a negative thing when it results in displacement of poor tenants by their landlords; however, when the renovation occurs primarily in abandoned buildings, or when government programs are in place to assist lower-income homeowners in renovating their buildings and subsidize rents so that lower-income tenants can afford their units when their building is renovated, the infusion of a sizable middle-class population may actually help to stabilize and strengthen the neighborhood.

Grandfathered. A passive verb used to describe how a zoning board is to regard buildings constructed before any zoning rules or rule-changes were put in effect. Example: A three-story office building stands on a lot that is now in an exclusively residential zone. (It was built ten years before the city had zoning at all.) It is *grandfathered*, meaning that as long as the building exists, it can continue to be used for commercial purposes. If, however, it should be destroyed by fire or flood, it could not be replaced; only residential structures could be built.

Granny flat. An apartment, often in the basement or built in a side or rear addition, in a single-family house. May also be called an in-law suite or English basement. Granny flats in single-family zone-districts are one of the most common types of zoning violations. Because today's smaller families seldom need all the space available in large old houses, and often need the extra rental income, some zoning boards have recognized the need to change zoning to allow easy conversion of single-family houses. The legalization of granny flats, however, can become a hotly contested issue between those who favor strict zoning and those who believe that zoning must be adjusted frequently to reflect the needs of the times.

Impact fees. Costs assessed against developers based on the anticipated government spending per square foot of new construction to provide needed services and capital improvements to an area experiencing residential or commercial growth.

Incentive zone. An area designated by federal, state, or local law in which unemployment is high and economic activity is low (measured according to criteria laid out in the incentive zone regulations). Once the area is declared, developers and other property owners may then be eligible for a variety of government aid programs, **tax abatements, tax credits,** and zoning **bonuses,** such as may be provided by the law under which application is made.

Infill. After a building plan has been completed on a parcel of land, subdivision of the leftover open space into new building lots to allow construction of new houses or other buildings.

Initiative. A question placed on the ballot at the voters' instigation, usually after a petition signed by a set percentage of registered voters has been received. Initiatives may result in legislation, they may be advisory to legislators or appointed commissioners, or they may be simply an expression of popular will, lacking the force of law. Compare **Referendum.**

Infrastructure. The supporting network of roads, power and sewer lines, educational system, and government and private social services required by the population of a specified area.

International style. A twentieth-century style of architecture, often used for skyscrapers, making frequent use of glass, steel, and reinforced concrete, usually devoid of ornamentation. Called International because buildings done in the style lack regional characteristics, looking much the same, whether found in New York or Nairobi.

Large-tract review. See **Site Plan Review.**

Linkage. The practice of linking permits for commercial construction to some other specified social goal; for example, requiring that X-many square feet of low-income housing be built for Y square feet of office space. Instead of actual construction of units, some jurisdictions with linkage laws require the developer to make a contribution to a government-administered trust fund, which may pay for such public benefits as subsidized housing, mass transportation systems, day-care, creation of parks, or cleaning up of polluted areas. Linkage may be mandatory, meaning that new permits depend on fulfillment of requirements, or voluntary, allowing developers to receive added density and/or building height in exchange for the public benefits offered.

Locally Unwanted Land Use. See **LULU.**

Lot occupancy. The allowable percentage of ground that a building can cover.

LULU. An acronym for Locally Unwanted Land Use, used to refer to a variety of facilities and installations (usually large-scale) that neighbors can be counted on to oppose, including: power plants (nuclear and conventional), incinerators, landfills, industries producing toxic waste or pollution, missile-silos, air force bomber testing ranges, oil-drilling rigs, and sewage treatment plants.

M-O-R. See **Matter-of-right.**

Map case. An application to a zoning panel to change the zone-classification of a specified parcel of land. Compare **text amendment.**

Master plan. A plan charting the course of development for a wide area, such as a city or county, over a long period of time (at least five years, and often as long as twenty years). A master plan may be adopted by the legislature as a set of binding policy directives, or it may simply be an advisory document, to be consulted by government planners; it may consist of a detailed map, containing prescriptions for all recorded parcels of land, or it may have a "soft-edged" map, classifying land in broad areas but not on a lot-by-lot basis. Some plans have lengthy accompanying texts, explaining the maps and giving rationales for the policies; others simply provide a legend to the colors, symbols, and patterns in use on the map. Also known as a Comprehensive Plan.

Matter-of-right. A synonym for **As-of-right.**

Mixed use. A zone allowing office, retail, residential, and sometimes light-industrial development to be built on the same lot, or in the same complex. In some jurisdictions, there is no mixed-use zoning, but developers may be granted permits to build mixed-use projects through the **PUD** process.

National Register of Historic Places. A list of designated landmarks and historic districts maintained by the National Park Service, according to the National Historic Preservation Act of 1966. Structures and districts may be included on the list through nomination by state and local landmarks commissions, or through designation by the federal government. Listing allows owners of rehabilitated commercial property to take a 20 percent tax credit for work done in accordance with the *Secretary of the Interior's Guidelines for Rehabilitation*.

NIMBY. An acronym for **Not In My Back Yard,** NIMBY can refer to a development project—usually a social-service facility such as a halfway house, a group home for the mentally retarded or emotionally disturbed, a homeless shelter, or a drug-treatment clinic—or it could be used to described the people opposed to such a project, or to the attitude itself.

Overlay. In zoning, a set of restrictions, requirements, or definitions applied to an area, over and above the zoning classification of the land. For example, in a C–1 zone with a Neighborhood-Commercial-Overlay, there could be a restriction on the number of bars and restaurants allowed, although in a C–1 zone without the overlay, no such restriction would apply; and rules mandating parking for shoppers, though an ordinary requirement in the C–1 zone, could be waived, to ensure that the zone remains pedestrian-oriented and that trees and shrubs are not removed to make room for more parking spaces.

PUD (also known as **PDA, PMUD, MUDA** and similar alphabetic combinations). Stands for **Planned Unit Development, Planned Development Area, Planned Mixed-Use Development, Mixed-Use Development Area,** respectively). A widely-used zoning technique intended to encourage development of superior quality to matter-of-right. The developer is allowed to apply for somewhat greater density and/or height, in exchange for which he is to include substantial **amenities** in his project.

Paper street. A street, lane, or alley shown on an official city or county map, which does not exist in reality. Generally speaking, some governmental action must be taken to close a paper street before development can occur on the land; however, a developer may be automatically entitled to build a real street when there is a paper one shown on the map.

Parking ratio. The number of parking spaces in relation to the amount of square footage, or number of residential units to be built. Minimum ratios are usually specified by the zoning code.

Party status. Recognition by the Zoning Board or court that one is a full participant in a case, with the right to call witnesses, cross-examine opposing witnesses, receive copies of filed documents, and offer opening and closing arguments.

Pastiche. French for "pasting," it describes the practice in architecture of attaching ornamentation of one style to a building predominantly done in a different style. Most commonly used as a term of criticism of Post-modernist buildings made of poured concrete and glass, but with a cut-out of a gable placed on the roof, a neo-classical colonnade along the sidewalk, or any other historical feature applied out of context.

Penthouse. A structure on top of a flat-roofed building housing ventilating equipment and other mechanical or electrical systems. Also called mechanical roof or **roof structure.** The term is also used to refer to a top-floor apartment, usually with its own elevator or private access.

Perspective drawing. A drawing showing a three-dimensional view of a building, usually from a distance.

Planned Development Area or **Planned Unit Development.** See **PUD.**

Plat. An official map showing the boundary lines of a lot or lots.

Point of measurement. The spot on a building lot from which the maximum allowable height is to be calculated. Some jurisdictions allow the developer to pick his own point of measurement (in which case he will be sure to pick the highest spot on his lot); other places specify that height must be figured from the center point of the front facade.

Pork-barrel. A government project designed primarily to benefit the voters and/or friends of a representative of a particular electoral district. A pork-barrel project is not *always* a **boondoggle,** but the two do tend to go hand in hand.

Post-modernism. A style of architecture employing traditional architectural forms, such as columns, pediments, and gables, to buildings of modern size and density, or made primarily of modern building materials, such as glass and concrete.

Public space. Sidewalks, roads, grass strips, or other land-areas that abut privately owned land, which, in some cases, may be incorporated into a private development plan. Air-space may also be involved, as when a developer proposes a sky-way—a pedestrian corridor raised above street level linking two separate buildings.

Puffing. The practice of real estate sales agents of describing deficits and flaws in a house or apartment in euphemistic terms. Puffing can be relatively benign—such as when a house located thirty miles from downtown is described as being "close in"—or it can be just short of fraudulent—as when the plan for a new, 1000–student elementary school next door to your house is described to you as "a little red schoolhouse."

REIT. See **Real Estate Investment Trust.**

R-O-W. See **Right-of-way.**

Real Estate Investment Trust. A common corporate structure for development companies or their financial backers (although becoming less so, now that Congress has removed certain tax shelters from the federal income tax code).

Redlining. An illegal, discriminatory banking practice, whereby a lending institution denies mortgages or commercial loans to all owners of property within a specified (usually minority and/or low-income) area.

Referendum. A measure placed on the ballot for direct voter approval or denial. While an initiative is generally a ballot item placed at the voters' instigation, a referendum is more often brought about because the city charter requires it (of all bond issues, for example) or because the legislature took an action needing to be ratified by a direct vote. The term could also be used to describe a ballot-item introduced through citizen-petition intended to reverse a law passed by the legislature. In common parlance, however, the word is used interchangeably with **initiative.**

Revolving door. The hiring of former government regulators by the same corporations they used to oversee. Also, the appointment to positions of regulatory authority of corporate executives who were only recently among the regulated. The revolving door inevitably leads to **conflicts of interest.**

Right-of-Way. A road, alley, path, or other piece of land used to reach a destination. Also used to refer to the land over which a railroad lays its tracks, or the air-space through which power-lines are strung. May be governed by public regulations or, if privately owned, by covenants and agreements among the parties.

Roof structures. Refers to all elements found on top of a building, whether in an enclosure (**penthouse**) or not. Examples: elevator pop-ups, satellite dishes, radio and TV antennas, vent-pipes, air-conditioning condensers, and weather balloons.

Run-off. Rainwater that washes from one parcel of land to another, which (if measures are not taken to prevent it) may carry pollutants and topsoil (causing erosion). Especially of concern if the area receiving the run-off is a natural preserve or a recreational area.

SHPDA. Stands for **State Health Planning and Development Agency** (pronounced "Shipda"). The agency that determines whether an application for a new hospital, or hospital expansion, nursing home, hospice, inpatient psychiatric care center, or other major health facility, is needed, meets standards, and so should receive a Certificate of Occupancy.

S-O-B zone. See **Sexually-oriented-business zone.**

Set-back. The amount of space that must be left open between the lot lines and the buildings. Not to be confused with setback, which is what your organization will suffer if a developer wins the right to build without any set-backs.

Sexually-oriented-business zone. A designated area in which property owners may get permits to operate bars featuring nude dancing or wrestling, strip shows, peep shows, pornographic movies and bookstores, massage parlors, and other "adult" entertainments. May be referred to colloquially as "The Strip," "The Block," "The Tenderloin," or "The Combat Zone."

Signage. Planners' jargon for any lettering or logos attached to or carved into a building. Signage can be of neon, back-lit plastic, individually attached letters, or in the form of a billboard. The term also covers signs put up to control traffic and parking, whether public or private ("No Left Turn," "No Parking Anytime," "Right Lane Must Turn Right," and so forth).

Site plan review. A requirement in some cities that certain development plans, which would otherwise be allowed routinely as a matter-of-right, undergo review by the city planning agency, which has the power to withhold permits if the plan does not meet certain standards. Site plan review may be reserved for development projects above a certain size (in which case it may be called **large-tract review**) or in a specified area (for example, near the city's waterfront, or in an urban renewal area).

Special exception. Used in some jurisdictions instead of **variance.**

Spot zoning. The application of a zone classification to one lot or small group of lots on a block, when there are others in the area that share the same general characteristics, but come under a different zone. Because it gives owners of similar properties dissimilar economic return, spot zoning has been found to violate the **uniformity principle** of fair zoning practice.

Square footage. Used for the measurement of **area,** and may be figured as **gross square footage,** meaning all of the built floor area, including parking levels, basement and roof areas, or the **net square footage,** the floor area after all the unrentable space has been subtracted. Calculations for zoning requirements are often based upon the net, not the gross.

Standing. Having a position that will be recognized by a court or zoning authority as reason to accept you as an applicant or a party to an action. Showing that you are representative of a legitimate, neighborhood organization is one way to establish standing in a zoning case; being a property owner of nearby land is another way; showing that the outcome will significantly affect your health, safety, or peace of mind would also be sufficient to prove standing in most jurisdictions.

State Health Planning and Development Agency. See **SHPDA.**

Stop-work order. An order issued by an administrative agency, such as a building inspections bureau, or by a court, usually in the form of an injunction or a **TRO** (temporary restraining order), bringing construction to a halt. Stop-work orders may be issued when construction is being done without a permit, or when the work described in the permit-application does not match what is actually being built, or when there are violations of health, safety, environmental, and other regulations.

Steering. The illegal, discriminatory practice of some real estate agents of showing their clients only those houses or apartments located in areas predominantly occupied by members of the client's ethnic group.

Street furniture. Term used for benches, telephone booths, parking meters, utility poles, vending machines, trash barrels, mail boxes, newspaper vending boxes—in short, anything affixed to the sidewalk or street that is neither a building nor a sign.

TDRs. See **Transfer development rights.**

TND overlay. See **Traditional Neighborhood Development Overlay.**

TRO. Stands for **Temporary restraining order,** discussed under **Stop-work order** (above).

TSM measures. See **Traffic system management measures.**

Taking. A term to describe the acquisition of property by the state without fair compensation to the owner, often used by developers in fighting the imposition of zoning or landmark regulations on their real estate.

Tax abatement. May be given in the form of a reduced assessment value for taxation of real estate, or in a reduction in the rate of taxation—usually to achieve desirable social ends, such as helping the elderly to remain in homes purchased many years ago when the values were much lower, or helping small business operators to remain in storefronts downtown and in other high-rent locations. Compare **tax credit.**

Tax credit. Similar in purpose to a tax abatement, but arrived at differently. The assessment of property value remains the same, and the rate is the same, but after the tax is figured, a certain percentage will be deducted from the total owed. One of the best-known and most-used tax credit programs is the Investment Tax Credit for the Rehabilitation of Historic Properties, available to owners of income-producing properties listed on the **National Register of Historic Places.**

Text amendment. A change in the zoning code, not to a specific area shown on the map (as in a **Map amendment**) but to the definitions or descriptions of the rules. Examples: Taking a list of all the commercial uses permitted in a low-density commercial zone, and excluding from it fast-food restaurants, as defined in the code; or changing the **point of measurement** so that the maximum allowable building height will be calculated from the lowest point of land on the site.

Traditional Neighborhood Development Overlay. A zoning plan devised by University of Maryland professor Roger Lewis, along with other planning professionals, to encourage the development of new subdivisions along the lines of the traditional American small town, rather than in the conventional, car-dependent patterns typical of suburbia today.

Traffic system management measures. A collection of techniques available to traffic engineers to control the volume and direction of traffic on the street system of any given area. TSM measures include: turn-prohibitions, one-way streets, reserved car-pool and bus-lanes, reversible lanes, "Do not enter" signs, rush hour restrictions, speed bumps, rumble-strips, barricades, and diverters.

Transfer development rights. A means by which a developer can be allowed to build greater density on one building-site, by building less (or nothing at all) on another. The unused development rights of one parcel are thus transferred (often in exchange for money) to the other, although the underlying restrictions of the zoning code should still be in force.

Turning movements studies. A way to determine how many cars are using an intersection and which way those cars are going. Traffic counters record each car that turns right, left, or goes straight within a given period of time (for example, the p.m. rush hour); if **Traffic System Management measures** (see above) are then tried out that change the use of the intersection, a second study can be ordered for the same time-period, and the results compared, so that the measures can be fairly evaluated.

UDAG. Stands for **Urban Development Action Grant.** A program of the Housing and Urban Development Department. Funds made available to cities and urbanized counties for neighborhood revitalization and stimulation of the local economy.

Uniformity principle. A doctrine of fairness in zoning, which dictates that lots sharing similar characteristics in close proximity to one another be similarly classified for zoning purposes. This ensures that no owner is singled out for greater restrictions on his property, nor given favored status.

Upzoning. Changing the zoning on a parcel of land from a less restrictive to a more restrictive category. Upzoning is what developers frequently apply for and get; **downzoning** is what neighborhoods want but seldom know how to pursue—so the trend in zoning in most communities is ever upward, to higher and higher densities.

Use. One of the factors determined by zoning. Different zoning codes classify uses differently, but the following general terms are widespread: residential (with different sub-classifications for levels of density, low to high); commercial (retail and/or office); industrial; institutional; farmland; parks, recreational areas and open space; and mixed-use (any of the above in combination).

Variance. An exception to the zoning rules for an area granted for a single property in that area. Also called **special exception.** Variances may be granted for use, height, density, percent of lot occupancy, or front, rear, or side-yard set-backs, or several of these in combination.

Vesting. The point at which a developer has established his right to build a particular plan on a lot, under the zoning rules governing that lot. Vesting may occur at different points under different systems. In some areas a developer will have a vested right to build up to the limits of zoning as soon as he files a complete set of plans with the government; in other places his right to build is not vested until the plan has been reviewed and a permit has been granted; in a few areas his rights will not be vested even then, but will be secure only after he has broken ground and begun to build the building described in his plan. At any time before vesting occurs, a neighborhood organization or government body could file for downzoning of the property, which, if granted, could preclude the developer from building the size of building contemplated under the old zoning.

Zoning. A system of regulation of development. Zoning determines: height, **density, lot occupancy, set-back,** and **use** (boldfaced words defined above).

Resource Guide

City Planning Organizations

American Planning Association
1776 Massachusetts Avenue, N.W.
Washington, D.C. 20036

American Public Transit Association
1201 New York Avenue, Suite 400
Washington, D.C. 20005

Citizens for a Quieter City
c/o Ralph M. Brozan
300 E. 42nd Street
New York, NY 10017

Federal Highway Administration
U.S. Department of Transportation
Washington, D.C. 20590

Federal Railroad Administration
U.S. Department of Transportation
Washington, D.C. 20590

National League of Cities
1301 Pennsylvania Avenue, N.W.
Washington, D.C. 20004

Urban Land Institute
1090 Vermont Avenue, N.W.
Washington, D.C. 20005

Architecture and Urban Design Contacts

American Society of Civil Engineers
345 E. 47th Street
New York, NY 10017

American Society of Landscape Architects
1733 Connecticut Avenue, N.W.
Washington, D.C. 20009

Association for Bridge Construction and
    Design
1301 Manor Building
564 Forbes Avenue
Pittsburgh, PA 15219

Center for Design Planning
1208 N. McKinley Street
Albany, GA 31701

Council on Tall Buildings and the Urban
    Habitat
Building 13
Lehigh University
Bethlehem, PA 18015

Institute for Community Design Analysis
66 Clover Road
Great Neck, NY 11021

Institute for Urban Design
Main P.O. Box 105
Purchase, NY 10577

Main Street Center
The National Trust for Historic Preservation
1785 Massachusetts Avenue, N.W.
Washington, D.C. 20036

Public Art Fund
25 Central Park West, Suite 25R
New York, NY 10023

Regional/Urban Design Assistance Teams
American Institute of Architects
1735 New York Avenue, N.W.
Washington, D.C. 20006

Site, Inc.
65 Bleecker Street 2nd Floor
New York, NY 10012

Neighborhood Networking, Fundraising, and Lobbying Assistance

ACORN (Association of Communities Organized for Reform Now)
1024 Elysian Fields Avenue
New Orleans, LA 70117

Center for Community Change
1000 Wisconsin Avenue, N.W.
Washington, D.C. 20007

Common Cause
2030 M Street, N.W.
Washington, D.C. 20036

Community Associations Institute
1423 Powhatan Street, Suite 7
Alexandria, VA 22314

The Foundation Center
79 Fifth Avenue
New York, NY 10003

The Grantsmanship Center
P.O. Box 6210
650 South Spring Street, Ste. 507
Los Angeles, CA 90014

Local Initiatives Support Corporation
The Ford Foundation
666 Third Avenue
New York, NY 10017

National Association of Community
Development Loan Funds
151 Montague City Road
Greenfield, MA 01301

National Association of Neighborhoods
1651 Fuller Street, N.W.
Washington, D.C. 20009

National Association of Towns and
Townships
1522 K Street, N.W., Suite 730
Washington, D.C. 20005

National Housing Law Project
1950 Addison Street
Berkeley, CA 94704

National Neighborhood Coalition
810 First Street, N.E.
Washington, D.C. 20002

National Self-Help Clearinghouse
33 W. 42nd Street, Room 62-0N
New York, NY 10036

Neighborhoods USA
4643 Amesborough
Dayton, OH 45420

Partners for Livable Places
1429 21st Street, N.W.
Washington, D.C. 20036

Small Towns Institute
P. O. Box 517
Ellensburg, WA 98926

Small Business Administration
1441 L Street, N.W.
Washington, D.C. 20416

Historic Preservation Organizations

General

Architectural History Foundation
350 Madison Avenue
New York, NY 10017

American Association for State and Local
History
172 Second Avenue
Nashville, TN 37201

Cooperative for the Preservation of Architectural Records
Prints and Photographs Department
Library of Congress
Washington, D.C. 20540

National Alliance of Preservation Commissions
Hall of the States
444 N. Capitol Street, N.W., Suite 322
Washington, D.C. 20001

National Alliance of Statewide Preservation
Organizations
c/o Historic Massachusetts, Inc.
Old City Hall

45 School Street
Boston, MA 02108

National Center for Preservation Law
1233 20th Street, N.W., Suite 501
Washington, D.C. 20036

National Register of Historic Places
Interagency Resources Division
National Park Service
P.O. Box 37127
U.S. Department of the Interior
Washington, D.C. 20013–7127

National Trust for Historic Preservation
1785 Massachusetts Avenue, N.W.
Washington, D.C. 20036

Preservation Action
1350 Connecticut Avenue, N.W.
Washington, D.C. 20009

Society of Architectural Historians
1232 Pine Street
Philadelphia, PA 19107

Specialized

Airports

American Aviation Historical Society
2333 Otis Street
Santa Ana, CA 92704

Archaeology

World Archaeological Society
HCR 1, Box 445
Hollister, MO 65672

Building Types

Art Deco Societies of America
P.O. Box 3384
Chicago, IL 60654

Classical America
227 E. 50th Street
New York, NY 10022

Friends of Cast-Iron Architecture
c/o Margot Gayle, President
235 E. 87th Street, Room 6–C
P.O. Box 57
New York, NY 10028

League of Historic American Theaters
1511 K Street, N.W., Suite 923
Washington, D.C. 20005

Literary Landmarks Association
The Thurber House
77 Jefferson Street
Columbus, OH 43215

Railway Station Historical Society
430 104th Avenue
Crete, NE 68333

Society for the Preservation of Old Mills
4841 Mill Brook Drive
Dunwoody, GA 30338

Theater Historical Society
2215 W. North Avenue
Chicago, IL 60647

U.S. Lighthouse Society
244 Kearney Street, 5th Floor
San Francisco, CA 94108

Vernacular Architecture Forum
P.O. Box 283
Annapolis, MD 21401

Victorian Society in America
219 S. 6th Street
Philadelphia, PA 19106

Cemeteries

Association for Gravestone Studies
c/o Rosalie F. Oakley
46 Plymouth Road
Needham, MA 02192

Civil War Sites

American Civil War Association
c/o Gary Griesmyer

P.O. Box 1865
Alexandria, VA 22313

Churches

Interfaith Forum on Religious Art and Architecture
1913 Architects Building
Philadelphia, PA 19103

Commercial Buildings

Society for Commercial Archaeology
National Museum of American History
Room 5010
Washington, D.C. 20560

Popular Culture Association
Popular Culture Center
Bowling Green University
Bowling Green, OH 43403

Farmland

Agricultural Historical Society
1301 New York Avenue, Room 1232
Washington, D.C. 20005

Settlement Histories

Association for the Study of Afro-American
Life and History
1407 14th Street, N.W.
Washington, D.C. 20005

Chinese Historical Society of America
650 Commercial Street
San Francisco, CA 94108

Immigration History Society
c/o Dr. M. Mark Stolarik
Balch Institute
18 South 7th Street
Philadelphia, PA 19106

Institute of Early American History and
Culture
P.O. Box 220
Williamsburg, VA 23187

Japanese-American Citizens League
1765 Sutter Street
San Francisco, CA 94115

Pioneer America Society
c/o Michael Roark
Department of Earth Science

Southeast Missouri State University
Cape Girardeau, MO 63701

Public Works

Public Works Historical Society
1313 E. 60th Street
Chicago, IL 60637

Parks, Open Space, and Environmental Advocates

American Farmland Trust
1920 N Street, N.W., Suite 400
Washington, D.C. 20036

American Forestry Association
1516 P Street, N.W.
Washington, D.C. 20005

American Shore and Beach Preservation
    Association
P.O. Box 279
Middletown, CT 95461

American Society of Consulting Arborists
700 Canterbury Road
Clearwater, FL 34624

American Trails Foundation
c/o Ray Sherman
P.O. Box 782
New Castle, CA 95658

Association of Conservation Engineers
c/o William P. Allinder
Alabama Department of Conservation
64 N. Union Street
Montgomery, AL 36130

Coastal Conservation Association
4801 Woodway, Suite 220 W.
Houston, TX 77056

The Conservation Foundation
1250 24th Street, N.W.
Washington, D.C. 20037

Defenders of Wildlife
1244 19th Street, N.W.
Washington, D.C. 20036

Earth First
P.O. Box 5871
Tucson, AZ 85703

Environmental Defense Fund
257 Park Avenue South
New York, NY 10010

Environmental Law Institute
1616 P Street, N.W., Suite 200
Washington, D.C. 20036

Frederick Law Olmstead Association
475 Riverside Drive
New York, NY 10115

Friends of the Earth
530 7th Street, SE
Washington, D.C. 20003

Greenpeace, USA
1436 U Street, N.W.
Washington, D.C. 20009

Greensward Foundation
104 Prospect Park North
Brooklyn, NY 11215

Land Trust Exchange
1017 Duke Street
Alexandria, VA 22314

National Audubon Society
950 Third Avenue
New York, NY 10022

National Park Service
U.S. Department of the Interior
Washington, D.C. 20013–7127

National Parks and Conservation
    Association
1015 31st Street, N.W.
Washington, D.C. 20007

National Register of Big Trees
American Forestry Association
1516 P Street, N.W.
Washington, D.C. 20005

National Resources Defense Council
40 W. 20th Street
New York, NY 10168

National Wildlife Federation
1400 16th Street, N.W.
Washington, D.C. 20036

Nature Conservancy
1815 N. Lynn Street
Arlington, VA 22209

North American Wildlife Foundation
102 Wilmot Road, #410
Deerfield, IL 60015

Project for Public Spaces
153 Waverly Place
New York, NY 10014

Sierra Club
730 Polk Street
San Francisco, CA 94109

Sierra Club Legal Defense Fund
2044 Fillmore Street
San Francisco, CA 94115

Soil and Water Conservation Society
7515 N.E. Ankeny Road
Ankeny, IA 50021

Treepeople
12601 Mulholland Drive
Beverly Hills, CA 90210

Trust for Public Land
116 New Montgomery Street, 4th Floor
San Francisco, CA 94105

U.S. Forest Service
U.S. Department of Agriculture
P. O. Box 2417
Washington, D.C. 20013

Wilderness Society
1400 I Street, N.W.
Washington, D.C. 20005

Wildlife Information Center
629 Green Street
Allentown, PA 18102

The Wildlife Society
5410 Grosvenor Lane
Bethesda, MD 20814

Index

About the Author:

Peggy Robin first confronted developers when she learned that bulldozers were poised to rip down the trees in the park across the street from her house to make room for 185 townhouses. That was eleven years ago. Now Robin is a veteran of the development wars in Washington, D.C., having organized numerous neighborhood conservation groups, and having served on the boards of directors of several citizens' advisory panels. Not only has she beaten back development time and again—including overly dense tract housing, massive office projects, shopping malls, and unwanted roads—but she has helped to save parks, tree-lined streets, and historic buildings as well.

Robin is proof that a degree in architecture or urban planning isn't required to succeed in fighting unwanted development. She earned a B.A. in Chinese History from the University of California at Berkeley before moving to Washington, D.C., where she lives with her husband, also a writer.